Life Studies

A Thematic Reader

Life Studies

A Thematic Reader

EDITED BY

David Cavitch
Tufts University

A Bedford Book

ST. MARTIN'S PRESS · NEW YORK

Library of Congress Catalog Card Number: 82-060460
Copyright © 1983 by St. Martin's Press, Inc.
All Rights Reserved.
Manufactured in the United States of America.
765
fed
For information, write St. Martin's Press, Inc.
175 Fifth Avenue, New York, N.Y. 10010
Editorial offices, Bedford Books of St. Martin's Press
29 Commonwealth Avenue, Boston, MA 02116

ISBN: 0-312-48484-4

Typography and Cover Design: Anna Post
Cover Photograph and Frontispiece: Ken Robert Buck

Part Opening Photographs

Self-Images (page 2): Frank Siteman
Family Ties (page 80): Burk Uzzle/ Magnum
Group Pictures (page 148): Joan C. Netherwood
Possessions (page 220): Robert Frank
Ambitions (page 274): Richard Howard
Love and Longings (page 340): Gilles Peress/ Magnum
Dilemmas (page 412): Michael Hayman/ Stock, Boston

Acknowledgments

James Agee, "Three Singers." From *Let Us Now Praise Famous Men,* by
James Agee and Walker Evans. Copyright 1939 and 1940 by James Agee.
Copyright © renewed 1969 by Mia Fritsch Agee. Reprinted by permission
of Houghton Mifflin Company.

*Acknowledgments and copyrights continue at the back of the book on pages
482–486, which constitute an extension of the copyright page.*

TO INSTRUCTORS

◊

The premise informing this composition reader is that good writing emerges from a strong desire to gain a better understanding of what we know, and from the pleasure we find in saying it well. Writers learn about themselves and their world by writing attentively, just as artists learn about their subjects by sketching them from different perspectives and in different settings. Hence the title *Life Studies*, for the works included here offer students varied perspectives on topics they care about, encouraging them to read carefully and to express their feelings and ideas clearly in writing.

The seven sections of the book treat a progression of human dimensions and experiences: our images of ourselves, our family ties, our behavior in groups, our relations to our possessions, our ambitions, our love and longing for others, our moral dilemmas. Each section contains the widest possible variety in views of the topic and in types of writing. The selections are all well-written and provocative, and most of them (even those by well-known writers) appear for the first time in a composition reader, along with several classic essays. Each section opens with a number of "Insights": succinct, often controversial statements by well-known writers whose colloquy of opinions offers a lively approach to the theme. The longer works that follow include contemporary essays, memoirs, orations, social criticism, letters, and journalism; they represent such diverse fields of knowledge as law, art, philosophy, computers, sports, and the social, behavioral, and animal sciences. In addition to essays, each section also contains one short story and one poem that develop the theme imaginatively. Then, at the end of each section, three or four pages of photographs and paintings — called "Images" — capture the theme visually and sometimes illuminate specific earlier selections.

To help students appreciate what they read, and especially to generate good writing, *Life Studies* contains detailed and extensive editorial apparatus. Preceding each selection is a biographical and introductory headnote. Following each selection are pointed and feasible questions and writing topics. These lead students to reexamine the selection's concepts and rhetorical methods, and they prompt substantive, intelligent responses in class discussions, in short written exercises, and in longer, more carefully planned essays. Additional writing topics at the end of each thematic section encourage analysis of the "Images" and further written consideration of the theme. A rhetorical index to the essays appears in the back of the book, and an instructor's manual offers both suggestions for dealing with each piece and more writing assignments.

Acknowledgments

The concept for this book took concrete form only with the wise, generous assistance of the experts at Bedford Books: Charles Christensen, the publisher; Joan Feinberg, the assistant publisher; Timothy J. Kenslea, the editor; and Anna Post, the book designer. Others who contributed valuable support include Laurel Anderson, Sylvan Barnet, Pembroke Herbert, Lynn Klampkin, Nancy Piore, and Carol Radov. My deepest gratitude is to Donna Hollenberg, who suggested many interesting pieces, who was willing to talk about all the ideas, good and bad, and who always maintained that *Life Studies* was a good idea.

CONTENTS

◊

1. SELF-IMAGES   3

INSIGHTS: *Susan Sontag, Rom Harre, Helen Keller*   4

Nora Ephron SHAPING UP ABSURD   6

A journalist's witty account of feeling tragically misfitted for life by the curse of flat-chestedness.

Suzanne Britt Jordan THAT LEAN AND HUNGRY LOOK   16

What's so good about being thin? This author reconsiders the delights and virtues of being pleasingly plump.

Mary McCarthy NAMES   20

A leading novelist and critic tells how in a girl's boarding school, names and nicknames acquire magical powers over the students' personalities.

Germaine Greer THE STEREOTYPE   29

A feminist denounces women's conventional role in society and explains the tyranny it has exercised over both women and men.

Erik Erikson THE SHAPE OF EXPERIENCE   37

In this experiment, one of the foremost psychoanalysts of our time observes children at play to learn where adult sex roles originate.

Jeremy Seabrook A TWIN IS ONLY HALF
                   A PERSON   47

An inability to communicate with his twin gives this young
Englishman a startling perspective on the whole question of personal identity.

James Thurber THE SECRET LIFE OF
                 WALTER MITTY (*story*)   53

Irrepressible dreams of glory guide American literature's most famous nonentity through the dreariness of his day.

Joan Didion IN BED   59

The chronic suffering brought on by migraine headaches gave
this essayist a deluded view of herself, until she separated fact
from fantasy.

Walt Whitman A NOISELESS PATIENT
               SPIDER (*poem*)   64

America's greatest poet observes a spider spinning its web and
draws a connection to his own life and work.

John Berger THE CHANGING VIEW OF MAN
              IN THE PORTRAIT   66

According to this contemporary art critic, the industrial revolution, the development of photography, and the wide acceptance
of the idea of equality all changed the way portraitists painted
and the way we see ourselves.

IMAGES: Judith D. Sedwick, *Twins*   73
         Alexander Gardner, *Abraham Lincoln*
         George P. A. Healy, *Abraham Lincoln*
         Four Views of Eleanor Roosevelt

Additional Writing Topics   77

2. FAMILY TIES   81

INSIGHTS: *Robert Nisbet, Leo Tolstoy, C. S. Lewis,*
  Francis Bacon   82

Margaret Mead FAMILY CODES   84

A famous anthropologist explains that American families vary greatly in codes of behavior and ways of communicating them.

Philip Slater SOCIAL CLIMBING BEGINS
  AT HOME   89

A sociologist views the nuclear family as a class system, and argues that growing up is the prototype of upward mobility.

Nancy Friday COMPETITION   93

The love between a mother and her two daughters is tempered by the fierce competition in beauty, intelligence, and accomplishment among all the three women, says the author of *My Mother/ My Self.*

Adrienne Rich THE ANGER OF A CHILD   99

A poet looks back at the angry, demanding father and the timid mother who dominated her youth.

Alexander Boswell LETTER OF ADVICE TO
  HIS SON JAMES   104

A disappointed eighteenth-century father tries to persuade his wayward son (later to become a famous biographer) to stop wasting his time and money on dissolute living, get a job, and make something of himself.

Robert Hayden THOSE WINTER SUNDAYS
  (*poem*)   109

A poet remembers the weekly ritual that perfectly symbolized his father's lonely devotion to his family.

John Updike STILL OF SOME USE (*story*)   *111*

> A man helps his ex-wife and his sons clean out their house on moving day. The artifacts of his former life — toys, games, a kerosene lamp — remind him of all that is over.

E. B. White ONCE MORE TO THE LAKE   *117*

> A father takes his son to the Maine vacation retreat to which his own father often brought him, and his confused sense of time unnerves him

Robert F. Sayre THE PARENTS' LAST LESSONS   *124*

> A writer examines the lives and deaths of the father, mother, and great-aunt who defined the world of his youth and learns something from each.

IMAGES: Owen Franken, *Harvard Graduation*   *143*
        Linda G. Rich, *Murty, Ananta, and Santhi Hejeebu*
        Michael Hayman, *Family — Byron, Michigan*

Additional Writing Topics   *146*

3. GROUP PICTURES   *149*

INSIGHTS: *John Donne, Ralph Waldo Emerson, Theodore Reik, Jean-Paul Sartre, W. E. B. DuBois*   *150*

Dean MacCannell THE TOURIST   *153*

> All of us become tourists at one time or another, but what makes a tourist? And what makes a tourist so uncomfortable?

Edward C. Martin BEING JUNIOR HIGH   *156*

> A teacher examines the anxious desire to belong and the beginnings of confusion about authority that characterize his twelve- to fourteen-year-old students.

Maya Angelou GRADUATION 162

A commencement speaker's prejudice threatens but cannot destroy the pride of a black community.

John Cheever EXPELLED (*story*) 175

A student examines the unthinking conformity and unquestioned beliefs that governed the students *and* faculty at a prep school from which he has just been expelled.

Maxine Hong Kingston THE MISERY OF SILENCE 186

The language barrier is the greater wall of China for this immigrant child raised in a small California city.

James Agee THREE SINGERS 192

On a dusty road in Alabama during the Great Depression, black and white meet — and a young white journalist learns a lesson about racial conflict, the legacy of history, and the pride of an oppressed people.

Desmond Morris TERRITORIAL BEHAVIOR 198

A zoologist maintains that groups exist in order to protect their own turf and that people realize who they are by noticing where they are.

Sylvia Plath MUSHROOMS (*poem*) 208

The ordinary behavior of a seemingly docile, unassertive fungus takes on eerie, threatening force.

Alexis de Tocqueville ARISTOCRACY AND DEMOCRACY 211

Few observers had a better grasp of what it means to be an American than this nineteenth-century Frenchman. Here he looks at some of the social changes that take place in a society without an aristocracy.

IMAGES: Peter Vandermark, *Junior High School*   214
Robert Frank, *Cocktail Party — New York City*
Elinor B. Cohn, *Celebration of Friendship*
Elinor B. Cohn, *Polish-American War Mothers*

Additional Writing Topics   *218*

4. POSSESSIONS   221

INSIGHTS: *Henry David Thoreau, Henry James,*
Matthew   222

William Ryan MINE, ALL MINE   223

A social psychologist finds the whole idea of *ownership* a little incredible.

E. M. Forster MY WOOD   230

An English novelist finds that owning a stretch of forest changes his view of it: being a landowner brings out unwelcome attitudes.

Flannery O'Connor THE KING OF THE BIRDS   234

A famous writer acknowledges her lifelong servitude to these regal, gorgeous, maddening peacocks.

Matthew THE LILIES OF THE FIELD (*poem*)   242

In the Sermon on the Mount, Jesus warns his listeners not to be overly concerned about property and gain, lest they lose sight of more important things.

John Kenneth Galbraith ACCOMMODATION TO
POVERTY   244

An economist points out that victims of mass poverty have no reason to try to improve themselves, when experience virtually guarantees that they won't succeed.

Kennedy Fraser MODESTY   247

> Each change in fashion exposes or conceals more flesh and constructs or removes more taboos. A fashion critic considers some historical changes, especially in women's swimwear, and ponders the "last frontier" of modesty.

Harry Crews THE CAR   252

> A southern writer recalls the period when he seemed to live entirely through his cars: They organized his activities and defined his personality.

John Ciardi A CADILLAC FULL OF
            DIAMONDS (*story*)   257

> The alarming allegory might well be a dramatization of Jesus' point in the Sermon on the Mount: In a man's mad quest for wealth and success, his possessions come to own him.

Jack Matthews A REASONABLE MADNESS   261

> The passion for book collecting gives this otherwise mild-mannered man a mission to rescue forgotten volumes from their dust.

IMAGES: Norman Sanders, *Andrew*   269
        Jeff Albertson, *Rolls-Royce*
        Linda G. Rich, *Miss May*

Additional Writing Topics   272

5. AMBITIONS   275

INSIGHTS: *Robert Browning, Vince Lombardi, Vincent van Gogh, John Keats*   276

Joseph Epstein THE VIRTUES OF AMBITION   277

> The editor of *The American Scholar* makes a large claim for the importance of ambition at the center of individual character and social order.

Andrew Carnegie HOW I SERVED MY
                 APPRENTICESHIP   283

> An industrial giant of the nineteenth century reveals how he started on the rise to success through diligence, thrift, and pluck.

Pauline Newman WORKING FOR THE UNION   288

> A union organizer speaks of her ambition to bring the fair rewards of hard work, not just to herself, but to a whole class of workers in the turbulent early decades of the twentieth century.

Richard Rodriguez READING FOR SUCCESS   296

> The author, raised in a home where English was not the first language, considers his drive to get an education — and the sacrifices he and his family had to make — in order to be a success in America.

Seymour Wishman A LAWYER'S GUILTY
                 SECRETS   302

> What it takes to be a good lawyer isn't always the same as what it takes to be a good person. A successful criminal lawyer reflects on the competition, the conflicts, and the compromises of his profession.

Fran Lebowitz THE LAST LAUGH   306

> A popular writer tells about the trials of "setting up shop" in the humor business.

Sherwood Anderson THE EGG (*story*)   311

> A boy observes what happens to his father when "the American passion for getting up in the world" takes hold of the family.

Ecclesiastes ALL IS VANITY (*poem*)   322

> A bleak but arresting biblical view of the futility of human endeavor.

Henry David Thoreau WHERE I LIVED,
                      AND WHAT I LIVED FOR   325

> America's most famous free spirit wants us to recognize that what we *do* in life becomes our life.

Virginia Woolf PROFESSIONS FOR WOMEN   329

> To learn to write truthfully, this novelist had to face inner obstacles, which she explains to other women entering any profession.

IMAGES: Donald Patterson, *Campaigning*   335
         David S. Strickler, *Showing Little Brother the Trophies*
         Peter Vandermark, *Piano Recital*

Additional Writing Topics   338

6. LOVE AND LONGINGS   341

INSIGHTS: *François de La Rochefoucauld, St. John, Walker Percy, anonymous, Selma Fraiberg*   342

Susan Allen Toth THE BOYFRIEND   344

> Having a boyfriend was a requirement in high school — but this one was special. An Iowa woman remembers her adolescence in the 1950s.

Wendell Berry GETTING MARRIED   352

> The symbolic place in which a marriage gets started continues to influence a couple's life together.

Katherine Mansfield SIX LOVE LETTERS   357

> From a foreign country, a writer tells her lover of her preparations and her longing for his imminent visit.

Robert Solomon "I-LOVE-YOU"   364

> What claims and what challenges do we make when we utter those three daring words? A philosopher considers words as actions

William Shakespeare WHEN, IN DISGRACE WITH
                    FORTUNE AND MEN'S EYES
                    (*poem*)   369

> "For thy sweet love rememb'red such wealth brings,
> That then I scorn to change my state with kings."

Raymond Carver WHAT WE TALK ABOUT WHEN
               WE TALK ABOUT LOVE (*story*)   371

> When the drinks begin to flow, two couples get more and more upset as they try to discuss what real love means.

D. H. Lawrence COUNTERFEIT LOVE   384

> A novelist laments the death of real emotion and its inevitable, terrible consequences.

Ernest van den Haag LOVE OR MARRIAGE?   388

> A psychoanalyst argues that we've got the idea of marriage all wrong, and our lives show it.

Jill Tweedie THE FUTURE OF LOVE   399

> A feminist tells us some of the things we mistake for love and imagines what we will need to learn in order to experience *real* love.

IMAGES: Frank Siteman, *At the Beach*   406
Frank Siteman, *At the Party*
Katrina Thomas, *Bride*
Samuel Cooper Studio, *Wedding Reception Line*

Additional Writing Topics   *410*

7. DILEMMAS   *413*

INSIGHTS: *anonymous, Konrad Lorenz, Sissela Bok, E. M. Forster, Roy Schafer*   *414*

Robert Frost THE ROAD NOT TAKEN (*poem*)   *416*

The poet looks back on a moment of decision.

Neil Chayet LAW AND MORALITY   *418*

A lawyer recounts a case in which what's right and what's legal are not the same.

Leo Rosten HOME IS WHERE TO LEARN HOW TO HATE   *420*

We've got to learn somewhere that anger contributes to our sense of right and wrong, says a leading essayist.

Willie Morris CAMPUS POLITICS   *427*

The editor of a college newspaper (later the editor of *Harper's*) faces, for the first time, pressure from influential outsiders to "kill" a story.

Patrick Henry LIBERTY OR DEATH!   *435*

At the dawn of the American Revolution, a Virginia legislator tries to convince his colleagues that the time for talking is over and the time for action is at hand.

George Orwell SHOOTING AN ELEPHANT   *439*

> An incident that might at first seem amusing teaches a young Englishman a lesson about the mutual fear, hatred, and suspicion that a colonial power and a native people feel toward each other.

William Carlos Williams THE USE OF FORCE
(*story*)   *448*

> In a troublesome case, a country doctor finds himself making all the right decisions for all the wrong reasons.

Jonathan Swift A MODEST PROPOSAL   *453*

> The great eighteenth-century satirist presents an extreme and shocking solution to the problem of poverty in Ireland.

Jonathan Schell THE CHOICE   *462*

> The nuclear arms race creates a horrifying situation that people do not want to face, but there is no way to avoid the problem.

Robert Jastrow AN END AND A BEGINNING   *471*

> Computers are growing more intelligent than people. It is just a matter of time before they redefine life as we know it.

IMAGES: Frank Johnston, *The Longest Walk*   *477*
Gary Kemper, *Ajax Bay, Falkland Islands: Cross Marks the Grave of Col. H. Jones*
Robert Capa, *France: Followed by Jeers and Marked by Her Shaved Head, a Woman Collaborator Carries Her Baby out of the Town of Chartres Following Its Capture by Allied Troops, 1944*

Additional Writing Topics   *480*

Rhetorical Index   *487*

TO STUDENTS

◊

The title of this book, *Life Studies*, alludes to the series of sketches an artist makes of the human figure in solitude and in society. Each selection in this book presents a different perspective on the individual. Taken together, the selections reveal the complexity of the individual in varied and deep connections with other people and also with objects, ideas, and nonhuman things in the natural world. Like the artist's studies, the essays can open up new ideas about your own and other people's experiences. By writing about the topics you can gain a clearer understanding of what you know and who you are, as the artist gains a clearer understanding of his or her subject by sketching it.

The selections in *Life Studies* examine matters that are probably important to you. They are organized into seven actions, covering our images of ourselves, our family relationships, our behavior in groups, our connection to valued possessions, our long-range desires and ambitions, our love and longings for other people, and our moral dilemmas. Besides offering diverse and fresh perspectives on significant subjects, the readings also present written language of remarkably high quality. Written language is different from spoken language, so it is acquired mainly through extensive reading. The written language is not the spoken "mother tongue" in which we express ourselves easily and directly to others. It is less tied to momentary situations, it is more compact and formal, and it offers a vastly increased vocabulary. In writing we use sentences that are more complex and diversified; even our thinking changes when we take time to develop precisely what we mean. Learning to write originally and effectively requires practice in reading as well as writing. This book guides you in both activities by providing well-written, interesting selections that suggest writing assignments on stimulating topics.

Whether humorous or solemn about their subject, the authors of the selections considered it important to formulate their viewpoint into words. They tried to be precise in their observations, and they seem to find pleasure — sometimes even great delight — in clarifying and sharing their ideas and feelings about the subject. They discover something through writing about it. By learning to write well, you too will discover something about your world.

Life Studies

A Thematic Reader

1

SELF-IMAGES

INSIGHTS

Photographs actively promote nostalgia. Photography is an elegiac art, a twilight art. Most subjects photographed are, just by virtue of being photographed, touched with pathos. An ugly or grotesque subject may be moving because it has been dignified by the attention of the photographer. A beautiful subject can be the object of rueful feelings, because it has aged or decayed or no longer exists. All photographs are *memento mori*. To take a photograph is to participate in another person's (or thing's) mortality, vulnerability, mutability. Precisely by slicing out this moment and freezing it, all photographs testify to time's relentless melt.

— SUSAN SONTAG

The nicknames children bestow on one another can confer power. Like ancient Rome, the playground republic marks off the inner core of citizens from barbarians. Those who have no nicknames have no social existence; they are the nonpeople. . . . To be nicknamed is to be seen as having an attribute that entitles one to social attention, even if that attention is unpleasant. Thus, it may be better to be called "Sewage" than merely John.

— ROM HARRE

I do not know what it is to see into the heart of a friend through that "window of the soul," the eye. I can only "see" through my finger tips the outline of a face. I can detect laughter, sorrow, and many other obvious emotions. I know my friends from the feel of their faces. But I cannot really picture their personalities by touch. I know their

4

personalities, of course, through other means, through the thoughts they express to me, through whatever of their actions are revealed to me. But I am denied that deeper understanding of them which I am sure would come through sight of them, through watching their reactions to various expressed thoughts and circumstances, through noting the immediate and fleeting reactions of their eyes and countenance.

— HELEN KELLER

Nora Ephron

SHAPING UP ABSURD

◊

NORA EPHRON (b. 1941) grew up in Hollywood amid an adult world of screenwriters, entertainers, and celebrities. This background may have had more to do with shaping her self-image than the physical trait of flat-chestedness that she writes about in this essay. She wanted to be a writer, and she began her career as a journalist in New York by writing for *Newsweek* and contributing articles to entertainment magazines. Her essays have been collected in *Wallflower at the Orgy* (1970) and *Crazy Salad* (1975). In this essay Ephron deals frankly with intimate personal experience that is not usually discussed openly. Her candor gives us a view of preadolescent girlhood that is full of humor and sympathy for the young. Furthermore, her observations about her adult experience suggest that people hold very peculiar attitudes, which accounts for some of her personal distress.

I have to begin with a few words about androgyny. In grammar 1 school, in the fifth and sixth grades, we were all tyrannized by a rigid set of rules that supposedly determined whether we were boys or girls. The episode in *Huckleberry Finn* where Huck is disguised as a girl and gives himself away by the way he threads a needle and catches a ball — that kind of thing. We learned that the way you sat, crossed your legs, held a cigarette and looked at your nails, your wristwatch, the way you did these things instinctively was absolute proof of your sex. Now obviously most children did not take this literally, but I did. I thought that just one slip, just one incorrect cross of my legs or flick of an imaginary cigarette ash would turn me from whatever I was into the other thing; that would be all it took, really. Even though I was outwardly a girl and had many of the trappings generally associated with the field of girldom — a girl's name, for example, and dresses, my own telephone, an autograph book — I spent the early years of my adolescence absolutely certain that I might at any point gum it up. I did not feel at all like a girl. I was boyish. I was athletic, ambitious, outspoken, competitive, noisy, rambunctious. I had scabs on my knees and my socks slid into my loafers and I could throw a football. I wanted desperately not to be that way, not to be a mixture of both things but instead just one, a girl, a definite indisputable girl. As soft and as pink as a nursery. And nothing would do that for me, I felt, but breasts.

I was about six months younger than everyone in my class, and so 2 for about six months after it began, for six months after my friends had begun to develop — that was the word we used, develop — I was not particularly worried. I would sit in the bathtub and look down at my breasts and know that any day now, any second now, they would start growing like everyone else's. They didn't. "I want to buy a bra," I said to my mother one night. "What for?" she said. My mother was really hateful about bras, and by the time my third sister had gotten to that point where she was ready to want one, my mother had worked the whole business into a comedy routine, "Why not use a Band-Aid instead?" she would say. It was a source of great pride to my mother that she had never even had to wear a brassiere until she had her fourth child, and then only because her gynecologist made her. It was incomprehensible to me that anyone would ever be proud of something like that. It was the 1950's, for God's sake. Jane Russell. Cashmere sweaters. Couldn't my mother see that? *"I am too old to wear an undershirt."* Screaming. Weeping. Shouting. "Then don't wear an undershirt," said my mother. "But I want to buy a bra." "What for?"

I suppose that for most girls, breasts, brassieres, that entire thing, 3 has more trauma, more to do with the coming of adolescence, of becoming a woman, than anything else. Certainly more than getting your period, although that too was traumatic, symbolic. But you could *see* breasts; they were there; they were visible. Whereas a girl could claim to have her period for months before she actually got it and nobody would ever know the difference. Which is exactly what I did. All you had to do was make a great fuss over having enough nickels for the Kotex machine and walk around clutching your stomach and moaning for three to five days a month about The Curse and you could convince anybody. There is a school of thought somewhere in the women's lib/women's mag/gynecology establishment that claims that menstrual cramps are purely psychological, and I lean toward it. Not that I didn't have them finally. Agonizing cramps, heating-pad cramps, go-down-to-the-school-nurse-and-lie-on-the-cot cramps. But unlike any pain I had ever suffered, I adored the pain of cramps, welcomed it, wallowed in it, bragged about it. "I can't go. I have cramps." "I can't do that. I have cramps." And most of all, gigglingly, blushingly: "I can't swim. I have cramps." Nobody ever used the hard-core word. Menstruation. God, what an awful word. Never that. "I have cramps."

The morning I first got my period, I went into my mother's bed- 4 room to tell her. And my mother, my utterly-hateful-about-bras mother, burst into tears. It was really a lovely moment, and I remember it so clearly not just because it was one of the two times I ever saw my mother cry on my account (the other was when I was caught being a six-year-old kleptomaniac), but also because the incident did not mean to me what it meant to her. Her little girl, her firstborn, had finally become a woman. That was what she was crying about. My reaction to the event, however, was that I might well be a woman in some scientific, textbook sense (and could at least stop faking every month and stop wasting all those nickels). But in another sense — in a visible sense — I was as androgynous and as liable to tip over into boyhood as ever.

I started with a 28AA bra. I don't think they made them any 5 smaller in those days, although I gather that now you can buy bras for five year olds that don't have any cups whatsoever in them; trainer bras they are called. My first brassiere came from Robinson's Department Store in Beverly Hills. I went there alone, shaking, positive they would look me over and smile and tell me to come back next year. An actual fitter took me into the dressing room and stood over me while I took off my blouse and tried the first one on. The little puffs stood out on my chest. "Lean over," said the fitter (to this day I am not sure what fitters in bra departments do except to tell you to lean over). I leaned over, with the fleeting hope that my breasts would miraculously fall out of my body and into the puffs. Nothing.

"Don't worry about it," said my friend Libby some months later, 6 when things had not improved. "You'll get them after you're married."

"What are you talking about?" I said.   7

"When you get married," Libby explained, "your husband will 8
touch your breasts and rub them and kiss them and they'll grow."
That was the killer. Necking I could deal with. Intercourse I could 9
deal with. But it had never crossed my mind that a man was going to
touch my breasts, that breasts had something to do with all that, petting, my God they never mentioned petting in my little sex manual
about the fertilization of the ovum. I became dizzy. For I knew in-
stantly — as naïve as I had been only a moment before — that only
part of what she was saying was true: the touching, rubbing, kissing
part, not the growing part. And I knew that no one would ever want to
marry me. I had no breasts. I would never have breasts.

My best friend in school was Diana Raskob. She lived a block from 10
me in a house full of wonders. English muffins, for instance. The Ras-
kobs were the first people in Beverly Hills to have English muffins for
breakfast. They also had an apricot tree in the back, and a badminton
court, and a subscription to *Seventeen* magazine, and hundreds of
games like Sorry and Parcheesi and Treasure Hunt and Anagrams.
Diana and I spent three or four afternoons a week in their den reading
and playing and eating. Diana's mother's kitchen was full of the most
colossal assortment of junk food I have ever been exposed to. My
house was full of apples and peaches and milk and homemade choco-
late-chip cookies — which were nice, and good for you, but-not-right-
before-dinner-or-you'll-spoil-your-appetite. Diana's house had nothing
in it that was good for you, and what's more, you could stuff it in right
up until dinner and nobody cared. Bar-B-Q potato chips (they were
the first in them, too), giant bottles of ginger ale, fresh popcorn with
melted butter, hot fudge sauce on Baskin-Robbins jamoca ice cream,
powdered-sugar doughnuts from Van de Kamps. Diana and I had
been best friends since we were seven; we were about equally popular
in school (which is to say, not particularly), we had about the same
success with boys (extremely intermittent), and we looked much the
same. Dark. Tall. Gangly.

It is September, just before school begins. I am eleven years old, 11
about to enter the seventh grade, and Diana and I have not seen each
other all summer. I have been to camp and she has been somewhere
like Banff with her parents. We are meeting, as we often do, on the
street midway between our two houses and we will walk back to
Diana's and eat junk and talk about what has happened to each of us

that summer. I am walking down Walden Drive in my jeans and my father's shirt hanging out and my old red loafers with the socks falling into them and coming toward me is . . . I take a deep breath . . . a young woman. Diana. Her hair is curled and she has a waist and hips and a bust and she is wearing a straight skirt, an article of clothing I have been repeatedly told I will be unable to wear until I have the hips to hold it up. My jaw drops, and suddenly I am crying, crying hysterically, can't catch my breath sobbing. My best friend has betrayed me. She has gone ahead without me and done it. She has shaped up.

Here are some things I did to help: 12
Bought a Mark Eden Bust Developer.   13
Slept on my back for four years.   14
Splashed cold water on them every night because some French ac-   15 tress said in *Life* magazine that that was what *she* did for her perfect bustline.

Ultimately, I resigned myself to a bad toss and began to wear pad-   16 ded bras. I think about them now, think about all those years in high school I went around in them, my three padded bras, every single one of them with different sized breasts. Each time I changed bras I changed sizes: one week nice perky but not too obtrusive breasts, the next medium-sized slightly pointed ones, the next week knockers, true knockers; all the time, whatever size I was, carrying around this rubberized appendage on my chest that occasionally crashed into a wall and was poked inward and had to be poked outward — I think about all that and wonder how anyone kept a straight face through it. My parents, who normally had no restraints about needling me — why did they say nothing as they watched my chest go up and down? My friends, who would periodically inspect my breasts for signs of growth and reassure me — why didn't they at least counsel consistency?

And the bathing suits. I die when I think about the bathing suits.   17 That was the era when you could lay an uninhabited bathing suit on the beach and someone would make a pass at it. I would put one on, an absurd swimsuit with its enormous bust built into it, the bones from the suit stabbing me in the rib cage and leaving little red welts on my body, and there I would be, my chest plunging straight downward absolutely vertically from my collarbone to the top of my suit and then suddenly, wham, out came all that padding and material and wiring absolutely horizontally.

Buster Klepper was the first boy who ever touched them. He was 18
my boyfriend my senior year of high school. There is a picture of him
in my high-school yearbook that makes him look quite attractive in a
Jewish, horn-rimmed glasses sort of way, but the picture does not
show the pimples, which were air-brushed out, or the dumbness.
Well, that isn't really fair. He wasn't dumb. He just wasn't terribly
bright. His mother refused to accept it, refused to accept the relent-
lessly average report cards, refused to deal with her son's inevitable
destiny in some junior college or other. "He was tested," she would
say to me, apropos of nothing, "and it came out 145. That's near-
genius." Had the word underachiever been coined, she probably
would have lobbed that one at me, too. Anyway, Buster was really
very sweet — which is, I know, damning with faint praise, but there it
is. I was the editor of the front page of the high-school newspaper and
he was editor of the back page; we had to work together, side by side,
in the print shop, and that was how it started. On our first date, we
went to see *April Love* starring Pat Boone. Then we started going together. Buster had a green coupe, a 1950 Ford with an engine he had
handchromed until it shone, dazzled, reflected the image of anyone
who looked into it, anyone usually being Buster polishing it or the
gas-station attendants he constantly asked to check the oil in order for
them to be overwhelmed by the sparkle on the valves. The car also
had a boot stretched over the back seat for reasons I never understood;
hanging from the rearview mirror, as was the custom, was a pair of an-
gora dice. A previous girl friend named Solange who was famous
throughout Beverly Hills High School for having no pigment in her
right eyebrow had knitted them for him. Buster and I would ride
around town, the two of us seated to the left of the steering wheel. I
would shift gears. It was nice.

There was necking. Terrific necking. First in the car, overlooking 19
Los Angeles from what is now the Trousdale Estates. Then on the
bed of his parents' cabana at Ocean House. Incredibly wonderful,
frustrating necking, I loved it, really, but no further than necking,
please don't, please, because there I was absolutely terrified of the
general implications of going-a-step-further with a near-dummy and
also terrified of his finding out there was next to nothing there (which
he knew, of course; he wasn't that dumb).

I broke up with him at one point. I think we were apart for about 20
two weeks. At the end of that time I drove down to see a friend at a

boarding school in Palos Verdes Estates and a disc jockey played *April Love* on the radio four times during the trip. I took it as a sign. I drove straight back to Griffith Park to a golf tournament Buster was playing in (he was the sixth-seeded teen-age golf player in Southern California) and presented myself back to him on the green of the 18th hole. It was all very dramatic. That night we went to a drive-in and I let him get his hand under my protuberances and onto my breasts. He really didn't seem to mind at all.

"Do you want to marry my son?" the woman asked me.   21

"Yes," I said.   22

I was nineteen years old, a virgin, going with this woman's son, this   23 *big strange woman who was married to a Lutheran minister in New Hampshire and pretended she was Gentile and had this son, by her first husband, this total fool of a son who ran the hero-sandwich concession at Harvard Business School and whom for one moment one December in New Hampshire I said — as much out of politeness as anything else — that I wanted to marry.*

"Fine," she said. "Now, here's what you do. Always make sure   24 *you're on top of him so you won't seem so small. My bust is very large, you see, so I always lie on my back to make it look smaller, but you'll have to be on top most of the time."*

I nodded. "Thank you," I said.   25

"I have a book for you to read," she went on. "Take it with you   26 *when you leave. Keep it." She went to the bookshelf, found it, and gave it to me. It was a book on frigidity.*

"Thank you," I said.   27

That is a true story. Everything in this article is a true story, but I   28 feel I have to point out that that story in particular is true. It happened on December 30, 1960. I think about it often. When it first happened, I naturally assumed that the woman's son, my boyfriend, was responsible. I invented a scenario where he had had a little heart-to-heart with his mother and confessed that his only objection to me was that my breasts were small; his mother then took it upon herself to help out. Now I think I was wrong about the incident. The mother was acting on her own, I think: that was her way of being cruel and competitive under the guise of being helpful and maternal. You have small breasts, she was saying; therefore you will never make him as happy as I have. Or you have small breasts; therefore you will doubtless have sexual problems. Or you have small breasts; therefore you are less woman than I am. She was, as it happens, only the first of what seems to me to be a never-ending string of women who have made competitive remarks to me about breast size. "I would love to wear a dress like that," my friend Emily says to me, "but my bust is too big." Like that. Why do women say these things to me? Do I attract these remarks the way other women attract married men or alcoholics or homosexuals? This summer, for example. I am at a party in East Hampton and I am introduced to a woman from Washington. She is a minor celebrity, very pretty and Southern and blonde and outspoken and I am flattered because she has read something I have written. We are talking animatedly, we have been talking no more than five minutes, when a man comes up to join us. "Look at the two of us," the woman says to the man, indicating me and her. "The two of us together couldn't fill an A cup." Why does she say that? It isn't even true, dammit, so why? Is she even more addled than I am on this subject? Does she honestly believe there is something wrong with her size breasts, which, it seems to me, now that I look hard at them, are just right? Do I unconsciously bring out competitiveness in women? In that form? What did I do to deserve it?

As for men.　　　　　　　　　　　　　　　　　29

There were men who minded and let me know they minded. There 30 were men who did not mind. In any case, I always minded.

And even now, now that I have been countlessly reassured that my 31 figure is a good one, now that I am grown up enough to understand that most of my feelings have very little to do with the reality of my shape, I am nonetheless obsessed by breasts. I cannot help it. I grew up in the terrible Fifties — with rigid stereotypical sex roles, the insistence that men be men and dress like men and women be women and dress like women, the intolerance of androgyny — and I cannot shake it, cannot shake my feelings of inadequacy. Well, that time is gone, right? All those exaggerated examples of breast worship are gone, right? Those women were freaks, right? I know all that. And yet, here I am, stuck with the psychological remains of it all, stuck with my own peculiar version of breast worship. You probably think I am crazy to go on like this: here I have set out to write a confession that is meant to hit you with the shock of recognition and instead you are sitting there thinking I am thoroughly warped. Well, what can I tell you? If I had had them, I would have been a completely different person. I honestly believe that.

After I went into therapy, a process that made it possible for me to 32 tell total strangers at cocktail parties that breasts were the hang-up of my life, I was often told that I was insane to have been bothered by my condition. I was also frequently told, by close friends, that I was extremely boring on the subject. And my girl friends, the ones with nice big breasts, would go on endlessly about how their lives had been far more miserable than mine. Their bra straps were snapped in class. They couldn't sleep on their stomachs. They were stared at whenever the word "mountain" cropped up in geography. And *Evangeline*, good God what they went through every time someone had to stand up and recite the Prologue to Longfellow's *Evangeline:* "*. . . stand like druids of eld . . . / With beards that rest on their bosoms.*" It was much worse for them, they tell me. They had a terrible time of it, they assure me. I don't know how lucky I was, they say.

I have thought about their remarks, tried to put myself in their 33 place, considered their point of view. I think they are full of shit.

CONSIDERATIONS

1. Ephron establishes a very informal, colloquial tone right from the first paragraph. Underline the key words and phrases in the opening paragraph that help set this tone. What is the correlation between this tone of voice and the subject of her essay?
2. As a child Ephron felt sure that her every distress would lead to a large, fateful disaster. In addition to her flat-chestedness, what else does she worry over? How does she express these worries?
3. What is the point of the section about her friend Diana? Does her name fit the effect that she has on Ephron? Similarly, what is the point of the section about Buster Klepper? And what are the connotations of his name? Did they fit his effect on her?
4. Both Nora Ephron and Mary McCarthy (see the third essay in this chapter, p. 20) suffered mortifications in their girlhood that they say affected their adult character. Compare the kinds of humiliation they endured. What were the aspirations that made each girl feel dissatisfied with herself?

5. WRITING TOPIC. Near the end of the essay, Ephron says, "If I had had them, I would have been a completely different person. I honestly believe that." Being unusually tall or short, thin or fat, red-haired, freckled, pretty, or thoroughly average, can seem to be the most important fact in your existence. Write a 500-word essay on how one trait came to have exaggerated importance for some period in your life.

Suzanne Britt Jordan

THAT LEAN
AND HUNGRY LOOK

◇

Suzanne Britt Jordan (b. 1946) is a free-lance writer who lives in Raleigh, North Carolina, where she has taught college English. She was educated at Salem College. Jordan writes a newspaper column and contributes articles to *Newsday*, the *New York Times*, and *Newsweek*, in which the following selection first appeared. Jordan expanded this humorous treatment of a plump person's view of thin people in her first book, *Skinny People Are Dull and Crunchy Like Carrots* (1982).

Caesar was right. Thin people need watching. I've been watching 1 them for most of my adult life, and I don't like what I see. When these narrow fellows spring at me, I quiver to my toes. Thin people come in all personalities, most of them menacing. You've got your "together" thin person, your mechanical thin person, your condescending thin person, your tsk-tsk thin person, your efficiency-expert thin person. All of them are dangerous.

In the first place, thin people aren't fun. They don't know how to 2 goof off, at least in the best, fat sense of the word. They've always got to be adoing. Give them a coffee break, and they'll jog around the block. Supply them with a quiet evening at home, and they'll fix the screen door and lick S&H green stamps. They say things like "there aren't enough hours in the day." Fat people never say that. Fat people think the day is too damn long already.

Thin people make me tired. They've got speedy little metabolisms 3 that cause them to bustle briskly. They're forever rubbing their bony hands together and eyeing new problems to "tackle." I like to surround myself with sluggish, inert, easygoing fat people, the kind who believe that if you clean it up today, it'll just get dirty again tomorrow.

Some people say the business about the jolly fat person is a myth, 4 that all of us chubbies are neurotic, sick, sad people. I disagree. Fat people may not be chortling all day long, but they're a hell of a lot *nicer* than the wizened and shriveled. Thin people turn surly, mean, and hard at a young age because they never learn the value of a hot-fudge sundae for easing tension. Thin people don't like gooey soft things because they themselves are neither gooey nor soft. They are crunchy and dull, like carrots. They go straight to the heart of the matter while fat people let things stay all blurry and hazy and vague, the way things actually are. Thin people want to face the truth. Fat people know there is no truth. One of my thin friends is always staring at complex, unsolvable problems and saying, "The key thing is. . . ." Fat people never say that. They know there isn't any such thing as the key thing about anything.

Thin people believe in logic. Fat people see all sides. The sides fat 5 people see are rounded blobs, usually gray, always nebulous and truly not worth worrying about. But the thin person persists. "If you con-sume more calories than you burn," says one of my thin friends, "you will gain weight. It's that simple." Fat people always grin when they hear statements like that. They know better.

Fat people realize that life is illogical and unfair. They know very 6 well that God is not in his heaven and all is not right with the world. If God was up there, fat people could have two doughnuts and a big orange drink anytime they wanted it.

Thin people have a long list of logical things they are always spout- 7 ing off to me. They hold up one finger at a time as they reel off these things, so I won't lose track. They speak slowly as if to a young child. The list is long and full of holes. It contains tidbits like "get a grip on yourself," "cigarettes kill," "cholesterol clogs," "fit as a fiddle," "ducks in a row," "organize," and "sound fiscal management." Phrases like that.

They think these 2,000-point plans lead to happiness. Fat people 8 know happiness is elusive at best and even if they could get the kind thin people talk about, they wouldn't want it. Wisely, fat people see that such programs are too dull, too hard, too off the mark. They are never better than a whole cheesecake.

Fat people know all about the mystery of life. They are the ones 9 acquainted with the night, with luck, with fate, with playing it by ear.

One thin person I know once suggested that we arrange all the parts of a jigsaw puzzle into groups according to size, shape, and color. He figured this would cut the time needed to complete the puzzle by at least 50 percent. I said I wouldn't do it. One, I like to muddle through. Two, what good would it do to finish early? Three, the jigsaw puzzle isn't the important thing. The important thing is the fun of four people (one thin person included) sitting around a card table, working a jigsaw puzzle. My thin friend had no use for my list. Instead of joining us, he went outside and mulched the boxwoods. The three remaining fat people finished the puzzle and made chocolate, double-fudged brownies to celebrate.

The main problem with thin people is they oppress. Their good intentions, bony torsos, tight ships, neat corners, cerebral machinations, and pat solutions loom like dark clouds over the loose, comfortable, spread-out, soft world of the fat. Long after fat people have removed their coats and shoes and put their feet up on the coffee table, thin people are still sitting on the edge of the sofa, looking neat as a pin, discussing rutabagas. Fat people are heavily into fits of laughter, slapping their thighs and whooping it up, while thin people are still politely waiting for the punch line. 10

Thin people are downers. They like math and morality and reasoned evaluation of the limitations of human beings. They have their skinny little acts together. They expound, prognose, probe, and prick. 11

Fat people are convivial. They will like you even if you're irregular and have acne. They will come up with a good reason why you never wrote the great American novel. They will cry in your beer with you. They will put your name in the pot. They will let you off the hook. Fat people will gab, giggle, guffaw, gallumph, gyrate, and gossip. They are generous, giving, and gallant. They are gluttonous and goodly and great. What you want when you're down is soft and jiggly, not muscled and stable. Fat people know this. Fat people have plenty of room. Fat people will take you in. 12

CONSIDERATIONS

1. One after another, the author presents a string of specific contrasts between thin and fat people. What kind of material would have to be added

if the author devoted the first half of the essay entirely to thin people and the second half to fat people? How would that method of contrast change the tone of the essay?

2. Do you think this essay is offensive to thin people? Why or why not?
3. What personality traits does Jordan value most highly? What traits does she find most objectionable?
4. WRITING TOPIC. Is there some truth in the view that red-haired people have bad tempers? Are short men apt to be aggressive? Are people with brown eyes more loving than blue-eyed people? Does a high forehead signify intelligence? Do long fingers indicate gentleness? Taking up one of these bits of popular body lore, explain in 500 words why it may seem to be true even though we know it is unfounded.

Mary McCarthy

NAMES

MARY MCCARTHY (b. 1912) writes sophisticated, satirical fiction about college life and young womanhood, such as *The Company She Keeps* (1942), *The Groves of Academe* (1952), and *The Group* (1963). She has also written penetrating social criticism and political reportage in books about the Vietnam war and the Watergate coverup. Educated at Vassar, she undertook a career in journalism in New York before turning to fiction writing and to mixing memories and fiction together in her memoirs. In this chapter from her *Memories of a Catholic Girlhood* (1957), she recalls the importance she attached to names, especially after she moved back from Minneapolis to Seattle, where as an orphan she was raised by her grandparents. She implies that the early difficulties of dealing with her names influenced her adult character.

Anna Lyons, Mary Louise Lyons, Mary von Phul, Emilie von Phul, 1 Eugenia McLellan, Marjorie McPhail, Marie-Louise L'Abbé, Mary Danz, Julia Dodge, Mary Fordyce Blake, Janet Preston — these were the names (I can still tell them over like a rosary) of some of the older girls in the convent: the Virtues and Graces. The virtuous ones wore wide blue or green moire good-conduct ribbons, bandoleer-style, across their blue serge uniforms; the beautiful ones wore rouge and powder or at least were reputed to do so. Our class, the eighth grade, wore pink ribbons (I never got one myself) and had names like Patricia ("Pat") Sullivan, Eileen Donohoe, and Joan Kane. We were inelegant even in this respect; the best name we could show, among us, was Phyllis ("Phil") Chatham, who boasted that her father's name, Ralph, was pronounced "Rafe" as in England.

Names had a great importance for us in the convent, and foreign 2 names, French, German, or plain English (which, to us, were foreign, because of their Protestant sound), bloomed like prize roses among a collection of spuds. Irish names were too common in the school to have any prestige either as surnames (Gallagher, Sheehan, Finn, Sullivan, McCarthy) or as Christian names (Kathleen, Eileen). Anything exotic had value: an "olive"complexion, for example. The pet girl of the convent was a fragile Jewish girl named Susie Lowenstein, who had pale red-gold hair and an exquisite retroussé nose, which, if we had had it, might have been called "pug." We liked her name too and the name of a child in the primary grades: Abbie Stuart Baillargeon. My favorite name, on the whole, though, was Emilie von Phul (pronounced "Pool"); her oldest sister, recently graduated, was called Celeste. Another name that appealed to me was Genevieve Albers, Saint Genevieve being the patron saint of Paris who turned back Attila from the gates of the city.

All these names reflected the still-pioneer character of the Pacific ₃ Northwest. I had never heard their like in the parochial school in Minneapolis, where "foreign" extraction, in any case, was something to be ashamed of, the whole drive being toward Americanization of first name and surname alike. The exceptions to this were the Irish, who could vaunt such names as Catherine O'Dea and the name of my second cousin, Mary Catherine Anne Rose Violet McCarthy, while an unfortunate German boy named Manfred was made to suffer for his. But that was Minneapolis. In Seattle, and especially in the convent of the Ladies of the Sacred Heart, foreign names suggested not immigration but emigration — distinguished exile. Minneapolis was a granary; Seattle was a port, which had attracted a veritable Foreign Legion of adventurers — soldiers of fortune, younger sons, gamblers, traders, drawn by the fortunes to be made in virgin timber and shipping and by the Alaska Gold Rush. Wars and revolutions had sent the defeated out to Puget Sound, to start a new life; the latest had been the Russian Revolution, which had shipped us, via Harbin, a Russian colony, complete with restaurant, on Queen Anne Hill. The English names in the convent, when they did not testify to direct English origin, as in the case of "Rafe" Chatham, had come to us from the South and represented a kind of internal exile; such girls as Mary Fordyce Blake and Mary McQueen Street (a class ahead of me; her sister was named Francesca) bore their double-barreled first names like titles of aristocracy from the ante-bellum South. Not all our girls, by any means, were Catholic; some of the very prettiest ones — Julia Dodge and Janet Preston, if I remember rightly — were Protestants. The nuns had taught us to behave with special courtesy to these strangers in our midst, and the whole effect was of some superior hostel for refugees of all the lost causes of the past hundred years. Money could not count for much in such an atmosphere; the fathers and grandfathers of many of our "best" girls were ruined men.

Names, often, were freakish in the Pacific Northwest, particularly 4 girls' names. In the Episcopal boarding school I went to later, in Tacoma, there was a girl called De Vere Utter, and there was a girl called Rocena and another called Hermonie. Was Rocena a mistake for Rowena and Hermonie for Hermione? And was Vere, as we called her, Lady Clara Vere de Vere? Probably. You do not hear names like those often, in any case, east of the Cascade Mountains; they belong to the frontier, where books and libraries were few and memory seems to have been oral, as in the time of Homer.

Names have more significance for Catholics than they do for other 5 people; Christian names are chosen for the spiritual qualities of the saints they are taken from; Protestants used to name their children out of the Old Testament and now they name them out of novels and plays, whose heroes and heroines are perhaps the new patron saints of a secular age. But with Catholics it is different. The saint a child is named for is supposed to serve, literally, as a model or pattern to imitate; your name is your fortune and it tells you what you are or must be. Catholic children ponder their names for a mystic meaning, like birthstones; my own, I learned, besides belonging to the Virgin and Saint Mary of Egypt, originally meant "bitter" or "star of the sea." My second name, Thérèse, could dedicate me either to Saint Theresa or to the saint called the Little Flower, Soeur Thérèse of Lisieux, on whom God was supposed to have descended in the form of a shower of roses. At Confirmation, I had added a third name (for Catholics then rename themselves, as most nuns do, yet another time, when they take orders); on the advice of a nun, I had taken "Clementina," after Saint Clement, an early pope — a step I soon regretted on account of "My Darling Clementine" and her number nine shoes. By the time I was in the convent, I would no longer tell anyone what my Confirmation name was. The name I had nearly picked was "Agnes," after a little Roman virgin martyr, always shown with a lamb, because of her purity. But Agnes would have been just as bad, I recognized in Forest Ridge Convent — not only because of the possibility of

"Aggie," but because it was subtly, indefinably *wrong* in itself. Agnes would have made me look like an ass.

The fear of appearing ridiculous first entered my life, as a governing motive, during my second year in the convent. Up to then, a desire for prominence had decided many of my actions and, in fact, still persisted. But in the eighth grade, I became aware of mockery and perceived that I could not seek prominence without attracting laughter. Other people could, but I couldn't. This laughter was proceeding, not from my classmates, but from the girls of the class just above me, in particular from two boon companions. Elinor Heffernan and Mary Harty, a clownish pair — oddly assorted in size and shape, as teams of clowns generally are, one short, plump, and baby-faced, the other tall, lean, and owlish — who entertained the high-school department by calling attention to the oddities of the younger girls. Nearly every school has such a pair of satirists, whose marks are generally low and who are tolerated just because of their laziness and non-conformity; one of them (in this case, Mary Harty, the plump one) usually appears to be half asleep. Because of their low standing, their indifference to appearances, the sad state of their uniforms, their clowning is taken to be harmless, which, on the whole, it is, their object being not to wound but to divert; such girls are bored in school. We in the eighth grade sat directly in front of the two wits in study hall, so that they had us under close observation; yet at first I was not afraid of them, wanting, if anything, to identify myself with their laughter, to be initiated into the joke. One of their specialties was giving people nicknames, and it was considered an honor to be the first in the eighth grade to be let in by Elinor and Mary on their latest invention. This often happened to me; they would tell me, on the playground, and I would tell the others. As their intermediary, I felt myself almost their friend and it did not occur to me that I might be next on their list.

I had achieved prominence not long before by publicly losing my faith and regaining it at the end of a retreat. I believe Elinor and Mary questioned me about this on the playground, during recess, and listened with serious, respectful faces while I told them about my conversations with the Jesuits. Those serious faces ought to have been an omen, but if the two girls used what I had revealed to make fun of me, it must have been behind my back. I never heard any more of it, and yet just at this time I began to feel something, like a cold breath on the nape of my neck, that made me wonder whether the new position I had won for myself in the convent was as secure as I imagined. I would turn around in study hall and find the two girls looking at me with speculation in their eyes.

It was just at this time, too, that I found myself in a perfectly ab- 8 surd situation, a very private one, which made me live, from month to month, in horror of discovery. I had waked up one morning, in my convent room, to find a few small spots of blood on my sheet; I had somehow scratched a trifling cut on one of my legs and opened it during the night. I wondered what to do about this, for the nuns were fussy about bedmaking, as they were about our white collars and cuffs, and if we had an inspection those spots might count against me. It was best, I decided, to ask the nun on dormitory duty, tall, stout Mother Slattery, for a clean bottom sheet, even though she might scold me for having scratched my leg in my sleep and order me to cut my toenails. You never know what you might be blamed for. But Mother Slattery, when she bustled in to look at the sheet, did not scold me at all; indeed, she hardly seemed to be listening as I explained to her about the cut. She told me to sit down: she would be back in a minute. "You can be excused from athletics today," she added, closing the door. As I waited, I considered this remark, which seemed to me strangely munificent, in view of the unimportance of the cut. In a moment, she returned, but without the sheet. Instead, she produced out of her big pocket a sort of cloth girdle and a peculiar flannel object which I first took to be a bandage, and I began to protest that I did not need or want a bandage; all I needed was a bottom sheet. "The sheet can wait," said Mother Slattery, succinctly, handing me two large safety pins. It was the pins that abruptly enlightened me; I saw Mother Slattery's mistake, even as she was instructing me as to how this flannel article, which I now understood to be a sanitary napkin, was to be put on.

"Oh, no, Mother," I said, feeling somewhat embarrassed. "You 9 don't understand. It's just a little cut, on my leg." But Mother, again, was not listening; she appeared to have grown deaf, as the nuns had a habit of doing when what you were saying did not fit in with their ideas. And now that I knew what was in her mind, I was conscious of a funny constraint; I did not feel it proper to name a natural process, in so many words, to a nun. It was like trying not to think of their going to the bathroom or trying not to see the straggling iron-gray hair coming out of their coifs (the common notion that they shaved their heads was false). On the whole, it seemed better just to show her my cut. But when I offered to do so and unfastened my black stocking, she only glanced at my leg, cursorily. "That's only a scratch, dear," she said. "Now hurry up and put this on or you'll be late for chapel. Have you any pain?" "No, no, Mother!" I cried. "You don't understand!" "Yes, yes, I understand," she replied soothingly, "and you will too, a little later. Mother Superior will tell you about it some time during the morning. There's nothing to be afraid of. You have become a woman."

"I know all about that," I persisted. "Mother, please listen. I just 10 cut my leg. On the athletic field. Yesterday afternoon." But the more excited I grew, the more soothing, and yet firm, Mother Slattery became. There seemed to be nothing for it but to give up and do as I was bid. I was in the grip of a higher authority, which almost had the power to persuade me that it was right and I was wrong. But of course I was not wrong; that would have been too good to be true. While Mother Slattery waited, just outside my door, I miserably donned the equipment she had given me, for there was no place to hide it, on account of drawer inspection. She led me down the hall to where there was a chute and explained how I was to dispose of the flannel thing, by. dropping it down the chute into the laundry. (The convent arrangements were very old-fashioned, dating back, no doubt, to the days of Louis Philippe.)

The Mother Superior, Madame MacIllvra, was a sensible woman, 11 and all through my early morning classes, I was on pins and needles, chafing for the promised interview with her which I trusted would clear things up. "*Ma Mère*," I would begin, "Mother Slattery thinks. . . ." Then I would tell her about the cut and the athletic field. But precisely the same impasse confronted me when I was summoned to her office at recess-time. *I* talked about my cut, and *she* talked about becoming a woman. It was rather like a round, in which she was singing "Scotland's burning, Scotland's burning," and I was singing "Pour on water, pour on water." Neither of us could hear the other, or, rather, I could hear her, but she could not hear me. Owing to our different positions in the convent she was free to interrupt me, whereas I was expected to remain silent until she had finished speaking. When I kept breaking in, she hushed me, gently, and took me on her lap. Exactly like Mother Slattery, she attributed all my references to the cut to a blind fear of this new, unexpected reality that had supposedly entered my life. Many young girls, she reassured me, were frightened if they had not been prepared. "And you, Mary, have lost your dear mother, who could have made this easier for you." Rocked on Madame MacIllvra's lap, I felt paralysis overtake me and I lay, mutely listening, against her bosom, my face being tickled by her white, starched, fluted wimple, while she explained to me how babies were born, all of which I had heard before.

There was no use fighting the convent. I had to pretend to have become a woman, just as, not long before, I had had to pretend to get my faith back — for the sake of peace. This pretense was decidedly awkward. For fear of being found out by the lay sisters downstairs in the laundry (no doubt an imaginary contingency, but the convent was so very thorough), I reopened the cut on my leg, so as to draw a little blood to stain the napkins, which were issued me regularly, not only on this occasion, but every twenty-eight days thereafter. Eventually, I abandoned this bloodletting, for fear of lockjaw, and trusted to fate. Yet I was in awful dread of detection; my only hope, as I saw it, was either to be released from the convent or to become a woman in reality, which might take a year at least, since I was only twelve. Getting out of athletics once a month was not sufficient compensation for the farce I was going through. It was not my fault; they had forced me into it; nevertheless, it was I who would look silly — worse than silly; half mad — if the truth ever came to light.

I was burdened with this guilt and shame when the nickname finally found me out. "Found me out," in a general sense, for no one ever did learn the particular secret I bore about with me, pinned to the linen band. "We've got a name for you," Elinor and Mary called out to me, one day on the playground. "What is it?" I asked half hoping, half fearing, since not all their sobriquets were unfavorable. "Cye," they answered, looking at each other and laughing. "Si?" I repeated, supposing that it was based on Simple Simon. Did they regard me as a hick? "C.Y.E.," they elucidated, spelling it out in chorus. "The letters stand for something. Can you guess?" I could not and I cannot now. The closest I could come to it in the convent was "Clean Your Ears." Perhaps that was it, though in later life I have wondered whether it did not stand, simply, for "Clever Young Egg" or "Champion Young Eccentric." But in the convent I was certain that it stood for something horrible, something even worse than dirty ears (as far as

I knew, my ears were clean), something I could never guess because it represented some aspect of myself that the world could see and I couldn't, like a sign pinned on my back. Everyone in the convent must have known what the letters stood for, but no one would tell me. Elinor and Mary had made them promise. It was like halitosis; not even my best friend, my deskmate, Louise, would tell me, no matter how much I pleaded. Yet everyone assured me that it was "very good," that is, very apt. And it made everyone laugh.

This name reduced all my pretensions and solidified my sense of 14 *wrongness*. Just as I felt I was beginning to belong to the convent, it turned me into an outsider, since I was the only pupil who was not in the know. I liked the convent, but it did not like me, as people say of certain foods that disagree with them. By this, I do not mean that I was actively unpopular, either with the pupils or with the nuns. The Mother Superior cried when I left and predicted that I would be a novelist, which surprised me. And I had finally made friends; even Emilie von Phul smiled upon me softly out of her bright blue eyes from the far end of the study hall. It was just that I did not fit into the convent pattern; the simplest thing I did, like asking for a clean sheet, entrapped me in consequences that I never could have predicted. I was not bad; I did not consciously break the rules; and yet I could never, not even for a week, get a pink ribbon, and this was something I could not understand, because I was trying as hard as I could. It was the same case as with the hated name; the nuns, evidently, saw something about me that was invisible to me.

The oddest part was all that pretending. There I was, a walking 15 mass of lies, pretending to be a Catholic and going to confession while really I had lost my faith, and pretending to have monthly periods by cutting myself with nail scissors; yet all this had come about without my volition and even contrary to it. But the basest pretense I was driven to was the acceptance of the nickname. Yet what else could I do? In the convent, I could not live it down. To all those girls, I had become "Cye McCarthy." That was who I was. That was how I had to identify myself when telephoning my friends during vacations to ask them to the movies: "Hello, this is Cye." I loathed myself when I said it, and yet I succumbed to the name totally, making myself over into a sort of hearty to go with it — the kind of girl I hated. "Cye" was my new patron saint. This false personality stuck to me, like the name, when I entered public high school, the next fall, as a freshman, having finally persuaded my grandparents to take me out of the convent, although they could never get to the bottom of my reasons, since, as I admitted, the nuns were kind, and I had made many nice new friends. What I wanted was a fresh start, a chance to begin life over again, but the first thing I heard in the corridors of the public high school was that name called out to me, like the warmest of welcomes: "Hi, there, Si!" That was the way they thought it was spelled. But this time I was resolute. After the first weeks, I dropped the hearties who called me "Si"and I never heard it again. I got my own name back and sloughed off Clementina and even Therese — the names that did not seem to me any more to be mine but to have been imposed on me by others. And I preferred to think that Mary meant "bitter" rather than "star of the sea."

CONSIDERATIONS

1. The first paragraph develops two pairs of contrasts: one between two sets of names and another between two sets of girls. What is the correlation between this structure and the main point of the paragraph?
2. How are the mistakes about the author's supposed first menstruation connected to the principal subject of names in this essay?
3. According to McCarthy, names exercise special powers over people's lives in the adult world of religion and society. She further demonstrates that names and nicknames also wield special powers in the children's world of school. To what different purposes do adults and children use the powers of names?
4. What influences did McCarthy's own various names have over her? How well did she accept or reject their powers?
5. WRITING TOPIC. What sort of a child is McCarthy in this essay? Think of three adjectives that describe her personality and then write a 400-word character sketch that presents your view of her as a child.
6. WRITING TOPIC. As a child did you ever create an imaginary name for yourself? If so, write a 700-word essay explaining its attractions and its advantages over your given name. How did you secretly, or openly, make use of your self-chosen name?

Germaine Greer

THE STEREOTYPE

◊

GERMAINE GREER (b. 1939) was raised and educated in Australia, where she taught at a girls' school before going to England to obtain a Ph.D. degree in English literature at Cambridge University. While teaching as a Shakespearean scholar, she also worked as a television comedy performer in London. She now teaches at the University of Tulsa. Her first book, *The Female Eunuch* (1970), raised a storm of controversy over whether she was aiding the cause of feminism or doing it a disservice by her charges that women's sexuality has been distorted into passivity and castratedness. Her second book, *The Obstacle Race: The Story of Women in Painting* (1979), argues that women were barred from opportunity to become painters. In this chapter from *The Female Eunuch* she denounces the false mask of female glamour that is imposed on women.

In that mysterious dimension where the body meets the soul the 1 stereotype is born and has her being. She is more body than soul, more soul than mind. To her belongs all that is beautiful, even the very word beauty itself. All that exists, exists to beautify her. The sun shines only to burnish her skin and gild her hair, the wind blows only to whip up the color in her cheeks; the sea strives to bathe her; flowers die gladly so that her skin may luxuriate in their essence. She is the crown of creation, the masterpiece. The depths of the sea are ransacked for pearl and coral to deck her; the bowels of the earth are laid open that she might wear gold, sapphires, diamonds, and rubies. Baby seals are battered with staves, unborn lambs ripped from their mothers' wombs, millions of moles, muskrats, squirrels, minks, ermines, foxes, beavers, chinchillas, ocelots, lynxes, and other small and lovely creatures die untimely deaths that she might have furs. Egrets, ostriches and peacocks, butterflies and beetles yield her their plumage.

29

Men risk their lives hunting leopards for her coats, and crocodiles for her handbags and shoes. Millions of silkworms offer her their yellow labors; even the seamstresses roll seams and whip lace by hand, so that she might be clad in the best that money can buy.

The men of our civilization have stripped themselves of the fineries 2 of the earth so that they might work more freely to plunder the universe for treasures to deck my lady in. New raw materials, new processes, new machines are all brought into her service. My lady must therefore be the chief spender as well as the chief symbol of spending ability and monetary success. While her mate toils in his factory, she totters about the smartest streets and plushest hotels with his fortune upon her back and bosom, fingers and wrists, continuing that essential expenditure in his house which is her frame and her setting, enjoying that silken idleness which is the necessary condition of maintaining her mate's prestige and her qualification to demonstrate it. Once upon a time only the aristocratic lady could lay claim to the title of crown of creation: only her hands were white enough, her feet tiny enough, her waist narrow enough, her hair long and golden enough; but every well-to-do burgher's wife set herself up to ape my lady and to follow fashion, until my lady was forced to set herself out like a gilded doll overlaid with monstrous rubies and pearls like pigeons' eggs. Nowadays the Queen of England still considers it part of her royal female role to sport as much of the family jewelry as she can manage at any one time on all public occasions, although the male monarchs have escaped such showcase duty, which devolves exclusively upon their wives.

At the same time as woman was becoming the showcase for wealth 3 and caste, while men were slipping into relative anonymity and "handsome is as handsome does," she was emerging as the central emblem of western art. For the Greeks the male and female body had beauty of a human, not necessarily a sexual, kind; indeed they may have marginally favored the young male form as the most powerful and perfectly proportioned. Likewise the Romans showed no bias towards the depiction of femininity in their predominantly monumental art. In the Renaissance the female form began to predominate, not only as the mother in the predominate emblem of *madonna col bambino*, but as an aesthetic study in herself. At first naked female forms took their chances in crowd scenes or diptychs of Adam and Eve, but gradually Venus claims ascendancy, Mary Magdalene ceases to be wizened and emaciated, and becomes nubile and ecstatic, portraits of anonymous young women, chosen only for their prettiness, begin to appear, are gradually disrobed, and renamed Flora or Primavera. Painters begin to paint their own wives and mistresses and royal consorts as voluptuous beauties, divesting them of their clothes if desirable, but not of their jewelry. Susanna keeps her bracelets on in the bath, and Hélène Fourment keeps ahold of her fur as well!

What happened to women in painting happened to her in poetry as 4 well. Her beauty was celebrated in terms of the riches which clustered around her: her hair was gold wires, her brow ivory, her lips ruby, her teeth gates of pearl, her breasts alabaster veined with lapis lazuli, her eyes as black as jet. The fragility of her loveliness was emphasized by the inevitable comparisons with the rose, and she was urged to employ her beauty in love-making before it withered on the stem. She was for consumption; other sorts of imagery spoke of her in terms of cherries and cream, lips as sweet as honey and skin white as milk, breasts like cream uncrudded, hard as apples. Some celebrations yearned over her finery as well, her lawn more transparent than morning mist, her lace as delicate as gossamer, the baubles that she toyed with and the favors that she gave. Even now we find the thriller hero describing his classy dame's elegant suits, cheeky hats, well-chosen accessories, and footwear; the imagery no longer dwells on jewels and flowers but the consumer emphasis is the same. The mousy secretary blossoms into the feminine stereotype when she reddens her lips, lets down her hair, and puts on something frilly.

Nowadays women are not expected, unless they are Paola di Liegi 5 or Jackie Onassis, and then only on gala occasions, to appear with a king's ransom deployed upon their bodies, but they are required to look expensive, fashionable, well-groomed, and not to be seen in the same dress twice. If the duty of the few may have become less onerous, it has also become the duty of the many. The stereotype marshals an army of servants. She is supplied with cosmetics, underwear, foundation garments, stockings, wigs, postiches, and hairdressing as well as her outer garments, her jewels and furs. The effect is to be built up layer by layer, and it is expensive. Splendor has given way to fit, line, and cut. The spirit of competition must be kept up, as more and more women struggle towards the top drawer, so that the fashion industry can rely upon an expanding market. Poorer women fake it, ape it, pick up on the fashions a season too late, use crude effects, mistaking the line, the sheen, the gloss of the high-class article for a garish simulacrum. The business is so complex that it must be handled by an expert. The paragons of the stereotype must be dressed, coifed, and painted by the experts and the style-setters, although they may be encouraged to give heart to the housewives studying their lives in pulp magazines by claiming a lifelong fidelity to their own hair and soap and water. The boast is more usually discouraging than otherwise, unfortunately.

As long as she is young and personable, every woman may cherish 6 the dream that she may leap up the social ladder and dim the sheen of luxury by sheer natural loveliness; the few examples of such a feat are kept before the eye of the public. Fired with hope, optimism, and ambition, young women study the latest forms of the stereotype, set out in *Vogue, Nova, Queen,* and other glossies, where the mannequins stare from among the advertisements for fabulous real estate, furs, and jewels. Nowadays the uniformity of the year's fashions is severely affected by the emergence of the pert female designers who direct their appeal to the working girl, emphasizing variety, comfort, and simple, striking effects. There is no longer a single face of the year. . . .

The stereotype is the Eternal Feminine. She is the Sexual Object 7 sought by all men, and by all women. She is of neither sex, for she has herself no sex at all. Her value is solely attested by the demand she excites in others. All she must contribute is her existence. She need achieve nothing, for she is the reward of achievement. She need never give positive evidence of her moral character because virtue is assumed from her loveliness, and her passivity. If any man who has no right to her be found with her she will not be punished, for she is morally neuter. The matter is solely one of male rivalry. Innocently she may drive men to madness and war. The more trouble she can cause, the more her stocks go up, for possession of her means more the more demand she excites. Nobody wants a girl whose beauty is imperceptible to all but him; and so men welcome the stereotype because it directs their taste into the most commonly recognized areas of value, although they may protest because some aspects of it do not tally with their fetishes. There is scope in the stereotype's variety for most fetishes. The leg man may follow miniskirts, the tit man can encourage see-through blouses and plunging necklines, although the man who likes fat women may feel constrained to enjoy them in secret. There are stringent limits to the variations on the stereotype, for nothing must interfere with her function as sex object. She may wear leather, as long as she cannot actually handle a motorbike: she may wear rubber, but it ought not to indicate that she is an expert diver or waterskier. If she wears athletic clothes the purpose is to underline her unathleticism. She may sit astride a horse, looking soft and curvy, but she must not crouch over its neck with her rump in the air.

Because she is the emblem of spending ability and the chief 8 spender, she is also the most effective seller of this world's goods. Every survey ever held has shown that the image of an attractive woman is the most effective advertising gimmick. She may sit astride the mudguard of a new car, or step into it ablaze with jewels; she may lie at a man's feet stroking his new socks; she may hold the petrol pump in a challenging pose, or dance through woodland glades in slow motion in all the glory of a new shampoo; whatever she does her image sells. The gynolatry of our civilization is written large upon its face, upon hoardings,* cinema screens, television, newspapers, magazines, tins, packets, cartons, bottles, all consecrated to the reigning deity, the female fetish. Her dominion must not be thought to entail the rule of women, for she is not a woman. Her glossy lips and mat complexion, her unfocused eyes and flawless fingers, her extraordinary hair all floating and shining, curling and gleaming, reveal the inhuman triumph of cosmetics, lighting, focusing and printing, cropping and composition. She sleeps unruffled, her lips red and juicy and closed, her eyes as crisp and black as if new painted, and her false lashes immaculately curled. Even when she washes her face with a new and creamier toilet soap her expression is as tranquil and vacant and her paint as flawless as ever. If ever she should appear tousled and troubled, her features are miraculously smoothed to their proper veneer by a new washing powder or a bouillon cube. For she is a doll: weeping, pouting or smiling, running or reclining, she is a doll. She is an idol, formed of the concatenation of lines and masses, signifying the lineaments of satisfied impotence.

Her essential quality is castratedness. She absolutely must be 9 young, her body hairless, her flesh buoyant, and *she must not have a sexual organ*. No musculature must distort the smoothness of the lines of her body, although she may be painfully slender or warmly cuddly.

---

* Billboards.

Her expression must betray no hint of humor, curiosity, or intelligence, although it may signify hauteur to an extent that is actually absurd, or smoldering lust, very feebly signified by drooping eyes and a sullen mouth (for the stereotype's lust equals irrational submission), or, most commonly, vivacity and idiot happiness. Seeing that the world despoils itself for this creature's benefit, she must be happy; the entire structure would topple if she were not. So the image of woman appears plastered on every surface imaginable, smiling interminably. An apple pie evokes a glance of tender beatitude, a washing machine causes hilarity, a cheap box of chocolates brings forth meltingly joyous gratitude, a Coke is the cause of a rictus of unutterable brilliance, even a new stick-on bandage is saluted by a smirk of satisfaction. A real woman licks her lips and opens her mouth and flashes her teeth when photographers appear: *she* must arrive at the premiere of her husband's film in a paroxysm of delight, or his success might be murmured about. The occupational hazard of being a Playboy Bunny is the aching facial muscles brought on by the obligatory smiles.

So what is the beef? Maybe I couldn't make it. Maybe I don't have 10 a pretty smile, good teeth, nice tits, long legs, a cheeky arse, a sexy voice. Maybe I don't know how to handle men and increase my market value, so that the rewards due to the feminine will accrue to me. Then again, maybe I'm sick of the masquerade. I'm sick of pretending eternal youth. I'm sick of belying my own intelligence, my own will, my own sex. I'm sick of peering at the world through false eyelashes, so everything I see is mixed with a shadow of bought hairs; I'm sick of weighting my head with a dead mane, unable to move my neck freely, terrified of rain, of wind, of dancing too vigorously in case I sweat into my lacquered curls. I'm sick of the Powder Room. I'm sick of pretending that some fatuous male's self-important pronouncements are the objects of my undivided attention, I'm sick of going to films and plays when someone else wants to, and sick of having no opinions of my own about either. I'm sick of being a transvestite. I refuse to be a female impersonator. I am a woman, not a castrate.

April Ashley was born male. All the information supplied by genes, 11 chromosomes, internal and external sexual organs added up to the same thing. April was a man. But he longed to be a woman. He longed for the stereotype, not to embrace, but to be. He wanted soft fabrics, jewels, furs, makeup, the love and protection of men. So he was impotent. He couldn't fancy women at all, although he did not particularly welcome homosexual addresses. He did not think of himself as a pervert, or even as a transvestite, but as a woman cruelly transmogrified into manhood. He tried to die, became a female impersonator, but eventually found a doctor in Casablanca who came up with a more acceptable alternative. He was to be castrated, and his penis used as the lining of a surgically constructed cleft, which would be a vagina. He would be infertile, but that has never affected the attribution of femininity. April returned to England, resplendent. Massive hormone treatment had eradicated his beard, and formed tiny breasts: he had grown his hair and bought feminine clothes during the time he had worked as an impersonator. He became a model, and began to illustrate the feminine stereotype as he was perfectly qualified to do, for he was elegant, voluptuous, beautifully groomed, and in love with his own image. On an ill-fated day he married the heir to a peerage, the Hon. Arthur Corbett, acting out the highest achievement of the feminine dream, and went to live with him in a villa in Marbella. The marriage was never consummated. April's incompetence as a woman is what we must expect from a castrate, but it is not so very different after all from the impotence of feminine women, who submit to sex without desire, with only the infantile pleasure of cuddling and affection, which is their favorite reward. As long as the feminine stereotype remains the definition of the female sex, April Ashley is a woman, regardless of the legal decision ensuing from her divorce. She is as much a casualty of the polarity of the sexes as we all are. Disgraced, unsexed April Ashley is our sister and our symbol.

CONSIDERATIONS

1. The first paragraph is packed full of examples — of what? Find the topic sentence; then consider what types of examples Greer has chosen to illustrate her point. Do they as a group refer to ordinary or uncommon events? What is the effect of her choosing such examples? What feelings does the first paragraph arouse?
2. What is the tone of Greer's voice in this essay? Pick out a few sentences that strike you as particularly good or effective. Do they contain words and phrases that seem characteristic of her style?
3. According to Greer, what is the purpose of stereotyping women? Does the essay develop a central argument?

4. In your view, what is attractive about women? About men? Is personal glamour what Greer says that it is?

5. In the last paragraph, Greer presents a special case that was the subject of news-gossip in the 1960s. Today, most readers do not know the person or the events she refers to. Is Greer's final paragraph outdated? Does the paragraph strengthen or weaken her essay now? Is April Ashley a "symbol," as Greer maintains?

6. WRITING TOPIC. In what way have you been stereotyped? Perhaps as "a brain" or "a jock"; or as a black, a Jew, an Italian; or as someone who is always "good-natured," or always "responsible." In a 700-word essay, examine the stereotype that falsifies and denigrates what is true in your nature.

Erik Erikson

THE SHAPE
OF EXPERIENCE

◊

ERIK ERIKSON (b. 1902) was born and educated in Germany, where he began a career as an art historian before changing to the profession of psychoanalysis. He has written extensively about the steps of growing up, including the possibilities of changing directions in one's life. Most widely known for his formulations about personal development such as "the identity crisis" and "the life cycle," Erikson has examined the ways people define their individuality within a variety of primitive and modern societies and in different historical periods. His books include *Young Man Luther* (1958), *Identity: Youth and Crisis* (1968), and *Gandhi's Truth* (1969). In this selection from his first book, *Childhood and Society* (1950), he considers some basic differences between the play activities of male and female children.

I set up a play table and a random selection of toys and invited the   1
boys and girls of the study, one at a time, to come in and to imagine that the table was a movie studio and the toys, actors and sets. I then asked them to "construct on the table an exciting scene out of an imaginary moving picture." This instruction was given to spare these children, the majority of whom were eleven years old, the indignity of having to play at "kids' stuff"; at the same time it was thought to be a sufficiently impersonal "stimulus" for an un–self-conscious use of the imagination. But here was the first surprise: although, for over a year and a half, about 150 children constructed about 450 scenes, not more than a half dozen of these were movie scenes, and only a few dolls were named after a particular actor. Instead, after a moment of thoughtfulness, the children arranged their scenes as if guided by an inner design, told me a brief story with more or less exciting content, and left me with the task of finding out what (if anything) these con-

structions "meant." I remembered, however, that years before, when I had tried out an analogous method on a smaller group of Harvard and Radcliffe students, all English majors, who were asked to construct a "dramatic" scene, not one scene was reminiscent of a Shakespearean or any other drama. It appears, then, that such vague instructions do accomplish what the encouragment to "associate freely" (i.e., to let thoughts wander and words flow without self-censorship) effects in a psychoanalytic interview, as does, indeed, the suggestion to play in interviews with children: seemingly arbitrary themes tend to appear which on closer study prove to be intimately related to the dynamics of the person's life history. In the present study, what I came to call "unique elements" often provided the key to such significance. For example, one of the few colored boys in the study, and the smallest of these, is the only child to build his scene *under* the table. He thus offers stark and chilling evidence of the meaning of his smiling meekness: he "knows his place." Or consider the only scene in which the piano chair is pushed under the piano so that it is quite clear that nobody is playing. Since the girl who constructed the scene is the only subject whose mother is a musician, it becomes probable that the dynamic meaning of musical noise in her childhood (if suggested in other data as well) deserves our attention. Finally, to mention one of the main instances where a child reveals in her play an awareness of something she was not supposed to know: a girl, since deceased, who suffered from a malignant blood disease was said to be ignorant of the fact that she was kept alive only by a new medical invention then in its experimental stages. She constructed the only ruin built by a girl and put in the center of her scene "a girl who miraculously returned to life after having been sacrificed to the gods." These examples do not touch on the difficult problem of interpreting unconscious content, but they indicate that the scenes often enough proved to be close to life. However, this is not what is to be discussed at this point. Here, I intend only to consider the manifestations of the power of organ modes in spatial modalities.

In order to convey a measure of my surprise in finding organ modes among what (in contrast to *unique* elements) I came to call the *common* elements in these children's constructions, it is necessary to claim what is probably hard to believe, namely, that I tried not to expect anything in particular, and was, in fact, determined to enjoy the freshness of the experience of working with so many children, and

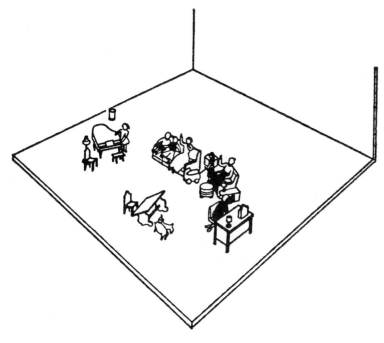

FIGURE 1

healthy ones. To be ready to be surprised belongs to the discipline of a clinician; for without it clinical "findings" would soon lose the instructive quality of new (or truly confirming) finds.

As one child after another concentrated with a craftsman's con- 3 scientiousness on configurations which had to be "just right" before he would announce that his task was done, I gradually became aware of the fact that I was learning to expect different configurations from boys than from girls. To give an example, . . . girls much more often than boys would arrange a room in the form of a circle of furniture, without walls. Sometimes a circular configuration of furniture was presented as being intruded upon by something threatening, even if funny, such as a pig (see Figure 1) or "father coming home riding on a lion." One day, a boy arranged such a "feminine" scene, with wild animals as intruders, and I felt that uneasiness which I assume often betrays to an experimenter what his innermost expectations are. And, indeed, on departure and already at the door, the boy exclaimed,

"There is something wrong here," came back, and with an air of relief arranged the animals along a tangent to the circle of furniture. Only one boy built and left such a configuration, and this twice. He was of obese and effeminate build. As thyroid treatment began to take effect, he built, in his third construction (a year and a half after the first) the highest and most slender of all towers — as was to be expected of a boy.

That this boy's tower, now that he himself had at last become 4 slimmer, was the slenderest, was one of those "unique" elements which suggested that some sense of one's physical self influenced the spatial modalities of these constructions. From here it was only one step to the assumption that the modalities *common* to either sex may express something of the sense of being male or female. It was then that I felt grateful for the kind of investigation which we had embarked on. For building blocks provide a wordless medium quite easily counted, measured, and compared in regard to spatial arrangement. At the same time, they seem so impersonally geometric as to be least compromised by cultural connotations and individual meanings. A block is *almost* nothing but a block. It seemed striking, then (unless one considered it a mere function of the difference in themes), that boys and girls differed in the *number* of blocks used as well as in the *configurations* constructed.

So I set out to define these configurations in the simplest terms, 5 such as towers, buildings, streets, lanes, elaborate enclosures, simple enclosures, interiors with walls, and interiors without walls. I then gave photographs of the play scenes to two objective observers to see whether they could agree on the presence or the absence of such configurations (and of combinations of them). They did agree "significantly," whereupon it could be determined how often these configurations were said by these observers (who did not know of my expectations) to have occurred in the constructions of boys and of girls. I will abstract their conclusions here in general terms. The reader may assume that each item mentioned occurs more (and often considerably more) than two thirds of the time in the constructions of the sex specified and that in the remaining one third special conditions prevail which often can be shown to "prove the rule."

The most significant sex difference was the tendency of boys to 6 erect structures, buildings, towers, or streets (see Figure 2); the girls tended to use the play table as the interior of a house, with simple, little, or no use of blocks (see Figure 1).

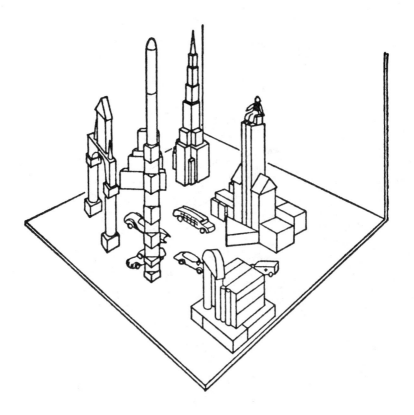

FIGURE 2

High structures, then, were prevalent in the configurations of the 7 boys. But the opposite of elevation, i.e., *downfall*, was equally typical for them: ruins or fallen-down structures were exclusively found among boys. (I quoted the one exception.) In connection with the very highest towers, something in the nature of a downward trend appears regularly, but in such diverse forms that only "unique" elements can illustrate it: one boy, after much indecision, took his extraordinarily high and well-built tower down in order to build a final configuration of a simple and low structure without any "exciting" content; another balanced his tower very precariously and pointed out that the immediate danger of collapse was the "exciting" element in his story,

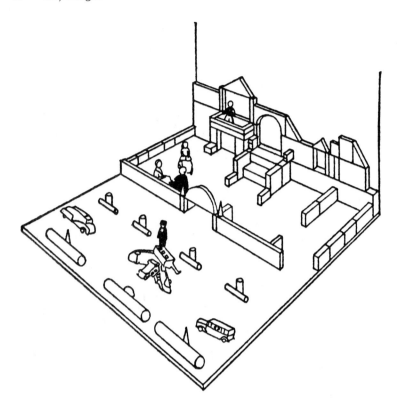

FIGURE 3

in fact, *was* his story. One boy who built an especially high tower laid a boy doll at the foot of it and explained that this boy had fallen from the top of the tower; another boy left the boy doll sitting high on one of several elaborate towers but said that the boy had had a mental breakdown (Figure 2). The very highest tower was built by the very smallest boy; and, as pointed out, a colored boy built his *under* the table. All these variations make it apparent that *the variable high-low is a masculine variable.* Having studied a number of the histories of these children I would add the clinical judgment that extreme height (in its combination with an element of breakdown or fall) reflects a need to overcompensate a doubt in, or a fear for, one's masculinity.

The boys' structures enclosed fewer people and animals inside a 8
house. Rather, they channeled the traffic of motorcars, animals, and
Indians. And they blocked traffic: the single policeman was the doll
used most often by boys! (Figure 3)

Girls rarely built towers. When they did, they made them lean 9
against, or stay close to, the background. The highest tower built by
any girl was not on the table at all but on a shelf in a niche behind the
table.

If "high" and "low" are masculine variables, "open" and "closed" 10
are feminine modalities. Interiors of houses without walls were built
by a majority of girls. In many cases the interiors were expressly peaceful. Where it was a home rather than a school, a little girl often played
the piano: a remarkably tame "exciting movie scene" for girls of that
age. In a number of cases, however, a disturbance occurred. An intruding pig throws the family in an uproar and forces the girl to hide
behind the piano; a teacher has jumped on a desk because a tiger has
entered the room. While the persons thus frightened are mostly
women, the intruding element is always a man, a boy, or an animal. If
it is a dog, it is expressly a boy's dog. Strangely enough, however, this
idea of an intruding creature does not lead to the defensive erection of
walls or to the closing of doors. Rather, the majority of these intrusions have an element of humor and of pleasurable excitement.

Simple enclosures with low walls and without ornaments were the
largest item among the configurations built by girls. However, these
enclosures often had an elaborate gate (Figure 4): the only configuration which girls cared to construct and to ornament richly. A blocking
of the entrance or a thickening of the walls could on further study be
shown to reflect acute anxiety over the feminine role.

The most significant sex differences in the use of the play space, 12
then, added up to the following modalities: in the boys, the outstand-
ing variables were height and downfall and strong motion (Indians,
animals, motorcars) and its channelization or arrest (policemen); in
girls, static interiors, which are open, simply enclosed, and peaceful or
intruded upon. Boys adorned high structures; girls, gates.

It is clear by now that the spatial tendencies governing these con- 13
structions [suggest] the *genital modes,* . . . and that they, in fact,
closely parallel the morphology of the sex organs: in the male, *external*
organs, *erectable* and *intrusive* in character, *conducting* highly *mobile*
sperm cells; *internal* organs in the female, with a vestibular *access*

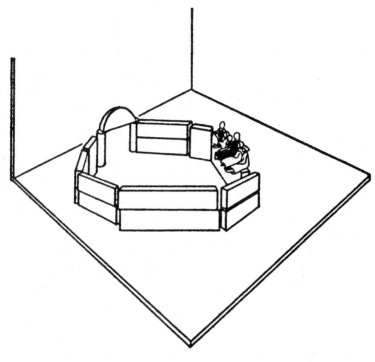

FIGURE 4

leading to *statically expectant* ova. Does this reflect an acute and temporary emphasis on the modalities of the sexual organs owing to the experience of oncoming sexual maturation? My clinical judgment (and the brief study of the "dramatic productions" of college students) incline me to think that the dominance of genital modes over the modalities of spatial organization reflects a profound difference in the sense of space in the two sexes, even as sexual differentiation obviously provides the most decisive difference in the ground plan of the human body which, in turn, codetermines biological experience and social roles.

Play construction can also be seen as spatial expression of a variety 14 of social connotations. A boy's tendency to picture outward and upward movement may, then, be only another expression of a general sense of obligation to prove himself strong and aggressive, mobile and independent in the world, and to achieve "high standing." The girls' representation of house interiors (which has a clear antecedent in their infantile play with dolls) would then mean that they are concentrating on the anticipated task of taking care of a home and of rearing children.

But this commonsense interpretation poses more questions than it 15 answers. If the boys, in building these scenes, think primarily of their present or anticipated roles, why are not boy dolls the figures most frequently used by them? The policeman is their favorite; yet it is safe to say that few anticipate being policemen or believe that we expect them to be. Why do the boys not arrange any sports fields in their play constructions? With the inventiveness born of strong motivation, this could have been accomplished, as could be seen in the contruction of one football field, with grandstand and all. But this was arranged by a girl who at the time was obese and tomboyish and wore "affectedly short-trimmed hair" — all of which suggests a unique determination in her case.

As mentioned before, World War II approached and broke out 16 during the early stages of the study; to be an aviator became one of the most intense hopes of many boys. Yet the pilot received preferred treatment only over the monk, and over the baby; while the policeman occurs twice as often as the cowboy, who certainly is the more immediate role-ideal of these Western boys and the one most in keeping with the clothes they wear and the attitudes they affect.

If the girls' prime motivation is the love of their present homes and 17 the anticipation of their future ones to the exclusion of all aspirations which they might be sharing with boys, it still would not immediately explain why the girls build fewer and lower walls around their houses. Love for home life might conceivably result in an increase in high walls and closed doors as guarantors of intimacy and security. The majority of the girl dolls in these peaceful family scenes are playing the piano or peacefully sitting with their families in the living room: could this really be considered representative of what they want to do or think they should pretend they want to do when asked to build an exciting movie scene?

If a piano-playing little girl seems as specific for the representation 18 of a peaceful interior in the girls' constructions as traffic halted by the policeman is for the boys' street scenes, the first can be understood to express *goodness indoors;* the second, *caution outdoors.* Such emphasis on goodness and caution, in response to the explicit instruction to construct an "exciting movie scene," suggests that in these responses dynamic dimensions and acute conflicts are expressed which are not explained by a theory of mere compliance with cultural and conscious ideals.

We may accept, then, the evidence of organ-modes in these constructions as a reminder of the fact that experience is anchored in the ground plan of the body. Beyond the organ-modes and their anatomical models, we see a suggestion of a male and a female experience of space. Its outlines become clearer if, instead of mere configurations, we note the specific functions emphasized in the various ways of using (or not using) blocks. Some constructions (lanes, tunnels, crossings) serve the *channelization* of traffic. Other structures are an expression of an *erecting, constructing,* and *elaborating* tendency. Simple walls, on the other hand, *include* and *enclose,* while open interiors *hold safely* without the necessity of an exclusion of the outside. 19

CONSIDERATIONS

1. Paraphrase the final sentence of the first paragraph. Take two or three sentences, if necessary, to clarify what Erikson says while avoiding his words. What audience is suggested by his choice of words? What audience is suggested by your choice of words in your paraphrase?
2. In setting up the experiment, how does Erikson try to avoid influencing the children's form of play? Considering that the experiment was conducted about thirty-five years ago, would you do any part of it differently now?
3. Summarize Erikson's findings from the experiment itself. Is there ample evidence for his generalizations? Are his generalizations formed to include all the details among the evidence?
4. How does Erikson respond to possible alternative explanations of his findings? Why does a "commonsense interpretation" seem inadequate to him?
5. Is Erikson imposing sexual stereotypes (see the preceding essay by Germaine Greer) on the children?
6. WRITING TOPIC. Become an unobtrusive observer at a playground or wherever you can watch children at play and take notes on their play acting or their game. How do the children interact? What keeps the play going? What brings the playing to an end? How do they act when it is over? Write a 700-word account of what you observe.

Jeremy Seabrook

A TWIN IS ONLY HALF
A PERSON

◊

JEREMY SEABROOK (b. 1939) is a British writer of plays for radio and television. He is also a social worker and sociologist who has written about modern English society in such books as *The Unprivileged* (1967) and *Homosexuals and Society* (1976). This excerpt from his memoirs, *Mother and Son* (1980), considers one of the causes of his feelings of alienation from himself and from other people.

Whenever I have told people I've met that I am a twin, there has 1 always come a change of expression in their eyes, a kind of re-focusing, which I came to recognize long before I detected its meaning. I think it is an attempt to discern in me my absent half: everybody knows that a twin is only half a person. There is a distinct withdrawal too, the readjustment people make when they discover someone they have been talking to freely and intimately is married. If you are a twin, people behave as though you are not worth making a relationship with; and they recoil, sensing perhaps that there is no reserve of feeling within you which you could possibly expend on them. They are interested and polite. They say "Oh is he like you?" and you can watch them adjust to the possibility of a replica of the individual they have just met; and your sense of uniqueness is assailed. They ask "Do you feel pain and joy on behalf of each other? If he is suffering, do you feel a pang, can you not bear to be apart?"

It has been nothing like that. 2

My twin has always been there. This may seem a very banal and 3 obvious thing to say; but he was there as a presence and not as a person. It is only now that we are well into our thirties that we have begun to exist for each other.

Our family made the same assumptions about us that are common 4

47

in the general response to twinning. The first was that there is a sense of symmetry in nature, and that in a twin situation human characteristics are distributed in compensating opposites: the absence of some feature in one of us was made good by the presence of another, which, in turn, was lacking in the other twin. There was a division of human qualities between us soon after birth, like a fairy-tale christening at which all the members of the family bestowed a gift upon us, or, in some cases, a curse, according to their disposition. And it seems to have occurred to no one that the same features might have been present in both of us. In this way, our natures were built by our relatives, an elaborate and ingenious construct which it has taken half a lifetime to demolish.

It was clear from the beginning that my brother was a good child 5
who didn't cry. All that remained for me was to be bad; but to make up for that, it was decided I would be clever. This implied that Jack would be dull; so it was decreed that he would be practical, skilled with his hands, which he became. This caused me to be clumsy and maladroit; and to make up for this, I was given a loving disposition, which I faithfully set about developing — even though I occasionally sensed guiltily that it wasn't true, and I longed to express my hatred of Aunt Maud and my loathing of bunny rabbits.

Our whole personalities were created rather than allowed to de- 6
velop, and the pace was forced. When one of us gave any sign of a preference or an ability, there was a rush to seek out its opposite in the other.

This meant over time that we became, each for the other, objects 7
of great mystery; and in this lay the deeper purpose of our contrived complementarity. The other was always endowed with what one didn't have, with what one lacked. My twin was a reproach to me for all the things I would never be. He was the beautiful one; and this meant, not simply that I was plain, or even of tolerably neutral appearance, but that I was ugly. For many years I observed people overcome what I imagined must be their revulsion before they could even bear to talk to me. But if I was bright, this implied that my brother was not merely average, but that he was backward. And we obliged by carrying out these determinants whispered over our cradle by malevolent adults. It was discovered — in early infancy somehow — that my brother would never be able to read or write. Later, when I went to the Grammar School, he was consigned to the C stream of the Sec-

ondary Modern in compliance with this melancholy fact. These roles pursued us far into adult life; and it wasn't until he was in the army, in Germany, that my brother realized, with wonder, that he was writing to his girl friend every day, letters he was amazed to find linguistically quite competent and marvellously rich in ideas.

In this way we grew up as strangers to each other; strangers who 8 had nothing in common and therefore no reason to make each other's acquaintance. The qualities which each of us possessed were not seen by the other as complementary. They had evolved to satisfy other people's sense of the rightness of things. We were immured in separate chambers of the body of the family, with our respective myths about ourselves and each other. It wouldn't be true to say that I disliked my brother. I regarded him with distant curiosity, as someone governed by quite different laws and values from myself — the kind of anthropological detachment which is normally brought to the observation of remote outlandish customs and practices. He was inaccessible, because apparently there was nothing we shared — not even our mother. She was a different person with each of us, as became someone with compassion for the monster of ugliness and the subnormal she had brought into the world.

But at the same time, my brother was the embodiment of all the 9 things I could never be. I grew up with my own deficiences constantly illuminated by the model of the child I understood him to be. The pain of this was made worse by our close relatives. Why can't you be more like Jack, I was asked with despairing insistence. It was a question I didn't have an answer to then. I do now, but it is thirty years too late to be of use to either of us.

If each of us was held up as an example of human perfection to the 10 other, it meant that we both grew up with a deepened sense of our own inadequacy. The relationship with our mother always seemed to take place privately, with only one at a time; and this didn't strike us as odd. Each of us was so dazzled by the vaunted perfection of the other, that he could only expect to wait, humble, patient, excluded from the mystical bond that existed between brother and mother. I often wondered what she said to him, as she washed him at night if I had been put to bed first and was waiting to go to sleep; or why she talked to me all the time about him if he were already washed and in bed. When he and I were together, we were like indifferent stepchildren, sullenly accepting each other's presence, but unable to find any

area of common interest. We had no idea then of our mother's resentment of what men had done to her. She must have dreaded above
all else that my brother and I might combine against her.

Mealtimes were the worst. I could never understand why other 11
families would spend perhaps an hour at table, when our meals were
such functional occasions, concerned with nothing but the assimila-
tion of food. My brother and I would sit in morose silence as we
played with the food on our plates, damming the gravy within an em-
bankment of mashed potato and waiting for the rampart to give way,
heads lowered, not even looking at each other. We simply eliminated
one another from our consciousness; and in order to survive, each had
to make light of the qualities the other had, and which were always
being set before him as an example. I learned to undervalue practical
ability in anything, so that I came to adulthood unable to pay a bill,
mend a fuse, change a plug, mow a lawn. And in our competitive
struggle I made a virtue of these things, because I was the only person
who sought my true good qualities in vain. If I was patient or kind, I
failed to observe it, or assumed patience and kindness to be of little
worth because they were mine; or perhaps I considered them deeply
contaminated by the fact that I was cowardly, ugly, and greedy. So I
had to diminish physical beauty. It was after all, I never ceased telling
myself, merely a shell; it indicated nothing of the person you really
were. I had to despise tractability and the quiet acceptance of the
adult timetable for sleep, food or play; I questioned the purpose of
these rituals endlessly, disputed them with tears and refusal, until the
adults despaired over my causeless grief.

My brother and I both tried to be as worthy as each suspected the 12
other of being of our mother's love; and it was given to us both to understand that each was always on the brink of ousting the preferred
other. This meant that neither finally gave up the struggle; neither
became totally indifferent or demoralized. A competitive tension persisted. I promised my mother that when I grew up, I would take her
away with me to live in Canada, not knowing that my brother had
promised to make a life for both of them in Australia.

So we grew, slightly deformed, like trees that have a common root 13
but have no room to grow to their full height side by side. We were
shadows cast over each other's childhood. I have a photograph of us at
the age of about seven. We are holding hands in front of the lilac
bush, and we are dressed identically. I have no recollection of the pic-

ture having been taken; only I am incredulous that we could ever have held hands. He was always there, with his beautiful violet eyes, silent and reproachful over his model-making, building aeroplanes with strips of frail balsa-wood, exuding a smell of pear drops from the adhesive he used. Once or twice he did initiate a clumsy attempt to get close to me. When Gran died, he tried to put an arm around me; when he was fourteen, he tried to talk to me about his loneliness. Terrified, I fled. It seemed like being molested by a stranger.

But now that we are grown up and our lives are separate in every   14 way — we sometimes don't meet for a year or more at a time — there remains, curiously, an ache and an absence. There is a sense of emptiness where he should have been and yet never was. When we are together, the old rivalry erupts readily in argument and misunderstanding; but when it doesn't there is a strange unspoken pain, which is present to a lesser degree with other members of the family — the scars of kinship.

At times I feel incomplete. The space he occupied has remained   15 vacant. It seems to me now that much of my adult life has been spent looking for people who resemble, not him but myself: a belated and doomed search for the things I ought to have shared with my twin. I remain with a persistent fear of being alone; and yet with others I feel inadequate, half a person. But it is half a person with no complement.

CONSIDERATIONS

1. Seabrook objects to people's instant curiosity about his being a twin. Explain why he would feel "assailed" by other people's expressions of interest.
2. How did their mother foster the twins' resentment of each other? Do you think she was aware of the effects of her actions? What does Seabrook seem to think about her?
3. Explain what Seabrook means at the end of the fourth paragraph when he says, "our natures were built by our relatives, an elaborate and ingenious construct which it has taken half a lifetime to demolish." What is a construct, and how do you suppose he demolished it?
4. What adjectives describe Seabrook's tone of voice in the selection? Find specific examples of his word-choice and sentence structure that help convey his tone to you.

5. WRITING TOPIC. Comparisons between people are often called "invidious" or "odious," because they are almost always displeasing in some way — even when they are meant to be favorable, and even when they have a mainly beneficial effect. When younger, were you often compared with other members of your family? Or were you compared with someone at summer camp? Or with other students in high school? What were such comparisons meant to show? Can you recall your response to them? Write a 700-word essay on the comparison to another person that you were fitted into, for better or worse, for an extended time.

6. WRITING TOPIC. The identical twins in the photograph on page 73 may appear to you to have different personalities despite their many similarities. Does Seabrook's memoir suggest ways of interpreting their relationship? How do specific details of their appearance and the background in the picture convey impressions of them as individuals and as sisters? In a 500-word essay, explain why and how this photograph leads you to particular inferences about their life as twins.

James Thurber

THE SECRET LIFE OF WALTER MITTY

◊

JAMES THURBER (1894–1961) was one of a number of urbane, witty writers about metropolitan life — others included Robert Benchley, Dorothy Parker, S. J. Perelman, E. B. White, Alexander Woollcott — whose essays and fiction appeared mainly in *The New Yorker* during the 1930s and 1940s. Thurber also drew cartoons for that magazine, which were memorable for their enormous dogs and for the fiercely battling little men and large-sized women. His essays, stories, and drawings are collected in such books as *The Owl in the Attic and Other Perplexities* (1931), *My Life and Hard Times* (1933), and *Men, Women, and Dogs* (1943). He also wrote a memoir of his career on *The New Yorker* staff, *My Years with Ross* (1959). The story of Walter Mitty, which was first published in 1939, created the character that popularly symbolizes the henpecked husband whose mind drifts away into daydreams of glory. Even his name, like other notorious fictional names — Uncle Tom, George Babbitt — has come to be a commonplace word for his specific type of personality.

"We're going through!" The Commander's voice was like thin ice 1 breaking. He wore his full-dress uniform, with the heavily braided white cap pulled down rakishly over one cold gray eye. "We can't make it, sir. It's spoiling for a hurricane, if you ask me." "I'm not asking you, Lieutenant Berg," said the Commander. "Throw on the power lights! Rev her up to 8,500! We're going through!" The pounding of the cylinders increased; ta-pocketa-pocketa-pocketa-*pocketa-pocketa*. The Commander stared at the ice forming on the pilot window. He walked over and twisted a row of complicated dials. "Switch on No. 8 auxiliary!" he shouted. "Switch on No. 8 auxiliary!" repeated Lieutenant Berg. "Full strength in No. 3 turret!" shouted

the Commander. "Full strength in No. 3 turret!" The crew, bending
to their various tasks in the huge, hurtling eight-engined Navy hydro-
plane, looked at each other and grinned. "The Old Man'll get us
through," they said to one another. "The Old Man ain't afraid of
Hell!" . . .

"Not so fast! You're driving too fast!" said Mrs. Mitty. "What are   2
you driving so fast for?"

"Hmm?" said Walter Mitty. He looked at his wife, in the seat be-   3
side him, with shocked astonishment. She seemed grossly unfamiliar,
like a strange woman who had yelled at him in a crowd. "You were up
to fifty-five," she said. "You know I don't like to go more than forty.
You were up to fifty-five." Walter Mitty drove on toward Waterbury
in silence, the roaring of the SN202 through the worst storm in
twenty years of Navy flying fading in the remote, intimate airways of
his mind. "You're tensed up again," said Mrs. Mitty. "It's one of your
days. I wish you'd let Dr. Renshaw look you over."

Walter Mitty stopped the car in front of the building where his   4
wife went to have her hair done. "Remember to get those overshoes
while I'm having my hair done," she said. "I don't need overshoes,"
said Mitty. She put her mirror back into her bag. "We've been all
through that," she said, getting out of the car. "You're not a young
man any longer." He raced the engine a little. "Why don't you wear
your gloves? Have you lost your gloves?" Walter Mitty reached in a
pocket and brought out the gloves. He put them on, but after she had
turned and gone into the building and he had driven on to a red light,
he took them off again. "Pick it up, brother," snapped a cop as the
light changed, and Mitty hastily pulled on his gloves and lurched
ahead. He drove around the streets aimlessly for a time, and then he
drove past the hospital on his way to the parking lot.

. . . "It's the millionaire banker, Wellington McMillan," said the   5
pretty nurse. "Yes?" said Walter Mitty, removing his gloves slowly.
"Who has the case?" "Dr. Renshaw and Dr. Benbow, but there
are two specialists here, Dr. Remington from New York and Dr.
Pritchard-Mitford from London. He flew over." A door opened down
a long, cool corridor and Dr. Renshaw came out. He looked distraught
and haggard. "Hello, Mitty," he said. "We're having the devil's own
time with McMillan, the millionaire banker and close personal friend
of Roosevelt. Obstreosis of the ductal tract. Tertiary. Wish you'd take
a look at him." "Glad to," said Mitty.

In the operating room there were whispered introductions: "Dr. 6
Remington, Dr. Mitty. Dr. Pritchard-Mitford, Dr. Mitty." "I've read
your book on streptothricosis," said Pritchard-Mitford, shaking hands.
"A brilliant performance, sir." "Thank you," said Walter Mitty.
"Didn't know you were in the States, Mitty," grumbled Remington.
"Coals to Newcastle, bringing Mitford and me up here for a tertiary."
"You are very kind," said Mitty. A huge, complicated machine, connected to the operating table, with many tubes and wires, began at
this moment to go pocketa-pocketa-pocketa. "The new anaesthetizer
is giving away!" shouted an interne. "There is no one in the East who
knows how to fix it!" "Quiet, man!" said Mitty, in a low, cool voice.
He sprang to the machine, which was now going pocketa-pocketa-
queep-pocketa-queep. He began fingering delicately a row of glistening dials. "Give me a fountain pen!" he snapped. Someone handed
him a fountain pen. He pulled a faulty piston out of the machine and
inserted the pen in its place. "That will hold for ten minutes," he said.
"Get on with the operation." A nurse hurried over and whispered to
Renshaw, and Mitty saw the man turn pale. "Coreopsis has set in,"
said Renshaw nervously. "If you would take over, Mitty?" Mitty
looked at him and at the craven figure of Benbow, who drank, and at
the grave, uncertain faces of the two great specialists. "If you wish,"
he said. They slipped a white gown on him; he adjusted a mask and
drew on thin gloves; nurses handed him shining. . . .

"Back it up, Mac! Look out for that Buick!" Walter Mitty jammed 7
on the brakes. "Wrong lane, Mac," said the parking-lot attendant,
looking at Mitty closely. "Gee. Yeh," muttered Mitty. He began cau-
tiously to back out of the lane marked "Exit Only." "Leave her sit
there," said the attendant. "I'll put her away." Mitty got out of the
car. "Hey, better leave the key." "Oh," said Mitty, handing the man
the ignition key. The attendant vaulted into the car, backed it up with
insolent skill, and put it where it belonged.

They're so damn cocky, thought Walter Mitty, walking along 8
Main Street; they think they know everything. Once he had tried to
take his chains off, outside New Milford, and he had got them wound
around the axles. A man had had to come out in a wrecking car and
unwind them, a young, grinning garage man. Since then Mrs. Mitty
always made him drive to a garage to have the chains taken off. The
next time, he thought, I'll wear my right arm in a sling; they won't
grin at me then. I'll have my right arm in a sling and they'll see I

couldn't possibly take the chains off myself. He kicked at the slush on
the sidewalk. "Overshoes," he said to himself, and he began looking
for a shoe store.

When he came out into the street again, with the overshoes in a   9
box under his arm, Walter Mitty began to wonder what the other
thing was his wife had told him to get. She had told him, twice before
they set out from their house for Waterbury. In a way he hated these
weekly trips to town — he was always getting something wrong.
Kleenex, he thought, Squibb's, razor blades? No. Toothpaste, toothbrush, bicarbonate, carborundum, initiative, and referendum? He
gave it up. But she would remember it. "Where's the what's-its-
name?" She would ask. "Don't tell me you forgot the what's-its-
name." A newsboy went by shouting something about the Waterbury
trial.

. . . "Perhaps this will refresh your memory." The District Attorney   10
suddenly thrust a heavy automatic at the quiet figure on the witness
stand. "Have you ever seen this before?" Walter Mitty took the gun
and examined it expertly. "This is my Webley-Vickers 50-80," he said
calmly. An excited buzz ran around the courtroom. The judge
rapped for order. "You are a crack shot with any sort of firearms, I
believe?" said the District Attorney, insinuatingly. "Objection!"
shouted Mitty's attorney. "We have shown that the defendant could
not have fired the shot. We have shown that he wore his right arm in
a sling on the night of the fourteenth of July." Walter Mitty raised his
hand briefly and the bickering attorneys were stilled. "With any
known make of gun," he said evenly, "I could have killed Gregory
Fitzhurst at three hundred feet *with my left hand.*" Pandemonium
broke loose in the courtroom. A woman's scream rose above the bed-
lam and suddenly a lovely, dark-haired girl was in Walter Mitty's
arms. The District Attorney struck at her savagely. Without rising
from his chair, Mitty let the man have it on the point of the chin.
"You miserable cur!"

"Puppy biscuit," said Walter Mitty. He stopped walking and the   11
buildings of Waterbury rose up out of the misty courtroom and surrounded him again. A woman who was passing laughed. "He said
'Puppy biscuit,' " she said to her companion. "That man said 'Puppy
biscuit' to himself." Walter Mitty hurried on. He went into an
A. & P., not the first one he came to but a smaller one farther up the
street. "I want some biscuit for small, young dogs," he said to the

clerk. "Any special brand, sir?" The greatest pistol shot in the world thought a moment. "It says 'Puppies Bark for It' on the box," said Walter Mitty.

His wife would be through at the hairdresser's in fifteen minutes, 12 Mitty saw in looking at his watch, unless they had trouble drying it; sometimes they had trouble drying it. She didn't like to get to the hotel first; she would want him to be there waiting for her as usual. He found a big leather chair in the lobby, facing a window, and he put the overshoes and the puppy biscuit on the floor beside it. He picked up an old copy of *Liberty* and sank down into the chair. "Can Germany Conquer the World through the Air?" Walter Mitty looked at the pictures of bombing planes and of ruined streets.

. . . "The cannonading has got the wind up in young Raleigh, sir," 13 said the sergeant. Captain Mitty looked up at him through tousled hair. "Get him to bed," he said wearily, "with the others. I'll fly alone." "But you can't, sir," said the sergeant anxiously. "It takes two men to handle that bomber and the Archies are pounding hell out of the air. Von Richtman's circus is between here and Saulier." "Somebody's got to get that ammunition dump," said Mitty. "I'm going over. Spot of brandy?" He poured a drink for the sergeant and one for himself. War thundered and whined around the dugout and battered at the door. There was a rending of wood and splinters flew through the room. "A bit of a near thing," said Captain Mitty carelessly. "The box barrage is closing in," said the sergeant. "We only live once, sergeant," said Mitty, with his faint, fleeting smile. "Or do we?" He poured another brandy and tossed it off. "I never see a man could hold his brandy like you, sir," said the sergeant. "Begging your pardon, sir." Captain Mitty stood up and strapped on his huge Webley-Vickers automatic. "It's forty kilometers through hell, sir," said the sergeant. Mitty finished one last brandy. "After all," he said softly, "what isn't?" The pounding of the cannon increased; there was the rat-tat-tatting of machine guns, and from somewhere came the menacing pocketa-pocketa-pocketa of the new flame-throwers. Walter Mitty walked to the door of the dugout humming "Après de Ma Blonde." He turned and waved to the sergeant. "Cheerio!" he said. . . .

Something struck his shoulder. "I've been looking all over this 14 hotel for you," said Mrs. Mitty. "Why do you have to hide in this old chair? How did you expect me to find you?" "Things close in," said

Walter Mitty vaguely. "What?" Mrs. Mitty said. "Did you get the what's-its-name? The puppy biscuit? What's in that box?" "Overshoes," said Mitty. "Couldn't you have put them on in the store?" "I was thinking," said Walter Mitty. "Does it ever occur to you that I am sometimes thinking?" She looked at him. "I'm going to take your temperature when I get you home," she said.

They went out through the revolving doors that made a faintly 15 derisive whistling sound when you pushed them. It was two blocks to the parking lot. At the drugstore on the corner she said, "Wait here for me. I forgot something. I won't be a minute." She was more than a minute. Walter Mitty lighted a cigarette. It began to rain, rain with sleet in it. He stood up against the wall of the drugstore, smoking. . . . He put his shoulders back and his heels together. "To hell with the handkerchief," said Walter Mitty scornfully. He took one last drag on his cigarette and snapped it away. Then, with that faint, fleeting smile playing about his lips, he faced the firing squad; erect and motionless, proud and disdainful, Walter Mitty the Undefeated, inscrutable to the last.

CONSIDERATIONS

1. Explain the statement "The Commander's voice was like thin ice breaking." Does it quite perfectly fit the impression that Mitty would like to give?

2. What is a *tertiary?* What is a *coreopsis?* Why does Thurber use these terms in Mitty's fantasy of being a surgeon?

3. Explain a few implications of Mrs. Mitty's statement, in the next-to-last paragraph, "I'm going to take your temperature when I get you home."

4. What personal qualities do Walter Mitty's fantasies of himself have in common? In addition to his wife, what other things in his actual life contradict his daydreams?

5. WRITING TOPIC. Write a 500-word essay on the daydreams or fantasy ambitions that preoccupied you when you were ten to twelve years old. To what extent did your daydreams incorporate current events and celebrities, and to what extent did they incorporate legendary or literary material?

Joan Didion

IN BED

◊

JOAN DIDION (b. 1934) was raised in California and graduated from the University of California at Berkeley in 1956. Her career in journalism has included work as an editor and columnist for such magazines as *Vogue* and *Saturday Evening Post,* and her essays have appeared in such national periodicals as *The American Scholar* and the *National Review.* She has written three novels, including *Play It As It Lays* (1971) and *A Book of Common Prayer* (1977). Her essays are collected in *Slouching Toward Bethlehem* (1969) and *The White Album* (1979). In this essay from the latter volume Didion gives a complex, double view of her suffering from migraine headaches.

Three, four, sometimes five times a month, I spend the day in bed 1 with a migraine headache, insensible to the world around me. Almost every day of every month, between these attacks, I feel the sudden irrational irritation and flush of blood into the cerebral arteries which tell me that migraine is on its way, and I take certain drugs to avert its arrival. If I did not take the drugs, I would be able to function perhaps one day in four. The physiological error called migraine is, in brief, central to the given of my life. When I was fifteen, sixteen, even twenty-five, I used to think that I could rid myself of this error by simply denying it, character over chemistry. "Do you have headaches *sometimes? frequently? never?*" the application forms would demand. "Check one." Wary of the trap, wanting whatever it was that the successful circumnavigation of that particular form could bring (a job, a scholarship, the respect of mankind and the grace of God), I would check one. *"Sometimes,"* I would lie. That in fact I spent one or two days a week almost unconscious with pain seemed a shameful secret, evidence not merely of some chemical inferiority but of all my bad attitudes, unpleasant tempers, wrongthink.

For I had no brain tumor, no eyestrain, no high blood pressure, 2 nothing wrong with me at all: I simply had migraine headaches, and migraine headaches were, as everyone who did not have them knew, imaginary. I fought migraine then, ignored the warnings it sent, went to school and later to work in spite of it, sat through lectures in Middle English and presentations to advertisers with involuntary tears running down the right side of my face, threw up in washrooms, stumbled home by instinct, emptied ice trays onto my bed and tried to freeze the pain in my right temple, wished only for a neurosurgeon who would do a lobotomy on house call, and cursed my imagination.

It was a long time before I began thinking mechanistically enough 3 to accept migraine for what it was: something with which I would be living, the way some people live with diabetes. Migraine is something more than the fancy of a neurotic imagination. It is an essentially hereditary complex of symptoms, the most frequently noted but by no means the most unpleasant of which is a vascular headache of blinding severity, suffered by a surprising number of women, a fair number of men (Thomas Jefferson had migraine, and so did Ulysses S. Grant, the day he accepted Lee's surrender), and by some unfortunate children as young as two years old. (I had my first when I was eight. It came on during a fire drill at the Columbia School in Colorado Springs, Colorado. I was taken first home and then to the infirmary at Peterson Field, where my father was stationed. The Air Corps doctor prescribed an enema.) Almost anything can trigger a specific attack of migraine: stress, allergy, fatigue, an abrupt change in barometric pressure, a contretemps over a parking ticket. A flashing light. A fire drill. One inherits, of course, only the predisposition. In other words I spent yesterday in bed with a headache not merely because of my bad attitudes, unpleasant tempers, and wrongthink, but because both my grandmothers had migraine, my father has migraine, and my mother has migraine.

No one knows precisely what it is that is inherited. The chemistry 4 of migraine, however, seems to have some connection with the nerve hormone named serotonin, which is naturally present in the brain. The amount of serotonin in the blood falls sharply at the onset of migraine, and one migraine drug, methysergide, or Sansert, seems to have some effect on serotonin. Methysergide is a derivative of lysergic acid (in fact Sandoz Pharmaceuticals first synthesized LSD-25 while looking for a migraine cure), and its use is hemmed about with so many contraindications and side effects that most doctors prescribe it only in the most incapacitating cases. Methysergide, when it is prescribed, is taken daily, as a preventive; another preventive which works for some people is old-fashioned ergotamine tartrate, which helps to constrict the swelling blood vessels during the "aura," the period which in most cases precedes the actual headache.

Once an attack is under way, however, no drug touches it. Migraine gives some people mild hallucinations, temporarily blinds others, shows up not only as a headache but as a gastrointestinal disturbance, a painful sensitivity to all sensory stimuli, an abrupt overpowering fatigue, a strokelike aphasia, and a crippling inability to make even the most routine connections. When I am in a migraine aura (for some people the aura lasts fifteen minutes, for others several hours), I will drive through red lights, lose the house keys, spill whatever I am holding, lose the ability to focus my eyes or frame coherent sentences, and generally give the appearance of being on drugs, or drunk. The actual headache, when it comes, brings with it chills, sweating, nausea, a debility that seems to stretch the very limits of endurance. That no one dies of migraine seems, to someone deep into an attack, an ambiguous blessing.

My husband also has migraine, which is unfortunate for him but fortunate for me: perhaps nothing so tends to prolong an attack as the accusing eye of someone who has never had a headache. "Why not take a couple of aspirin," the unafflicted will say from the doorway, or "I'd have a headache, too, spending a beautiful day like this inside with all the shades drawn." All of us who have migraine suffer not only from the attacks themselves but from this common conviction that we are perversely refusing to cure ourselves by taking a couple of aspirin, that we are making ourselves sick, that we "bring it on ourselves." And in the most immediate sense, the sense of why we have a headache this Tuesday and not last Thursday, of course we often do. There certainly is what doctors call a "migraine personality," and that personality tends to be ambitious, inward, intolerant of error, rather rigidly organized, perfectionist. "You don't look like a migraine personality," a doctor once said to me. "Your hair's messy. But I suppose you're a compulsive housekeeper." Actually my house is kept even more negligently than my hair, but the doctor was right nonetheless: perfectionism can also take the form of spending most of a week writing and rewriting and not writing a single paragraph.

But not all perfectionists have migraine, and not all migrainous 7 people have migraine personalities. We do not escape heredity. I have tried in most of the available ways to escape my own migrainous heredity (at one point I learned to give myself two daily injections of histamine with a hypodermic needle, even though the needle so frightened me that I had to close my eyes when I did it), but I still have migraine. And I have learned now to live with it, learned when to expect it, how to outwit it, even how to regard it, when it does come, as more friend than lodger. We have reached a certain understanding, my migraine and I. It never comes when I am in real trouble. Tell me that my house is burned down, my husband has left me, that there is gunfighting in the streets and panic in the banks, and I will not respond by getting a headache. It comes instead when I am fighting not an open but a guerrilla war with my own life, during weeks of small household confusions, lost laundry, unhappy help, canceled appointments, on days when the telephone rings too much and I get no work done and the wind is coming up. On days like that my friend comes uninvited.

And once it comes, now that I am wise in its ways, I no longer fight 8 it. I lie down and let it happen. At first every small apprehension is magnified, every anxiety a pounding terror. Then the pain comes, and I concentrate only on that. Right there is the usefulness of migraine, there in that imposed yoga, the concentration on the pain. For when the pain recedes, ten or twelve hours later, everything goes with it, all the hidden resentments, all the vain anxieties. The migraine has acted as a circuit breaker, and the fuses have emerged intact. There is a pleasant convalescent euphoria. I open the windows and feel the air, eat gratefully, sleep well. I notice the particular nature of a flower in a glass on the stair landing. I count my blessings.

CONSIDERATIONS

1. Why did Didion for many years try to ignore her migraines and to deny having them? What realizations finally changed her mind?

2. In paragraphs 4 and 5, Didion gives an objective account of migraines, and at the same time she also suggests her subjective responses as a migraine sufferer. What words and phrases give us her personal response, despite the air of objective detachment?
3. What is a "migraine personality"? Does Didion believe that she has one?
4. In the final two paragraphs Didion personifies her migraines as she learns to live with her affliction. How does the personification help make her problem more tolerable?
5. WRITING TOPIC. Children generally assume that any emotional or physical pain that they suffer is caused by some fault in themselves. In a 500-word essay, recall a period of illness or affliction in which you felt guilty, or to blame, for being distressed. How did other people reinforce or dispel your feelings?

Walt Whitman

A NOISELESS
PATIENT SPIDER

◊

WALT WHITMAN (1819–1892) worked as a printer, an editor, a school-teacher, a carpenter, and he also drifted a lot until he began to write the kind of poetry that he felt defined his true self. He believed that one's individual personality gave meaning to the contradictory terms of nineteenth-century American life, such as democracy and slavery, nature and commerce, westward expansion and civil war. He worked chiefly on one book of poems, *Leaves of Grass*, from his early thirties to his death at age seventy-two. He constantly expanded the volume with new poems and revised its overall organization. In this poem he notices a similarity between himself and a spider.

A noiseless patient spider,
I mark'd where on a little promontory it stood isolated,
Mark'd how to explore the vacant vast surrounding,
It launch'd forth filament, filament, filament, out of
    itself,
Ever unreeling them, ever tirelessly speeding them.

And you O my soul where you stand,
Surrounded, detached, in measureless oceans of space,
Ceaselessly musing, venturing, throwing, seeking the
    spheres to connect them,   10
Till the bridge you will need be form'd, till the
    ductile anchor hold,
Till the gossamer thread you fling catch somewhere,
    O my soul.

CONSIDERATIONS

1. Notice the amount of repetition of words and sounds in the first stanza. What qualities of the spider are emphasized by the repetition? Is the image repellent or fascinating or both?
2. In stanza two, what is Whitman implicitly saying to his soul? Why doesn't he say it explicitly? What is the tone of his voice in the second stanza?
3. What is "the gossamer thread" that issues from his soul? Where might he "fling" it? And where might it "catch" on to something? Does the diction sound careless and casual?
4. WRITING TOPIC. In about 300 words, describe in clear detail a nonhuman thing that suggests an image of your essential self. When relevant to your purpose, include description of the movements and surroundings of your subject.

John Berger

THE CHANGING VIEW
OF MAN
IN THE PORTRAIT

◊

JOHN BERGER (b. 1926) was born in London and educated in art schools for his first career as a painter and teacher of drawing. He is also a prominent art critic, novelist, and screenwriter, who brings to his work a Marxist interpretation of the way individuals are affected by the basic structures of their society. His fiction includes *A Painter of Our Time* (1958) and the prize-winning *G* (1972); his books on the visual arts include *The Success and Failure of Picasso* (1965), *The Moment of Cubism* (1969), and *The Look of Things* (1974), from which this essay is taken. In comparing painted portraits and photographs, he maintains that photographs reflect a more modern view of human nature.

It seems to me unlikely that any important portraits will ever be 1
painted again. Portraits, that is to say, in the sense of portraiture as we
now understand it. I can imagine multi-medium memento-sets devoted to the character of particular individuals. But these will have
nothing to do with the works now in the National Portrait Gallery.

I see no reason to lament the passing of the portrait — the talent 2
once involved in portrait painting can be used in some other way to
serve a more urgent, modern function. It is, however, worth while in-
quiring why the painted portrait has become outdated; it may help us
to understand more clearly our historical situation.

The beginning of the decline of the painted portrait coincided 3
roughly speaking with the rise of photography, and so the earliest answer to our question — which was already being asked towards the
end of the nineteenth century — was that the photographer had

taken the place of the portrait painter. Photography was more accurate, quicker, and far cheaper; it offered the opportunity of portraiture to the whole of society: previously such an opportunity had been the privilege of a very small elite.

To counter the clear logic of this argument, painters and their patrons invented a number of mysterious, metaphysical qualities with which to prove that what the painted portrait offered was incomparable. Only a man, not a machine (the camera), could interpret the soul of a sitter. An artist dealt with the sitter's destiny: the camera with mere light and shade. An artist judged: a photographer recorded. Etcetera, etcetera.

All this was doubly untrue. First, it denies the interpretative role of the photographer, which is considerable. Secondly, it claims for painted portraits a psychological insight which ninety-nine per cent of them totally lack. If one is considering portraiture as a genre, it is no good thinking of a few extraordinary pictures but rather of the endless portraits of the local nobility and dignitaries in countless provincial museums and town halls. Even the average Renaissance portrait — although suggesting considerable presence — has very little psychological content. We are surprised by ancient Roman or Egyptian portraits, not because of their *insight,* but because they show us very vividly how little the human face has changed. It is a myth that the portrait painter was a revealer of souls. Is there a qualitative difference between the way Velazquez painted a face and the way he painted a bottom? The comparatively few portraits that reveal true psychological insight (certain Raphaels, Rembrandts, Davids, Goyas) suggest personal, obsessional interests on the part of the artist which simply cannot be accommodated within the *professional* role of the portrait painter. Such pictures have the same kind of intensity as self-portraits. They are in fact works of self-discovery.

Ask yourself the following hypothetical question. Suppose that there is somebody in the second half of the nineteenth century in whom you are interested but of whose face you have never seen a picture. Would you rather find a painting or a photograph of this person? And the question itself posed like that is already highly favourable to painting, since the logical question should be: would you rather find a painting or a whole album of photographs?

Until the invention of photography, the painted (or sculptural) portrait was the only means of recording and presenting the likeness of a person. Photography took over this role from painting and at the same time raised our standards for judging how much an informative likeness should include.

This is not to say that photographs are *in all ways* superior to 8 painted portraits. They are more informative, more psychologically revealing, and in general more accurate. But they are less tensely unified. Unity in a work of art is achieved as a result of the limitations of the medium. Every element has to be transformed in order to have its proper place within these limitations. In photography the transformation is to a considerable extent mechanical. In a painting each transformation is largely the result of a conscious decision by the artist. Thus the unity of a painting is permeated by a far higher degree of intention. The total effect of a painting (as distinct from its truthfulness) is less arbitrary than that of a photograph; its construction is more intensely socialized because it is dependent on a greater number of human decisions. A photographic portrait may be more revealing and more accurate about the likeness and character of the sitter; but it is likely to be less persuasive, less (in the very strict sense of the word) conclusive. For example, if the portraitist's intention is to flatter or idealize, he will be able to do so far more convincingly with a painting than with a photograph.

From this fact we gain an insight into the actual function of por- 9 trait painting in its heyday: a function we tend to ignore if we concentrate on the small number of exceptional "unprofessional" portraits by Raphael, Rembrandt, David, Goya, etc. The function of portrait painting was to underwrite and idealize a chosen social role of the sitter. It was not to present him as "an individual" but, rather, as an individual monarch, bishop, landowner, merchant and so on. Each role had its accepted qualities and its acceptable limit of discrepancy. (A monarch or a pope could be far more idiosyncratic than a mere gentleman or courtier.) The role was emphasized by pose, gesture, clothes, and background. The fact that neither the sitter nor the successful professional painter was much involved with the painting of these parts is not to be entirely explained as a matter of saving time: they were thought of and were meant to be read as the accepted attributes of a given social stereotype.

The hack painters never went much beyond the stereotype; the 10 good professionals (Memlinck, Cranach, Titian, Rubens, Van Dyck, Velazquez, Hals, Philippe de Champaigne) painted individual men, but they were nevertheless men whose character and facial expressions were seen and judged in the exclusive light of an ordained social role. The portrait must fit like a hand-made pair of shoes, but the type of shoe was never in question.

The satisfaction of having one's portrait painted was the satisfaction of being personally recognized and *confirmed in one's position:* it had nothing to do with the modern lonely desire to be recognized "for what one really is." 11

If one were going to mark the moment when the decline of portraiture became inevitable by citing the work of a particular artist, I would choose the two or three extraordinary portraits of lunatics by Géricault, painted in the first period of romantic disillusion and defiance which followed the defeat of Napoleon and the shoddy triumph of the French bourgeoisie. The paintings were neither morally anecdotal nor symbolic: they were straight portraits, traditionally painted. Yet their sitters had no social role and were presumed to be incapable of fulfilling any. In other pictures Géricault painted severed human heads and limbs as found in the dissecting theatre. His outlook was bitterly critical: to choose to paint dispossessed lunatics was a comment on men of property and power; but it was also an assertion that the essential spirit of man was independent of the role into which society forced him. Géricault found society so negative that, although sane himself, he found the isolation of the mad more meaningful than the social honour accorded to the successful. He was the first and, in a sense, the last profoundly anti-social portraitist. The term contains an impossible contradiction. 12

After Géricault, professional portraiture degenerated into servile and crass personal flattery, cynically undertaken. It was no longer possible to believe in the value of the social roles chosen or allotted. Sincere artists painted a number of "intimate" portraits of their friends or models (Corot, Courbet, Degas, Cézanne, Van Gogh), but in these the social role of the sitter is reduced to *that of being painted.* The implied social value is either that of personal friendship (proximity) or that of being seen in such a way (being "treated") by an original artist. In either case the sitter, somewhat like an arranged still life, becomes subservient to the painter. Finally it is not his personality or his role which impress us but the artist's vision. 13

Toulouse-Lautrec was the one important latter-day exception to this general tendency. He painted a number of portraits of tarts and 14 cabaret personalities. As we survey them, they survey us. A social reciprocity is established through the painter's mediation. We are presented neither with a disguise — as with official portraiture — nor with mere creatures of the artist's vision. His portraits are the only late nineteenth-century ones which are persuasive and conclusive in the sense that we have defined. They are the only painted portraits in whose social evidence we can believe. They suggest not the artist's studio, but "the world of Toulouse-Lautrec": that is to say a specific and complex social milieu. Why was Lautrec such an exception? Because in his own eccentric manner he believed in the social roles of his sitters. He painted the cabaret performers because he admired their performances: he painted the tarts because he recognized the usefulness of their trade.

Increasingly for over a century fewer and fewer people in capitalist 15 society have been able to believe in the social value of the social roles offered. This is the second answer to our original question about the decline of the painted portrait.

The second answer suggests, however, that given a more confident 16 and coherent society, portrait painting might revive. And this seems unlikely. To understand why, we must consider the third answer.

The measures, the scale-change of modern life, have changed the 17 nature of individual identity. Confronted with another person today, we are aware, through this person, of forces operating in directions which were unimaginable before the turn of the century, and which have only become clear relatively recently. It is hard to define this change briefly. An analogy may help.

We hear a lot about the crisis of the modern novel. What this in- 18 volves, fundamentally, is a change in the mode of narration. It is scarcely any longer possible to tell a straight story sequentially unfolding in time. And this is because we are too aware of what is continually traversing the story-line laterally. That is to say, instead of being aware of a point as an infinitely small part of a straight line, we are aware of it as an infinitely small part of an infinite number of lines, as the centre of a star of lines. Such awareness is the result of our constantly having to take into account the simultaneity and extension of events and possibilities.

Something similar but less direct applies to the painted portrait. 19 We can no longer accept that the identity of a man can be adequately established by preserving and fixing what he looks like from a single viewpoint in one place. (One might argue that the same limitation applies to the still photograph, but as we have seen, we are not led to expect a photograph to be as conclusive as a painting.) Our terms of recognition have changed since the heyday of portrait painting. We may still rely on "likeness" to identify a person, but no longer to explain or place him. To concentrate upon "likeness" is to isolate falsely. It is to assume that the outermost surface *contains* the man or object: whereas we are highly conscious of the fact that nothing can contain itself.

It seems that the demands of a modern vision are incompatible with the singularity of viewpoint which is the prerequisite for a static painted "likeness." The incompatibility is connected with a more general crisis concerning the meaning of individuality. Individuality can no longer be contained within the terms of manifest personality traits. In a world of transition and revolution individuality has become a problem of historical and social relations, such as cannot be revealed by the mere characterizations of an already established social stereotype. Every mode of individuality now relates to the whole world. 20

CONSIDERATIONS

1. Berger rejects the opinion that painted portraits are superior to photographs. What are the arguments that favor portraits, and how does Berger refute them?
2. According to Berger, in what specific ways are photographs superior to portraits? Does he have a general preference for one over the other?
3. In the essay, Berger develops three reasons for the decline of portrait painting. Write a one-paragraph synopsis of his argument.
4. Berger maintains that the truly great portraits express the painter more fully than they represent the sitter: "They are in fact works of self-discovery." Does Berger mean that you can deduce the personality of the artist by examining his works? What is your own view of that inference?
5. WRITING TOPIC. In a 700-word essay, describe a painted portrait, or a self-portrait, such as you might find in a book of art prints or at a museum. Try to explain which details in the painting indicate the sitter's social role and which details seem mainly individualizing. Consider whether, in Berger's sense, the painting has "unity," that is, whether every element of the portrait has been fitted into a general effect.
6. WRITING TOPIC. In a 700-word essay, compare the photograph and the

painted portrait of Abraham Lincoln on pages 74–75. What features are emphasized in each likeness — such as hands, eyes, hair, posture, clothing — and what qualities of character are suggested by these and other details? Does Lincoln seem to be significantly changed in these two images? Or do you find that despite the different visual materials, the pictures convey similar impressions of the man? Which picture do you like better, and why?

IMAGES

Judith D. Sedwick, Twins. (*The Picture Cube*)

Alexander Gardner, Abraham Lincoln, *1863.*
(*The Abraham Lincoln Museum, Lincoln Memorial University*)

George P. A. Healy, Abraham Lincoln, *1866–1870.*
(*Chicago Historical Society*)

Four Views of Eleanor Roosevelt: 1903, 1928, 1946, 1959. (Wide World)

ADDITIONAL WRITING TOPICS

◇

SELF-IMAGES

1. Write a 500-word essay on the way people are portrayed in the drawings and paintings that young children do when they are about six to eight years old. (Perhaps you can remember some of your own at that time.) What features are especially prominent? Is there a sense of movement and purpose in the figures? How do you know who they are?

2. In the past, slaves, serfs, peasants, and subjugated minorities often did not have family names, or even first names with legal standing, because such classes did not have full legal rights as national citizens or subjects. At present, everyone residing in the United States, as in most other literate societies, is required by government regulations to have a name. Does such a requirement increase or reduce personal freedom? Write a 500-word essay explaining how your sense of identity is affected — perhaps both positively and negatively — by the legal status of your name.

3. Write an account in 700 words of how your overall view of someone was changed by your recognition of particular new qualities about the person. The person may have been a stranger who gave you an impression that was modified upon further observation; or the person may be someone long familiar to you in a different way. Was the person aware of your earlier view and your later view? Was the person's reaction part of the process or circumstance of the change? Strive to be precise about your former view and your revised view, and be sure to include enough details to show how this change came about.

4. Write a 700-word essay about looking at old photographs. Perhaps you used to look through an album including pictures of yourself among many photographs of other people. What feelings about yourself were stimulated by this assortment of pictures? Since seeing other people in photographs may evoke reactions different from your responses to them as actual people, try to explain the effect of seeing them and yourself as photographic images.

5. What is *self-respect*? Write a 500-word essay that defines this quality of personal experience. Try to write concretely about this abstraction. You

77

may find it useful to include explanations of how self-respect is lost (did you ever feel ashamed of something that you really are?), and you might consider what role other people have in diminishing or restoring one's self-respect.

6. If you were going to write an autobiography, where would you start? In a 700-word essay, explain your reasons for deciding on a particular beginning for your life story. In other words, do not write the beginning of your autobiography — write an essay explaining why you would begin one at that particular point.

7. The four photographs of Eleanor Roosevelt on page 76 suggest more than merely the changes caused by aging. Her character appears to change; her sense of herself and her outlook toward other people visibly differ in these four stages of her life. Consider the details of her expressions as well as her choice of clothing and hair styles. What significant traits continue through her life? Which traits grow more pronounced, and which soften or disappear? What attitudes and feelings can you discern in her? Does she seem to acquire a new dimension to her character in any or all of the pictures? In a 1,000-word essay, explain all that you perceive about her identity in the series of photographs. (To relate these photographs to Eleanor Roosevelt's life history, you may choose to consult a biographical reference work, such as *The McGraw-Hill Encyclopedia of World Biography* or *Notable American Women: The Modern Period.* In any case, keep your essay focused on the photographs you are interpreting. Write your own life study of the personality you see pictured there.)

2

FAMILY TIES

INSIGHTS

The family, not the individual, is the real molecule of society, the key link in the social chain of being.

– ROBERT NISBET

All happy families are alike; but an unhappy family is unhappy in its own way.

– LEO TOLSTOY

We hear a great deal about the rudeness of the rising generation. I am an oldster myself and might be expected to take the oldsters' side, but in fact I have been far more impressed by the bad manners of parents to children than by those of children to parents. Who has not been the embarrassed guest at family meals where the father or mother treated their grown-up offspring with an incivility which, offered to any other young people, would simply have terminated the acquaintance? Dogmatic assertions on matters which the children understand and their elders don't, ruthless interruptions, flat contradictions, ridicule of things the young take seriously — sometimes of their religion — insulting references to their friends, all provide an easy answer to the question "Why are they always out? Why do they like every house better than their home?" Who does not prefer civility to barbarism?

– C. S. LEWIS

He that hath wife and children hath given hostages to fortune; for they are impediments to great enterprises, either of virtue or mischief. Certainly the best works, and of greatest merit for the public, have proceeded from the unmarried or childless men, which both in affection and means have married and endowed the public.

— FRANCIS BACON

Margaret Mead

FAMILY CODES

◊

MARGARET MEAD (1901–1978) grew up in Philadelphia and went to Barnard College, where she discovered the subject of anthropology. By her mid-twenties she was doing field work studying adolescent girls in Samoa, a research project that led to her first book, *Coming of Age in Samoa* (1928), and to her Ph.D. from Columbia University. She continued writing about adolescence in primitive societies in *Growing Up in New Guinea* (1930), and the topics of sexual development and family life occupy much of her voluminous writing throughout her distinguished career as a professor, field worker, and highly popular author and lecturer. In *Male and Female* (1949) she examines contemporary society with the trained eye of an anthropologist looking at her own culture. In this excerpt from that book she points out that modern Americans face a particularly difficult problem in learning how to live together in families.

In the United States the striking characteristic is that each set of parents is different from each other set, that no two have exactly the same memories, that no two families could be placed side by side and it could be said: "Yes, these four parents ate the same food, played the same games, heard the same lullabies, were scared by the same bogeys, taught that the same words were taboo, given the same picture of what they would be as men and women, made ready to hand on unimpaired the tradition they received, whole, unravelled, unfaded, from their parents."

Every home is different from every other home, every marriage, even within the same class, in the same clique, contains contrasts between the partners as superficially striking as the difference between one New Guinea tribe and another. "In our family we never locked the bathroom door." "In our family you never entered another person's room without knocking." "Mother always asked to see our letters, even after we were grown." "The smallest scrap of paper on which one had written something was returned unread." "We were never allowed to mention our legs." "Father said that 'sweat' was a good deal honester word than 'perspiration,' but to be careful not to say it when we went to Aunt Alice's." "Mother said my hands would get rough if I climbed trees." "Mother said girls ought to stretch their legs and get some exercise while they were young." Side by side, next-door neighbours, children of first cousins, sometimes children of sisters or brothers, the ways of each household diverge, one family bringing up the children to prudery, privacy, and strongly marked sex roles, another to an open give-and-take that makes the girls seem tomboys. Then again comes marriage between the children with the different upbringings, and again the clash, the lack of timing, the lack of movement in step, of the new set of parents. Every home is different from every other home; no two parents, even though they were fed their cereal from silver porringers of the same design, were fed it in quite the same way. The gestures of the feeding hands, whether of mother, grandmother, Irish cook, English nurse, Negro mammy, country-bred hired girl, are no longer the assured, the highly patterned gestures of the member of a homogeneous society. The recently come foreigner's hand is unsure as it handles unfamiliar things and tries to thrust a spoon into the mouth of a child who acts and speaks strangely; the old American's hand bears marks of such uncertainties in former generations, and may tremble or clench anew over some recent contact with some newly arrived and little-understood stranger.

But just because every home is different from every other home, 3 because no husband and wife can move effortlessly in step to the same remembered cradle-songs, so also is every home alike. The anthropologist who has studied a New Guinea tribe can often predict down to the smallest detail what will go on in each family if there is a quarrel, what will be said when there is a reconciliation, who will make it, with what words and what gestures. No anthropologist can ever hope to do the same thing for the United States. What the quarrel will be, who will make up and how, will differ in every home; what the highest moment between parents and child will be will differ. But the form, the kind of quarrel, the kind of reconciliation, the kind of love, the kind of misunderstandings, will be alike in their very difference. In

one home the husband will indicate his importunate desire by bringing flowers, in another by kicking the cat playfully as he enters, in a
third by making a fuss over the baby, in a fourth by getting very busy
over the radio, while the wife may indicate her acceptance or rejection
of his erotic expectation by putting on more lip-stick or by rubbing off
the lip-stick she has on, by getting very busy tidying up the room or by
sinking in a soft dream into the other overstuffed chair, playing idly
with her baby's curly hair. There is no pattern, no simple word or gesture that has been repeated by all husbands in the presence of all the
small children who are to be future husbands, and all the small girls
who are to be wives, so that when they grow up they will be letter-
perfect in a ballet of approach or retreat.

In America the language of each home is different, there is a code 4
in each family that no one else knows. And that is the essential likeness, the essential regularity, among all these apparent differences.
For in each American marriage there is a special code, developed from
the individual pasts of the two partners, put together out of the accidents of honeymoon and parents-in-law, finally beaten into a language
that each understands imperfectly. For here is another regularity.
When a code, a language, is shared by every one in the village, spoken
by the gracious and the grim, by the flexible-tongued and the stubborn, by the musical voice and the halting and stammering voice, the
language becomes beautifully precise, each sound sharply and perfectly differentiated from each other sound. The new-born baby, first
babbling happily through his whole possible range of lovely and unlovely noise, listens, and narrows his range. Where he once babbled a
hundred nuances of sound, he limits himself to a bare half-dozen, and
practices against the perfection, the sureness, of his elders. Later, he
too, however stumbling his tongue or poor his ear, will speak the language of his people so that all can understand him. The perfected
model made by the lips and tongues of many different sorts of people
speaking the same words holds the speech of each new-comer clear
and sharp enough for communication. And as with speech, so with
gesture, so with the timing of initiative, of response, of command and
obedience. The toddler falls in step with the multitude around him
and cannot fail to learn his part.

But in a culture like modern America, the child does not see any 5
such harmonious, repetitive behaviour. All men do not cross their legs
with the same assured masculinity, or squat on wooden stools to

protect themselves from a rear-guard attack. All women do not walk with little mincing steps, or sit and lie with thighs drawn close together, even in sleep. The behaviour of each American is itself a composite, an imperfectly realized version, of the behaviour of others who in turn had, not a single model — expressed in many voices and many ways, but still a single model — but a hundred models, each different, each an individually developed style, lacking the authenticity, the precision, of a group style. The hand held out in greeting, to still a tear, or to help up a strange child that has stumbled, is not sure that it will be taken, or if taken, taken in the sense in which it is offered. Where patterns of courtship are clear, a girl knows the outcome if she smiles, or laughs, casts down her eyes, or merely walks softly by a group of harvesting youths cradling a red ear of corn in her arms. But in America, the same smile may evoke a casual answering grin, embarrassed averted eyes, an unwelcome advance, or may even mean being followed home along a deserted street, not because each boy who answers feels differently about the girl, but because each understands differently the cue that she gives.

CONSIDERATIONS

1. Mead maintains that in modern America "Every home is different from every other home." Consider the illustrations she gives in the second paragraph to demonstrate differences among families. Are they superficial or significant details? Can you add others that illustrate her point? Throughout this essay, when Mead generalizes, how does she support her points?
2. Why is it necessary to devise codes and models of expression? From a social scientist's viewpoint, why isn't it sufficient just to say what we mean and do what we intend?
3. If it is true that American families must develop a code of communication that a primitive society provides ready-made for all its families, how are we more "advanced" than New Guinea tribesmen? Are we occupied in reinventing the wheel, so to speak? Are there personal and social advantages in our situation over theirs?
4. WRITING TOPIC. At home, how long can you talk on the telephone without raising objections from your family? Where is your stereo set, and what is the acceptable volume level around the house? How are you

praised for your academic achievements? And for what things can you give praise to your parents? How do you know when you can feel assured of privacy in your home? With the eyes of an anthropologist observing a primal (if not primitive) society, write a 500-word essay that deciphers the code only your family members would fully comprehend regarding one significant issue of family life.

Philip Slater

SOCIAL CLIMBING
BEGINS AT HOME

◊

PHILIP SLATER (b. 1927) was educated at Harvard and taught sociology at Brandeis University until 1971, when he joined a private organization for social and ecological change. He is the author of *The Pursuit of Loneliness: American Culture at the Breaking Point* (1970), a book that combines sociological and psychoanalytic perspectives on American society. In this selection from *Earthwalk* (1974) he continues his examination of why modern man is "driven."

It is customary to blame the isolated-nuclear-family system for many of America's social ills, despite the fact that it does exactly what it is supposed to do: socialize children to live in an individualistic society. To change it would be to change everything, and yet it is changing. Most of us will not live to see this transfiguration proceed any great distance, but if such things can be said to have a beginning, it has begun. I am speaking here, by the way, of real social change, not merely changes in intellectual fashion, such as are annually announced by academics and news commentators. Real social change is like geological change, while media-defined social change — the kind that makes one feel, in 1974, that 1968 belonged to a different era — is like the loose dirt daily blown about by the afternoon wind, subsiding in a slightly different place. . . . The transmission belt for these phenomena, as for most social processes, is the family. For while the family by no means transmits all of our culture from one generation to the next, it does transmit what is most elemental: the way feelings and close relationships are dealt with. Television, school, and other institutions may talk of these things and teach the child how to conceptualize them, but this is only as important as words like "balance," "wheel," "handlebar," and "falling off" are to someone trying to learn to ride a bicycle. Parents don't teach the culture, they *are* the culture. No matter what they do or how many child rearing manuals they read, they will transmit in spite of themselves the accepted cultural mode of mangling feelings and distorting relationships. This is not to say parents are helpless — only that they cannot disguise what they are, and that this is the only thing a child pays close attention to. The parents' insistence that a child *not* pay attention to this is what makes children schizophrenic.

The nuclear family is a social system with two castes — male and female — and two classes — adult and child. In the class system there is an avenue of social mobility, which is called growing up. In American families, the lower-class term for the higher class is, in fact, "grown-up," although the higher class itself uses the label "adult."

The adult class has certain privileges and powers. As in all class systems — since the family is the model for all class systems — the basic contract is one involving responsibility and the obligation to protect, in return for power, narcissistic rewards, and a disproportionate share of scarce resources. But . . . all such contracts are in part a protection racket: "If you do as I say I will protect you against my own wrath." It always seems like a terrible bargain, and yet is often accepted with pleasure by the oppressed, so repugnant is the burden of responsibility. If it were not for the extreme intensity of human dependency needs, political oppression would be a rare event.

What is unique to this prototypical class system is that social mobility is so complete. Almost every child who lives long enough becomes an adult. Furthermore, this mobility is not only expected but carefully prepared for: Each child is carefully indoctrinated into the behavior appropriate to her eventual initiation into the higher class.

This does not mean that other class systems have deviated in any essential way from the model. The adult class is constantly losing members, and any social class faced with the same problem of diminution behaves in exactly the same way — replenishing itself with energetic (if crude) new blood from the lower classes. Any ruling class that fails to do this is doomed.

Class behavior is learned in the nuclear family. By this I mean not only the specific behavior appropriate to one's social class, but also the underlying concept of social division, the whole minuet of interclass behavior, the fundamental contract between classes, and what it feels like to live in each one. This learning is not intellectual, but emotional and experiential. It is like learning to play baseball by simply being asked to play every position in turn. By the time the child reaches school she knows all about how class systems work, and while she may be naïve about the particular social class system of her own society and how she fits into it, the essential structure of all such systems is bred into her very bones by her family experiences.

One learns, for example, that those in the lower class are expected 7 to be deferential to those above, and that when the highers boss them around they are not expected to be insulted or humiliated. The use of different terms of address (first name vs. Mr. and Mrs.) between members of different classes is also derived from the family, in which children are usually called by first names and parents by titles (such as "Mom" and "Dad") which call attention to their parental function. Control and allocation of resources is largely reserved to the higher class, which is then expected to protect and ensure some minimum provision for the child-serf class.

Class distinctions within the family tend gradually to decline over 8 time, and each child ultimately graduates into the higher class (i.e., becomes adult). There is considerable variation in the timing of these changes ("You'll always be my baby" vs. "You're old enough to support yourself now"), but the rule holds. In this miniature two-class society proper social mobility behavior is learned by virtually every member of the lower class. All children know how to be social climbers, although they are seldom able to use this knowledge in the far less receptive outside world. Every child is expected to become an adult, but serfs are not expected to become nobles, and workers are not expected to become managers. There is a place for each child in the adult world, but most members of the lower social orders already have the only place they are likely to have — they are expected to "know their place." There is no vacuum for them to fill. Ordinarily, then, each individual is socially mobile within the family but not outside. Yet there are some individuals who use their mobility knowledge very aggressively outside the family, without any particular societal encouragement or demand for new blood. What motivates these people who do not "know their place"?

Family patterns vary a good deal from one society to another, and 9 most of the prerogatives usually reserved to the parent are permitted the child in some society or other. There is one adult prerogative, however, that is clutched with particular intensity in virtually every society: the monopoly on sexual intercourse within the nuclear family. The family class system, in other words, is maintained by the incest taboo — the most fiercely endorsed taboo of our species. By the same token, since the nuclear family molds our social responses, it is highly unlikely that such a thing as a classless society could ever exist so long as there is an incest taboo.

CONSIDERATIONS

1. According to Slater, how do families transmit culture and social change? How do they differ from schools, government, and other institutions that define a society?
2. In his view, what are some of the essential features of a class system? Can you add other details of family life that illustrate the concept of social division?
3. What is your reaction to Slater's style? Would you call his writing aggressive or mild in tone? Find specific indications of his tone in his diction, his sentence structure, and his organization of paragraphs. Do you think that his style should be modified in one way or another?
4. If we can never have a completely classless society (because of the incest taboo in families), how can changes in family life affect social order? What does Slater seem to be foreseeing as a possible improvement in family and society? What possible inferences about better ways of growing up can you draw from this selection?
5. WRITING TOPIC. Are kids kicked around? Write a 700-word essay on children as the underclass. Use information from beyond your own experience, such as publications by UNESCO or other service organizations, to help you consider childhood in this special perspective.

Nancy Friday

COMPETITION

◊

NANCY FRIDAY (b. 1937) worked as a journalist after attending Wellesley College. As a feminist writer, she has helped reexamine woman's identity by writing about the way sexual roles are enforced and expressed in everyday life. Her first book, *My Secret Garden* (1973), considered the prominence of fantasies in the sexual development of young people. This excerpt from her autobiography, *My Mother/My Self* (1977), recounts the way that as an early adolescent she reacted to the presence of older, more sexually defined and attractive women in her family.

Although I didn't realize it at the time, my mother was getting 1 prettier. My sister was a beauty. My adolescence was the time of our greatest estrangement.

I have a photo of the three of us when I was twelve: my mother, my 2 sister Susie, and I, on a big chintz sofa, each on a separate cushion, leaning away from one another with big spaces in between. I grew up fired with a sense of family spirit, which I loved and needed, with aunts and uncles and cousins under the omnipotent umbrella of my grandfather. "All for one and one for all," he would say at summer reunions, and no one took it more seriously than I. I would have gone to war for any one of them, and believed they would do the same for me. But within our own little nucleus, the three of us didn't touch much.

Now, when I ask her why, my mother sighs and says she supposes it 3 was because that was how she was raised. I remember shrinking from her Elizabeth Arden night-cream kiss, mumbling from under the blanket that yes, I had brushed my teeth. I had not. I had wet the toothbrush in case she felt it, feeling that would get even with her. For what? The further we all get from childhood, the more physically affectionate we try to be with one another. But we are still shy after all these years.

I was a late bloomer, like my mother. But my mother bloomed so 4
late, or had such a penetrating early frost, that she believed it even less
than I would in my turn. When she was a freckled sixteen and sitting
shyly on her unfortunate hands, her younger sister was already a famous beauty. That is still the relationship between them. Grandmothers both, in their eyes my aunt is still the sleek-haired belle of the
ball, immaculately handsome on a horse. My mother's successes do
not count. They will argue at 2:00 A.M. over whether one of my aunt's
many beaux ever asked my mother out. My mother could never make
up a flattering story about herself. I doubt that she so much as heard
the nice things men told her once she had grown into the fine-looking
woman who smiles at me in family photos. But she always gives in to
my aunt, much I'm sure as she gave in to the old self-image after my
father died. He — that one splendidly handsome man — may have
picked her out from all the rest, but his death just a few years later
must have felt like some punishment for having dared to believe for a
moment that her father was wrong: who could possibly want her? She
still blushes at a compliment.

I think she was at her prettiest in her early thirties. I was twelve and 5
at my nadir. Her hair had gone a delicate auburn red and she wore it
brushed back from her face in soft curls. Seated beside her and Susie,
who inherited a raven version of her beautiful hair, I look like an
adopted person. But I had already defended myself against my looks.
They were unimportant. There was a distance between me and the
mirror commensurate with the growing distance between me and my
mother and sister. My success with my made-up persona was proof: I
didn't need them. My titles at school, my awards and achievements,
so bolstered my image of myself that until writing this book I genuinely believed that I grew up feeling sorry for my sister. What chance
had she alongside The Great Achiever and Most Popular Girl in the
World? I even worked up some guilt about outshining her. Pure survival instinct? My dazzling smile would divert the most critical observer from comparing me to the cute, petite girls with whom I grew
up. I switched the contest: don't look at my lank hair, my 5' 10",
don't notice that my right eye wanders bizarrely (though the eye doctor said it was useless to keep me in glasses); watch me tap dance,
watch me win the game, let me make you happy! When I describe
myself in those days my mother laughs. "Oh, Nancy, you were such a
darling little girl." But I wasn't little any more.

I think my sister, Susie, was born beautiful, a fact that affected my 6
mother and me deeply, though in different ways. I don't think it mat-
tered so much until Susie's adolescence. She turned so lush one ached
to look at her. Pictures of Susie then remind me of the young Elizabeth Taylor in *A Place in the Sun.* One has to almost look away from
so much beauty. It scared my mother to death. Whatever had gone on
between them before came to a head and has never stopped. Their
constant friction determined me to get away from this house of
women, to be free of women's petty competitions, to live on a bigger
scale. I left home eventually but I've never gotten away from feeling
how wonderful to be so beautiful your mother can't take her eyes off
you, even if only to nag.

I remember an amazing lack of any feeling about my only sibling, 7
with whom I shared a room for years, whose clothes were identical to
mine until I was ten. Except for feelings of irritation when she tried to
cuddle me when I was four, bursts of anger that erupted into fist fights
which I started and won at ten, and after that, indifference, a calcu-
lated unawareness that has resulted in a terrible and sad absence of
my sister in my life.

My husband says his sister was the only child his father ever paid 8
any attention to: "You have done to Susie what I did to my sister," he
says. "You made her invisible." Me, jealous of Susie, who never won a
single trophy or had as many friends as I? I must have been insanely
jealous.

I only allowed myself to face it twice. Both times happened in that 9
twelfth year, when my usual defenses couldn't take the emotional
cross currents of adolescence. When I did slash out it wasn't very glorious, no well-chosen words or contest on the tennis courts. I did it
like a thief in the night. Nobody ever guessed it was I who poured the
red nail polish down the front of Susie's new white eyelet evening
dress the day of her first yacht club dance. When I stole her summer
savings and threw her wallet down the sewer, mother blamed Susie for
being so careless. I watched my sister accept the criticism with her
mother's own resignation, and I felt some relief from the angry emotions that had hold of me.

When Susie went away to boarding school, I made jokes about how 10
glad I was to be rid of her. It was our first separation. Conflicting
urges, angers, and envies were coming at me from every direction; I had
nothing left over to handle my terrible feelings of loss at her going.

It was the summer I was plagued by what I called "my thoughts."

I read every book in the house as a talisman against thinking. I was   11
afraid that if my brain were left idle for even one minute, these
"thoughts" would take over. Perhaps I feared they already had. Was
my sister's going away the fulfillment of my own murderous wishes
against her? I wrote in my first and only diary: "Susie, come home,
please come home!!!!!!! I'm sorry, I'm sorry!!!!!!!"

When I outgrew the Nancy Drew books for perfect attendance at   12
Sunday school, and the Girl Scout badges for such merits as selling
the most rat poison door to door, I graduated to prizes at the community theater. I won a plastic wake-up radio for the I Speak for Democracy contest. I was captain of the athletic association, president of the
student government, and had the lead in the class play, all in the same
year. In fact, I wrote the class play. It might have been embarrassing,
but no one else wanted these prizes. Scoring home runs and getting
straight A's weren't high on the list of priorities among my friends.
(The South takes all prizes for raising noncompetitive women.) In the
few cases where anyone did give me a run for the money, I had an unbeatable incentive: my grandfather's applause. It was he for whom I
ran.

I can't remember ever hearing my grandfather say to my mother,   13
"Well done, Jane." I can't remember my mother ever saying to my
sister, "Well done, Susie." And I never gave my mother the chance to
say it to me. She was the last to hear of my achievements, and when
she did, it was not from me but from her friends. Did she really notice
so little that I was leaving her out? Was she so hurt that she pretended
not to care? My classmates who won second prize or even no prize at
all asked their families to attend the award ceremonies. I, who won
first prize, always, did so to the applause of no kin at all. Was I spiting
her? I know I was spiting myself. Nothing would have made me happier than to have her there; nothing would induce me to invite her. It
is a game I later played with men: "Leave!" I would cry, and when
they did, "How could you hurt me so?" I'd implore.

If I deprived her of the chance to praise me, she never criticized   14
me. Criticism was the vehicle by which she could articulate her relationship to my sister. No matter what it was, Susie could never get it
right — in my mother's eyes. It continues that way to this day. Difficult as it is to think of my mother as competitive with anyone, how
else could she have felt about her beautiful, ripe fourteen-year-old

daughter? My mother was coming into her own mature, full bloom but perhaps that only made her more sensitive to the fact that Susie was simultaneously experiencing the same sexual flush. A year later, my mother remarried. Today, only the geography has changed: the argument begins as soon as they enter the same room. But they are often in the same room. They have never been closer.

How often the dinner table becomes the family battleground. When I met Bill he had no table you could sit around in his vast bachelor apartment. The dinner table was where his father waged war; it was the one time the family was together. In Charleston, dinner was served at 2:00. I have this picture of our midday meals: Susie on my right, mother on my left, and me feeling that our cook, Ruth, had set this beautiful table for me alone.

No one else seemed to care about the golden squash, the crisp chicken, the big silver pitcher of iced tea. While I proceeded to eat my way from one end of the table to the other, Susie and mother would begin: "Susie, that lipstick is too dark. . . . Must you pluck your eyebrows? . . . Why did you buy high-heeled, open-toe shoes when I told you to get loafers? . . . Those pointy bras make you look a, like a — " But my mother couldn't say the word. At this point one of them would leave the table in tears, while the other shuddered in despair at the sound of the slammed bedroom door. Meanwhile, I pondered my problem of whose house to play at that afternoon. I would finish both their desserts and be gone before Ruth had cleared the table. Am I exaggerating? Did it only happen once a week? Does it matter?

I was lucky to have escaped those devastating battles. "I never had to worry about Nancy," my mother has always said. "She could always take care of herself." It became true. Only my husband has been allowed to see the extent of my needs. But the competitive drive that made me so self-sufficient was fired by more than jealousy of my sister. If my mother wasn't going to acknowledge me, her father would. If she couldn't succeed in his eyes, I would. It's my best explanation for all those years of trophies and presidencies, for my ability to "reach" my grandfather as my mother never could. I not only won what she had wanted all her life — his praise — I learned with the canniness of the young that this great towering man loved to be loved, to be touched. He couldn't allow himself to reach out first to those he loved most, but he couldn't resist an overture of affection.

I greeted his visits with embraces, took the kisses I had won and sat 18
at his feet like one of his Dalmatians, while my sister stood shyly in
the background and my mother waited for his criticism. But I was no
more aware of competing with my mother than of being jealous of my
sister. Two generations of women in my family have struggled for my
grandfather's praise. Perhaps I became his favorite because he sensed
I needed it most. The price I paid was that I had to beat my mother
and my sister. I am still guilty for that.

In the stereotyping of the sexes, men are granted all the competi- 19
tive drives, women none. The idea of competitive women evokes disturbing images — the darker, dykey side of femininity, or cartoons of
"ladies" in high heels, flailing at each other ineffectively with their
handbags. An important step has been left out of our socialization:
mother raises us to win people's love. She gives us no training in the
emotions of rivalry that would lose it for us. With no practical experience in the rules that make competition safe, we fear its ferocity.
Never having been taught to win, we do not know how to lose.
Women are not raised to compete like gentlemen.

CONSIDERATIONS

1. What sort of person was the author as a twelve-year-old? Describe her appearance and personality. How was she different at that age from Nora
   Ephron (see "Shaping Up Absurd," p. 6) or from Mary McCarthy (see
   "Names," p. 20)?
2. Identify some specific signs of a "family code" (see the preceding selection) that functions for all three generations. To what extent did Friday
   practice the code, and to what extent, if at all, did she alter it?
3. What does Friday's mother fear? Identify several things in her life that
   contribute to those fears. Do Friday's insights to her mother's character
   seem fair?
4. What do you think the author's guiding purpose is in this selection? Does
   Friday want to influence her reader's attitudes about competitiveness? Or
   is she mainly interested in understanding her own past? Or is there another purpose that guides the tone and direction of her writing?
5. WRITING TOPIC. Write a 500-word essay that explains the difference between "hating to lose" and "loving to win."

Adrienne Rich

THE ANGER OF
A CHILD

◊

A<small>DRIENNE</small> R<small>ICH</small> (b. 1929) published her first book of poems before she
was graduated from Radcliffe. Her early volumes, such as *A Change of
World* (1951), *Snapshots of a Daughter-in-Law* (1963), and *The Will
to Change* (1971), reflect her youth and marriage, her growing consciousness of womanhood, and the coming of middle age. In the 1970s
Rich became an activist in the women's movement, and in addition to
poetry she wrote literary criticism and essays on patriarchy in our culture. In this excerpt from her book about motherhood, *Of Woman
Born* (1976), she gives a thumbnail sketch of her parents and her upbringing that left some deep resentments smoldering even in the adult
woman.

It is hard to write about my mother. Whatever I do write, it is my 1
story I am telling, my version of the past. If she were to tell her own
story other landscapes would be revealed. But in my landscape or hers,
there would be old, smoldering patches of deep-burning anger. Before
her marriage, she had trained seriously for years both as a concert pianist and a composer. Born in a southern town, mothered by a strong,
frustrated woman, she had won a scholarship to study with the director at the Peabody Conservatory in Baltimore, and by teaching at
girls' schools had earned her way to further study in New York, Paris,
and Vienna. From the age of sixteen, she had been a young belle, who
could have married at any time, but she also possessed unusual talent,
determination, and independence for her time and place. She read —
and reads — widely and wrote — as her journals from my childhood
and her letters of today reveal — with grace and pungency.

She married my father after a ten years' engagement during which 2
he finished his medical training and began to establish himself in aca-

demic medicine. Once married, she gave up the possibility of a concert career, though for some years she went on composing, and she is still a skilled and dedicated pianist. My father, brilliant, ambitious, possessed by his own drive, assumed that she would give her life over to the enhancement of his. She would manage his household with the formality and grace becoming to a medical professor's wife, though on a limited budget; she would "keep up" her music, though there was no question of letting her composing and practice conflict with her duties as a wife and mother. She was supposed to bear him two children, a boy and a girl. She had to keep her household books to the last penny — I still can see the big blue gray ledgers, inscribed in her clear, strong hand; she marketed by streetcar, and later, when they could afford a car, she drove my father to and from his laboratory or lectures, often awaiting him for hours. She raised two children, and taught us all our lessons, including music. (Neither of us was sent to school until the fourth grade.) I am sure that she was made to feel responsible for all our imperfections.

My father, like the transcendentalist Bronson Alcott, believed that 3 he (or rather, his wife) could raise children according to his unique moral and intellectual plan, thus proving to the world the values of enlightened, unorthodox child-rearing. I believe that my mother, like Abigail Alcott, at first genuinely and enthusiastically embraced the experiment, and only later found that in carrying out my father's intense, perfectionist program, she was in conflict with her deep instincts as a mother. Like Abigail Alcott, too, she must have found that while ideas might be unfolded by her husband, their daily, hourly practice was going to be up to her. (" 'Mr. A. aids me in general principles, but nobody can aid me in the detail,' she mourned. . . . Moreover her husband's views kept her constantly wondering if she were doing a good job. 'Am I doing what is right? Am I doing enough? Am I doing too much?' " The appearance of "temper" and "will" in Louisa, the second Alcott daughter, was blamed by her father on her inheritance from her mother.) Under the institution of motherhood, the mother is the first to blame if theory proves unworkable in practice, or if anything whatsoever goes wrong. But even earlier, my mother had failed at one part of the plan: she had not produced a son.

For years, I felt my mother had chosen my father over me, had sac- 4 rificed me to his needs and theories. When my first child was born, I was barely in communication with my parents. I had been fighting my father for my right to an emotional life and a selfhood beyond his needs and theories. We were all at a draw. Emerging from the fear, exhaustion, and alienation of my first childbirth, I could not admit even to myself that I wanted my mother, let alone tell her how much I wanted her. When she visited me in the hospital neither of us could uncoil the obscure lashings of feeling that darkened the room, the tangled thread running backward to where she had labored for three days to give birth to me, and I was not a son. Now, twenty-six years later, I lay in a contagious hospital with my allergy, my skin covered with a mysterious rash, my lips and eyelids swollen, my body bruised and sutured, and, in a cot beside my bed, slept the perfect, golden, male child I had brought forth. How could I have interpreted her feelings when I could not begin to decipher my own? My body had spoken all too eloquently, but it was, medically, just my body. I wanted her to mother me again, to hold my baby in her arms as she had once held me; but that baby was also a gauntlet flung down: *my son.* Part of me longed to offer him for her blessing; part of me wanted to hold him up as a badge of victory in our tragic, unnecessary rivalry as women.

But I was only at the beginning. I know now as I could not possibly know then, that among the tangle of feelings between us, in that crucial yet unreal meeting, was her guilt. Soon I would begin to understand the full weight and burden of maternal guilt, that daily, nightly, hourly, *Am I doing what is right? Am I doing enough? Am I doing too much?* The institution of motherhood finds all mothers more or less guilty of having failed their children; and my mother, in particular, had been expected to help create, according to my father's plan, a perfect daughter. This "perfect" daughter, though gratifyingly precocious, had early been given to tics and tantrums, had become permanently lame from arthritis at twenty-two; she had finally resisted her father's Victorian paternalism, his seductive charm and controlling cruelty, had married a divorced graduate student, had begun to write "modern," "obscure," "pessimistic" poetry, lacking the fluent sweetness of Tennyson, had had the final temerity to get pregnant and bring a living baby into the world. She had ceased to be the demure and precocious child or the poetic, seducible adolescent. Something, in my father's view, had gone terribly wrong. I can imagine that whatever else my mother felt (and I know that part of her *was* mutely on my side) she also was made to feel blame. Beneath the "numbness"

that she has since told me she experienced at that time, I can imagine
the guilt of Everymother, because I have known it myself.

But I did not know it yet. And it is difficult for me to write of my   6
mother now, because I have known it too well. I struggle to describe
what it felt like to be her daughter, but I find myself divided, slipping
under her skin; a part of me identifies too much with her. I know deep
reservoirs of anger toward her still exist: the anger of a four-year-old
locked in the closet (my father's orders, but my mother carried them
out) for childish misbehavior; the anger of a six-year-old kept too long
at piano practice (again, at his insistence, but it was she who gave the
lessons) till I developed a series of facial tics. (As a mother I know
what a child's facial tic is — a lancet of guilt and pain running
through one's own body.) And I still feel the anger of a daughter,
pregnant, wanting my mother desperately and feeling she had gone
over to the enemy.

And I know there must be deep reservoirs of anger in her; every   7
mother has known overwhelming, unacceptable anger at her children.
When I think of the conditions under which my mother became a
mother, the impossible expectations, my father's distaste for pregnant
women, his hatred of all that he could not control, my anger at her
dissolves into grief and anger *for* her, and then dissolves back again
into anger at her: the ancient, unpurged anger of the child.

My mother lives today as an independent woman, which she was   8
always meant to be. She is a much-loved, much-admired grandmother, an explorer in new realms; she lives in the present and future,
not the past. I no longer have fantasies — they are the unhealed
child's fantasies, I think — of some infinitely healing conversation
with her, in which we could show all our wounds, transcend the pain
we have shared as mother and daughter, say everything at last. But in
writing these pages, I am admitting, at least, how important her existence is and has been for me.

CONSIDERATIONS

1. According to the author, why didn't her mother continue to develop her
   extraordinary talents and potentials for a creative, artistic life? What became of her mother's abilities?

2. Given what Rich mentions, what concrete details would you like to see filled into this portrait of Rich's mother? How might such details affect our view of the mother? Or of the author?

3. What is the author's view of her father? Was he important in her early life?

4. Describe the kind of mothering that the daughter received. Explain why the author still feels "the ancient, unpurged anger of the child." What is she angry about?

5. WRITING TOPIC. In 500 words, compare Rich's sketch of her parents with Nancy Friday's sketch (see the preceding selection) of her mother and grandfather. In which family does life seem more bearable to the child?

Alexander Boswell

LETTER OF ADVICE
TO HIS SON JAMES

◊

ALEXANDER BOSWELL, Lord Auchinleck (1706–1782), a judge in the
Scottish circuit courts, was disappointed that his oldest son, James, did
not pursue a respectable career but chose, instead, to leave his native
Scotland and lead a relatively bohemian life in London among writers
and theater people. James further tarnished the family honor by keeping a candid journal of his unseemly adventures and allowing his
friends to read entertaining portions, some of which were printed in
London magazines. To his father it seemed that James was destroying
himself in scandalous behavior, but to posterity James developed into
the foremost diarist of the eighteenth century, who achieved fame as
the author of a great biography of his older friend, Dr. Samuel Johnson. In this excerpt from a letter, Lord Auchinleck is trying to persuade
James, as yet only twenty-two years old, to return to his senses and plan
a decent life for the future.

If you'll at all reflect, you must be sensible what I suffer by your 1
means. Is it not hard that after all the tenderness I have shown you
and the expense and labour I have bestowed upon you, you should not
only neglect your own reputation, but do what you can to bring me to
shame on your account? The offices I hold entitle me to some respect,
and I get it beyond my merit from all that know me except from you,
who by the laws of God, nature, gratitude, and interest are bound to
do what you can to make me happy, in place of striving, as it were, to
find out the things will be most galling to me and making these your
pursuit. What I have said will account for my not having wrote you
these three months. Indeed, finding that I could be of no use to you, I
had determined to abandon you, to free myself as much as possible
from sharing your ignominy, and to take the strongest and most pub-

lic steps for declaring to the world that I was come to this resolution. But I have been so much importuned by your excellent mother, the partaker of my distresses and shame on your account, again to write to you, and your last letter, which I received at Ayr when on the Circuit, is wrote in a strain that is becoming and speaks out that you are satisfied of some of your errors; therefore it is that you receive this from me in answer to those you sent me since the Session rose.

As in yours you desire me to give you my advice with freedom, you 2 cannot be dissatisfied with the introduction to this letter. Every wise man would rather be informed for what things he is censured, that he may correct them, than be flattered when he don't deserve it; and he alone is a true friend who informs us of our faults. It is true such a friend is rarely to be met with, but you have had such friend in me.

You are under a mistake in your last when you write I have been 3 struggling for authority over you. I have a right to it, indeed, but it is a thing I never wished or desired. And every step in my conduct has shown that to be the case. I always used you with lenity and tenderness; and though you were behaving in a way highly disrespectful to me, settled an annuity upon you for life and so put you in a state of independency. You say that you was struggling for independency. What you mean by becoming independent I am at a loss to conceive, for it would seem to be something very different from what anybody else would aim at. Your notion of independency seems to consist in contemning your relations and your native country, where and from whom you have a natural right to receive regard and friendship, and to live in dependence upon strangers in another country, where you have no title to notice, and from whom you have nothing to expect but fair words. They have their relations to provide, their political connections to keep up, and must look on one who comes from Scotland as an idle person to have no right to share of their bounty; in the same way that we here would never think of bestowing anything upon a vaguing Englishman except a dinner or a supper. When you left this, I told you that you would find this to be true on trial. You would not then believe it, but now you candidly own you have found the thing turn out according as I said it would do.

You desire my advice as to your after schemes in life. As to this, I 4 have already told you I have no authority; and the mention I have made of sundry things in your conduct that vex and distress me and every friend and acquaintance of yours who has common sense, is not from authority but from friendship. I am bound by the ties of nature to love you; and though it is disagreeable still to be finding fault, I should be wanting in my duty not to tell you my mind. If you'll call to remembrance sundry of your past schemes which I advised you against and were happily disappointed, you must be sensible how dangerous it is for a young man to propose to give himself up to be governed by whims. You have escaped from a variety of ruinous snares that you were quite bent upon, and now are convinced were such as behoved to have brought you to misery. This should make you cautious in time coming. The poet says, "Felix quem faciunt aliena pericula cautum," but he must be unhappy indeed who won't learn from his own past dangers. To come more close to the point in your letter wherein you ask my advice as to what scheme of life you should follow, I shall convince you that I do not insist on authority, for though you tell me you will return to Scotland if I tell you your absence from it makes me unhappy, I will not insist either on one thing or another, but fairly and candidly lay matters before you. All that ever I insisted upon was that you should behave as the young gentlemen of your station do and act with prudence and discretion. If you set up in the character of my eldest son, you may expect regard and respect, but in the style of a vagrant must meet with the reverse. Be assured of this; for even I, who am your father and who, while you trod the paths of virtue and discretion was bound up in you and carried on all my projects with a view to you in whom I flattered myself to find a representative worthy of this respectable family — I say, even I by your strange conduct had come to the resolution of selling all off, from the principle that it is better to snuff a candle out than leave it to stink in a socket. And this purpose, though interrupted at present by your last letters being wrote in a strain that gives hopes of amendment, upon my being disappointed in that hope, I should certainly carry into execution.

As for your manner of life, I never declared positively against any 5 kind of life except that of dissipation and vice, and as a consequence against your going into the Guards. But I told you if you chose to be a soldier and make that your business in good earnest, though I did not like the business, I should procure you a commission in a marching regiment, and had one pressed upon me by my good friend General Sinclair, now no more. But you signified your unwillingness to serve in a marching regiment, so that scheme went over and you fell to the study of the law; and I can say with truth, showed as much genius for it when you applied as any ever I knew. Be assured that your following the study of the law, whether as a lawyer or as a gentleman, to fit you to be useful in the world, is what to me is most agreeble and what I verily think is the only thing will make you go through life agreeably; for as you well observe, without some pursuit that is rational, one of your turn can never be happy. In the plan I propose you have for your objects being respected, being useful with your advice, getting into Parliament, and having the power of conferring places, instead of going about begging one. And to these I may add, you have the satisfaction of making your parents happy and adding more lustre to the family you have the honour to be come of. And if you were truly fixed on this plan, I would make no difficulty, when you were a little settled from your reelings, to let you go abroad for a while. But if you are bent on the Army, as you say you have the offer of an ensigncy in a marching regiment, though I am far from liking the thing, if better cannot be, take it, and hold by that as your business for life. But be more on your guard for the future against mimicry, journals, and publications, still acting with prudence and discretion, which is as necessary for a soldier as for a man of any other employment. I would further recommend to you to endeavour to find out some person of worth who may be a friend, not one who will say as you say when with you and when he is away will make a jest of you as much as of any other.

Your mother is in her ordinary, so is Johnny. Both remember you 6 with affection.

Farewell. It is in your power to make us all happy and yourself too. 7 May God dispose you to the best.

CONSIDERATIONS

1. Judging from details in the first paragraph, what has been happening between father and son for at least the past three months? Reconstruct the situation.
2. James and his father appear to disagree over what is meant by *independence* and *dependency*. Define these terms from both the son's and the father's viewpoints, explaining the difference in their usage of the words.
3. The father says that if James acts properly, he "may expect regard and respect." Does the father in this letter show regard and respect for James? Present evidence for your opinion about his attitude.

4. WRITING TOPIC. Write a letter of response to Lord Auchinleck as if he were your own father. Try to make him understand how the tone and substance of his letter affect you, and how you feel about choosing a career. By going into detail about his letter and your attitudes, you will probably want to write at least 700 words.

5. WRITING TOPIC. Read portions of *Boswell's London Journal, 1762–1763* (published in 1950) for a direct view of the life that young James was leading and that so exasperated his father. Perhaps you will find James strong-minded, foolish, conceited, dedicated, indulgent, untrustworthy, generous, courageous, or a jerk. In an appendix to the volume, you will find his father's complete letter, from which this shortened selection was taken. With a fuller understanding of both personalities and the main issues between them, write a 700-word essay on James Boswell in relation to his father.

Robert Hayden

THOSE WINTER SUNDAYS

◊

ROBERT HAYDEN (1913–1980) grew up in Detroit and was educated there at Wayne State University. He taught poetry writing at Fisk University and the University of Michigan. His poems often center on vivid characterizations, such as the following recollection of his father. Hayden's poems were collected in *Selected Poems* (1966), the same year that he won the Grand Prize for Poetry at the Dakar World Festival of the Arts.

Sundays too my father got up early
and put his clothes on in the blueblack cold,
then with cracked hands that ached
from labor in the weekday weather made
banked fires blaze. No one ever thanked him.

I'd wake and hear the cold splintering, breaking.
When the rooms were warm, he'd call,
and slowly I would rise and dress,
fearing the chronic angers of that house,

Speaking indifferently to him,   10
who had driven out the cold
and polished my good shoes as well.
What did I know, what did I know
of love's austere and lonely offices?

CONSIDERATIONS

1. How is the father characterized in the long first sentence of the first stanza? Why is there such a difference in length between this opening sentence and the short sentence that ends the stanza?
2. What was the boy's attitude toward his family and home life? How did he express his attitude?
3. What is the effect of the repetition in the next-to-last line? How would the meaning change if the phrase occurred only once?
4. What is the meaning of "offices" in the final line? As an oddly used word, how does it illuminate the adult poet's memory of his father?
5. WRITING TOPIC. In 500 words, write a character study of the most solitary or the most private person in your extended family (which can include aunts, uncles, cousins, grandparents). Give details that will make the person vivid to the reader and try to explain or present the relative separateness that is a way of life for this person.

John Updike

STILL OF SOME USE

◊

JOHN UPDIKE (b. 1932) was raised in a small town in Pennsylvania and was graduated with highest honors from Harvard. He joined the staff of *The New Yorker*, contributing stories, poems, and essays even to this day, though he soon moved away from the city to another small town, this one on the Massachusetts shore. His main novels are about a commonplace member of an unremarkable society, Harry "Rabbit" Angstrom, who is the dubious but sympathetic hero of *Rabbit, Run* (1960), *Rabbit Redux* (1971), and *Rabbit Is Rich* (1981). Updike's fiction usually includes an outlook of deep uneasiness mixed with humor over the transformations of relationships within a family. This story about a divorced couple and their family appeared in *The New Yorker*.

When Foster helped his ex-wife clean out the attic of the house 1 where they had once lived and which she was now selling, they came across dozens of forgotten, broken games. Parcheesi, Monopoly, Lotto; games aping the strategies of the stock market, of crime detection, of real-estate speculation, of international diplomacy and war; games with spinners, dice, lettered tiles, cardboard spacemen, and plastic battleships; games bought in five-and-tens and department stores feverish and musical with Christmas expectations; games enjoyed on the afternoon of a birthday and for a few afternoons thereafter and then allowed, shy of one or two pieces, to drift into closets and toward the attic. Yet, discovered in their bright flat boxes between trunks of outgrown clothes and defunct appliances, the games presented a forceful semblance of value: the springs of their miniature launchers still reacted, the logic of their instructions would still generate suspense, given a chance. "What shall we do with all these games?" Foster shouted, in a kind of agony, to his scattered family as they moved up and down the attic stairs.

"Trash 'em," his younger son, a strapping nineteen, urged. 2

"Would the Goodwill want them?" asked his ex-wife, still wife 3
enough to think that all of his questions deserved answers. "You used
to be able to give things like that to orphanages. But they don't call
them orphanages anymore, do they?"

"They call them normal American homes," Foster said.   4

His older son, now twenty-two, with a cinnamon-colored beard, of- 5
fered, "They wouldn't work anyhow; they all have something missing.
That's how they got to the attic."

"Well, why didn't we throw them away at the time?" Foster asked, 6
and had to answer himself. Cowardice, the answer was. Inertia.
Clinging to the past.

His sons, with a shadow of old obedience, came and looked over his 7
shoulder at the sad wealth of abandoned playthings, silently groping
with him for the particular happy day connected to this and that pattern of coded squares and colored arrows. Their lives had touched
these tokens and counters once; excitement had flowed along the
paths of these stylized landscapes. But the day was gone, and scarcely
a memory remained.

"Toss 'em," the younger decreed, in his manly voice. For these 8
days of cleaning out, the boy had borrowed a pickup truck from a
friend and parked it on the lawn beneath the attic window, so the
smaller items of discard could be tossed directly into it. The bigger
items were lugged down the stairs and through the front hall and out;
already the truck was loaded with old mattresses, broken clock-radios,
obsolete skis, and boots. It was a game of sorts to hit the truck bed
with objects dropped from the height of the house. Foster flipped
game after game at the target two stories below. When the boxes hit,
they exploded, throwing a spray of dice, tokens, counters, and cards
into the air and across the lawn. A box called Mousetrap, its lid showing laughing children gathered around a Rube Goldberg device,
drifted sideways, struck one side wall of the truck, and spilled its plastic components into a flower bed. As a set of something called Drag
Race! floated gently as a snowflake before coming to rest, much di-
minished, on a stained mattress, Foster saw in the depth of downward
space the cause of his melancholy: he had not played enough with
these games. Now no one wanted to play.

Had he and his wife avoided divorce, of course, these boxes would 9
have continued to gather dust in an undisturbed attic, their sorrow

unexposed. The toys of his own childhood still rested in his mother's attic. At his last visit, he had wound the spring of a tin Donald Duck that had responded with an angry clack of its bill and a few stiff strokes on its drum. A tin shield with concentric grooves for marbles still waited in a bushel basket with his alphabet blocks and lead airplanes — waited for his childhood to return.

His ex-wife paused where he squatted at the attic window and asked him, "What's the matter?" 10

"Nothing. These games weren't used much." 11

"I know. It happens fast. You better stop now; it's making you too sad." 12

Behind him, his family had cleaned out the attic; the slant-ceilinged rooms stood empty, with drooping insulation. "How can you bear it?" he asked her, of the emptiness. 13

"Oh, it's fun, once you get into it. Off with the old, on with the new. The new people seem nice. They have little children." 14

He looked at her and wondered if she was being brave or truly hardhearted. The attic trembled slightly. "That's Ted," she said. 15

She had acquired a boyfriend, a big athletic banker fleeing from domestic embarrassments in a neighboring town. When Ted slammed the kitchen door two stories below, the glass shade of a kerosene lamp that, though long unused, Foster hadn't had the heart to throw out of the window vibrated in its copper clips, emitting a thin note like a trapped wasp's song. Time to go. Foster's dusty knees creaked when he stood. His ex-wife's eager steps raced ahead of him down through the emptied house. He followed, carrying the lamp, and set it finally on the bare top of a bookcase he had once built, on the first-floor landing. He remembered screwing the top board, a prize piece of knot-free pine, into place from underneath, so not a nailhead marred its smoothness. 16

After all the vacant rooms and halls, the kitchen seemed indecently full of heat and life. "Dad, want a beer?" the red-bearded son asked. "Ted brought some." The back of the boy's hand, holding forth the dewy can, blazed with fine ginger hairs. His girlfriend, wearing gypsy earrings and a "No Nukes" sweatshirt, leaned against the disconnected stove, her hair in a bandanna and a black smirch becomingly placed on one temple. From the kind way she smiled at Foster, he felt this party was making room for him. 17

"No, I better go." 18

Ted shook Foster's hand, as he always did. He had a thin pink skin   19
and silver hair whose fluffy waves seemed mechanically induced. Foster could look him in the eye no longer than he could gaze at the sun.
He wondered how such a radiant brute had got into such a tame line
of work. Ted had not helped with the attic today because he had been
off in his old town, visiting his teen-age twins. "I hear you did a splendid job today," he announced.

"They did," Foster said. "I wasn't much use. I just sat there   20
stunned. All those things I had forgotten buying."

"Some were presents," his son reminded him. He passed the can   21
his father had snubbed to his mother, who took it and tore up the tab
with that defiant-sounding *pssff*. She had never liked beer, yet tipped
the can to her mouth.

"Give me one sip," Foster begged, and took the can from her and   22
drank a long swallow. When he opened his eyes, Ted's big hand was
cupped under Mrs. Foster's chin while his thumb rubbed away a
smudge of dirt along her jaw which Foster had not noticed. This protective gesture made her face look small, pouty, frail, and somehow
parched. Ted, Foster noticed now, was dressed with a certain comical
perfection in a banker's Saturday outfit — softened bluejeans, crisp
tennis sneakers, lumberjack shirt with cuffs folded back. The youthful
outfit accented his age, his hypertensive flush. Foster saw them suddenly as a touching, aging couple, and this perception seemed permission to go.

He handed back the can.   23

"Thanks for your help," his former wife said.   24

"Yes, we do thank you," Ted said.   25

"Talk to Tommy," she unexpectedly added. She was still sending   26
out trip wires to slow his departures. "This is harder on him than he
shows."

Ted looked at his watch, a fat, black-faced thing he could swim un-   27
derwater with. "I said to him coming in, 'Don't dawdle till the dump
closes.' "

"He loafed all day," his brother complained, "mooning over old   28
stuff, and now he's going to screw up getting to the dump."

"He's very sensi-tive," the visiting gypsy said, with a strange chim-   29
ing brightness, as if repeating something she had heard.

Outside, the boy was picking up litter that had fallen wide of the   30 truck. Foster helped him. In the grass there were dozens of tokens and dice. Some were engraved with curious little faces — Olive Oyl, Snuffy Smith, Dagwood — and others with hieroglyphs — numbers, diamonds, spades, hexagons — whose code was lost. He held out a handful for Tommy to see. "Can you remember what these were for?"

"Comic-Strip Lotto," the boy said without hesitation. "And a 31 game called Gambling Fools there was a kind of slot machine for." The light of old chances and payoffs flickered in his eyes as he gazed down at the rubble in his father's hand. Though Foster was taller, the boy was broader in the shoulders, and growing. "Want to ride with me to the dump?" Tommy asked.

"I would, but I better go." He, too, had a new life to lead. By being 32 on this forsaken property at all, Foster was in a sense on the wrong square, if not *en prise*. Once, he had begun to teach this boy chess, but in the sadness of watching him lose — the little bowed head frowning above his trapped king — the lessons had stopped.

Foster tossed the tokens into the truck; they rattled to rest on the 33 metal. "This depress you?" he asked his son.

"Naa." The boy amended, "Kind of." 34

"You'll feel great," Foster promised him, "coming back with a 35 clean truck. I used to love it at the dump, all that old happiness heaped up, and the sea-gulls."

"It's changed since you left. They have all these new rules. The 36 lady there yelled at me last time, for putting stuff in the wrong place."

"She did?" 37

"Yeah. It was scary." Seeing his father waver, he added, "It'll only 38 take twenty minutes." Though broad of build, Tommy had beardless cheeks and, between thickening eyebrows, a trace of that rounded, faintly baffled blankness babies have, that wrinkles before they cry.

"O.K.," Foster said, greatly lightened. "I'll protect you." 39

CONSIDERATIONS

1. What is the significance of the diversity and the condition of all those games? Do they suggest anything about the past?
2. Not many names are used in the story. Instead, characters are designated as "his ex-wife," "the younger son," "the red-bearded son," "the visiting

gypsy," "the boy." What is the atmosphere of the situation that this form of reference suggests?

3. Mrs. Foster's boyfriend, Ted, and the older son's girlfriend are the only characters whose physical appearance is fully described. How do they appear to Foster?

4. At the end, are Foster and Tommy serious or joking? Or both? How can you tell?

5. WRITING TOPIC. In a 500-word essay, clarify the attitude that Updike appears to be taking toward divorce and new relationships.

E. B. White

ONCE MORE TO
THE LAKE

◊

E. B. WHITE (b. 1899) joined the staff of *The New Yorker* (see the headnote on James Thurber, p. 53) soon after he was graduated from Cornell University. He contributed regularly to the "Talk of the Town" section and contributed other essays to the magazine. In later years he wrote essays for *Harper's,* many of which are collected in *One Man's Meat* (1942), *The Second Tree from the Corner* (1953), and the *Essays of E. B. White* (1977). He also wrote the classic children's books, *Stuart Little* (1945) and *Charlotte's Web* (1952). In 1938 he moved with his wife and son to Maine, to the region that he loved since boyhood. In this essay, a visit with his son to a scene of his own youthful summers with his father brings on vivid memories and a keen sense of the sequence of generations.

One summer, along about 1904, my father rented a camp on a lake 1 in Maine and took us all there for the month of August. We all got ringworm from some kittens and had to rub Pond's Extract on our arms and legs night and morning, and my father rolled over in a canoe with all his clothes on; but outside of that the vacation was a success and from then on none of us ever thought there was any place in the world like that lake in Maine. We returned summer after summer — always on August 1 for one month. I have since become a salt-water man, but sometimes in summer there are days when the restlessness of the tides and the fearful cold of the sea water and the incessant wind that blows across the afternoon and into the evening make me wish for the placidity of a lake in the woods. A few weeks ago this feeling got so strong I bought myself a couple of bass hooks and a spinner and returned to the lake where we used to go, for a week's fishing and to revisit old haunts.

I took along my son, who had never had any fresh water up his nose 2
and who had seen lily pads only from train windows. On the journey
over to the lake I began to wonder what it would be like. I wondered
how time would have marred this unique, this holy spot — the coves
and streams, the hills that the sun set behind, the camps and the
paths behind the camps. I was sure that the tarred road would have
found it out, and I wondered in what other ways it would be deso-
lated. It is strange how much you can remember about places like that
once you allow your mind to return into the grooves that lead back.
You remember one thing, and that suddenly reminds you of another
thing. I guess I remembered clearest of all the early mornings, when
the lake was cool and motionless, remembered how the bedroom
smelled of the lumber it was made of and of the wet woods whose
scent entered through the screen. The partitions in the camp were
thin and did not extend clear to the top of the rooms, and as I was
always the first up I would dress softly so as not to wake the others,
and sneak out into the sweet outdoors and start out in the canoe,
keeping close along the shore in the long shadows of the pines. I remembered being very careful never to rub my paddle against the gun-
wale for fear of disturbing the stillness of the cathedral.

The lake had never been what you would call a wild lake. There 3
were cottages sprinkled around the shores, and it was in farming country although the shores of the lake were quite heavily wooded. Some
of the cottages were owned by nearby farmers, and you would live at
the shore and eat your meals at the farmhouse. That's what our family
did. But although it wasn't wild, it was a fairly large and undisturbed
lake and there were places in it that, to a child at least, seemed infinitely remote and primeval.

I was right about the tar: it led to within half a mile of the shore. 4
But when I got back there, with my boy, and we settled into a camp
near a farmhouse and into the kind of summertime I had known, I
could tell that it was going to be pretty much the same as it had been
before — I knew it, lying in bed the first morning, smelling the bedroom and hearing the boy sneak quietly out and go off along the shore
in a boat. I began to sustain the illusion that he was I, and therefore,
by simple transposition, that I was my father. This sensation persisted,
kept cropping up all the time we were there. It was not an entirely
new feeling, but in this setting it grew much stronger. I seemed to be
living a dual existence. I would be in the middle of some simple act, I

would be picking up a bait box or laying down a table fork, or I would be saying something, and suddenly it would be not I but my father who was saying the words or making the gesture. It gave me a creepy sensation.

We went fishing the first morning. I felt the same damp moss covering the worms in the bait can, and saw the dragonfly alight on the tip of my rod as it hovered a few inches from the surface of the water. It was the arrival of this fly that convinced me beyond any doubt that everything was as it always had been, that the years were a mirage and that there had been no years. The small waves were the same, chucking the rowboat under the chine as we fished at anchor, and the boat was the same boat, the same color green and the ribs broken in the same places, and under the floorboards the same fresh-water leavings and debris — the dead helgramite, the wisps of moss, the rusty discarded fishhook, the dried blood from yesterday's catch. We stared silently at the tips of our rods, at the dragonflies that came and went. I lowered the tip of mine into the water, tentatively, pensively dislodging the fly, which darted two feet away, poised, darted two feet back, and came to rest again a little farther up the rod. There had been no years between the ducking of this dragonfly and the other one — the one that was part of memory. I looked at the boy, who was silently watching his fly, and it was my hands that held his rod, my eyes watching. I felt dizzy and didn't know which rod I was at the end of.

We caught two bass, hauling them in briskly as though they were mackerel, pulling them over the side of the boat in a businesslike manner without any landing net, and stunning them with a blow on the back of the head. When we got back for a swim before lunch, the lake was exactly where we had left it, the same number of inches from the dock, and there was only the merest suggestion of a breeze. This seemed an utterly enchanted sea, this lake you could leave to its own devices for a few hours and come back to, and find that it had not stirred, this constant and trustworthy body of water. In the shallows, the dark, water-soaked sticks and twigs, smooth and old, were undulating in clusters on the bottom against the clean ribbed sand, and the track of the mussel was plain. A school of minnows swam by, each minnow with its small individual shadow, doubling the attendance, so clear and sharp in the sunlight. Some of the other campers were in swimming, along the shore, one of them with a cake of soap, and the water felt thin and clear and unsubstantial. Over the years there had been this person with the cake of soap, this cultist, and here he was. There had been no years.

Up to the farmhouse to dinner through the teeming, dusty field, 7 the road under our sneakers was only a two-track road. The middle track was missing, the one with the marks of the hooves and the splotches of dried, flaky manure. There had always been three tracks to choose from in choosing which track to walk in; now the choice was narrowed down to two. For a moment I missed terribly the middle alternative. But the way led past the tennis court, and something about the way it lay there in the sun reassured me; the tape had loosened along the backline, the alleys were green with plantains and other weeds, and the net (installed in June and removed in September) sagged in the dry noon, and the whole place steamed with midday heat and hunger and emptiness. There was a choice of pie for dessert, and one was blueberry and one was apple, and the waitresses were the same country girls, there having been no passage of time, only the illusion of it as in a dropped curtain — the waitresses were still fifteen; their hair had been washed, that was the only difference — they had been to the movies and seen the pretty girls with the clean hair.

Summertime, oh, summertime, pattern of life indelible, the fade- 8 proof lake, the woods unshatterable, the pasture with the sweetfern and the juniper forever and ever, summer without end; this was the background, and the life along the shore was the design, the cottagers with their innocent and tranquil design, their tiny docks with the flagpole and the American flag floating against the white clouds in the blue sky, the little paths over the roots of the trees leading from camp to camp and the paths leading back to the outhouses and the can of lime for sprinkling, and at the souvenir counters at the store the miniature birch-bark canoes and the postcards that showed things looking a little better than they looked. This was the American family at play, escaping the city heat, wondering whether the newcomers in the camp at the head of the cove were "common" or "nice," wondering whether it was true that the people who drove up for Sunday dinner at the farmhouse were turned away because there wasn't enough chicken.

It seemed to me, as I kept remembering all this, that those times 9 and those summers had been infinitely precious and worth saving. There had been jollity and peace and goodness. The arriving (at the beginning of August) had been so big a business in itself, at the railway station the farm wagon drawn up, the first smell of the pine-laden air, the first glimpse of the smiling farmer, and the great importance of the trunks and your father's enormous authority in such matters, and the feel of the wagon under you for the long ten-mile haul, and at the top of the last long hill catching the first view of the lake after eleven months of not seeing this cherished body of water. The shouts and cries of the other campers when they saw you, and the trunks to be unpacked, to give up their rich burden. (Arriving was less exciting nowadays, when you sneaked up in your car and parked it under a tree near the camp and took out the bags and in five minutes it was all over, no fuss, no loud wonderful fuss about trunks.)

Peace and goodness and jollity. The only thing that was wrong 10 now, really, was the sound of the place, an unfamiliar nervous sound of the outboard motors. This was the note that jarred, the one thing that would sometimes break the illusion and set the years moving. In those other summertimes all motors were inboard; and when they were at a little distance, the noise they made was a sedative, an ingredient of summer sleep. They were one-cylinder and two-cylinder engines, and some were make-and-break and some were jump-spark, but they all made a sleepy sound across the lake. The one-lungers throbbed and fluttered, and the twin-cylinder ones purred and purred, and that was a quiet sound, too. But now the campers all had outboards. In the daytime, in the hot mornings, these motors made a petulant, irritable sound; at night, in the still evening when the afterglow lit the water, they whined about one's ears like mosquitoes. My boy loved our rented outboard, and his great desire was to achieve singlehanded mastery over it, and authority, and he soon learned the trick of choking it a little (but not too much), and the adjustment of the needle valve. Watching him I would remember the things you could do with the old one-cylinder engine with the heavy flywheel, how you could have it eating out of your hand if you got really close to it spiritually. Motorboats in those days didn't have clutches, and you would make a landing by shutting off the motor at the proper time and coasting in with a dead rudder. But there was a way of reversing them, if you learned the trick, by cutting the switch and putting it on again exactly on the final dying revolution of the flywheel, so that it would kick back against compression and begin reversing. Approaching a dock in a strong following breeze, it was difficult to slow up sufficiently by the ordinary coasting method, and if a boy felt he had complete mastery over his motor, he was tempted to keep it running beyond its time and then reverse it a few feet from the dock. It took a cool nerve, because if you threw the switch a twentieth of a second too soon you would catch the flywheel when it still had speed enough to go up past center, and the boat would leap ahead, charging bull-fashion at the dock.

We had a good week at the camp. The bass were biting well and 11 the sun shone endlessly, day after day. We would be tired at night and lie down in the accumulated heat of the little bedrooms after the long hot day and the breeze would stir almost imperceptibly outside and the smell of the swamp drift in through the rusty screens. Sleep would come easily and in the morning the red squirrel would be on the roof, tapping out his gay routine. I kept remembering everything, lying in bed in the mornings — the small steamboat that had a long rounded stern like the lip of a Ubangi, and how quietly she ran on the moonlight sails, when the older boys played their mandolins and the girls sang and we ate doughnuts dipped in sugar, and how sweet the music was on the water in the shining night, and what it had felt like to think about girls then. After breakfast we would go up to the store and the things were in the same place — the minnows in a bottle, the plugs and spinners disarranged and pawed over by the youngsters from the boys' camp, the Fig Newtons and the Beeman's gum. Outside, the road was tarred and cars stood in front of the store. Inside, all was just as it had always been, except there was more Coca-Cola and not so much Moxie and root beer and birch beer and sarsaparilla. We would walk out with a bottle of pop apiece and sometimes the pop would backfire up our noses and hurt. We explored the streams, quietly, where the turtles slid off the sunny logs and dug their way into the soft bottom; and we lay on the town wharf and fed worms to the tame bass. Everywhere we went I had trouble making out which was I, the one walking at my side, the one walking in my pants.

One afternoon while we were there at that lake a thunderstorm 12 came up. It was like the revival of an old melodrama that I had seen long ago with childish awe. The second-act climax of the drama of the electrical disturbance over a lake in America had not changed in any important respect. This was the big scene, still the big scene. The whole thing was so familiar, the first feeling of oppression and heat and a general air around camp of not wanting to go very far away. In mid-afternoon (it was all the same) a curious darkening of the sky, and a lull in everything that had made life tick; and then the way the boats suddenly swung the other way at their moorings with the coming of a breeze out of the new quarter, and the premonitory rumble. Then the kettle drum, then the snare, then the bass drum and cymbals, then crackling light against the dark, and the gods grinning and licking their chops in the hills. Afterward the calm, the rain steadily rustling in the calm lake, the return of light and hope and spirits, and the campers running out in joy and relief to go swimming in the rain, their bright cries perpetuating the deathless joke about how they were getting simply drenched, and the children screaming with delight at the new sensation of bathing in the rain, and the joke about getting drenched linking the generations in a strong indestructible chain. And the comedian who waded in carrying an umbrella.

When the others went swimming, my son said he was going in, too. 13 He pulled his dripping trunks from the line where they had hung all through the shower and wrung them out. Languidly, and with no thought of going in, I watched him, his hard little body, skinny and bare, saw him wince slightly as he pulled up around his vitals the small, soggy, icy garment. As he buckled the swollen belt, suddenly my groin felt the chill of death.

CONSIDERATIONS

1. White and his son are more used to the ocean than to the inland lakes. What is the point of the many contrasts between the two bodies of water? Comment on the essay's title.
2. When his son does exactly the same things he used to do, why does White begin to feel "dizzy" and to have "a creepy sensation"?
3. In the first half of the essay, the past floods in on him; then, in the second half, time ebbs away. Can you discern at which point in the essay the tide turns? What does White express at the very moment before it turns?
4. WRITING TOPIC. Young as well as older people experience nostalgia — it doesn't seem to require a long, distant past. Nostalgia is a broad feeling that can include being homesick for some place or lonely for someone, but it also seems to go beyond such particular objects to a general illusion. A movie, a book, or music can make us feel "nostalgic" over an imaginary life. In a 700-word essay, explain what you find to be nostalgic in a book or movie.

Robert F. Sayre

THE PARENTS' LAST LESSONS

◊

ROBERT F. SAYRE (b. 1933) is a professor of English at the University of Iowa. Educated at Wesleyan and Yale, he has written widely on topics in American literature, with a special interest in the autobiographies of Benjamin Franklin, Henry Adams, and others who saw their own lives as illustrating their society. In this memoir of his parents, Sayre considers their contrasting ways of dying.

One of the common experiences of people in their early forties, 1 which they seem to need to talk about, is having parents who are in their sixties and seventies. The situation itself is only a biological and statistical inevitability, at least in contemporary American culture. But I have been surprised, just the same, at the frequency with which discussion of parents now comes up among people I know. Ten years ago, when we were in our early thirties, we talked about our children — about pregnancies and births, bottles versus breast-feeding, how to get "them" to sleep through the night, and then about toilet-training and schools. We were primarily parents, and our own parents were secondary subjects. They were just grandparents and in-laws who were or were not helpful or demanding, visiting, vacationing, or whatnot. Only in the last four or five years, I realize, have I been telling and hearing stories about *parents,* usually with friends, but sometimes with people I have just met, if they are my age.

This is, I suppose, one of the features of a "mid-life crisis," as the 2 psychologists call it. But I will call it by its older name — "middle age." I now realize that I am in that period because I am in the middle, between my children, who are six, eight, and ten, and my parents, who died in 1974, in their late seventies. In fact, maybe beyond the middle, for as my brother and sisters and I observed to one another at my mother's funeral, we are now the oldest generation. *Our* children know no Sayres who are older than we and our cousins.

Therefore, I would like to talk about my parents and my great-aunt, 3 who lived in my parents' family when I was young, and about my own perceptions of their "aging" now that I, too, am "aging." Four persons in three generations. It is, by definition, a senescent topic. It won't have much appeal to that large "youth audience" we used to hear about! For, as I just noted, talk about one's old or recently dead parents is mostly for the middle-aged and beyond.

The reasons why we in our early forties talk so much about our par- 4 ents are, I think, two. First, we suddenly bear a responsibility for them which we never expected to have. All through our own childhood and even our early adulthood (though I realize that the extent of this period can vary widely), we usually thought of ourselves first. Our lives were full of problems, theirs were predictable and secure. They knew what they were doing, because they were telling us what to do. Only on rare occasions did we worry about them or for them — when they were very sick or when a father lost a job. Unless we were very foresighted or unless *they* told us, we did not anticipate the day when we would have to tell *them* what to do. So the burden of a sick or indigent or incompetent parent is a surprise. And it is sometimes a heavy burden, financially, psychologically, or both. Second, as we see them grow old and die, we realize as we never did before that we are mortal, too. What is happening to them will, in a few short decades, happen to us. Time is different when you are forty, and you know that in a short while you will be sixty or seventy yourself. And so you look to your sixty- or seventy-year-old parents for your last lessons: how to go on living and how to die. If they are healthy and active and contented, you are happy for them and you seek to imitate them. If they are miserable, you try to help them, but you also hope that you will not imitate them. One way or another, they are your inheritance: your blessing or your curse.

The case for my brother, sisters, and me is one of exactly this am- 5 bivalence. Our father, Harrison Sayre, lived to be almost eighty. On the evening of 15 May 1974, he went over to our sister Dixie's house for supper. He had a drink with her and praised the view he liked so much from her living-room windows — the lawn, the trees, the sunset over the city. Then, as he frequently did, he lay down for a nap, while

Dixie prepared supper. When she tried to wake him, she could not. May 21, six days later, would have been his eightieth birthday; and we had been planning a large celebration for him. Instead of the party, we had a memorial service. But it was not a gloomy one, for he had died, as a friend said, "easily and with dignity — the way he lived." "It makes you realize," my brother said, "that death can have dignity."

Mother died on 19 October, five months later. She was seventy-   6
seven, and for six years she had been in rest homes, excluded from a normal life because of a relentless decline in her memory. She had an obscure neural ailment known as Alzheimer's disease, and though it was not what killed her (the "cause" was pneumonia), it had brought on her slow death to the world. At first, back in the late 1950s and early 1960s, she had begun to forget friends' names. Then she began doing daft things like going out to deliver something to a friend's house and getting lost. A companion-housekeeper was hired, but the disease continued. By the time she was in the first rest home, she could not remember her grandchildren's names. Later she barely recognized us children. When told of her husband's death, she only asked, as if she had never heard of him, "Hal?"

I think that anyone can see the extremes of dignity and degradation   7
represented by these two fates. Given the choice, one would prefer to grow old and die like Harrison Sayre: no senility, no decline in his mental faculties, and only a slight reduction in his physical strength. The few ailments that he had had were skillfully treated by expert doctors, and he then maintained his health by regularly taking his pills, carefully watching his diet, and getting plenty of mild exercise. Finally, by dying quickly and painlessly, he even cheated the doctors and the hospitals of those expensive fees for terminal care. Mother's rest-home care, on the other hand, cost between ten and fifteen thousand dollars a year, and if it prolonged her life, it did so for what? She was happy, in a simple, childlike way. She was warm and well fed. She had nurses to look out for her, and put her on the toilet and change her diapers. She watched television and talked in a polite, vacuous way with the other patients. When we went to visit her, we sang old college songs and World War I patriotic tunes. She apparently did not even recognize her own pitiable state. But I know that her condition gave Dad and the rest of us a great deal of sadness. Had we been right to put her in the rest homes? Was there anything we and she could have done in the years before to have prevented this depressing end?

The assumption of most men and women is that how we age and 8
how we die must be consequences of how we live. A plane crash, a
virus, a bullet, or one slip of the wheel on a narrow road — these may
happen to anyone. But they cannot destroy this basic faith. Those
people who are leading satisfying, healthy lives normally expect to go
on with them. When doctors and actuaries tell them that their life
expectancy is seventy or seventy-five, they believe it. People who
smoke and drink excessively, who are tense or overweight, and who
feel generally dissatisfied and gloomy are likewise assured that they
run higher-than-average risks of cancer, heart disease, and the other
causes of early death or old-age distress. Thus, most people at the age
of thirty-five or forty-five begin to feel some responsibility for their
later fate. They diet, exercise, get annual physical examinations, and
try to be more moderate in their habits. This, as I myself realize, is
one of the major causes of that legendary middle-aged conservatism. If
you want to live to seventy, to see the maturity of your children, and
to complete the goals you have set for yourself, you cannot go on living like Lord Byron or Scott Fitzgerald.

Therefore, the questions which I have repeatedly asked are: where 9
was Mother wrong, and Dad right? If we are responsible for our old
age, in what ways did Dad prepare for it, and in what ways was
Mother irresponsible? For even though Mother's Alzheimer's disease
may have been unavoidable — an accident like a plane crash or a
congenital defect like her colorblindness (which I share) — I would
still prefer not to think that I am helpless before the same fate. As I
have learned to live with the colorblindness by looking very carefully
at stoplights, I would also like to circumvent Alzheimer's disease.
Such precautions may ultimately be as vain as those of Oedipus's parents, but doing nothing is obviously not the answer either.

Mother grew up in Columbus, Ohio, and lived there all her life. 10
She was an only child, but her parents, James White and Maude
Hanna White, seem to have been related to half of the city. As I imagine them, they were all members of that Middle Western business
middle class: McKinley Republicans, American Victorians, who con-
fidently believed that America was the best country on earth, Ohio
the leading state, and Columbus the best city. They had their local aristocracy of old and leading families, to which Mother looked up, and
they had their rigid Victorian customs and taboos, which were honored as "good taste." But Mother's generation was perhaps the first to

belong to what Thorstein Veblen called the "leisure class." She had time for tennis tournaments (as a girl she was a city champion), for dances and parties, and she eventually went to Vassar College to prepare for her later roles in the YWCA, the Junior League, and other volunteer groups and charities. When I was a child, Mother's stories of her childhood, including the little electric car her parents gave her when she was only twelve, all seemed long, long ago. But today I realize that the differences between her childhood and mine were superficial, not essential. Neighborhoods and addresses changed, like fashions, but neighbors and family life did not. The secure complacency, the supposed good breeding, the comfort and conformity, and the energetic pleasures in which she was raised endured in the Columbus in which I was raised, too.

Dad's childhood in Newark, New Jersey, was several steps lower 11 economically, and more old-fashioned culturally. Before the First World War, Newark was a small town. His father and mother belonged to its plain, Presbyterian majority. Sayres had been in northern New Jersey since the early eighteenth century, but Dad's own relatives had not prospered. Both of his grandfathers had died before the end of the Civil War, so that both his father and mother were raised by widows. Neither of his parents, he said later, was much aware of the changing industrial world of their times. The stories he heard as a boy were family stories from the American Revolution. He grew up serious and thrifty. Poor eyesight kept him out of sports, though as an adolescent he was over six feet tall. He went on to work his way through Wesleyan University by selling aluminum cooking ware. In three years he graduated, Phi Beta Kappa, and stayed an extra year as a high school debating coach and an assistant in philosophy. He was a lieutenant in the First World War, and then moved to Columbus, Ohio, to be a salesman in his cousin Fred Freeman's bond brokerage business.

He and Mother married in 1921, and with money from Mother's 12 family, Dad was able in 1923 to buy an interest in the American Education Press and become an editor of its small line of teaching materials for junior and senior high schools, the most important of which was *Current Events*. Preston Davis, the manager and major owner of the company, was a perceptive but retiring man who gave his close associates encouragement in developing their own ideas. One of Dad's, which had been suggested to him by the teachers he visited, was a weekly paper like *Current Events* that could be used in lower grades to teach reading. In 1928 he and Preston Davis started *My Weekly Reader,* and it became, as Dad said, "a children's favorite, a publisher's miracle." Its subscription price was only twenty cents a semester, so low that each child could have his own copy — and no competitor could undercut the company. It became Depression-proof. Editions were added to supply all the lower grades, and each autumn an avalanche of orders poured in. "Following the successful launching of the *Weekly Reader,*" Dad recalled, "Preston doubled my salary, recommended my name for inclusion in *Who's Who in America* . . . and nominated me for presidency of all three companies in our corporate complex. . . . Dividends from the Educational Printing House were so liberal that I never asked for another salary increase. In return, Preston gave me free hand to do the community work — which after 1931 I felt was all-important."

His was an American success story, but with some subtle varia- 13
tions. In 1931 he was only thirty-seven years old — very young for a businessman to decide that "community work . . . was all-important," even if he considered his income sufficient. Benjamin Franklin, whom he often regarded as a model, did not retire until he was in his midforties. To be sure, Dad had not retired. He remained president of the American Education Press until it was sold to Wesleyan University in 1949. But in 1931 the Japanese invasion of Manchuria and the failure by the League of Nations to oppose it looked to him, he said later, like terrifying omens. Perhaps in these later reflections he was boasting a little of his foresight, but he did genuinely believe by the 1930s that there was no security for him or for other people which was not dependent on world order. And feeling ineffectual in promoting world order, he concentrated his energies, time, and ability on promoting the health and betterment of the communities in which he lived. He was what people in Columbus called "community-minded," and the words "community" and "citizen" had profound meaning to him. Thus, he was not a typical businessman, rushed, tense, and absorbed in daily affairs. His nearest modern equivalent might be one of those vice-presidents for public relations, as some companies call them, who devote most of their time to community service. Such service does not bring in business, but it does enhance the company's reputation and bring a different voice to the boardroom. Ideally, such men have wide interests and a sense of history. They are not moles; they are eagles.

Not only did Dad believe in this kind of work; it also brought him great satisfaction. He grew in it, and I think that it contributed to the greater patience and mellowness he developed in his sixties and seventies. He was definitely not the kind of businessman who works hard till age sixty-five and then retires to play golf and raise roses.

Had someone looked at him and Mother in 1940, however, when 14 they were still only forty-six and forty-four, respectively, it would have been much harder to see this about him or to see what was so different about her. I raise this point because obviously none of us can yet look back on ourselves. Our lives are in process, and therefore we should try to understand the lives of our parents as they were at our own present ages, not just as they later reconstructed them from the position of age sixty-five or seventy-five. This is all the more important with Mother because her loss of memory prevented her ever having that retrospective view of herself, whereas Dad took time in his seventies to perfect his. He wrote his autobiography, in the form of three hundred pages of disjointed chapters which he called *Random Recollections*. And though these are a great help to me in reconstructing his past, I have nothing like them for Mother. Nor is she mentioned much in his *Recollections*. He found it painful to think about her, and he did not like dwelling on her failures (though I know he thought about them often).

But as a means of recapturing Dad and Mother in the late 1930s 15 and early 1940s, I have looked at several reels of old home movies which Dad took; and they are magical recreations. For instance, they show me at age three or four playing in the sand on the beach at Point O'Woods, New York, where we went in the summer. They show my twin sisters, Babs and Jean, at age nine or ten, dressed to go to an evening movie or children's dance; and they show our big brother and sister, Jimmy and Dixie, sailing the eighteen-foot Cape Cod Knockabout that was bought in 1938. Characteristic glimpses "as we were," and as Mother and Dad liked to see us. But these proud parents also took a few shots of themselves "as they were," and these are the most precious, because until I saw them I had forgotten (or never known) how youthful Mother and Dad–Harrison and Mary Sayre then were.

Some shots of Mother show her in a bathing suit, reading in the 16 shade of a beach umbrella. Her figure is trim, her hair a dark brown just turning to black, and her motions quick and a little shy, camera-shy. She waves a hand in front of her face, and I can hear her saying, "Oh now, Hal, now really! Point that at the children, not me." But the camera does not move, and she soon smiles, a lovely and satisfied, shy, girlish smile. She is/was a warm, gentle person.

Dad is not photographed on the beach. (Perhaps he wanted no one 17 else's wet and sandy hands to grasp his expensive gadget.) But about five o'clock one afternoon, he was caught in his white shirt and white-duck slacks as he and Mother were off to a party. He stands on the boardwalk in front of the cottage, grinning like a monkey and grotesquely chomping his jaws. For a moment I cannot figure out what he is doing. But then I see. He is mocking the motions of some of us children chewing gum! Chewing with our mouths open! "Close your mouth when you chew" was something he frequently told us at dinner. And if that command failed, he got sarcastic. He mocked us, as here! He was very funny; but he was also a little frightening. As a child (and long after), I was as much afraid of his mockery and sarcasm as I was of his ordinary reproofs. At that time I never felt close to him.

In these old films, I find the revealing (if extremely selective) evi- 18 dence that Mother in her mid-forties was the more pleasant person. Had someone taken bets then on which would live the longer, more joyful life, I suspect that most people would have guessed she would. He was twinkly, but also a little nasty. She seemed naturally happy. He had to work at it. He clowned in his light moments, but he also teased. And his teasing seemed to suggest the suppressed criticism, the dissatisfactions with the people around him. He was, I imagine, as displeased by habits in Columbus City Hall and the world at large as by children chewing with their mouths open — and made equally strenuous objections to both. The more cynical or worldly of his friends probably regarded him as an idealist. "Hal Sayre," I hear them saying, "is a perfectionist, while Mary is good-natured. Oh, they are an attractive couple," the voices go on, "religious, honest. Neither drinks; they serve no liquor in their home. But they are not Prohibitionists — just staunch Presbyterians. It's hard to know which is the more determined on this. I guess it's Mary, since Hal will have a beer now and then. But in most ways she is the lighthearted one. She's nervous sometimes, but when she relaxes she is lots of fun. She has more fun at parties without tasting a drop than other people do on three highballs. He has some interesting ideas, but he wants to change the world!"

Studied from this perspective, Mother's premature senility and the 19
dignity of Dad's old age are hard to explain. This view also makes
Mother's degradation even more pathetic. How could life turn on
someone who seemed to love it so much? Everything that was youthful and happy in Mary Sayre appears, in the end, to have folded back
on her and turned her into a helpless child all over again. Where his
life was a rising diagonal line, hers was a circle. She went from youth
into a still-vivacious middle age, and then back into a dependent,
timeless childhood.

But there are more things which must have been on Mother's and 20
Dad's minds when they were in their middle age. Wouldn't they, indeed, have thought sometimes of *their* parents just as I am now
thinking of mine? I know they did, for in 1936 Mother's mother,
Grandmother White, died, and soon afterward Dad's maternal aunt,
Miss Adelaide Browne, who had briefly lived with Grandmother,
came to live with us. She would have been a constant reminder to him
of his parents and his ancestry. In 1942 he researched and privately
published a slim volume of genealogy called *The Descendants of
Ephraim Sayre.* He was thinking not just of his parents but of all his
ancestors. And I remember trips which he and Mother made a few
years later to country towns and villages in eastern Ohio from which
Mother's father had come. They may have even planned a White-
Hanna genealogy to match the Sayre one. Being only ten or so then
myself, I was not interested in this. It bored me. But now I have sympathy for what they were doing.

Both of them, moreover, must have had fears like mine. Mother's 21
mother had been afflicted with "hardening of the arteries" and high
blood pressure, and in her final years she lost her memory. One of her
habits was to ask all her grandchildren for a kiss; and one day she kept
repeating this demand to my brother, Jim, who was about eight or ten.
"But Grandma," he said, on each new demand, "I just kissed you."

"Oh that doesn't matter," she answered. "Kiss me again." 22

But on the fifth or sixth request, he stayed where he was and said, 23
sweetly but firmly, "I'm all out of kissing juice." The story was repeated in the late 1950s, when Mother was losing *her* memory and
asking for repeated kisses from *her* grandchildren.

Dad's ancestral fear came from his father, and though *he* had died 24
much earlier, in 1915, it was probably an even heavier burden. He
never told us about it until 1968 or 1969, when he was working on his

Random Recollections. His father, Joseph Sayre, had had epilepsy, which in the nineteenth century carried all the awful superstitions we are aware of from Dostoevsky and was believed to be hereditary. The possibility of seizures was so great that Dad, as a little boy, used to have to accompany his father on business errands around Newark. And he was so afraid of passing the curse along to his own children that before he and Mother married he made a special trip to New York to get expert advice. The doctor told him not to worry; and neither he nor any of us has ever had the disease. But the consequence of watching his father in those terrifying fits was "a lifelong distaste for losing consciousness." "I fainted while making a speech in high school once," he wrote in the *Recollections*, "and, on the doctor's advice, willingly abstained from red meats for more than three years. I saw enough drunkenness in the streets of Newark and heard enough about it among family connections to make me prefer sobriety. I dislike the thought of anyone's losing control of himself." And control himself he did, all his life. Mother had nothing near his firm resolution and steely self-discipline.

But Mother also had different responsibilities. While Dad in the 25 early 1940s was a little like his exemplary Benjamin Franklin, a successful tradesman whose income permitted him to work for Columbus as Franklin had worked for Philadelphia, Mother still had all the daily chores of managing a large household. This Dad readily acknowledged. He called her "the manager," and he always deferred to her on household matters. But what was especially difficult for her was the care of Aunt Adelaide, who was a model of old-age vitality to Dad but a competitor and a burden to Mother. Thus, Aunt Adelaide's story seems to belong here, too, because it further illustrates how generations respond to one another.

Aunt Adelaide Browne, Dad's mother's unmarried younger sister, 26 was born in 1857. For thirty-three years she was a missionary in India, where she founded an orphanage which grew into an elementary school, a middle school, and eventually a high school for hundreds of children. In 1937, when she came to live with us at 264 North Drexel, she was already 80 years old, and I do not imagine that anyone expected her to live more than another five years. She was barely five feet tall and very frail-looking. But she was alert and peppery, and she lived on and on — for twenty-two years. She did not die until 1959, at nearly 102. For most of that time Mother could never leave the house, whether for a vacation, a weekend, or, toward the end, an afternoon, without making sure that someone was on hand to be with Aunt Adelaide. Before the Second World War, when servants could be hired for five dollars a week plus room and board, this was not so hard, but by the 1950s, when live-in "help" was no longer available — yet needed all the more for Aunt Adelaide — this was a constant worry. Mother thought that she had to keep someone on hand every hour of the day. In the morning a maid or one of us brought Aunt Adelaide breakfast in bed. Mother was downstairs by 7:00 or 7:30 to have breakfast and plan the day. At lunch Dad was downtown eating with his men friends. Mother was usually eating at home with *his* Aunt Adelaide, hearing unending stories about distant Sayre and Browne relatives or about retired missionaries. After lunch Aunt Adelaide napped. Then Mother tore out of the house to meetings, on errands, to pick up children, or maybe just to get away. At dinner, we could seldom have a raucous family fight. No one, as far as I remember, ever got mad or loud, or blew up, as I eventually discovered other families did. Sitting on one side of the table was always that calm, saintly missionary. Every dinner was like a Sunday-noon dinner, with the minister present. The aunt who came to dinner stayed twenty-two years.

Dad, all this time, had no cause for exasperation with this amazing 27 little woman. He knew only her jolly wit, her kind and clever flattery, the lessons of her experience, and an unceasing devotion verging on the maternal. I think I only now see what a peculiar advantage he had from her, from Aunt Adee, as he boyishly called her. From his mid-forties to his mid-sixties, he still had a doting mother-stand-in who praised his every achievement. For a time I think she even kept a scrapbook about him. But she was no simpleton of a protective, fawning mother, but a wise and accomplished person, who had lived abroad, learned another language, and once had the responsibilities of a school headmistress. Thus, any interesting news or perplexing decision could be discussed with her more easily — and probably more profitably — than with Mother. He, an educational publisher, had a retired expert teacher right there at home. Yet I am sure she never intruded, for I know that her way of teaching was always to say little until asked and then to answer with her own questions. "Well what do *you* think? What are *your* reasons?"

It is also interesting that even living in American luxury, this 28 bright, quick person practiced a kind of Oriental asceticism. She liked to say, with a little sassiness, "A third of what you eat keeps you alive; the rest is for the doctors and the undertakers." But she was not withdrawn from society. During the war she knitted over one hundred heavy wool sweaters for soldiers and refugees. Every fall Saturday, she listened to the radio broadcasts of Ohio State football games. She cared about her favorite players, though she never saw them, as if they were her own distant students. Her cries over touchdowns and fumbles were so intense that people sometimes thought that the long-expected heart attack had suddenly come. ("Hundred-Year-Old Missionary Dies Listening to Michigan Game" would certainly have been the Columbus headline.) And with all her piety and scrupulosity she was never much troubled, as far as I could see, over the scandals of recruiting, secret payments, riotous fans, and the rest of the seamy side of the game. "No one can live in Columbus without an interest in football," she would say, in a tone that was so matter-of-fact that it was at once beyond irony and the very essence of satire. She had a saint's power to delight in the good and coldly ignore the bad.

Yet, like Dad, she had a sharp tongue when she wanted to use it. 29 Her scorn for Franklin Roosevelt when he ran for a third term was expressed in two words: "Mr. Indispensable." I remember her pointing to his picture on the cover of a *Life* magazine that came in the fall of 1940. It was the first time I had heard the word "indispensable," and I had no idea what she meant. "But that's Roosevelt," I said in my seven-year-old's voice. "He's the President of the United States," I kept repeating. "That's Mr. Indispensable," she repeated, "and no one's Indispensable. No One's Indispensable." I was just more confused. Did No One now have a name, Mr. Indispensable? How could the President of the United States be No One? I'm sure that she eventually gave me a simple explanation, for I did at least realize that she was saying that none of us is so useful or wise or precious that the world cannot get along without him. But this shows how stubborn she could be, too. At eighty-three, teaching herself that *she* was not indispensable, she would not give in easily. She stabbed at Roosevelt's nose as if her finger were a dagger. "Mr. Indispensable."

Aside from a few memories like this one, I could never really see, as 30 a child, what was so amazing about her. She used to help us with our spelling lessons. She would invite us to her room and give us candy (especially peppermint Life Savers), and she would praise me when I later did little things like fix a lamp cord, or "fix" her radio by plugging it in. But she also had a contrariness that was unpredictable. If you were late in doing something she had asked, she would keep after you. She combined extremes of selfless humility and proud conviction. She once showed me a dime that she said had been given her by Mr. Rockefeller. I by then knew who he was and asked, "Only a *dime*, with all his money?" She answered that he gave much more money away than that. She seemed to like having actually met the richest man in the world. Or was it that she had that thin sliver of his fortune? Millions for him, a dime for her, and it made no difference to her. But I particularly remember how one of Dad's and Mother's maids used to be amazed every summer at Aunt Adelaide's way of protecting raspberries from the birds. In a long white dress she would sit beside the bushes for hours on end with her knitting and the family cat, undaunted by the heat and sun. Edith Daniels, the maid, perspired buckets herself and, having grown up on farms, had a sensible respect for the Midwestern summer sun. "That Miss Browne," Edith would say. "I don't know how she does it." "Oh, I used to live in India, you know," was her answer. And so the next day she would be back at her post, a little living scarecrow, happy and laughing, proud to be doing her duty, however humble.

Having this presence in the house for twenty-two years was hard on 31 Mother. Aunt Adelaide could wear Mother's cast-off dresses and look fine in them. The most intelligent guests would come to Sunday dinner, then go upstairs and spend an hour or more being enchanted by Miss Browne and have to be dragged out to join other people. Later they would praise Mother's hospitality, but Aunt Adelaide's company. In those years, I think, Mother was most interested in details and things, in family plans, furniture, and all the business of running a house (she had to be); Dad was most interested in projects and improvements of society — in ideas; and Aunt Adelaide was most interested in people. In her idiosyncratic way, she defined "personality" as meaning "an interest in persons." And she had it. Quarterbacks, missionaries, Indian students and professors visiting the United States, my sister's boyfriends, distant relatives she could only write to — she followed them all. People reciprocated with an interest in her, and she was like the unknown guest from out of town who stole all the dates. Ninety, ninety-five, and finally one hundred years old, with her wrinkled face and her white hair held up in pearl-colored pins, with her mohair shawl and dresses below her knees, she had more essential charm than any debutante who ever danced till dawn.

But Mother never learned to share in Aunt Adelaide's popularity. 32 Mother, unfortunately, had not only to arrange sitters and meals for Aunt Adelaide, but also to compete with her. The good side of the competition may have been that for these twenty-two long years, Mother had to stay young. Youth and beauty and energy were her assets against the charm and serenity and occasional sharp tongue of a woman twice her age. So Mother stayed in control: if Mother got sick, Aunt Adelaide might secretly begin taking over the household. Keeping her household (and her husband) seemed to require being the manager and nursing the rival. Aunt Adelaide was elderly. Aunt Adelaide must have breakfast in bed. Would someone please take up her tray? Aunt Adelaide must have naps, quiet, a nice room, care and consideration. And when I think of the strain this must have put on Mother, I wonder at how she did it. She seldom cracked, seldom broke down and pampered herself, though when she did she would verge, I think, on the hysterical. Then she had to have breakfast in bed, naps, doctors, enemas, special diets, and the whole panoply of Victorian neurasthenic care. For Mother sick was a demanding, petulant person, even more powerful, in a way, than Mother well. No one, not even Dad, could overrule her whining fury and senseless whims. But these moods came only after she had been driven to desperation. Most of the time she suppressed this urge to pamper and baby herself by pampering Aunt Adelaide. It was Aunt Adelaide who was frail and weak. Mother was young and strong.

The further consequence, however, was that when Aunt Adelaide 33 finally died, Mother, at age sixty-three, no longer had to keep this battle going. Nor had she had the opportunity to begin to relax her nerves and prepare for her own old age. There was no longer Aunt Adelaide against whom to be young and active and beautiful. Mother's aging began, fast. We children had grown up and left her, and having fewer of the outside interests that absorbed Dad, she had little to do. She suddenly became that saddest of sights, the overprotected middle-class grandmother in an age of two generation families where grandmothers have no function. Of course, she was proud of being "Mama." In the early 1960s she and Dad had thirteen grandchildren, and at every holiday she wanted "a family reunion." But when the children came, they made her nervous. Dad, on the other hand, began imitating the old Aunt Adee tricks. He gave chess lessons, taught puzzles and word games, and always kept a big jar of licorice drops near his desk. Mother admired his skill, but did not have it herself. She had belonged to a culture where nurses fed the children, brought them in for one respectful "goodnight from Grandmama," and then hustled them off to bed.

It would be an oversimplification to imply that the long burden of 34 Aunt Adelaide and the sudden change after her death were the only things that brought on Mother's senility. After all, many people have had elderly relatives living with them, even in this age of the two-generation family, and though some may have suffered from the experience, others have enjoyed and learned from it. Dad loved Aunt Adelaide not simply because she was his relative. Nor did Mother resent her only because she was *not* her relative. The point is, rather, that Aunt Adelaide was a kind of catalyst, an agent who brought out opposing tendencies in each of them, and the same or nearly the same tendencies would probably have come out anyway. In fact, as we could see later, Mother's response to grandchildren was pretty much the same—they were darlings and so on, but they made her nervous. Her response to some of Dad's friends, particularly if they were involved in work she did not understand, was cold and formal. She did not try to understand their work and regarded meeting them merely as an obligation. The older she got, the greater her resistance to change. It shocked her that her daughters came back from the hospital only six, five, three, days after delivering babies. Her confinements had lasted two weeks, and that was the "right" way. If we took coaches rather than Pullmans, we endangered our health. When we began to stop taking any trains and took planes, we seemed to Mother to be taking horrendous risks.

Dad's reactions to these failures in Mother made matters worse. I 35 remember one day before Christmas in the middle 1960s, when Dad was in bed with a cold and Mother was trying to locate a box of handkerchiefs which she had bought to give a friend. She knew this was an instance of her loss of memory, and she was distraught. "Hal," she kept saying, as she circled in and out of her bedroom, "where *did* I put those handkerchiefs?" I helped her, but could only follow her aimless quest. Dad meanwhile sat in bed, increasingly impatient with her. "Think, Mary," was all he could say. "Where did you put them when you brought them home?" He did not console her by telling her patiently that the handkerchiefs would turn up, and not to worry. He did not understand what had really happened. He was utterly frustrated with her and scowled at her as if she were a dumb schoolgirl. She just needed to "think." Then, with a groan, he got out of bed and joined the search, while she cried that he shouldn't, that he was sick. They were working against each other like two motors turning in opposite directions. He thought her problem was a mere failure of will, and his severity just made her the more flustered. Finally Mother and I went to another room to wrap other presents, forgetting the handkerchiefs and letting Dad go back to bed.

In September of 1968 Dad had a stroke, and in the ensuing treatment the doctors discovered a heart fibrillation. We children flew to Columbus from all directions and had a conference. When and if Dad recovered, we decided, he should not go back to the big house at 264 North Drexel. He and Mother alone did not need so much room, and maintaining the house was a burden. The trouble was that Mother was so attached to the old house — after thirty-two years — that she would not want to move. We had to choose between her wish to stay and Dad's need for something more manageable (for she was no longer "manager"). Moving might dreadfully unsettle her; staying might soon bring him another stroke.   36

What clinched the decision, at least for me, was the proposal, supported by Mother's doctors, that she go in the meantime to a psychiatric rest home. There she might have tests to determine exactly what her disease was and the treatments to arrest it, if possible. While she was there, the house would be sold, and Dad would move to a large apartment, with room enough for Mother should she recover. The decision was harsh, but I think it was the right one. As I watched Dad in his hospital bed, seeing him in tears one moment and telling jokes the next, I had an overwhelming sense of his determined will to live. He would readily accept any changes, do anything to be well and back on his feet. Mother, I had to recognize, scarcely knew what had happened to him. And when I recalled that absurd and dreadful fuss about the handkerchiefs, I recognized that separating them might save them both. With their currents working against each other, an overload, a short circuit and blackout for both, seemed inevitable.   37

So the decision was executed, and while Mother was in the rest home, Dad underwent a miraculous operation in which his heart was   38 stopped and then electrically stimulated to set it again in a normal beat. Dixie and Babs, the two sisters living in Columbus, went to work, methodically clearing out 264 North Drexel, emptying its dozens of closets and drawers and cupboards, basement to attic, of the accumulations of several generations — our old toys and sailing trophies; Mother's and Dad's clothes, books, furniture, dishes, and so on; and heirlooms of Whites and Hannas, Sayres and Brownes. This was not just a sale and a move, it was the end of an era. And Dixie and Babs proceeded so efficiently and carefully that Dad scarcely needed to do anything. He just sat in the library, gleefully sending off bundle after bundle of his once-prized papers and speeches to the trash. He was being reborn. And he loved it.

By the spring of 1969 he was begun on his new life. His apartment 39 had been beautifully furnished with the best of the things from 264, and he entertained proudly. He kept Mother's nurse-companion for a time, in gratitude for what she had done and in case Mother might return. But when that was seen to be impossible, he let her go. Alice Brown, his and Mother's former maid, came in daily to clean and prepare some meals; but he got on very well alone. He was constantly going out to meetings, to luncheons, and to dinner parties, and I think he wore his distinguished tuxedo more in those last five years than in the previous twenty.

But most gratifying to him was the growth of the Columbus Foun- 40 dation, the focus, finally, of all his decades of community service. He had started this civic foundation long ago in 1943, with some money from Preston Davis, and for twenty years or more it grew modestly, acquiring more good will than money. But in the late 1960s it began to receive bequests of a staggering size, some of over a million dollars. Its long-awaited success and the prospect of the numerous civic projects which it could support gave him immense gratification. There was nothing that contributed more to his culminating sense of usefulness to his city.

As he told me one night of the foundation's latest bequests, I asked 41 him how he had first heard of the idea. I knew the story, but I liked hearing it. He told it well, and it illustrated how a seed would root in his mind and maybe not flower for years, but then bloom like an orchard in May. So he repeated the story of how, shortly after he and Mother were married, they went to Cleveland to visit Freda Goff, a friend of Mother's from Vassar. Her father, Frederick H. Goff, was a lawyer and banker and had recently started the Cleveland Foundation, the first community foundation in America. Dad listened to Mr. Goff's persuasive arguments for this new institution, which was more versatile than the separate charities to which people usually made bequests and yet could still be used to support them; and Dad resolved that if the opportunity ever came, he would help start one in Columbus. But as he told this story, what suddenly struck me was that Mother had been the essential intermediary. Without her friendship with Freda Goff, he would never have met Mr. Goff. So I asked what Mother had thought of the idea and whether she had had any part in its development in Columbus.

No, he said, she hadn't. She had never taken much interest in it. 42 "What a pity," I said, "because if she had, you and she would now share this reward." My suggestion seemed to strike him like an arrow, making him involuntarily give up something he had long been holding back. He had privately thought of such a shared final purpose with Mother, I think, but when it did not occur, he did not talk about it. Typically, he kept his disappointments to himself. So, after a dark moment of hesitation, he looked up at me and said, in an earnest, husky voice, "Your mother is thought-less."

He seemed so close to tears that I hesitated to continue. But he had 43 said something that pained me. Mother *thoughtless?* A person who had spent twenty-two years taking care of *his* aunt, who had raised us five children, run his house for him, and been generous, considerate, and self-sacrificing until she was exhausted . . . ? "I always believed," I told him, "that Mother was very thought*ful.* I can't think of any word which is less appropriate!"

"No," he answered, repeating himself very slowly. "She is 44 thought-less."

"You mean now?" I replied. "That may be true now — and how 45 ironic, when you think of what she was."

"No," he said. "I mean before, too. Your mother has always been 46 thought-less."

He would say no more. And after a while I perceived his emphasis 47 and the meaning he was giving to the word. He meant that Mother did not *think.* She never *thought* — thought deeply, thought ahead, planned her life — in the profound philosophical way that he did. And so from his perspective the Alzheimer's disease was no accident or unpreventable disability. It was a fulfillment of her tragic flaw.

"What a cold person he could be," I exclaimed to myself. And what suffering he endured because of his coldness! For it was now plain to me how much he had wished to make Mother thoughtful, in his passionately rational way. But the more he tried, the more exhausted she must have become, and so the more futile her efforts, to her. Yet as a Christian, he loved her still. So he tried to refrain from judgments. He held to faith in his way, hope that she would see it, love for her nevertheless.

And refraining from judgments was right. For in judging her, he 48 implicitly revealed and commented upon himself. But he knew the Scripture better than I: Judge not that ye be not judged. So neither of us said any more.

CONSIDERATIONS

1. The father is brought into the essay by the story of his achievements. How is the mother initially presented? Make your answer explicit and detailed.
2. Sayre tries to understand the earlier life of his parents from a variety of perspectives. Whose viewpoints does he include besides his own? What kinds of evidence does he use to build up their characterizations? What is gained by partly fictionalizing them?
3. What are Sayre's insights to Aunt Adelaide's effects on each of his parents? Do you think that Sayre's parents would have had a better or a worse marriage if Aunt Adelaide had not lived with them for twenty-two years?
4. At the beginning of paragraph five, Sayre speaks of "ambivalence." What precisely does he mean by the word "ambivalence," and how does it apply to each of his parents?
5. WRITING TOPIC. The theme of taking care of others, including being taken care of by others, seems to define the central values and issues of the Sayres' family life. Conflicting or complex attitudes about caring and serving are prominent in all four generations, permeating their public and private experience. In 700 words, write on this theme as it is visible in your family and social environment. How does it enter into discussions and activities at home and in the community? Is it connected to other values that may conflict with caretaking?

IMAGES

Owen Franken, Harvard Graduation. (*Stock, Boston*)

Linda G. Rich, Murty, Ananta, and Santhi Hejeebu, *1977.*

Michael Hayman, Family — Byron, Michigan.
(*Stock, Boston*)

ADDITIONAL
WRITING TOPICS

◊

FAMILY TIES

1. Consider the literal meanings of a few family names, such as Carmichael, Hessberg, O'Connor, Rosenthal, Sanchez, or Sylvester. Using a dictionary of family names, look up the origins of the names on both sides of your family for the preceding two or three generations. Write a 700-word essay on the two or three relevant names that best indicate the background and present traits of your family. Some reference works that may be useful are Elsdon Smith, *Dictionary of American Family Names* (1956); Edward MacLysaght, *Irish Families* (1957); P. H. Reaney, *A Dictionary of British Surnames* (1958); and Benzion Kaganoff, *A Dictionary of Jewish Names and Their History* (1977). Your reference librarian may be able to help you to other sources as well.

2. Is family life portrayed differently on television and in the movies? In a 700-word essay, compare the views of the family in these two forms of popular entertainment. Choose fairly current examples, and focus mainly on one movie and one television show.

3. Write a review of a book about one of the notable American families that has received a great deal of public attention and serious study. You might choose one about the Adams family, the Guggenheims, the James family, the Kennedys, or the Rockefellers. In a 700-word essay, explain the author's insight into what makes this family cohere; that is, what is the book's viewpoint toward this particular family's ideals, goals, leaders, and style of living?

4. In about 700 words write a family biography of your pet.

5. Do you have too many brothers and sisters, or too few? Almost everyone sometimes wishes for a few changes in that area of fate. Would some sibling revisions improve your life? In 500 words, explain how your personality would be changed by changing the number, sex, and ages of your siblings.

6. Consider the family values that are expressed in the photographs on pages 143–145. All the details of personal expression, clothing, objects, background, and arrangement of the group indicate what the families take for

granted about themselves and how they wish to be seen by others. Each family is pictured at a moment that seems to sum up its daily concerns and style of life as well as its ambitions and expectations. The photographs may even suggest to you something about the fears and limits that affect each family. In 800 to 1,000 words, clarify the kind of family experience that each photograph indicates. Be sure to connect all your points to observations of specific details.

3

GROUP
PICTURES

INSIGHTS

No man is an island, entire of itself; every man is a piece of the continent, a part of the main; if a clod be washed away by the sea, Europe is the less, as well as if a promontory were, as well as if a manor of thy friends or of thine own were; any man's death diminishes me, because I am involved in mankind; and therefore never send to know for whom the bell tolls: it tolls for thee.

— JOHN DONNE

Society everywhere is in conspiracy against the manhood of every one of its members. Society is a joint-stock company, in which the members agree, for the better securing of his bread to each shareholder, to surrender the liberty and culture of the eater. The virtue in most request is conformity. Self-reliance is its aversion. It loves not realities and creators, but names and customs. Whoso would be a man, must be a nonconformist.

— RALPH WALDO EMERSON

Being ashamed of one's parents is, psychologically, not identical with being ashamed of one's people. I believe every one of us will, if he but digs deeply enough into the realm of unconscious memories, remember having been ashamed of his parents. Being ashamed of our people must have another psychological meaning. It must be the expression of a tendency to disavow the most essential part of ourself. To be ashamed of being Jewish means not only to be a coward and insincere in disavowing the proud inheritance of an old people who have made an eternal contribution to the civilization of mankind. It also means to disavow the best and the most precious part we get from

150

our parents, their parents, and their ancestors, who continue to live in us. It means, furthermore, to renounce oneself. Without self-respect and dignity no man or woman can live. When the Jewish proverb proclaims that he who is ashamed of his family will have no luck in life, it must mean just that: he cannot have that self-confidence which makes life worth living. Strange that the folklore of an oriental people coincides here with the viewpoint of Goethe: any life can be lived if one does not miss oneself, if one but remains oneself.

The thought that my children are sometimes ashamed of the human faults and failings of their father does not sadden me; but, for their own sake, I wish that they will never be ashamed that their father was Jewish. The one feeling concerns only the personal shortcomings of an individual who was striving, sometimes succeeding and often failing. The other shame concerns something superpersonal, something beyond the narrow realm of the individual. It concerns the community of fate, it touches the bond that ties one generation to those preceding it and those following it.

– THEODOR REIK

Hell is other people.
– JEAN-PAUL SARTRE

It is difficult to let others see the full psychological meaning of caste segregation. It is as though one, looking out from a dark cave in a side of an impending mountain, sees the world passing and speaks to it; speaks courteously and persuasively, showing them how these entombed souls are hindered in their natural movement, expression, and development; and how their loosening from prison would be a matter not simply of courtesy, sympathy, and help to them, but aid to all the world. One talks on evenly and logically in this way, but notices that the passing throng does not even turn its head, or if it does, glances curiously and walks on. It gradually penetrates the minds of the prisoners that the people passing do not hear; that some thick sheet of invisible but horribly tangible plate glass is between them and the world. They get excited; they talk louder; they gesticulate. Some of the passing world stop in curiosity; these gesticulations seem so pointless; they laugh and pass on. They still either do not hear at all, or hear but dimly, and even what they hear, they do not understand. Then the people within may become hysterical. They may scream and hurl themselves against the barriers, hardly realizing in their bewilderment that they are screaming in a vacuum unheard and that their antics may actually seem funny to those outside looking in. They may even, here and there, break through in blood and disfigurement, and find themselves faced by a horrified, implacable, and quite overwhelming mob of people frightened for their own very existence.

– W. E. B. DUBOIS

Dean MacCannell

THE TOURIST

◊

DEAN MACCANNELL (b. 1940) graduated from the University of California at Berkeley and earned a Ph.D. at Cornell University, where he did research for a book on *The Tourist* (1976), from which this selection is taken. MacCannell has traveled extensively throughout Europe and has taught at the American College in Paris, where students from many countries sometimes felt like tourists, as this excerpt indicates. MacCannell teaches behavioral science at the University of California at Davis. His most recent book, written with Juliet Flower MacCannell, interprets contemporary culture as *The Time of the Sign* (1982).

It is intellectually chic nowadays to deride tourists. An influential 1 theoretician of modern leisure, Daniel J. Boorstin, approvingly quotes a nineteenth-century writer at length:

> The cities of Italy [are] now deluged with droves of these creatures, for they never separate, and you see them forty in number pouring along a street with their director — now in front, now at the rear, circling round them like a sheep dog — and really the process is as like herding as may be. I have already met three flocks, and anything so uncouth I never saw before, the men, mostly elderly, dreary, sad-looking; the women, somewhat younger, travel-tossed but intensely lively, wide-awake and facetious.

Claude Lévi-Strauss writes simply: Travel and travelers are two things I loathe — and yet here I am, all set to tell the story of my expeditions." A student of mine in Paris, a young man from Iran dedicated to the revolution, half stammering, half shouting, said to me, "Let's face it, we are all tourists!" Then, rising to his feet, his face contorted with what seemed to me to be self-hatred, he concluded dramatically in a hiss: "Even *I* am a tourist."

I think it significant that people who are actually in accord are 2 struggling to distance themselves from themselves via this moral stereotype of the tourist. When I was eighteen years old, I returned a date to her home on a little resort-residential island. As the ferry approached the slip, I reached for the ignition key. She grabbed my hand, saying vehemently, "Don't do that! Only *tourists* start their cars before we dock!"

The rhetoric of moral superiority that comfortably inhabits this ₃ talk about tourists was once found in unconsciously prejudicial statements about other "outsiders," Indians, Chicanos, young people, blacks, women. As these peoples organize into groups and find both a collective identity and a place in the modern totality, it is increasingly difficult to manufacture morality out of opposition to them. The modern consciousness appears to be dividing along different lines against itself. Tourists dislike tourists. God is dead, but man's need to appear holier than his fellows lives. . . .

The modern critique of tourists is not an analytic reflection on the ₄ problem of tourism — it is a part of the problem. Tourists are not criticized by Boorstin and others for leaving home to see sights. They are reproached for being satisfied with superficial experiences of other peoples and other places. An educated respondent told me that he and his wife were "very nervous" when they visited the Winterthur museum because they did not know "the proper names of all the different styles of antiques," and they were afraid their silence would betray their ignorance. In other words, touristic shame is not based on being a tourist but on not being tourist enough, on a failure to see everything the way it "ought" to be seen. The touristic critique of tourism is based on a desire to go beyond the other "mere" tourists to a more profound appreciation of society and culture, and it is by no means limited to intellectual statements. All tourists desire this deeper involvement with society and culture to some degree; it is a basic component of their motivation to travel.

CONSIDERATIONS

1. According to MacCannell why do people not want to be thought of as tourists? Do you accept his explanation?
2. As a traveler, have you experienced "touristic shame"? What did you do

about it, and what do you now wish you had done at the time? In a paragraph or two, reconstruct the situation and recount your experience.

3. WRITING TOPIC. On campus, you are usually able to recognize visiting outsiders, such as pre-freshmen interviewees or groups from another college. In about 300 words, describe one such group of "tourists" and recall your attitude toward them at the time.

4. WRITING TOPIC. In a 500-word essay, relate one incident that occurred to you or around you during freshman orientation. Refer to yourself only in the third person, by your first name. That is, instead of writing "I saw," write "Michael saw," instead of writing "I felt sick," write "Michelle felt sick." Try to relate the interaction among strangers — including yourself — that made the incident stay in your memory.

Edward C. Martin

BEING JUNIOR HIGH

◊

EDWARD C. MARTIN (b. 1937) is an educational administrator and an author of such social science textbooks as *The People Make a Nation* (1971). He has taught in both high schools and junior high schools. In this essay on the early adolescent student, he discusses some of the special difficulties that a twelve- to fourteen-year-old has in being an individual and also a member of a group. This essay is a condensation of an article that originally appeared under the title "Reflections on the Early Adolescent in School."

What is it like to be in school if you are twelve to fourteen years of 1 age? What does and doesn't it mean to you?

... Fundamentally, for most American twelve-year-olds, school is 2 *where it's at*. School occupies the time and concerns of all the people you know — your friends, your parents, people you meet. People are always asking what you do in school and how you like school. School is often a source of contention between you and adults. Why did you get low grades? Why did you play hooky? Why don't you play school sports or join clubs or work harder or work less, and so forth? You are always telling people you don't like school, but often you don't mean it because school is comfortable and they at least want you around. Also you think school is important and even fun. But these things can't be said too openly.

Friends and enemies are a large part of school, perhaps the largest. 3 One comes to school to see friends, one fears school because enemies are there also. Some of the most important parts of the school day are the walk or ride there, changing between classes, the few minutes before the class gets started, the study hall, and the end of school. These times are the intense periods of "seeing the other kids," or realizing you have no one to see. One of those unwritten rules of teaching is "begin the class on time." It makes the teacher appear efficient and purposeful and gives the task to be done a sense of importance. When I started teaching in junior high I still believed this rule, until I began to realize how much there is to learn about students by observing or participating in the three minutes before class started. . . . My interest in the friendship group has been not to join it but to figure out ways to tap it when it made sense to do so. The usual separation of the interests of these groups and the classroom is not necessarily a bad separation. Doing the peer group's thing all the time would be as deadly as doing the teacher's thing all the time.

The case of a student staying home, being ill, or skipping a class 4 because he fears some group of students is more common than most adults imagine. Threats are used frequently by students although fortunately not often carried through. For two weeks a group of girls were harassing another girl in and out of classes. The girl under attack was literally terrified, although she sought to hold her ground by appearing casual and unafraid. When this failed she would seek the help of adults or just burst into tears. For the group of antagonists, this aggressiveness was a source of unity and camaraderie. They relished the times of confrontation and the times of subtle teasing. Individuals took pride and received group praise devising more exciting methods of taunting their foe. There was always the daring aspect of avoiding that line where the full force of adult intervention would be imposed. The several adults involved did not know what to do. One teacher tried to give some perspective on the situation by showing the long-run absurdity of such behavior, another by attempting disciplinary tactics — essentially tongue-lashing and keeping the aggressive group after school. The guidance counselor tried to talk it through with all the students involved. The situation improved on the surface, but we all knew the individual girl's fear remained and the group's resentment toward her and power over her continued. We also realized that there was very little we could do about it but make sure it did not become violent. I am always surprised at how brutal students this age can be toward each other. It reminds me again of how important a book Golding's novel *Lord of the Flies* is for teachers.

The intense friendship groupings in junior high obviously have an- 5 other side — the youngster who has no friends, no group to which he has allegiance or which sees him as a part. Several kinds of students in my experience fall into this category and it means different things to each. John was an outgoing intellectual student who spoke in an affected way and assumed he had the right answers. Other students saw him as a "freak" and made it clear to him that was how they regarded him. Sharon was a quiet withdrawn girl who talked with no one and to whom no one talked. She seemed not to be bothered by this isolation. Bob was a class leader. He demanded everyone's attention and when he did not get it was bound to provoke it. Although the students saw him as an important person to be reckoned with, he was really not a part of any group. Adults at one time or another are isolated from others by choice or happenstance, but the isolation of a twelve-, thirteen-, or fourteen-year-old is particularly difficult. There is a pain brought on by not being like everyone else when it is important that you be like others. This comes at a time in physical, emotional, and intellectual development when change is so rapid that many individual youngsters are either behind or ahead of the mass of their peers. Aggravating these gaps is the intolerance of this age group toward diversity and their delight in making an issue over those who are different. The boy who does not start to spurt in physical stature is called a "shrimp" and sees himself as a shrimp. The girl who gets seriously interested in a boy does not quite fit with her giggly friends. The peer group of the twelve- to fourteen-year-old has most of the mechanisms of keeping members in line but often lacks the moral, ethical, and intellectual substance of the so-called "youth culture" of older students. . . .

In schools, the classroom is seen as the center of the educational 6
experience. Whether or not it is in effect is beside the point. Students
see it as such. . . .
In the center of the classroom experience is the teacher. Students 7
most often describe and define their courses in terms of the teacher.
He or she is the one who makes a class great or terrible. Curriculum
reform projects of the past ten years in the academic disciplines have
tried to improve schools by producing better materials, some of which
could be taught by *any* teacher. Most of them now realize that with a
bad teacher students will feel the new course is as bad as the old. Parents, principals, and guidance counselors keep telling youngsters it
should not matter who the teacher is. They say you should be able to
learn from someone you do not like. This is true only when personal
dislike is mild and is overpowered by respect for the teacher's fairness
and competence. Most teachers accept the necessity of being liked by

their students; some turn this into an end in itself. Students want a positive personal relationship with their teachers, but they want more.

The teacher, whether or not he considers himself a benevolent des- 8 pot or a partner in learning, is a model. He is usually the only adult in a room of thirty people. He is the one most different and the one who is expected to do something to make that class good. If he does not, he is not a good teacher. He is the one turned to when the going gets rough. One day I brought six candy bars into class for a lesson on the distribution of goods. I put the candy bars on the desk and told the class they were welcome to have them and should agree on how to divide them. For the rest of the period and part of the next, alternatives were presented and discussed. Several boys from the track team suggested, only half in jest, that the candy be placed at one end of the room and the class race for it. Generally, this solution was opposed. Other proposals were made including equal division, grades, fighting, working, bidding, and drawing lots. None, by the way, suggested that I as teacher decide. Finally, drawing lots was agreed upon as the best method. As I moved the candy bars to another spot in the room, the elected class chairman grabbed at one. I asked him why, since all had agreed to do the division by lots. He said he wanted one. I held out the bars and he took one, opened it, and proceeded to eat it. The universal reaction of the class was silent confusion. I thought they would be outraged and I suppose they were, but in this case they expected me to take action, to stop the violation of their hard-reached decision. I finally did ask the boy why he disregarded the class's decision, rather mildly chewed him out, and ruled him out of the drawing of lots.

The incident illustrates many things and raises many questions. 9 Clearly I had violated the expectations of the students, either by letting their classmate take the candy or by not acting when he did. They expected me to handle this situation even though all but the assignment of the task was in their control and they had made the decisions. Perhaps I had asked them to step too far out of their notions of authority and the security that a teacher is expected to provide in the classroom. Another reason I was surprised at the class's lack of reaction was their usual strong reactions to injustice. Students measure teachers, generally with a high degree of accuracy, on a continuum from just to unjust in treatment of people. Twelve-year-olds often use a double standard — canons of fairness are strictly applied to others, much less strictly applied to themselves. Connected to both the security and justice issues is the whole question of authority. Although much less sensitive about authority than sixteen-year-olds, the twelve-year-old in school is keenly aware of who makes decisions and what role he has in the process. In the case of the candy bars, I was expected to act as the authority. No doubt I was naïve about how students viewed the authority relationships in class to think they would exercise some control on their classmate. This age student is more committed to the distinction between himself and adults. He is more willing to go along with the authorities, but is beginning to question. By the time he leaves junior high school, the question of legitimate authority is a central part of things about which he is "bugged."

A final point about the candy bar incident. The actions of the boy 10 represent, in the extreme, a serious problem for most youngsters in junior high school: *How do I establish and develop individuality in an institution that treats me as one of a group with similar characteristics?* Most of the students I teach want to be seen as individuals, just as we all do. A school is a difficult if not impossible place to get a great deal of individual treatment. The students want to be members of the group, but they also want to be someone unique. Since all the children have this problem and since there is considerable pressure toward group conformity, they are not much able to give each other this sense of individuality. The teacher is often the only one able to legitimatize pluralism, but he is hampered because he deals with so many children and almost always as a group.

CONSIDERATIONS

1. Martin recognizes that "seeing the other kids" is important in the school day, but he does not look into what makes it important. Based on your own observations, what interests and activities do seventh and eighth graders share with friends in school? How do they spend time together? Are they always with the same friends?
2. What are the qualities that junior high students generally expect from a teacher? How did Martin meet or fail their expectations?
3. Throughout the essay, Martin mentions several differences between junior high students and older, high school students. What are the differences he notes, and do you find his observations accurate?
4. In the final sentence what does Martin mean by "legitimatize pluralism"?

Paraphrase Martin and add an illustration of how the teacher might be able to do this. Why don't the students do the same for one another?

5. WRITING TOPIC. In a 500-word paper, present a specific example of the pressure you once felt to conform to a group. Give enough details of the situation to show that you were being pressured, and not left free to act individually. Show that the situation was of some importance to you. Even choosing a flavor of ice cream can be important if you feel that you are being bullied over making up your mind.

6. WRITING TOPIC. Write a 500-word analysis of the photograph on page 214, taking as your theme Martin's statement in the final paragraph that "students want to be members of the group, but they also want to be someone unique." Identify in detail the standards that define the group. What are the accepted expressions of uniqueness among them? Are there indications that anyone may be violating the codes of behavior? How does the background relate to the students' attitudes about themselves? What population groups and social classes are present? What does this tell you about the neighborhood or town where the school is located? How does this affect the way students group themselves and express themselves?

Maya Angelou

GRADUATION

◊

MAYA ANGELOU (b. 1928) was raised by her grandmother, who ran a small store for blacks in the town of Stamps, Arkansas. She survived a childhood that seemed certain to defeat her, and as she once told an interviewer: "One would say of my life — born loser — had to be; from a broken family, raped at eight, unwed mother at sixteen." During her adult life, she became a dancer, an actress, a poet, a television writer and producer, and a coordinator in Martin Luther King's Southern Christian Leadership Conference. She is most widely known for her four autobiographical books, beginning with *I Know Why the Caged Bird Sings* (1970) from which this selection is taken. Her most recent memoir is *The Heart of a Woman* (1981).

The children in Stamps trembled visibly with anticipation. Some 1 adults were excited too, but to be certain the whole young population had come down with graduation epidemic. Large classes were graduating from both the grammar school and the high school. Even those who were years removed from their own day of glorious release were anxious to help with preparations as a kind of dry run. The junior students who were moving into the vacating classes' chairs were tradition-bound to show their talents for leadership and management. They strutted through the school and around the campus exerting pressure on the lower grades. Their authority was so new that occasionally if they pressed a little too hard it had to be overlooked. After all, next term was coming, and it never hurt a sixth grader to have a play sister in the eighth grade, or a tenth-year student to be able to call a twelfth grader Bubba. So all was endured in a spirit of shared understanding. But the graduating classes themselves were the nobility. Like travelers with exotic destinations on their minds, the graduates were remarkably forgetful. They came to school without their books, or tablets, or even pencils. Volunteers fell over themselves to secure replacements for the missing equipment. When accepted, the willing workers might or might not be thanked, and it was of no importance to the pregraduation rites. Even teachers were respectful of the now quiet and aging seniors, and tended to speak to them, if not as equals, as beings only slightly lower than themselves. After tests were returned and grades given, the student body, which acted like an extended family, knew who did well, who excelled, and what piteous ones had failed.

Unlike the white high school, Lafayette County Training School 2 distinguished itself by having neither lawn, nor hedges, nor tennis court, nor climbing ivy. Its two buildings (main classrooms, the grade school and home economics) were set on a dirt hill with no fence to limit either its boundaries or those of bordering farms. There was a large expanse to the left of the school which was used alternately as a baseball diamond or a basketball court. Rusty hoops on the swaying poles represented the permanent recreational equipment, although bats and balls could be borrowed from the P.E. teacher if the borrower was qualified and if the diamond wasn't occupied.

Over this rocky area relieved by a few shady tall persimmon trees 3 the graduating class walked. The girls often held hands and no longer bothered to speak to the lower students. There was a sadness about them, as if this old world was not their home and they were bound for higher ground. The boys, on the other hand, had become more friendly, more outgoing. A decided change from the closed attitude they projected while studying for finals. Now they seemed not ready to give up the old school, the familiar paths and classrooms. Only a small percentage would be continuing on to college — one of the South's A & M (agricultural and mechanical) schools, which trained negro youths to be carpenters, farmers, handymen, masons, maids, cooks, and baby nurses. Their future rode heavily on their shoulders, and blinded them to the collective joy that had pervaded the lives of the boys and girls in the grammar school graduating class.

Parents who could afford it had ordered new shoes and ready-made 4 clothes for themselves from Sears and Roebuck or Montgomery Ward. They also engaged the best seamstresses to make the floating graduating dresses and to cut down secondhand pants which would be pressed to a military slickness for the important event.

Oh, it was important, all right. Whitefolks would attend the cere- 5 mony, and two or three would speak of God and home, and the

Southern way of life, and Mrs. Parsons, the principal's wife, would play the graduation march while the lower-grade graduates paraded down the aisles and took their seats below the platform. The high school seniors would wait in empty classrooms to make their dramatic entrance.

In the Store I was the person of the moment. The birthday girl. 6 The center. Bailey* had graduated the year before, although to do so he had had to forfeit all pleasures to make up for his time lost in Baton Rouge.

My class was wearing butter-yellow piqué dresses, and Momma 7 launched out on mine. She smocked the yoke into tiny crisscrossing puckers, then shirred the rest of the bodice. Her dark fingers ducked in and out of the lemony cloth as she embroidered raised daisies around the hem. Before she considered herself finished she had added a crocheted cuff on the puff sleeves, and a pointy crocheted collar.

I was going to be lovely. A walking model of all the various styles of 8 fine hand sewing and it didn't worry me that I was only twelve years old and merely graduating from the eighth grade. Besides, many teachers in Arkansas Negro schools had only that diploma and were licensed to impart wisdom.

The days had become longer and more noticeable. The faded beige 9 of former times had been replaced with strong and sure colors. I began to see my classmates' clothes, their skin tones, and the dust that waved off pussy willows. Clouds that lazed across the sky were objects of great concern to me. Their shiftier shapes might have held a message that in my new happiness and with a little bit of time I'd soon decipher. During that period I looked at the arch of heaven so religiously my neck kept a steady ache. I had taken to smiling more often, and my jaws hurt from the unaccustomed activity. Between the two physical sore spots, I suppose I could have been uncomfortable, but that was not the case. As a member of the winning team (the graduating class of 1940) I had outdistanced unpleasant sensations by miles. I was headed for the freedom of open fields.

Youth and social approval allied themselves with me and we tram- 10 meled memories of slights and insults. The wind of our swift passage

---

* The author's brother. The children help out in their grandmother's store.

remodeled my features. Lost tears were pounded to mud and then to dust. Years of withdrawal were brushed aside and left behind, as hanging ropes of parasitic moss.

My work alone had awarded me a top place and I was going to be 11 one of the first called in the graduating ceremonies. On the classroom blackboard, as well as on the bulletin board in the auditorium, there were blue stars and white stars and red stars. No absences, no tardinesses, and my academic work was among the best of the year. I could say the preamble to the Constitution even faster than Bailey. We timed ourselves often: "WethepeopleoftheUnitedStatesinordertoform-amoreperfectunion . . ." I had memorized the Presidents of the United States from Washington to Roosevelt in chronological as well as alphabetical order.

My hair pleased me too. Gradually the black mass had lengthened 12 and thickened, so that it kept at last to its braided pattern, and I didn't have to yank my scalp off when I tried to comb it.

Louise and I had rehearsed the exercises until we tired out our- 13 selves. Henry Reed was class valedictorian. He was a small, very black boy with hooded eyes, a long, broad nose and an oddly shaped head. I had admired him for years because each term he and I vied for the best grades in our class. Most often he bested me, but instead of being disappointed I was pleased that we shared top places between us. Like many Southern Black children, he lived with his grandmother, who was as strict as Momma and as kind as she knew how to be. He was courteous, respectful, and soft-spoken to elders, but on the playground he chose to play the roughest games. I admired him. Anyone, I reckoned, sufficiently afraid or sufficiently dull could be polite. But to be able to operate at a top level with both adults and children was admirable.

His valedictory speech was entitled "To Be or Not to Be." The 14 rigid tenth-grade teacher had helped him to write it. He'd been working on the dramatic stresses for months.

The weeks until graduation were filled with heady activities. A 15 group of small children were to be presented in a play about buttercups and daisies and bunny rabbits. They could be heard throughout the building practicing their hops and their little songs that sounded like silver bells. The older girls (non-graduates, of course) were assigned the task of making refreshments for the night's festivities. A tangy scent of ginger, cinnamon, nutmeg, and chocolate wafted around the home economics building as the budding cooks made samples for themselves and their teachers.

In every corner of the workshop, axes and saws split fresh timber as 16 the woodshop boys made sets and stage scenery. Only the graduates were left out of the general bustle. We were free to sit in the library at the back of the building or look in quite detachedly, naturally, on the measures being taken for our event.

Even the minister preached on graduation the Sunday before. His 17 subject was, "Let your light so shine that men will see your good works and praise your Father, Who is in Heaven." Although the sermon was purported to be addressed to us, he used the occasion to speak to backsliders, gamblers, and general ne'er-do-wells. But since he had called our names at the beginning of the service we were mollified.

Among Negroes the tradition was to give presents to children going 18 only from one grade to another. How much more important this was when the person was graduating at the top of the class. Uncle Willie and Momma had sent away for a Mickey Mouse watch like Bailey's. Louise gave me four embroidered handkerchiefs. (I gave her three crocheted doilies.) Mrs. Sneed, the minister's wife, made me an underskirt to wear for graduation, and nearly every customer gave me a nickel or maybe even a dime with the instruction "Keep on moving to higher ground," or some such encouragement.

Amazingly the great day finally dawned and I was out of bed before 19 I knew it. I threw open the back door to see it more clearly, but Momma said, "Sister, come away from that door and put your robe on."

I hoped the memory of that morning would never leave me. Sun- 20 light was itself still young, and the day had none of the insistence maturity would bring it in a few hours. In my robe and barefoot in the backyard, under cover of going to see about my new beans, I gave myself up to the gentle warmth and thanked God that no matter what evil I had done in my life He had allowed me to live to see this day. Somewhere in my fatalism I had expected to die, accidentally, and never have the chance to walk up the stairs in the auditorium and gracefully receive my hard-earned diploma. Out of God's merciful bosom I had won reprieve.

Bailey came out in his robe and gave me a box wrapped in 21 Christmas paper. He said he had saved his money for months to pay for it. It felt like a box of chocolates, but I knew Bailey wouldn't save money to buy candy when we had all we could want under our noses.

He was as proud of the gift as I. It was a soft-leather-bound copy of 22 a collection of poems by Edgar Allan Poe, or, as Bailey and I called him, "Eap." I turned to "Annabel Lee" and we walked up and down the garden rows, the cool dirt between our toes, reciting the beautifully sad lines.

Momma made a Sunday breakfast although it was only Friday. 23 After we finished the blessing, I opened my eyes to find the watch on my plate. It was a dream of a day. Everything went smoothly and to my credit. I didn't have to be reminded or scolded for anything. Near evening I was too jittery to attend to chores, so Bailey volunteered to do all before his bath.

Days before, we had made a sign for the Store and as we turned out 24 the lights Momma hung the cardboard over the doorknob. It read clearly: CLOSED. GRADUATION.

My dress fitted perfectly and everyone said that I looked like a sun- 25 beam in it. On the hill, going toward the school, Bailey walked behind with Uncle Willie, who muttered, "Go on, Ju." He wanted him to walk ahead with us because it embarrassed him to have to walk so slowly. Bailey said he'd let the ladies walk together, and the men would bring up the rear. We all laughed, nicely.

Little children dashed by out of the dark like fireflies. Their crepe- 26 paper dresses and butterfly wings were not made for running and we heard more than one rip, dryly, and the regretful "uh uh" that followed.

The school blazed without gaiety. The windows seemed cold and 27 unfriendly from the lower hill. A sense of ill-fated timing crept over me, and if Momma hadn't reached for my hand I would have drifted back to Bailey and Uncle Willie, and possibly beyond. She made a few slow jokes about my feet getting cold, and tugged me along to the now-strange building.

Around the front steps, assurance came back. There were my fel- 28 low "greats," the graduating class. Hair brushed back, legs oiled, new dresses and pressed pleats, fresh pocket handkerchiefs and little handbags, all homesewn. Oh, we were up to snuff, all right. I joined my comrades and didn't even see my family go in to find seats in the crowded auditorium.

The school band struck up a march and all classes filed in as had 29 been rehearsed. We stood in front of our seats, as assigned, and on a signal from the choir director, we sat. No sooner had this been accomplished than the band started to play the national anthem. We rose again and sang the song, after which we recited the pledge of allegiance. We remained standing for a brief minute before the choir director and the principal signaled to us, rather desperately I thought, to take our seats. The command was so unusual that our carefully rehearsed and smooth-running machine was thrown off. For a full minute we fumbled for our chairs and bumped into each other awkwardly. Habits change or solidify under pressure, so in our state of nervous tension we had been ready to follow our usual assembly pattern: the American National Anthem, then the pledge of allegiance, then the song every Black person I knew called the Negro National Anthem. All done in the same key, with the same passion and most often standing on the same foot.

Finding my seat at last, I was overcome with a presentiment of 30 worse things to come. Something unrehearsed, unplanned, was going to happen, and we were going to be made to look bad. I distinctly remember being explicit in the choice of pronoun. It was "we," the graduating class, the unit, that concerned me then.

The principal welcomed "parents and friends" and asked the Bap- 31 tist minister to lead us in prayer. His invocation was brief and punchy, and for a second I thought we were getting back on the high road to right action. When the principal came back to the dais, however, his voice had changed. Sounds always affected me profoundly and the principal's voice was one of my favorites. During assembly it melted and lowed weakly into the audience. It had not been in my plan to listen to him, but my curiosity was piqued and I straightened up to give him my attention.

He was talking about Booker T. Washington, our "late great 32 leader," who said we can be as close as the fingers on the hand, etc. . . . Then he said a few vague things about friendship and the friendship of kindly people to those less fortunate than themselves. With that his voice nearly faded, thin, away. Like a river diminishing to a stream and then to a trickle. But he cleared his throat and said, "Our speaker tonight, who is also our friend, came from Texarkana to deliver the commencement address, but due to the irregularity of the train schedule, he's going to, as they say, 'speak and run.' " He said that we understood and wanted the man to know that we were most grateful for the time he was able to give us and then something about how we were willing always to adjust to another's program, and without more ado — "I give you Mr. Edward Donleavy."

Not one but two white men came through the door offstage. The 33 shorter one walked to the speaker's platform, and the tall one moved over to the center seat and sat down. But that was our principal's seat, and already occupied. The dislodged gentleman bounced around for a long breath or two before the Baptist minister gave him his chair, then with more dignity than the situation deserved, the minister walked off the stage.

Donleavy looked at the audience once (on reflection, I'm sure that 34 he wanted only to reassure himself that we were really there), adjusted his glasses, and began to read from a sheaf of papers.

He was glad "to be here and to see the work going on just as it was 35 in the other schools."

At the first "Amen" from the audience I willed the offender to im- 36 mediate death by choking on the word. But Amens and Yes, sir's began to fall around the room like rain through a ragged umbrella.

He told us of the wonderful changes we children in Stamps had in 37 store. The Central School (naturally, the white school was Central) had already been granted improvements that would be in use in the fall. A well-known artist was coming from Little Rock to teach art to them. They were going to have the newest microscopes and chemistry equipment for their laboratory. Mr. Donleavy didn't leave us long in the dark over who made these improvements available to Central High. Nor were we to be ignored in the general betterment scheme he had in mind.

He said that he had pointed out to people at a very high level that 38 one of the first-line football tacklers at Arkansas Agricultural and Mechanical College had graduated from good old Lafayette County Training School. Here fewer Amen's were heard. Those few that did break through lay dully in the air with the heaviness of habit.

He went on to praise us. He went on to say how he had bragged 39 that "one of the best basketball players at Fisk sank his first ball right here at Lafayette County Training School."

The white kids were going to have a chance to become Galileos 40 and Madame Curies and Edisons and Gauguins, and our boys (the girls weren't even in on it) would try to be Jesse Owenses and Joe Louises.

Owens and the Brown Bomber were great heroes in our world, but 41
what school official in the white-goddom of Little Rock had the right
to decide that those two men must be our only heroes? Who decided
that for Henry Reed to become a scientist he had to work like George
Washington Carver, as a bootblack, to buy a lousy microscope? Bailey
was obviously always going to be too small to be an athlete, so which
concrete angel glued to what country seat had decided that if my
brother wanted to become a lawyer he had to first pay penance for his
skin by picking cotton and hoeing corn and studying correspondence
books at night for twenty years?

The man's dead words fell like bricks around the auditorium and 42
too many settled in my belly. Constrained by hard-learned manners I
couldn't look behind me, but to my left and right the proud graduating class of 1940 had dropped their heads. Every girl in my row had
found something new to do with her handkerchief. Some folded the
tiny squares into love knots, some into triangles, but most were wad-
ding them, then pressing them flat on their yellow laps.

On the dais, the ancient tragedy was being replayed. Professor Par- 43
sons sat, a sculptor's reject, rigid. His large, heavy body seemed devoid
of will or willingness, and his eyes said he was no longer with us. The
other teachers examined the flag (which was draped stage right) or
their notes, or the windows which opened on our now-famous playing
diamond.

Graduation, the hush-hush magic time of frills and gifts and con- 44
gratulations and diplomas, was finished for me before my name was
called. The accomplishment was nothing. The meticulous maps,
drawn in three colors of ink, learning and spelling decasyllabic words,
memorizing the whole of *The Rape of Lucrece*—it was nothing.
Donleavy had exposed us.

We were maids and farmers, handymen and washerwomen, and 45
anything higher that we aspired to was farcical and presumptuous.
Then I wished that Gabriel Prosser and Nat Turner had killed all
whitefolks in their beds and that Abraham Lincoln had been assassi-
nated before the signing of the Emancipation Proclamation, and that
Harriet Tubman had been killed by that blow on her head and Christopher Columbus had drowned in the *Santa Maria.*

It was awful to be Negro and have no control over my life. It was 46
brutal to be young and already trained to sit quietly and listen to
charges brought against my color with no chance of defense. We

should all be dead. I thought I should like to see us all dead, one on top of the other. A pyramid of flesh with the whitefolks on the bottom, as the broad base, then the Indians with their silly tomahawks and teepees and wigwams and treaties, the Negroes with their mops and recipes and cotton sacks and spirituals sticking out of their mouths. The Dutch children should all stumble in their wooden shoes and break their necks. The French should choke to death on the Louisiana Purchase (1803) while silkworms ate all the Chinese with their stupid pigtails. As a species, we were an abomination. All of us.

Donleavy was running for election, and assured our parents that if 47 he won we could count on having the only colored paved playing field in that part of Arkansas. Also — he never looked up to acknowledge the grunts of acceptance — also, we were bound to get some new equipment for the home economics building and the workshop.

He finished, and since there was no need to give any more than the 48 most perfunctory thank-you's, he nodded to the men on the stage, and the tall white man who was never introduced joined him at the door. They left with the attitude that now they were off to something really important. (The graduation ceremonies at Lafayette County Training School had been a mere preliminary.)

The ugliness they left was palpable. An uninvited guest who 49 wouldn't leave. The choir was summoned and sang a modern arrangement of "Onward, Christian Soldiers," with new words pertaining to graduates seeking their place in the world. But it didn't work. Elouise, the daughter of the Baptist minister, recited "Invictus," and I could have cried at the impertinence of "I am the master of my fate, I am the captain of my soul."

My name had lost its ring of familiarity and I had to be nudged to 50 go and receive my diploma. All my preparations had fled. I neither marched up to the stage like a conquering Amazon, nor did I look in the audience for Bailey's nod of approval. Marguerite Johnson, I heard the name again, my honors were read, there were noises in the audience of appreciation, and I took my place on the stage as rehearsed.

I thought about colors I hated: ecru, puce, lavender, beige, and 51 black.

There was shuffling and rustling around me, then Henry Reed was 52 giving his valedictory address, "To Be or Not to Be." Hadn't he heard the whitefolks? We couldn't *be*, so the question was a waste of time.

Henry's voice came out clear and strong. I feared to look at him. Hadn't he got the message? There was no "nobler in the mind" for Negroes because the world didn't think we had minds, and they let us know it. "Outrageous fortune"? Now, that was a joke. When the ceremony was over I had to tell Henry Reed some things. That is, if I still cared. Not "rub," Henry, "erase." "Ah, there's the erase." Us.

Henry had been a good student in elocution. His voice rose on tides   53 of promise and fell on waves of warnings. The English teacher had helped him to create a sermon winging through Hamlet's soliloquy. To be a man, a doer, a builder, a leader, or to be a tool, an unfunny joke, a crusher of funky toadstools. I marveled that Henry could go through with the speech as if we had a choice.

I had been listening and silently rebutting each sentence with my   54 eyes closed; then there was a hush, which in an audience warns that something unplanned is happening. I looked up and saw Henry Reed, the conservative, the proper, the A student, turn his back to the audience and turn to us (the proud graduating class of 1940) and sing, nearly speaking,

> Lift ev'ry voice and sing
> Till earth and heaven ring
> Ring with the harmonies of Liberty . . .

It was the poem written by James Weldon Johnson. It was the music composed by J. Rosamond Johnson. It was the Negro National Anthem. Out of habit we were singing it.

Our mothers and fathers stood in the dark hall and joined the   55 hymn of encouragement. A kindergarten teacher led the small children onto the stage and the buttercups and daisies and bunny rabbits marked time and tried to follow:

> Stony the road we trod
> Bitter the chastening rod
> Felt in the days when hope, unborn, had died.
> Yet with a steady beat
> Have not our weary feet
> Come to the place for which our fathers sighed?

Every child I knew had learned that song with his ABC's and along   56 with "Jesus Loves Me This I Know." But I personally had never heard it before. Never heard the words, despite the thousands of times I had sung them. Never thought they had anything to do with me.

On the other hand, the words of Patrick Henry had made such an 57
impression on me that I had been able to stretch myself tall and
trembling and say, "I know not what course others may take, but as
for me, give me liberty or give me death."

And now I heard, really for the first time: 58

> We have come over a way that with tears has been watered,
> We have come, treading our path through the blood of the
> slaughtered.

While echoes of the song shivered in the air, Henry Reed bowed 59
his head, said "Thank you," and returned to his place in the line. The
tears that slipped down many faces were not wiped away in shame.

We were on top again. As always, again. We survived. The depths 60
had been icy and dark, but now a bright sun spoke to our souls. I was
no longer simply a member of the proud graduating class of 1940; I
was a proud member of the wonderful, beautiful Negro race.

Oh, Black known and unknown poets, how often have your auc- 61
tioned pains sustained us? Who will compute the lonely nights made
less lonely by your songs, or by the empty pots made less tragic by
your tales?

If we were a people much given to revealing secrets, we might raise 62
monuments and sacrifice to the memories of our poets, but slavery
cured us of that weakness. It may be enough, however, to have it said
that we survive in exact relationship to the dedication of our poets
(include preachers, musicians, and blues singers).

CONSIDERATIONS

1. What changes come over the student body as the time for graduation approaches? What phrases convey a special atmosphere? What changes
   come over Angelou in particular?
2. What details indicate the involvement of the entire black community in
   the student graduations? Does the selection seem to exaggerate the public
   importance of the event, or is the account entirely believable? Does Angelou as an eighth grader appear too impressionable to be storing up accurate memories?
3. What details in the narrative contribute to the suspense and the worry

that something might go wrong? What kind of a calamity are we led to anticipate?

4. How do you explain Angelou's immediate response to Donleavy's speech? Does it seem excessive?

5. In what sense is this graduation truly a "commencement" for Angelou? Make your answer detailed and explicit.

6. WRITING TOPIC. What roots in history and tradition affect your pride? Beyond your immediate family, the national, ethnic, and religious groups that comprise your background contribute personality models and stereotypes to your developing identity. In 700 words, explain the mixed positive and negative effects of a group identification that you experience. (Like Angelou, you may find that songs and other forms of entertainment, such as jokes, games, and stories, convey personal messages.)

John Cheever

EXPELLED

◇

JOHN CHEEVER (1912–1982) attended a prep school in Massachusetts and was expelled. The event launched his notable literary career, for he gave his view of the school in his first published story, the following selection, which was written when he was seventeen. During his adult life Cheever wrote television scripts and occasionally taught writing courses, but he devoted himself mainly to writing stories and novels, including such collections as *The Way Some People Live* (1943), *The Enormous Radio* (1953), and *The Housebreaker of Shady Hill* (1958). His best-known novels are *The Wapshot Chronicle* (1957) and *The Wapshot Scandal* (1964).

It didn't come all at once. It took a very long time. First I had a 1 skirmish with the English department and then all the other departments. Pretty soon something had to be done. The first signs were cordialities on the part of the headmaster. He was never nice to anybody unless he was a football star, or hadn't paid his tuition, or was going to be expelled. That's how I knew.

He called me down to his office with the carved chairs arranged in a 2 semicircle and the brocade curtains resting against the vacant windows. All about him were pictures of people who had got scholarships at Harvard. He asked me to sit down.

"Well, Charles," he said, "some of the teachers say you aren't get- 3 ting very good marks."

"Yes," I said, "that's true." I didn't care about the marks. 4

"But Charles," he said, "you know the scholastic standard of this 5 school is very high and we have to drop people when their work becomes unsatisfactory." I told him I knew that also. Then he said a lot of things about the traditions, and the elms, and the magnificent military heritage from our West Point founder.

175

It was very nice outside of his room. He had his window pushed 6
open halfway and one could see the lawns pulling down to the road
behind the trees and the bushes. The gravy-colored curtains were too
heavy to move about in the wind, but some papers shifted around on
his desk. In a little while I got up and walked out. He turned and
started to work again. I went back to my next class.

The next day was very brilliant and the peach branches were full 7
against the dry sky. I could hear people talking and a phonograph
playing. The sounds came through the peach blossoms and crossed
the room. I lay in bed and thought about a great many things. My
dreams had been thick. I remembered two converging hills, some dry
apple trees, and a broken blue egg cup. That is all I could remember.

I put on knickers and a soft sweater and headed toward school. My 8
hands shook on the wheel. I was like that all over.

Through the cloudy trees I could see the protrusion of the new 9
tower. It was going to be a beautiful new tower and it was going to
cost a great deal of money. Some thought of buying new books for the
library instead of putting up a tower, but no one would see the books.
People would be able to see the tower five miles off when the leaves
were off the trees. It would be done by fall.

When I went into the building the headmaster's secretary was 10
standing in the corridor. She was a nice sort of person with brown
funnels of hair furrowed about a round head. She smiled. I guess she
must have known.

The Colonel

Every morning we went up into the black chapel. The brisk head- 11
master was there. Sometimes he had a member of the faculty with
him. Sometimes it was a stranger.

He introduced the stranger, whose speech was always the same. In 12
the spring life is like a baseball game. In the fall it is like football. That
is what the speaker always said.

The hall is damp and ugly with skylights that rattle in the rain. The 13
seats are hard and you have to hold a hymnbook in your lap. The
hymnbook often slips off and that is embarrassing.

On Memorial Day they have the best speaker. They have a mayor 14 or a Governor. Sometimes they have a Governor's second. There is very little preference.

The Governor will tell us what a magnificent country we have. He will tell us to beware of the Red menace. He will want to tell us that the goddam foreigners should have gone home a hell of a long time ago. That they should have stayed in their own goddam countries if they didn't like ours. He will not dare say this though.

If they have a mayor the speech will be longer. He will tell us that our country is beautiful and young and strong. That the War is over, but that if there is another war we must fight. He will tell us that war is a masculine trait that has brought present civilization to its fine condition. Then he will leave us and help stout women place lilacs on graves. He will tell them the same thing.

One Memorial Day they could not get a Governor or a mayor. There was a colonel in the same village who had been to war and who had a chest thick with medals. They asked him to speak. Of course he said he would like to speak.

He was a thin colonel with a soft nose that rested quietly on his face. He was nervous and pushed his wedding ring about his thin finger. When he was introduced he looked at the audience sitting in the uncomfortable chairs. There was silence and the dropping of hymn-books like the water spouts in the aftermath of a heavy rain.

He spoke softly and quickly. He spoke of war and what he had seen. Then he had to stop. He stopped and looked at the boys. They were staring at their boots. He thought of the empty rooms in the other buildings. He thought of the rectangles of empty desks. He thought of the curtains on the stage and the four Windsor chairs behind him. Then he started to speak again.

He spoke as quickly as he could. He said war was bad. He said that there would never be another war. That he himself should stop it if he could. He swore. He looked at the young faces. They were all very clean. The boys' knees were crossed and their soft pants hung loosely. He thought of the empty desks and began to whimper.

The people sat very still. Some of them felt tight as though they wanted to giggle. Everybody looked serious as the clock struck. It was time for another class.

People began to talk about the colonel after lunch. They looked behind them. They were afraid he might hear them.

It took the school several weeks to get over all this. Nobody said 23
anything, but the colonel was never asked again. If they could not get
a Governor or a mayor they could get someone besides a colonel.
They made sure of that.

Margaret Courtwright

Margaret Courtwright was very nice. She was slightly bald and 24
pulled her pressed hair down across her forehead. People said that she
was the best English teacher in this part of the country, and when
boys came back from Harvard they thanked her for the preparation
she had given them. She did not like Edgar Guest, but she did like
Carl Sandburg. She couldn't seem to understand the similarity. When
I told her people laughed at Galsworthy she said that people used to
laugh at Wordsworth. She did not believe people were still laughing
at Wordsworth. That was what made her so nice.

She came from the West a long time ago. She taught school for so 25
long that people ceased to consider her age. After having seen twenty-
seven performances of "Hamlet" and after having taught it for sixteen
years, she became a sort of immortal. Her interpretation was the one
accepted on college-board papers. That helped everyone a great deal.
No one had to get a new interpretation.

When she asked me for tea I sat in a walnut armchair with grapes 26
carved on the head and traced and retraced the arms on the tea caddy.
One time I read her one of my plays. She thought it was wonderful.
She thought it was wonderful because she did not understand it and
because it took two hours to read. When I had finished, she said,
"You know that thing just took right hold of me. Really it just swept
me right along. I think it's fine that you like to write. I once had a Japanese pupil who liked to write. He was an awfully nice chap until one
summer he went down to Provincetown. When he came back he was
saying that he could express a complete abstraction. Fancy . . . a complete abstraction. Well, I wouldn't hear of it and told him how absurd
it all was and tried to start him off with Galsworthy again, but I guess
he had gone just too far. In a little while he left for New York and
then Paris. It was really too bad. One summer in Provincetown just
ruined him. His marks fell down . . . he cut classes to go to sym-
phony. . . ." She went into the kitchen and got a tray of tarts.

The pastries were flaky and covered with a white coating that made 27
them shine in the dead sunlight. I watched the red filling burst the
thin shells and stain the triangles of bright damask. The tarts were
good. I ate most of them.

She was afraid I would go the way of her Japanese pupil. She 28
doubted anyone who disagreed with Heine on Shakespeare and Croce
on expression.

One day she called me into her antiseptic office and spoke to me of 29
reading Joyce. "You know, Charles," she said, "this sex reality can be
quite as absurd as a hypercritical regard for such subjects. You know
that, don't you? Of course, you do." Then she went out of the room.
She had straight ankles and wore a gold band peppered with diamond
chips on her ring finger. She seemed incapable of carrying the weight
of the folds in her clothing. Her skirt was askew, either too long in
front or hitching up on the side. Always one thing or the other.

When I left school she did not like it. She was afraid I might go too 30
near Provincetown. She wished me good luck and moved the blotter
back and forth on her desk. Then she returned to teaching "Hamlet."

Late in February Laura Driscoll got fired for telling her history 31
pupils that Sacco and Vanzetti were innocent. In her farewell appearance the headmaster told everyone how sorry he was that she was
going and made it all quite convincing. Then Laura stood up, told
the headmaster that he was a damned liar, and waving her fan-spread
fingers called the school a hell of a dump where everyone got into
a rut.

Miss Courtwright sat closely in her chair and knew it was true. She 32
didn't mind much. Professor Rogers with his anti-feminization movement bothered her a little, too. But she knew that she had been
teaching school for a long time now and no movement was going to
put her out of a job overnight — what with all the boys she had
smuggled into Harvard and sixteen years of "Hamlet."

Laura Driscoll

History classes are always dead. This follows quite logically, for 33
history is a dead subject. It has not the death of dead fruit or dead
textiles or dead light. It has a different death. There is not the timeless
quality of death about it. It is dead like scenery in the opera. It is on

cracked canvas and the paint has faded and peeled and the lights are too bright. It is dead like old water in a zinc bathtub.

"We are going to study ancient history this year," the teacher will 34 tell the pupils. "Yes, ancient history will be our field.

"Now of course, this class is not a class of children any longer. I 35 expect the discipline to be the discipline of well bred young people. We shall not have to waste any time on the scolding of younger children. No. We shall just be able to spend all our time on ancient history.

"Now about questions. I shall answer questions if they are impor- 36 tant. If I do not think them important I shall not answer them, for the year is short, and we must cover a lot of ground in a short time. That is, if we all cooperate and behave and not ask too many questions we shall cover the subject and have enough time at the end of the year for review.

"You may be interested in the fact that a large percentage of this 37 class was certified last year. I should like to have a larger number this year. Just think, boys: wouldn't it be fine if a very large number — a number larger than last year — was certified? Wouldn't that be fine? Well, there's no reason why we can't do it if we all cooperate and behave and don't ask too many questions.

"You must remember that I have twelve people to worry about and 38 that you have only one. If each person will take care of his own work and pass in his notebook on time it will save me a lot of trouble. Time and trouble mean whether you get into college or not, and I want you all to get into college.

"If you will take care of your own little duties, doing what is as- 39 signed to you and doing it well, we shall all get along fine. You are a brilliant-looking group of young people, and I want to have you all certified. I want to get you into college with as little trouble as possible.

"Now about the books. . . ."   40

I do not know how long history classes have been like this. One 41 time or another I suppose history was alive. That was before it died its horrible fly-dappled unquivering death.

Everyone seems to know that history is dead. No one is alarmed. 42 The pupils and the teachers love dead history. They do not like it when it is alive. When Laura Driscoll dragged history into the class-

room, squirming and smelling of something bitter, they fired Laura
and strangled the history. It was too tumultuous. Too turbulent.

In history one's intellect is used for mechanical speculation on a 43
probable century or background. One's memory is applied to a list of
dead dates and names. When one begins to apply one's intellect to
the mental scope of the period, to the emotional development of its
inhabitants, one becomes dangerous. Laura Driscoll was terribly dangerous. That's why Laura was never a good history teacher.

She was not the first history teacher I had ever had. She is not the 44
last I will have. But she is the only teacher I have ever had who could
feel history with an emotional vibrance — or, if the person was too
oblique, with a poetic understanding. She was five feet four inches
tall, brown-haired, and bent-legged from horseback riding. All the
boys thought Laura Driscoll was a swell teacher.

She was the only history teacher I have ever seen who was often ec- 45
statical. She would stand by the boards and shout out her discoveries
on the Egyptian cultures. She made the gargoylic churnings of
Chartres in a heavy rain present an applicable meaning. She taught
history as an interminable flood of events viewed through the distortion of our own immediacy. She taught history in the broad-handed
rhythms of Hauptmann's drama, in the static melancholy of Egypt
moving before its own shadow down the long sand, in the fluted symmetry of the Doric culture. She taught history as a hypothesis from
which we could extract the evaluation of our own lives.

She was the only teacher who realized that, coming from the West, 46
she had little business to be teaching these children of New England.

"I do not know what your reaction to the sea is," she would say. 47
"For I have come from a land where there is no sea. My elements
are the fields, the sun, the plastic cadence of the clouds and the
cloudlessness. You have been brought up by the sea. You have
been coached in the cadence of the breakers and the strength of the
wind.

"My emotional viewpoints will differ from yours. Do not let me 48
impose my perceptions upon you."

However, the college-board people didn't care about Chartres as 49
long as you knew the date. They didn't care whether history was
looked at from the mountains or the sea. Laura spent too much time
on such trivia and all of her pupils didn't get into Harvard. In fact,

very few of her pupils got into Harvard, and this didn't speak well for her.

While the other members of the faculty chattered over Hepple- 50 white legs and Duncan Phyfe embellishments, Laura was before five-handed Siva or the sexless compassion glorious in its faded polychrome. Laura didn't think much of America. Laura made this obvious and the faculty heard about it. The faculty all thought America was beautiful. They didn't like people to disagree.

However, the consummation did not occur until late in February. 51 It was cold and clear and the snow was deep. Outside the windows there was the enormous roaring of broken ice. It was late in February that Laura Driscoll said Sacco and Vanzetti were undeserving of their treatment.

This got everyone all up in the air. Even the headmaster was dis- 52 concerted.

The faculty met.   53

The parents wrote letters.   54

Laura Driscoll was fired.   55

"Miss Driscoll," said the headmaster during her last chapel at the 56 school, "has found it necessary to return to the West. In the few months that we have had her with us, she has been a staunch friend of the academy, a woman whom we all admire and love and who, we are sure, loves and admires the academy and its elms as we do. We are all sorry Miss Driscoll is leaving us. . . ."

Then Laura got up, called him a damned liar, swore down the 57 length of the platform and walked out of the building.

No one ever saw Laura Driscoll again. By the way everyone talked, 58 no one wanted to. That was all late in February. By March the school was quiet again. The new history teacher taught dates. Everyone carefully forgot about Laura Driscoll.

"She was a nice girl," said the headmaster, "but she really wasn't 59 made for teaching history. . . . No, she really wasn't a born history teacher."

Five Months Later

The spring of five months ago was the most beautiful spring I have 60 ever lived in. The year before I had not known all about the trees and the heavy peach blossoms and the tea-colored brooks that shook down over the brown rocks. Five months ago it was spring and I was in school.

In school the white limbs beyond the study hall shook out a green- 61 ness, and the tennis courts became white and scalding. The air was empty and hard, and the vacant wind dragged shadows over the road. I knew all this only from the classrooms.

I knew about the trees from the window frames. I knew the rain 62 only from the sounds on the roof. I was tired of seeing spring with walls and awnings to intercept the sweet sun and the hard fruit. I wanted to go outdoors and see the spring. I wanted to feel and taste the air and be among the shadows. That is perhaps why I left school.

In the spring I was glad to leave school. Everything outside was 63 elegant and savage and fleshy. Everything inside was slow and cool and vacant. It seemed a shame to stay inside.

But in a little while the spring went. I was left outside and there 64 was no spring. I did not want to go in again. I would not have gone in again for anything. I was sorry, but I was not sorry over the fact that I had gone out. I was sorry that the outside and the inside could not have been open to one another. I was sorry that there were roofs on the classrooms and trousers on the legs of the instructors to insulate their contacts. I was not sorry that I had left school. I was sorry that I left for the reasons that I did.

If I had left because I had to go to work or because I was sick 65 it would not have been so bad. Leaving because you are angry and frustrated is different. It is not a good thing to do. It is bad for everyone.

Of course it was not the fault of the school. The headmaster and 66 faculty were doing what they were supposed to do. It was just a preparatory school trying to please the colleges. A school that was doing everything the colleges asked it to do.

It was not the fault of the school at all. It was the fault of the sys- 67 tem—the noneducational system, the college-preparatory system. That was what made the school so useless.

As a college-preparatory school it was a fine school. In five years 68 they could make raw material look like college material. They could clothe it and breed it and make it say the right things when the colleges asked it to talk. That was its duty.

They weren't prepared to educate anybody. They were members of 69
a college-preparatory system. No one around there wanted to be educated. No sir.

They presented the subjects the colleges required. They had math, 70
English, history, languages, and music. They once had had an art department but it had been dropped. "We have enough to do," said the
headmaster, "just to get all these people into college without trying to
teach them art. Yes sir, we have quite enough to do as it is."

Of course there were literary appreciation and art appreciation and 71
musical appreciation, but they didn't count for much. If you are
young, there is very little in Thackeray that is parallel to your own
world. Van Dyke's "Abbé Scaglia" and the fretwork of Mozart quar-
tets are not for the focus of your ears and eyes. All the literature and
art that holds a similarity to your life is forgotten. Some of it is even
forbidden.

Our country is the best country in the world. We are swimming in 72
prosperity and our President is the best president in the world. We
have larger apples and better cotton and faster and more beautiful
machines. This makes us the greatest country in the world. Unemployment is a myth. Dissatisfaction is a fable. In preparatory school
America is beautiful. It is the gem of the ocean and it is too bad. It is
bad because people believe it all. Because they become indifferent.
Because they marry and reproduce and vote and they know nothing.
Because the tempered newspaper keeps its eyes ceilingwards and does
not see the dirty floor. Because all they know is the tempered newspaper.

But I will not say any more. I do not stand in a place where I can 73
talk.

And now it is August. The orchards are stinking ripe. The tea- 74
colored brooks run beneath the rocks. There is sediment on the stone
and no wind in the willows. Everyone is preparing to go back to
school. I have no school to go back to.

I am not sorry. I am not at all glad. 75

It is strange to be so very young and to have no place to report to at 76
nine o'clock. That is what education has always been. It has been
laced curtseys and perfumed punctualities.

But now it is nothing. It is symmetric with my life. I am lost in it. 77
That is why I am not standing in a place where I can talk.

The school windows are being washed. The floors are thick with 78
fresh oil.

Soon it will be time for the snow and the symphonies. It will be 79
time for Brahms and the great dry winds.

CONSIDERATIONS

1. Describe Charles's manner of behaving and his manner of writing. Are they alike?
2. Why was the colonel an embarrassment to everyone, students and faculty, on Memorial Day? What did Charles think of him in contrast to the usual speakers?
3. In the sketch of the English teacher, what are some indications of her attitude toward ideas? What seems to be important to her?
4. Did Laura Driscoll teach *history*? What high school teacher of your own most closely resembles her in intellectual and moral attitudes? In professional status with other teachers and administrators?
5. Charles becomes fed up with school during "the most beautiful spring I have ever lived in." What bearing does nature have on his attitude and actions in school?
6. How does Charles feel five months later in midsummer? How does he foresee his future?
7. WRITING TOPIC. Does a school really do much to develop a student's identity? How? By imparting skills and knowledge? Ideas? Values? By aiding self-discipline? Social development? What is the most important thing that a school gives its students? In a 750-word essay, establish an order of importance for two or three things that a good school does for its students.

Maxine Hong Kingston

THE MISERY OF
SILENCE

◊

MAXINE HONG KINGSTON (b. 1940) grew up in a Chinese immigrant community in Stockton, California, where her parents ran a laundry. As a first-generation American, Kingston had to learn how to live in two distinctly contrasting societies. This was confusing and difficult for a five- to seven-year-old child, as she recalls in this selection from her autobiography, *The Woman Warrior: Memories of a Girlhood among Ghosts* (1976). The immigrants regarded all non-Chinese as "ghosts" — pale, insubstantial, and threatening. Kingston was graduated from the University of California at Berkeley. She now lives in Hawaii and teaches writing at the University of Hawaii. Her latest book is *China Men* (1980).

When I went to kindergarten and had to speak English for the first 1
time, I became silent. A dumbness — a shame — still cracks my voice in two, even when I want to say "hello" casually, or ask an easy question in front of the check-out counter, or ask directions of a bus driver. I stand frozen, or I hold up the line with the complete, grammatical sentence that comes squeaking out at impossible length. "What did you say?" says the cab driver, or "Speak up," so I have to perform again, only weaker the second time. A telephone call makes my throat bleed and takes up that day's courage. It spoils my day with self-disgust when I hear my broken voice come skittering out into the open. It makes people wince to hear it. I'm getting better, though. Recently I asked the postman for special-issue stamps; I've waited since childhood for postmen to give me some of their own accord. I am making progress, a little every day.

My silence was thickest — total — during the three years that I 2 covered my school paintings with black paint. I painted layers of black over houses and flowers and suns, and when I drew on the blackboard, I put a layer of chalk on top. I was making a stage curtain, and it was the moment before the curtain parted or rose. The teachers called my parents to school, and I saw they had been saving my pictures, curling and cracking, all alike and black. The teachers pointed to the pictures and looked serious, talked seriously too, but my parents did not understand English. ("The parents and teachers of criminals were executed," said my father.) My parents took the pictures home. I spread them out (so black and full of possibilities) and pretended the curtains were swinging open, flying up, one after another, sunlight underneath, mighty operas.

During the first silent year I spoke to no one at school, did not ask 3 before going to the lavatory, and flunked kindergarten. My sister also said nothing for three years, silent in the playground and silent at lunch. There were other quiet Chinese girls not of our family, but most of them got over it sooner than we did. I enjoyed the silence. At first it did not occur to me I was supposed to talk or to pass kindergarten. I talked at home and to one or two of the Chinese kids in class. I made motions and even made some jokes. I drank out of a toy saucer when the water spilled out of the cup, and everybody laughed, pointing at me, so I did it some more. I didn't know that Americans don't drink out of saucers.

I liked the Negro students (Black Ghosts) best because they 4 laughed the loudest and talked to me as if I were a daring talker too. One of the Negro girls had her mother coil braids over her ears Shanghai-style like mine; we were Shanghai twins except that she was covered with black like my paintings. Two Negro kids enrolled in Chinese school, and the teachers gave them Chinese names. Some Negro kids walked me to school and home, protecting me from the Japanese kids, who hit me and chased me and stuck gum in my ears. The Japanese kids were noisy and tough. They appeared one day in kindergarten, released from concentration camp, which was a tic-tac-toe mark, like barbed wire, on the map.

It was when I found out I had to talk that school became a misery, 5 that the silence became a misery. I did not speak and felt bad each time that I did not speak. I read aloud in first grade, though, and heard the barest whisper with little squeaks come out of my throat.

"Louder," said the teacher, who scared the voice away again. The other Chinese girls did not talk either, so I knew the silence had to do with being a Chinese girl.

Reading out loud was easier than speaking because we did not have to make up what to say, but I stopped often, and the teacher would think I'd gone quiet again. I could not understand "I." The Chinese "I" has seven strokes, intricacies. How could the American "I," assuredly wearing a hat like the Chinese, have only three strokes, the middle so straight? Was it out of politeness that this writer left off strokes the way a Chinese has to write her own name small and crooked? No, it was not politeness; "I" is a capital and "you" is lower-case. I stared at that middle line and waited so long for its black center to resolve into tight strokes and dots that I forgot to pronounce it. The other troublesome word was "here," no strong consonant to hang on to, and so flat, when "here" is two mountainous ideographs. The teacher, who had already told me every day how to read "I" and "here," put me in the low corner under the stairs again, where the noisy boys usually sat.

When my second grade class did a play, the whole class went to the auditorium except the Chinese girls. The teacher, lovely and Hawaiian, should have understood about us, but instead left us behind in the classroom. Our voices were too soft or nonexistent, and our parents never signed the permission slips anyway. They never signed anything unnecessary. We opened the door a crack and peeked out, but closed it again quickly. One of us (not me) won every spelling bee, though.

I remember telling the Hawaiian teacher, "We Chinese can't sing 'land where our fathers died.'" She argued with me about politics, while I meant because of curses. But how can I have that memory when I couldn't talk? My mother says that we, like the ghosts, have no memories.

After American school, we picked up our cigar boxes, in which we had arranged books, brushes, and an inkbox neatly, and went to Chinese school, from 5:00 to 7:30 P.M. There we chanted together, voices rising and falling, loud and soft, some boys shouting, everybody reading together, reciting together and not alone with one voice. When we had a memorization test, the teacher let each of us come to his desk and say the lesson to him privately, while the rest of the class practiced copying or tracing. Most of the teachers were men. The boys who were so well behaved in the American school played tricks on them and talked back to them. The girls were not mute. They screamed and yelled during recess, when there were no rules; they had fistfights. Nobody was afraid of children hurting themselves or of children hurting school property. The glass doors to the red and green balconies with the gold joy symbols were left wide open so that we could run out and climb the fire escapes. We played capture-the-flag in the auditorium, where Sun Yat-sen and Chiang Kai-shek's pictures hung at the back of the stage, the Chinese flag on their left and the American flag on their right. We climbed the teak ceremonial chairs and made flying leaps off the stage. One flag headquarters was behind the glass door and the other on stage right. Our feet drummed on the hollow stage. During recess the teachers locked themselves up in their office with the shelves of books, copybooks, inks from China. They drank tea and warmed their hands at a stove. There was no play supervision. At recess we had the school to ourselves, and also we could roam as far as we could go — downtown, Chinatown stores, home — as long as we returned before the bell rang.

At exactly 7:30 the teacher again picked up the brass bell that sat 10 on his desk and swung it over our heads, while we charged down the stairs, our cheering magnified in the stairwell. Nobody had to line up.

Not all of the children who were silent at American school found 11 voice at Chinese school. One new teacher said each of us had to get up and recite in front of the class, who was to listen. My sister and I had memorized the lesson perfectly. We said it to each other at home, one chanting, one listening. The teacher called on my sister to recite first. It was the first time a teacher had called on the second-born to go first. My sister was scared. She glanced at me and looked away; I looked down at my desk. I hoped that she could do it because if she could, then I would have to. She opened her mouth and a voice came out that wasn't a whisper, but it wasn't a proper voice either. I hoped that she would not cry, fear breaking up her voice like twigs underfoot. She sounded as if she were trying to sing though weeping and strangling. She did not pause or stop to end the embarrassment. She kept going until she said the last word, and then she sat down. When it was my turn, the same voice came out, a crippled animal running on broken legs. You could hear splinters in my voice, bones rubbing jagged against one another. I was loud, though. I was glad I didn't whisper.

How strange that the emigrant villagers are shouters, hollering face 12
to face. My father asks, "Why is it I can hear Chinese from blocks
away? Is it that I understand the language? Or is it they talk loud?"
They turn the radio up full blast to hear the operas, which do not
seem to hurt their ears. And they yell over the singers that wail over
the drums, everybody talking at once, big arm gestures, spit flying.
You can see the disgust on American faces looking at women like
that. It isn't just the loudness. It is the way Chinese sounds, ching-
chong ugly, to American ears, not beautiful like Japanese sayonara
words with the consonants and vowels as regular as Italian. We make
guttural peasant noise and have Ton Duc Thang names you can't remember. And the Chinese can't hear Americans at all; the language is
too soft and western music unhearable. I've watched a Chinese audience laugh, visit, talk-story, and holler during a piano recital, as if the
musician could not hear them. A Chinese-American, somebody's son,
was playing Chopin, which has no punctuation, no cymbals, no
gongs. Chinese piano music is five black keys. Normal Chinese
women's voices are strong and bossy. We American-Chinese girls had
to whisper to make ourselves American-feminine. Apparently we whispered even more softly than the Americans. Once a year the teachers
referred my sister and me to speech therapy, but our voices would
straighten out, unpredictably normal, for the therapists. Some of us
gave up, shook our heads, and said nothing, not one word. Some of us
could not even shake our heads. At times shaking my head no is more
self-assertion than I can manage. Most of us eventually found some
voice, however faltering. We invented an American-feminine speaking personality.

CONSIDERATIONS

1. What was the connection between Kingston's silence and her paintings?
   What did the paintings signify to *her*?
2. Why did the English pronouns "I" and "you" strike Kingston as unnatural? How do they differ from their Chinese equivalents? What looks
   wrong about the word "here"?
3. Kingston was obviously a "problem student" in class. If you had been her
   teacher, what might you have done? How might the problem have been

handled by a teacher like Edward Martin? (See "Being Junior High," p. 156.)

4. Does this account reinforce a stereotype of the Oriental woman? What does Kingston suggest that Chinese women are like when they are among Chinese?

5. In one paragraph, describe the "speaking personality" of a friend or relative. Try to give your reader a direct impression of the voice and manner of the speaker.

6. WRITING TOPIC. At the beginning of this selection, Kingston says that even today she has trouble speaking up in public situations. Does her style of writing indicate any hesitation or absence of assertiveness in using English for writing to the public? Is her language easy or hard to read? What is the tone of her voice? Write 500 words on Kingston's style in relation to her childhood experience.

James Agee

THREE SINGERS

◊

JAMES AGEE (1909–1955) was born in Knoxville, Tennessee, a place memorably evoked in his Pulitzer prize–winning, posthumous novel *A Death in the Family* (1957). He was graduated from Harvard, worked for *Fortune* magazine, and then wrote reviews of books and films for *Time* and *The Nation*. He was among the first reviewers to take a serious critical interest in films, and he wrote scripts for several movies, among them *The African Queen*. As a documentary journalist, Agee investigated the lives of white, tenant farmers in Alabama during the Depression years of the 1930s in *Let Us Now Praise Famous Men* (1941). With Walker Evans, who took photographs that are included in the book, Agee lived among the impoverished sharecroppers and came to know their experience close at hand. In this excerpt, he is drawn into the reinforcement of racism as it existed in daily life within that particular society at that time.

They came into the Coffee Shoppe while we were finishing break- 1
fast, and Harmon introduced the other, whose name I forget, but
which had a French sound. He was middle-sized and dark, beginning
to grizzle, with the knotty, walnut kind of body and a deeply cut, not
unkindly monkey's face. He wore dark trousers, a starched freshly
laundered white collarless shirt, and a soft yellow straw hat with a
band of flowered cloth. His shoes were old, freshly blacked, not polished; his suspenders were nearly new, blue, with gold lines at the
edge. He was courteous, casual, and even friendly, without much
showing the element of strain: Harmon let him do the talking and
watched us from behind the reflecting lenses of his glasses. People
in the street slowed as they passed and lingered their eyes upon us.
Walker said it would be all right to make pictures, wouldn't it, and
he said, Sure, of course, take all the snaps you're a mind to; that is, if

you can keep the niggers from running off when they see a camera. When they saw the amount of equipment stowed in the back of our car, they showed that they felt they had been taken advantage of, but said nothing of it.

Harmon drove out with Walker, I with the other, up a loose wide 2 clay road to the northwest of town in the high glittering dusty Sunday late morning heat of sunlight. The man I drove with made steady conversation, in part out of nervous courtesy, in part as if to forestall any questions I might ask him. I was glad enough of it; nearly all his tenants were negroes and no use to me, and I needed a rest from asking questions and decided merely to establish myself as even more easygoing, casual, and friendly than he was. It turned out that I had not been mistaken in the French sound of his name; ancestors of his had escaped an insurrection of negroes in Haiti. He himself, however, was entirely localized, a middling well-to-do landowner with a little more of the look of the direct farmer about him than the average. He was driving a several-years-old tan sedan, much the sort of car a factory worker in a northern city drives, and was pointing out to me how mean the cotton was on this man's land, who thought he could skimp by on a low grade of fertilizer, and how good it was along this pocket and high lift, that somehow caught whatever rain ran across this part of the country, though that was no advantage to cotton in a wet year or even an average; it was good in a drowt year like this one, though; his own cotton, except for a stretch of it along the bottom, he couldn't say yet it was going to do either very good or very bad; here we are at it, though.

A quarter of a mile back in a flat field of short cotton a grove of 3 oaks spumed up and a house stood in their shade. Beyond, as we approached, the land sank quietly away toward woods which ran tendrils along it, and was speckled near and far with nearly identical two-room shacks, perhaps a dozen, some in the part shade of chinaberry bushes, others bare to the brightness, all with the color in the sunlight and frail look of the tissue of hornets' nests. This nearest four-room house we were approaching was the foreman's. We drew up in the oak shade as the doors of this house filled. They were negroes. Walker and Harmon drew up behind us. A big iron ring hung by a chain from the low branch of an oak. A heavy strip of iron leaned at the base of the tree. Negroes appeared at the doors of the two nearest tenant houses. From the third house away, two of them were approaching. One was in clean overalls; the other wore black pants, a white shirt, and a black vest unbuttoned.

Here at the foreman's home we had caused an interruption that 4 filled me with regret: relatives were here from a distance, middle-aged and sober people in their Sunday clothes, and three or four visiting children, and I realized that they had been quietly enjoying themselves, the men out at the far side of the house, the women getting dinner, as now, by our arrival, they no longer could. The foreman was very courteous, the other men were non-committal, the eyes of the women were quietly and openly hostile; the landlord and the foreman were talking. The foreman's male guests hovered quietly and respectfully in silence on the outskirts of the talk until they were sure what they might properly do, then withdrew to the far side of the house, watching carefully to catch the landowner's eyes, should they be glanced after, so that they might nod, smile, and touch their foreheads, as in fact they did, before they disappeared. The two men from the third house came up; soon three more came, a man of forty and a narrow-skulled pair of sapling boys. They all approached softly and strangely until they stood within the shade of the grove, then stayed their ground as if floated, their eyes shifting upon us sidelong and to the ground and to the distance, speaking together very little, in quieted voices: it was as if they had been under some sort of magnetic obligation to approach just this closely and to show themselves. The landlord began to ask of them through the foreman, How's So-and-So doing, all laid by? Did he do that extra sweeping I told you? — and the foreman would answer, Yes sir, yes sir, he do what you say to do, he doin all right; and So-and-So shifted on his feet and smiled uneasily while, uneasily, one of his companions laughed and the others held their faces in the blank safety of deafness. And you, you ben doin much coltn lately, you horny old bastard? — and the crinkled, old, almost gray-mustached negro who came up tucked his head to one side looking cute, and showed what was left of his teeth, and whined, tittering, Now Mist So-and-So, you know I'm settled down, married-man, you wouldn't — and the brutal negro of forty split his face in a villainous grin and said, He too *ole*, Mist So-and-So, he don't got no sap lef in him; and everyone laughed, and the landowner said, These yer two yere, colts yourn ain't they — and the old man said they were, and the landowner said, Musta found *them* in the woods, strappin young niggers as that; and the old man said, No sir, he got the both of them lawful married, Mist So-and-So; and the landowner said that eldest on em looks to be ready for a piece himself, and the negroes laughed, and the two boys twisted their beautiful bald gourdlike skulls in a unison of shyness and their faces were illumined with maidenly smiles of shame, delight and fear; and meanwhile the landowner had loosened the top two buttons of his trousers, and he now reached his hand in to the middle of the forearm, and, squatting with bent knees apart, clawed, scratched, and rearranged his genitals.

By now three others stood in the outskirts who had been sent for by 5 a running child; they were young men, only twenty to thirty, yet very old and sedate; and their skin was of that sootiest black which no light can make shine and with which the teeth are blue and the eyeballs gold. They wore pressed trousers, washed shoes, brilliantly starched white shirts, bright ties, and carried newly whited straw hats in their hands, and at their hearts were pinned the purple and gilded ribbons of a religious and burial society. They had been summoned to sing for Walker and for me, to show us what nigger music is like (though we had done all we felt we were able to spare them and ourselves this summons), and they stood patiently in a stiff frieze in the oak shade, their hats and their shirts shedding light, and were waiting to be noticed and released, for they had been on their way to church when the child caught them; and now that they were looked at and the order given they stepped forward a few paces, not smiling, and stopped in rigid line, and, after a constricted exchange of glances among themselves, the eldest tapping the clean dirt with his shoe, they sang. It was as I had expected, not in the mellow and euphonious Fisk Quartette style, but in the style I have heard on records by Mitchell's Christian Singers, jagged, tortured, stony, accented as if by hammers and cold-chisels, full of a nearly paralyzing vitality and iteration of rhythm, the harmonies constantly splitting the nerves; so that of western music the nearest approach to its austerity is in the first two centuries of polyphony. But here it was entirely instinctual; it tore itself like a dance of sped plants out of three young men who stood sunk to their throats in land, and whose eyes were neither shut nor looking at anything; the screeching young tenor, the baritone, stridulant in the height of his register, his throat tight as a fist, and the bass, rolling the iron wheels of his machinery, his hand clenching and loosening as he tightened

and relaxed against the spraining of his ellipses: and they were
abruptly silent; totally wooden; while the landowner smiled coldly.
There was nothing to say. I looked them in the eyes with full and
open respect and said, that was fine. Have you got time to sing us another? Their heads and their glances collected toward a common center, and restored, and they sang us another, a slow one this time; I had
a feeling, through their silence before entering it, that it was their favorite and their particular pride; the tenor lifted out his voice alone in
a long, plorative* line that hung like fire on heaven, or whistle's echo,
sinking, sunken, along descents of a modality I had not heard before,
and sank along the arms and breast of the bass as might a body sunken
from a cross; and the baritone lifted a long black line of comment; and
they ran in a long and slow motion and convolution of rolling as at the
bottom of a stormy sea, voice meeting voice as ships in dream, re-
treated, met once more, much woven, digressions and returns of time,
quite tuneless, the bass, over and over, approaching, drooping, the
same declivity, the baritone taking over, a sort of metacenter, murmuring along monotones between major and minor, nor in any deter-
minable key, the tenor winding upward like a horn, a wire, the flight
of a bird, almost into full declamation, then failing it, silencing; at
length enlarging, the others lifting, now, alone, lone, and largely,
questioning, alone and not sustained, in the middle of space, stopped;
and now resumed, sunken upon the bosom of the bass, the head de-
clined; both muted, droned; the baritone makes his comment, unresolved, that is a question, all on one note: and they are quiet, and do
not look at us, nor at anything.

The landlord objected that that was too much howling and too 6
much religion on end and how about something with some life to it,
they knew what he meant, and then they could go.

They knew what he meant, but it was very hard for them to give it 7
just now. They stiffened in their bodies and hesitated, several seconds,
and looked at each other with eyes ruffled with worry; then the bass
nodded, as abruptly as a blow, and with blank faces they struck into a
fast, sassy, pelvic tune whose words were loaded almost beyond translation with comic sexual metaphor; a refrain song that ran like a rapid
wheel, with couplets to be invented, progressing the story; they sang it
through four of the probably three dozen tunes they knew, then bit

* Wailing, or pealing.

it off sharp and sharply, and for the first time, relaxed out of line, as if they knew they had earned the right, with it, to leave.

Meanwhile, and during all this singing, I had been sick in the 8 knowledge that they felt they were here at our demand, mine and Walker's, and that I could communicate nothing otherwise; and now, in a perversion of self-torture, I played my part through. I gave their leader fifty cents, trying at the same time, through my eyes, to communicate much more, and said I was sorry we had held them up and that I hoped they would not be late; and he thanked me for them in a dead voice, not looking me in the eye, and they went away, putting their white hats on their heads as they walked into the sunlight.

CONSIDERATIONS

1. In the first paragraph, what details establish the social context of rural poor whites?
2. In the middle of the third paragraph, as Agee is approaching the shacks, he notices people coming out to stand in their doorways. His next sentence is very short: "They were negroes." What is the effect of the shortness of that sentence? What does it tell us about his perception of them? How does it change the tone of the essay?
3. There is a great deal of sexual joking and innuendo reported in this account. What is Agee's attitude toward it?
4. Why does Agee give such a lengthy, detailed description of the religious songs that the black trio performed for him? What qualities does he find in the music and the singers?
5. At what moments in the essay does Agee want to react against the role that he accepts?
6. WRITING TOPIC. Anything that is called a "documentary" is likely to be suggestive and to appeal to our emotions more directly than to our intellect; that is, a documentary tries to give provocative evidence and yet avoid explicit interpretations and conclusive judgments. In a 500-word essay, analyze two or three illustrations of Agee's documentary method.

Desmond Morris

TERRITORIAL BEHAVIOR

◊

DESMOND MORRIS (b. 1928) is a British zoologist whose scientific research into animal behavior at Oxford University and as the curator of
mammals at the London Zoo stirs his interest in explaining predictable
patterns in human activity. In addition to his scholarly papers, he has
written best-selling books for the general reader, such as *The Naked
Ape* (1967), *The Human Zoo* (1970), *Intimate Behaviour* (1972), and
Manwatching (1977) from which this selection is taken. He seems to
see groups of people as if they are all in cages — which might be not
only true but also the safest place to be.

A territory is a defended space. In the broadest sense, there are 1
three kinds of human territory: tribal, family and personal.

It is rare for people to be driven to physical fighting in defense of 2
these "owned" spaces, but fight they will, if pushed to the limit. The
invading army encroaching on national territory, the gang moving
into a rival district, the trespasser climbing into an orchard, the bur-
glar breaking into a house, the bully pushing to the front of a queue,
the driver trying to steal a parking space, all of these intruders are liable to be met with resistance varying from the vigorous to the savagely violent. Even if the law is on the side of the intruder, the urge to
protect a territory may be so strong that otherwise peaceful citizens
abandon all their usual controls and inhibitions. Attempts to evict
families from their homes, no matter how socially valid the reasons,
can lead to siege conditions reminiscent of the defence of a medieval
fortress.

The fact that these upheavals are so rare is a measure of the success 3
of Territorial Signals as a system of dispute prevention. It is sometimes cynically stated that "all property is theft," but in reality it is

198

the opposite. Property, as owned space which is *displayed* as owned space, is a special kind of sharing system which reduces fighting much more than it causes it. Man is a co-operative species, but he is also competitive, and his struggle for dominance has to be structured in some way if chaos is to be avoided. The establishment of territorial rights is one such structure. It limits dominance geographically. I am dominant in my territory and you are dominant in yours. In other words, dominance is shared out spatially, and we all have some. Even if I am weak and unintelligent and you can dominate me when we meet on neutral ground, I can still enjoy a thoroughly dominant role as soon as I retreat to my private base. Be it ever so humble, there is no place like a home territory.

Of course, I can still be intimidated by a particularly dominant in- 4 dividual who enters my home base, but his encroachment will be dangerous for him and he will think twice about it, because he will know that here my urge to resist will be dramatically magnified and my usual subservience banished. Insulted at the heart of my own territory, I may easily explode into battle — either symbolic or real — with a result that may be damaging to both of us.

In order for this to work, each territory has to be plainly advertised 5 as such. Just as a dog cocks its leg to deposit its personal scent on the trees in its locality, so the human animal cocks its leg symbolically all over his home base. But because we are predominantly visual animals we employ mostly visual signals, and it is worth asking how we do this at the three levels: tribal, family, and personal.

First: the Tribal Territory. We evolved as tribal animals, living in 6 comparatively small groups, probably of less than a hundred, and we existed like that for millions of years. It is our basic social unit, a group in which everyone knows everyone else. Essentially, the tribal territory consisted of a home base surrounded by extended hunting grounds. Any neighboring tribe intruding on our social space would be repelled and driven away. As these early tribes swelled into agricultural super-tribes, and eventually into industrial nations, their territorial defence systems became increasingly elaborate. The tiny, ancient home base of the hunting tribe became the great capital city, the primitive warpaint became the flags, emblems, uniforms, and regalia of the specialized military, and the war-chants became national anthems, marching songs and bugle calls. Territorial boundary-lines hardened into fixed borders, often conspicuously patrolled and punctuated with defensive structures — forts and lookout posts, checkpoints and great walls, and, today, customs barriers.

Today each nation flies its own flag, a symbolic embodiment of its 7 territorial status. But patriotism is not enough. The ancient tribal hunter lurking inside each citizen finds himself unsatisfied by membership in such a vast conglomeration of individuals, most of whom are totally unknown to him personally. He does his best to feel that he shares a common territorial defense with them all, but the scale of the operation has become inhuman. It is hard to feel a sense of belonging with a tribe of fifty million or more. His answer is to form sub-groups, nearer to his ancient pattern, smaller and more personally known to him — the local club, the teenage gang, the union, the specialist society, the sports association, the political party, the college fraternity, the social clique, the protest group, and the rest. Rare indeed is the individual who does not belong to at least one of these splinter groups, and take from it a sense of tribal allegiance and brotherhood. Typical of all these groups is the development of Territorial Signals — badges, costumes, headquarters, banners, slogans, and all the other displays of group identity. This is where the action is, in terms of tribal territorialism, and only when a major war breaks out does the emphasis shift upwards to the higher group level of the nation.

Each of these modern pseudo-tribes sets up its own special kind of 8 home base. In extreme cases non-members are totally excluded, in others they are allowed in as visitors with limited rights and under a control system of special rules. In many ways they are like miniature nations, with their own flags and emblems and their own border guards. The exclusive club has its own "customs barrier": the doorman who checks your "passport" (your membership card) and prevents strangers from passing in unchallenged. There is a government: the club committee; and often special displays of the tribal elders: the photographs or portraits of previous officials on the walls. At the heart of the specialized territories there is a powerful feeling of security and importance, a sense of shared defense against the outside world. Much of the club chatter, both serious and joking, directs itself against the rottenness of everything outside the club boundaries — in that "other world" beyond the protected portals.

In social organizations which embody a strong class system, such as 9 military units and large business concerns, there are many territorial rules, often unspoken, which interfere with the official hierarchy. High-status individuals, such as officers or managers, could in theory enter any of the regions occupied by the lower levels in the peck order, but they limit this power in a striking way. An officer seldom enters a sergeant's mess or a barrack room unless it is for a formal inspection. He respects those regions as alien territories even though he has the power to go there by virtue of his dominant role. And in businesses, part of the appeal of unions, over and above their obvious functions, is that with their officials, headquarters, and meetings they add a sense of territorial power for the staff workers. It is almost as if each military organization and business concern consists of two warring tribes: the officers versus the other ranks, and the management versus the workers. Each has its special home base within the system, and the territorial defence pattern thrusts itself into what, on the surface, is a pure social hierarchy. Negotiations between managements and unions are tribal battles fought out over the neutral ground of a boardroom table, and are as much concerned with territorial display as they are with resolving problems of wages and conditions. Indeed, if one side gives in too quickly and accepts the other's demands, the victors feel strangely cheated and deeply suspicious that it may be a trick. What they are missing is the protracted sequence of ritual and counter-ritual that keeps alive their group territorial identity.

Likewise, many of the hostile displays of sports fans and teenage 10 gangs are primarily concerned with displaying their group image to rival fan-clubs and gangs. Except in rare cases, they do not attack one another's headquarters, drive out the occupants, and reduce them to a submissive, subordinate condition. It is enough to have scuffles on the borderlands between the two rival territories. This is particularly clear at football matches, where the fan-club headquarters becomes temporarily shifted from the club-house to a section of the stands, and where minor fighting breaks out at the unofficial boundary line between the massed groups of rival supporters. Newspaper reports play up the few accidents and injuries which do occur on such occasions, but when these are studied in relation to the total numbers of displaying fans involved it is clear that the serious incidents represent only a tiny fraction of the overall group behavior. For every actual punch or kick there are a thousand war-cries, war-dances, chants, and gestures.

Second: The Family Territory. Essentially, the family is a breeding 11 unit and the family territory is a breeding ground. At the center of this space, there is the nest — the bedroom — where, tucked up in bed, we feel at our most territorially secure. In a typical house the bedroom is upstairs, where a safe nest should be. This puts it farther away from the entrance hall, the area where contact is made, intermittently, with the outside world. The less private reception rooms, where intruders are allowed access, are the next line of defense. Beyond them, outside the walls of the building, there is often a symbolic remnant of the ancient feeding grounds — a garden. Its symbolism often extends to the plants and animals it contains, which cease to be nutritional and become merely decorative — flowers and pets. But like a true territorial space it has a conspicuously displayed boundary-line, the garden fence, wall, or railings. Often no more than a token barrier, this is the outer territorial demarcation, separating the private world of the family from the public world beyond. To cross it puts any visitor or intruder at an immediate disadvantage. As he crosses the threshold, his dominance wanes, slightly but unmistakably. He is entering an area where he senses that he must ask permission to do simple things that he would consider a right elsewhere. Without lifting a finger, the territorial owners exert their dominance. This is done by all the hundreds of small ownership "markers" they have deposited on their family territory: the ornaments, the "possessed" objects positioned in the rooms and on the walls; the furnishings, the furniture, the colors, the patterns, all owner-chosen and all making this particular home base unique to them.

It is one of the tragedies of modern architecture that there has been 12 a standardization of these vital territorial living units. One of the most important aspects of a home is that it should be similar to other homes only in a general way, and that in detail it should have many differences, making it a *particular* home. Unfortunately, it is cheaper to build a row of houses, or a block of flats, so that all the family living-units are identical, but the territorial urge rebels against this trend and house-owners struggle as best they can to make their mark on their mass-produced properties. They do this with garden-design, with front-door colors, with curtain patterns, with wallpaper and all the other decorative elements that together create a unique and different family environment. Only when they have completed this nest-building do they feel truly "at home" and secure.

When they venture forth as a family unit they repeat the process in 13 a minor way. On a day-trip to the seaside, they load the car with personal belongings and it becomes their temporary, portable territory. Arriving at the beach they stake out a small territorial claim, marking it with rugs, towels, baskets, and other belongings to which they can return from their seaboard wanderings. Even if they all leave it at once to bathe, it retains a characteristic territorial quality and other family groups arriving will recognize this by setting up their own "home" bases at a respectful distance. Only when the whole beach has filled up with these marked spaces will newcomers start to position themselves in such a way that the inter-base distance becomes reduced. Forced to pitch between several existing beach territories they will feel a momentary sensation of intrusion, and the established "owners" will feel a similar sensation of invasion, even though they are not being directly inconvenienced.

The same territorial scene is being played out in parks and fields 14 and on riverbanks, wherever family groups gather in their clustered units. But if rivalry for spaces creates mild feelings of hostility, it is true to say that, without the territorial system of sharing and space-limited dominance, there would be chaotic disorder.

Third: the Personal Space. If a man enters a waiting-room and sits 15 at one end of a long row of empty chairs, it is possible to predict where the next man to enter will seat himself. He will not sit next to the first man, nor will he sit at the far end, right away from him. He will choose a position about halfway between these two points. The next man to enter will take the largest gap left, and sit roughly in the middle of that, and so on, until eventually the latest newcomer will be forced to select a seat that places him right next to one of the already seated men. Similar patterns can be observed in cinemas, public urinals, airplanes, trains, and buses. This is a reflection of the fact that we all carry with us, everywhere we go, a portable territory called a Personal Space. If people move inside this space, we feel threatened. If they keep too far outside it, we feel rejected. The result is a subtle series of spatial adjustments, usually operating quite unconsciously and producing ideal compromises as far as this is possible. If a situation becomes too crowded, then we adjust our reactions accordingly and allow our personal space to shrink. Jammed into an elevator, a rush-hour compartment, or a packed room, we give up altogether and allow body-to-body contact, but when we relinquish our Personal Space in this way, we adopt certain special techniques. In essence, what we do is to convert these other bodies into "nonpersons." We studiously ignore them, and they us. We try not to face them if we can possibly avoid it. We wipe all expressiveness from our faces, letting them go blank. We may look up at the ceiling or down at the floor, and we reduce body movements to a minimum. Packed together like sardines in a tin, we stand dumbly still, sending out as few social signals as possible.

Even if the crowding is less severe, we still tend to cut down our social interactions in the presence of large numbers. Careful observations of children in play groups revealed that if they are high-density groupings there is less social interaction between the individual children, even though there is theoretically more opportunity for such contacts. At the same time, the high-density groups show a higher frequency of aggressive and destructive behavior patterns in their play. Personal Space — "elbow room" — is a vital commodity for the human animal, and one that cannot be ignored without risking serious trouble. 16

Of course, we all enjoy the excitement of being in a crowd, and this reaction cannot be ignored. But there are crowds and crowds. It is pleasant enough to be in a "spectator crowd," but not so appealing to find yourself in the middle of a rush-hour crush. The difference between the two is that the spectator crowd is all facing in the same direction and concentrating on a distant point of interest. Attending a theatre, there are twinges of rising hostility toward the stranger who sits down immediately in front of you or the one who squeezes into the seat next to you. The shared armrest can become a polite, but distinct, territorial boundary-dispute region. However, as soon as the show begins, these invasions of Personal Space are forgotten and the attention is focused beyond the small space where the crowding is taking place. Now, each member of the audience feels himself spatially related, not to his cramped neighbors, but to the actor on the stage, and this distance is, if anything, too great. In the rush-hour crowd, by contrast, each member of the pushing throng is competing with his neighbors all the time. There is no escape to a spatial relation with a distant actor, only the pushing, shoving bodies all around. 17

Those of us who have to spend a great deal of time in crowded conditions become gradually better able to adjust, but no one can ever become completely immune to invasions of Personal Space. This is because they remain forever associated with either powerful hostile or equally powerful loving feelings. All through our childhood we will 18 have been held to be loved and held to be hurt, and anyone who invades our Personal Space when we are adults is, in effect, threatening to extend his behavior into one of these two highly charged areas of human interaction. Even if his motives are clearly neither hostile nor sexual, we still find it hard to suppress our reactions to his close approach. Unfortunately, different countries have different ideas about exactly how close is close. It is easy enough to test your own "space reaction": when you are talking to someone in the street or in any open space, reach out with your arm and see where the nearest point on his body comes. If you hail from western Europe, you will find that he is at roughly fingertip distance from you. In other words, as you reach out, your fingertips will just about make contact with his shoulder. If you come from eastern Europe you will find you are standing at "wrist distance." If you come from the Mediterranean region you will find that you are much closer to your companion, at little more than "elbow distance."

Trouble begins when a member of one of these cultures meets and 19 talks to one from another. Say a British diplomat meets an Italian or an Arab diplomat at an embassy function. They start talking in a friendly way, but soon the fingertips man begins to feel uneasy. Without knowing quite why, he starts to back away gently from his companion. The companion edges forward again. Each tries in his way to set up a Personal Space relationship that suits his own background. But it is impossible to do. Every time the Mediterranean diplomat advances to a distance that feels comfortable for him, the British diplomat feels threatened. Every time the Briton moves back, the other feels rejected. Attempts to adjust this situation often lead to a talking pair shifting slowly across a room, and many an embassy reception is dotted with western-European fingertip-distance men pinned against the walls by eager elbow-distance men. Until such differences are fully understood and allowances made, these minor differences in "body territories" will continue to act as an alienation factor which may interfere in a subtle way with diplomatic harmony and other forms of international transaction.

If there are distance problems when engaged in conversation, then 20 there are clearly going to be even bigger difficulties where people must work privately in a shared space. Close proximity of others, pressing against the invisible boundaries of our personal body-territory, makes it difficult to concentrate on non-social matters. Flat-mates, students sharing a study, sailors in the cramped quarters of a ship, and office staff in crowded work-places, all have to face this problem. They solve it by "cocooning." They use a variety of devices to shut themselves off from the others present. The best possible cocoon, of course, is a small private room — a den, a private office, a study, or a studio — which physically obscures the presence of other nearby territory-owners. This is the ideal situation for non-social work, but the space-sharers cannot enjoy this luxury. Their cocooning must be symbolic. They may, in certain cases, be able to erect small physical barriers, such as screens and partitions, which give substance to their invisible Personal Space boundaries, but when this cannot be done, other means must be sought. One of these is the "favored object." Each space-sharer develops a preference, repeatedly expressed until it becomes a fixed pattern, for a particular chair, or table, or alcove. Others come to respect this, and friction is reduced. This system is often formally arranged (this is my desk, that is yours), but even where it is not, favored places soon develop. Professor Smith has a favorite chair in the library. It is not formally his, but he always uses it and others avoid it. Seats around a mess-room table, or a boardroom table, become almost personal property for specific individuals. Even in the home, father has his favorite chair for reading the newspaper or watching television. Another device is the blinkers-posture. Just as a horse that over-reacts to other horses and the distractions of the noisy race-course is given a pair of blinkers to shield its eyes, so people studying privately in a public place put on pseudo-blinkers in the form of shielding hands. Resting their elbows on the table, they sit with their hands screening their eyes from the scene on either side.

A third method of reinforcing the body-territory is to use personal markers. Books, papers, and other personal belongings are scattered around the favored site to render it more privately owned in the eyes of companions. Spreading out one's belongings is a well-known trick in public-transport situations, where a traveller tries to give the impression that seats next to him are taken. In many contexts carefully arranged personal markers can act as an effective territorial display, even in the absence of the territory owner. Experiments in a library revealed that placing a pile of magazines on the table in one seating position successfully reserved that place for an average of 77 minutes. If a sports-jacket was added, draped over the chair, then the "reservation effect" lasted for over two hours.

In these ways, we strengthen the defences of our Personal Spaces, 22 keeping out intruders with the minimum of open hostility. As with all territorital behavior, the object is to defend space with signals rather than with fists and at all three levels — the tribal, the family, and the personal — it is a remarkably efficient system of space-sharing. It does not always seem so, because newspapers and newscasts inevitably magnify the exceptions and dwell on those cases where the signals have failed and wars have broken out, gangs have fought, neighboring families have feuded, or colleagues have clashed, but for every territorial signal that has failed, there are millions of others that have not. They do not rate a mention in the news, but they nevertheless constitute a dominant feature of human society — the society of a remarkably territorial animal.

CONSIDERATIONS

1. How does Morris view human beings in relation to other animals? What are the key words and phrases in the first five paragraphs that indicate his perspective on human actions?
2. What is the main purpose of displaying "Territorial Signals"? Do you accept his explanation as it applies to human behavior?
3. What are the most often used, main signals for indicating each of the three types of territorial behavior?
4. To what type of territorial behavior does Morris give his fullest attention? Does this emphasis make his points easier or harder to confirm?
5. What explanation would Morris give for the phenomenon of "touristic shame" that MacCannell mentions in "The Tourist," p. 153?
6. Does Morris define territorial behavior as sociable or antisocial? Do his examples adequately support his general point?
7. WRITING TOPIC. Writing as an observer of territorial behavior, analyze in 500 words the events at a freshman mixer, or at the first dorm meeting of the year, or at a large wedding reception, or during an overnight delay you experienced at an airport, or any similar assembly of strangers in partly unallocated spaces.

Sylvia Plath

MUSHROOMS

◊

Sylvia Plath (1932–1963) developed the art of expressing both love and anger sardonically in her poetry, which often treats painful subjects with grotesque, biting humor. She made two suicide attempts before she took her life at the age of thirty. Yet, outwardly, her experience seemed ordinary and reasonably happy, as she progressed through public schools in Massachusetts and went on to Smith College where she earned honors and wrote poems and fiction. She married and had two children. Most of her work was published posthumously, including the poems in *Ariel* (1965). In this poem Plath finds surprisingly human characteristics in the way mushrooms seem to spring up overnight.

Overnight, very
Whitely, discreetly,
Very quietly

Our toes, our noses
Take hold on the loam,
Acquire the air.

Nobody sees us,
Stops us, betrays us;
The small grains make room.

Soft fists insist on   10
Heaving the needles,
The leafy bedding,

Even the paving.
Our hammers, our rams,
Earless and eyeless,

Perfectly voiceless,
Widen the crannies,
Shoulder through holes. We

Diet on water,
On crumbs of shadow,   20
Bland-mannered, asking

Little or nothing.
So many of us!
So many of us!

We are shelves, we are
Tables, we are meek,
We are edible,

Nudgers and shovers
In spite of ourselves.
Our kind multiplies: 30

We shall by morning
Inherit the earth.
Our foot's in the door.

CONSIDERATIONS

1. What are the verbs that indicate the actions of the mushrooms? What personal characteristics of mushrooms do they suggest?
2. What is the appearance of the mushrooms? How does it contrast with their actions?
3. What kind of people are implied by the biblical reference in the next-to-last line? Has this personification of the mushrooms been suggested earlier in the poem?
4. Why does Plath speak in a first-person voice as if she is one of the mushrooms? What effect does this method have on the reader's response?
5. Do you think that this poem implies a political outlook, or would such an interpretation narrow down Plath's point about people?

6. WRITING TOPIC. In approximately 200 words, portray a certain group or kind of people by describing them as vegetables, perhaps in stages of growing, decaying, or in use. Use active verbs as well as adjectives and adverbs to indicate their vital characteristics. Once you have your people and vegetable in mind, concentrate on the vegetable in order to find the right words to describe the people.

Alexis de Tocqueville

ARISTOCRACY AND DEMOCRACY

◊

ALEXIS DE TOCQUEVILLE (1805–1859) was raised in a liberal-minded, aristocratic family that had narrowly escaped destruction during the reign of terror in the French Revolution. He prepared for a career as a jurist, but as a young man in his twenties he was far more interested in political and social theorizing than in arguing or hearing legal cases. He was sent to America in 1831 to survey the penal system, and he made use of the opportunity to develop his ideas about society. Upon his return to France he wrote *Democracy in America* (1835) from which this selection is taken. Tocqueville saw the absolute power of the old French monarchy and the potential for mob rule in the new American democracy as comparable dangers to the practice of freedom.

Among aristocratic nations families maintain the same station for 1 centuries and often live in the same place. So there is a sense in which all the generations are contemporaneous. A man almost always knows about his ancestors and respects them; his imagination extends to his great-grandchildren, and he loves them. He freely does his duty by both ancestors and descendants and often sacrifices personal pleasures for the sake of beings who are no longer alive or are not yet born.

Moreover, aristocratic institutions have the effect of linking each 2 man closely with several of his fellows.

Each class in an aristocratic society, being clearly and permanently 3 limited, forms, in a sense, a little fatherland for all its members, to which they are attached by more obvious and more precious ties than those linking them to the fatherland itself.

Each citizen of an aristocratic society has his fixed station, one 4 above another, so that there is always someone above him whose protection he needs and someone below him whose help he may require.

So people living in an aristocratic age are almost always closely in- 5 volved with something outside themselves, and they are often inclined to forget about themselves. It is true that in these ages the general conception of *human fellowship* is dim and that men hardly ever think of devoting themselves to the cause of humanity, but men do often make sacrifices for the sake of certain other men.

In democratic ages, on the contrary, the duties of each to all are 6 much clearer but devoted service to any individual much rarer. The bonds of human affection are wider but more relaxed.

Among democratic peoples new families continually rise from 7 nothing while others fall, and nobody's position is quite stable. The woof of time is ever being broken and the track of past generations lost. Those who have gone before are easily forgotten, and no one gives a thought to those who will follow. All a man's interests are limited to those near himself.

As each class catches up with the next and gets mixed with it, its 8 members do not care about one another and treat one another as strangers. Aristocracy links everybody, from peasant to king, in one long chain. Democracy breaks the chain and frees each link.

As social equality spreads there are more and more people who, 9 though neither rich nor powerful enough to have much hold over others, have gained or kept enough wealth and enough understanding to look after their own needs. Such folk owe no man anything and hardly expect anything from anybody. They form the habit of thinking of themselves in isolation and imagine that their whole destiny is in their own hands.

Thus, not only does democracy make men forget their ancestors, 10 but also clouds their view of their descendants and isolates them from their contemporaries. Each man is forever thrown back on himself alone, and there is danger that he may be shut up in the solitude of his own heart.

CONSIDERATIONS

1. According to Tocqueville, what social bonds are formed in a hereditary aristocracy? How are the lower classes included?

2. What is the chief weakness that he sees in democracy? Restate his criticism in your own words.
3. Tocqueville's views are not derived from examples. Can you refute or confirm his deductions by offering examples of social bonds in democratic life?
4. WRITING TOPIC. Tocqueville's views were formed 150 years ago. As one of the present-day descendants of the democrats he observed, write a 700-word letter to Tocqueville bringing him up to date on the American character. Focus on one or two traits that are visible in both society and the individual.

IMAGES

Peter Vandermark, Junior High School.

Robert Frank, Cocktail Party — New York City.

Elinor B. Cohn, Celebration of Friendship: Boy Scout
Camporee Awards Presentation, Baltimore, 1979.

Elinor B. Cohn, Polish-American War Mothers,
St. Casimir's Church, Baltimore, *1979*.

ADDITIONAL
WRITING TOPICS

◊

GROUP PICTURES

1. Part of the fun of spectator sports is in being part of the crowd of spectators. There are customs associated with attending certain sports that
amount to another set of "the rules of the game" for the fans who are
present. A crowd at a hockey game, for instance, behaves differently from
a crowd watching a marathon race. Crowds in a football stadium are different from crowds in baseball parks. Fans at a track meet adopt a different style when they go to basketball games. People's individual behavior
changes as the crowd differs from sport to sport. Write a 500-word essay
that gives instruction on the sport of "spectatoring." Explain the appropriate actions for a member of the crowd at a particular sports event. Or, you
may want to contrast spectator styles for two different sports.

2. In the photograph on page 215, a conversation at a cocktail party reveals
complicated social behavior. What roles does each woman adopt? What
personal responses are communicated by their expressions? What varied
social positions and occupations are suggested by the clothes and by the
arrangement of the group? Why aren't the men inclined slightly forward,
as the women are? In a 500-word essay, interpret the personalities and
their interactions at this moment, as if you were explaining this photograph to your associates in a detective or intelligence agency.

3. Young people in school often devise special ways of talking with members
of their clique or set. Their lingo identifies them as a separate group, and
often the language they speak seems to give individuals a certain distinction or flair that distinguishes them. Writing as an observer or as a member of such a group, analyze its lingo in a 700-word essay. Give samples of
the vocabulary, and explain the usages and describe the inflections or into-
nations of three or four key words. Try to illustrate your points with bits of
dialogue, if useful.

4. What groups do children like to pretend they are part of? When children
play-act adult roles, they imagine themselves as part of some easily recog-
nizable group; they seldom pick solitary roles for themselves. "Cowboys
and Indians" used to be popular, but probably it is not played any longer,

218

and only people well over thirty would remember it. Younger adults and present-day children grow up creating different imaginary groups. Drawing on your recollections or your direct observations of children at play, in a 500-word essay define one or two social types that children play-act. Where do the roles come from? What sort of games do children play in these roles?

5. Being ashamed of one's parents for one reason or another is part of almost everyone's experience for a time. What was it about your parents, either one or both of them, that caused you embarrassment or shame for a while? What group or standard did they fail to measure up to? In whose eyes (in addition to your own) did you think that they looked bad? How did you express your embarrassment toward them, and how did they react to your behavior? If you can discuss this difficult, and probably troubling, subject with some sympathy now for all the people involved (including yourself at the time), write a 750-word essay on your social embarrassment over your parents. To what extent were you perhaps struggling with social allegiances outside your family?

6. Compare the lyrics of two patriotic songs that generate pride in being an American. "America The Beautiful" and "The Star-Spangled Banner," for instance, express attitudes about the country and its history that make us proud of our national identity. These and other patriotic songs — such as "America," "The Battle Hymn of the Republic," "Yankee Doodle," and "Dixie" — include references to burdens and weaknesses that help to bond people together and give them pride in unity against dangers. In a 500-word essay, explain what sources of group pride and peril are celebrated in two patriotic songs.

7. The photographs on pages 216 and 217 were taken by the same photographer, who has a particular interest in group pictures. Many contrasts between the two subjects are evident. But what are the not so obvious similarities that these photographs reveal? Consider the differences and similarities in the clothing, the occasions, the arrangement of people, the objects included, and the suggestions about the origins and purposes of such groups. In an essay of 500 to 700 words, compare and contrast the photographs as the work of one photographer who sees special meaning in group pictures.

4

POSSESSIONS

INSIGHTS

A man is rich in proportion to the number of things which he can afford to let alone.

— HENRY DAVID THOREAU

I call people rich when they're able to meet the requirements of their imagination.

— HENRY JAMES

It is easier for a camel to go through the eye of a needle, than for a rich man to enter into the kingdom of God.

— MATTHEW 19:24

William Ryan

MINE, ALL MINE

◊

WILLIAM RYAN (b. 1923) is a professor of psychology at Boston College. His special interest in the psychological stresses of modern American life is reflected in his earlier books, *Distress in the City* (1969) and *Blaming the Victim* (1971). This selection is from *Equality* (1981), in which Ryan argues that the concept of property ownership and the amassing of great wealth are linked to insecurities over individual identity.

How do you get to own something? Well, you usually buy it. But 1 how did the fellow you bought it from get to own it? Where did the idea of *owning* come from? Or was it always there, perhaps in the mind of God?

No one really knows, of course. The idea of owning and property 2 emerged in the mists of unrecorded history. One can try to imagine the scene. Some Cro-Magnon innovator, seized with a fit of entrepreneurial passion, took his club and drew a line in the earth and called out, "Okay, you guys! Everything inside this line is mine. It belongs to me. I own it." Now, very likely, this first would-be landowner was a skinny, little, near-sighted Cro-Magnon who couldn't throw a spear straight and was able to drag by the hair only the homeliest girls of the tribe. A couple of his fellow cavemen may have kicked sand in his face, but most of the others probably laughed indulgently, kidding him about his intellectual pretensions, his ways of using big words like "belong" and "own" that nobody else knew the meaning of. "That Herman! A regular walking dictionary!" And they rubbed out Herman's line on the ground. (I am counting on a fair amount of good humor among the Cro-Magnons; another telling of the story might assume more malevolence and end with their rubbing out Herman himself.)

But, as we all know, a good idea never dies, and sooner or later a   3
hefty, well-respected caveman who carried a big club picked up Herman's notion, drew his own line in the earth, and made his claim
stick. Others drew their lines, taking possession of the land merely by
outlining its boundaries, and then talked about what they owned and
what belonged to them. The forcible seizure of what had been until
then common property, if property at all, led first to emulation, as
others also seized portions of land, and ultimately to the development
of ideas and relationships that could be thought to coincide with the
new reality. Rather than having men who had the muscle power to
seize and men who had not, we had landowners and the landless; instead of loot from the seizure, we had "property," then property laws
by the chapter, and finally the revelation that the institution of private
property had been ordained by God. These concepts — landowner,
property, and property rights — became common currency, unquestioned and unquestionable ideas, as natural and expected as the sun-
rise or as water flowing downhill, which we take for granted and don't
give another thought. And that is the central nature of ideology.

If you do stop and think about it, it's quite remarkable. An individ-   4
ual human being, occupying a blip on the screen of time, has the incredible gall to stand up and say, "*I* own this land; this land is *mine*."
He's talking about an acre or a hundred acres of the *earth*, a piece of
the *planet*! And he says it's *his*! Isn't that really an incredible claim to
make?

And he doesn't just say he owns the earth, he also says that he owns   5
what comes out of it and what is buried beneath it. The owner of the
land lays claim to the grain and the grass that spring up from it and to
the cattle that feed on the grain and the grass. He lays claim to the oil
and the iron that lie beneath the ground and then to the steel made
from the iron and to the automobile made from the steel and to the
gasoline made from the oil. He counts as his property the tree that
grows on the land and the wood of the tree and the buildings on the
land made from the wood. He *owns* those things, he says; they *belong*
to him. And we all act as if it were true, so it must be true. But behind
all these claims, supporting and upholding them — and our willingness to believe them — is the big club of the hefty Cro-Magnon who
made the first claim and dared his fellows to oppose him. The club is
smaller and neater now, hanging from the belt of the policeman, but
the principle remains the same.

Is it possible that the ideas we have today about ownership and property rights have been so universal in the human mind that it is truly as if they had sprung from the mind of God? By no means. The ancient Jews, for one, had a very different outlook on property and ownership, viewing it as something much more temporary and tentative than we do. Mosaic law with respect to ownership of land (the only significant productive property of the time) is unambiguous:

> And the land shall not be sold in perpetuity; for the land is Mine; for ye are strangers and settlers with Me. And in all the land of your possession ye shall grant a redemption for the land. (Lev. 25:23–24)

The buying and selling of land was based on principles very different from those we know. It was not, in fact, the land itself that changed hands, but rather the right to use the land to cultivate crops. The price of the land was determined by the number of years, and therefore the number of crops, remaining until the next jubilee year, when the land reverted to the family that originally possessed it. Under such a law, buying land is similar to the process we call leasing.

The institution of the jubilee year was a specific mechanism for rectifying the inequities that had accumulated, for simultaneously restoring liberty *and* equality for all:

> And ye shall hallow the fiftieth year, and proclaim liberty throughout the land unto all the inhabitants thereof; it shall be a jubilee unto you; and ye shall return every man unto his possession, and ye shall return every man unto his family. (Lev. 25:10)

There is no doubt that these laws were violated. Prophet after prophet condemned as violations efforts to accumulate wealth unjustly:

> Woe unto them that join house to house, that lay field to field, till there be no place, that they may be placed alone in the midst of the earth! (Isaiah, 5:8)

But that the law was violated and the violation condemned is a demonstration of its existence and applicability. Although the law of jubilee was evaded more and more and ultimately fell into disuse, there can be no doubt that it was adhered to for many generations.

Similarly, the tenure of land in the agrarian feudal ages was hedged all about with restrictions and accompanied by specific obligations that the landowner owed to his tenants. These restrictions and obligations, too, were frequently evaded and violated — perhaps more often than they were honored — but they were unquestionably part of the structure of law and custom until the dawn of the modern era, when the very idea of land began to change and when land began to be equated with capital, as the new commercial classes began to impose their own view of private property as something with which one could do more or less what one pleased.

A bit later, Europeans invented a new method of earning riches, that of "discovery," and they came to America and claimed the land — on the grounds that they had never seen it before — and then went through the arduous labor of possessing by bounding. To most of the Native American tribes, the land was not subject to "ownership" by individuals. Their thinking was expressed eloquently by a Blackfeet chief:

> As long as the sun shines and the waters flow, this land will be here to give life to man and animals. We cannot sell the lives of men and animals; therefore we cannot sell this land. It was put here by the Great Spirit and we cannot sell it because it does not belong to us.

The Europeans' peculiar ideas about individuals' claiming exclusive ownership of specific portions of God's earth seemed strange, at first incomprehensible and then irksomely eccentric. The Indians eventually learned to their sorrow that it was no eccentricity, but rather a murderous mania.

In modern times, of course, we have the example of socialist countries where private ownership of any significant amount of property that constitutes "means of production" is prohibited as antisocial and antihuman.

So, the ideas we have in America (and in the majority of the world's nations) about the private ownership of productive property as a natural and universal right of mankind, perhaps of divine origin, are by no means universal and must be viewed as an invention of man rather than a decree of God. Of course, we are completely trained to accept the idea of ownership of the earth and its products, raw and transformed. it seems not at all strange; in fact, it is quite difficult to imagine a society without such arrangements. If someone, some *individual*, didn't own that plot of land, that house, that factory, that machine, that tower of wheat, how would we function? What would the rules be? How would we know how to act? Whom would we buy from and how would we sell?

It is important to acknowledge a significant difference between 12 achieving ownership simply by taking or claiming property and owning what we tend to call the "fruits of labor." If I, alone or together with my family, work on the land and raise crops, or if I make something useful out of natural material, it seems reasonable and fair to claim that the crops or the objects belong to me or my family, are my property, at least in the sense that I have first claim on them. Hardly anyone would dispute that. In fact, some of the early radical workingmen's movements made [an ownership] claim on those very grounds. As industrial organization became more complex, however, such issues became vastly more intricate. It must be clear that in modern society the social heritage of knowledge and technology and the social organization of manufacture and exchange account for far more of the productivity of industry and the value of what is produced than can be accounted for by the labor of any number of individuals. Hardly any person can now point and say, "That — that right there — is the fruit of *my* labor." We *can* say, as a society, as a nation — as a world, really — that what is produced is the fruit of *our* labor, the product of the whole society as a collectivity. . . .

No one man could conceivably build a house with only twelve 13 times the amount of time and effort that twelve men expend in building the same house. Yet we ignore this evident reality. Even the workmen, though their experience makes them aware of it, have no way of thinking and talking about it. So, when the man who bought the land, the lumber, the nails, and the wire comes around at the end and gives them each a check for the "value of their labor" — and then even has the chutzpah to bestow upon himself the title "builder" — no one doubts that he, that individual, now is the rightful owner of that house. It has become his property.

With all of this distortion and overemphasis on individual action, 14 the idea of private property and ownership of pieces of the earth is still pretty much limited to that portion of the earth that is actually land. We cannot readily imagine buying a piece of air or seeking a mortgage on a segment of ocean. The idea of owning the air and the seas seems as incomprehensible to us as the idea of owning his own factory must seem to a Russian (although we are beginning to see a rapidly growing interest in extending the idea of ownership to these elements, particularly as the oceans come to be seen more clearly as a means of production, not only of fish, but of other food, of oil, and perhaps of minerals).

We would have a similar feeling if we watched someone sailing out 15 into the Atlantic and marking out a line of buoys to the north, east, south, and west and then proclaiming to whoever might listen, "These waves are mine. I own this piece of ocean. This water and the fish therein and the plankton and the salt and the seaweed belong to me. The water is mine and the fullness thereof." Hardly anyone would agree with him or honor his claim, no matter how much he might talk about the divine rights of man to own the ocean.

We have to recognize that the right of private individual ownership 16 of property is man-made and constantly dependent on the extent to which those without property believe that the owner can make his claim stick.

One way of making the claim stick is to remove it from the realm of 17 human agreements, to mystify it, to clothe it in myths, of which the most important with respect to the so-called right of private ownership of social product and the things that make this product possible is the myth of the lone "supernormal" individual. It is only by saying — louder and louder, over and over again — "I! I! I!" that we can then get away with saying "my" and "mine."

CONSIDERATIONS

1. Ryan begins with an anecdote about cavemen in order to illustrate the possible origin of private property. Does the anecdote *simplify* his point, or is it *simplistic*? That is, does it help us understand his explanation, or does it divert us from noticing other possible origins? Do other explanations sound more or less plausible to you?
2. In the fourth paragraph, the phrase "a blip on the screen of time" is a figure of speech that makes a metaphor out of what object? Is it appropriate to Ryan's tone?
3. According to Ryan, how did people formerly uphold their vast claims of property ownership? What historical exceptions and restrictions to the concept of private ownership does he mention?
4. Ryan says: "It must be clear that in modern society the social heritage of

knowledge and technology and the social organization of manufacture and exchange account for far more of the productivity of industry and the value of what is produced than can be accounted for by the labor of any number of individuals." Obviously, it isn't all that "clear" or else Ryan's sentence would be easier to understand. Paraphrase what he is saying, and add your own illustrations to clarify his point.

5. What is the main means through which contemporary society upholds the concept of private ownership of property? How does it differ from past societies?

6. WRITING TOPIC. If you were designing a utopian society, what would you allow individuals to own privately? In a 500-word essay, explain why your utopian plan for ownership would be good for people.

E. M. Forster

MY WOOD

E. M. FORSTER (1879–1970) was a British novelist and essayist who was educated at Cambridge University. Except for periods of travel to India and the Mediterranean, where he was deeply affected by his contacts with ancient cultures, he continued to live at his college through most of his adulthood. His fiction is often about conventionally educated young English people discovering something unconventional in themselves in response to symbolic places, such as other countries or old houses. Even the titles of his novels suggest traveling to take up a fresh perspective on things: *Where Angels Fear to Tread* (1905), *The Longest Journey* (1907), *A Room with a View* (1908), *Howards End* (1910), and *Passage to India* (1924), which is the book Forster mentions in the first sentence of this selection from his collection of essays *Abinger Harvest* (1936).

A few years ago I wrote a book which dealt in part with the diffi- 1
culties of the English in India. Feeling that they would have had no difficulties in India themselves, the Americans read the book freely. The more they read it the better it made them feel, and a cheque to the author was the result. I bought a wood with the cheque. It is not a large wood — it contains scarcely any trees, and it is intersected, blast it, by a public footpath. Still, it is the first property that I have owned, so it is right that other people should participate in my shame, and should ask themselves, in accents that will vary in horror, this very important question: What is the effect of property upon the character? Don't let's touch economics; the effect of private ownership upon the community as a whole is another question — a more important question, perhaps, but another one. Let's keep to psychology. If you own things, what's their effect on you? What's the effect on me of my wood?

In the first place, it makes me feel heavy. Property does have this 2

230

effect. Property produces men of weight, and it was a man of weight who failed to get into the Kingdom of Heaven. He was not wicked, that unfortunate millionaire in the parable, he was only stout; he stuck out in front, not to mention behind, and as he wedged himself this way and that in the crystalline entrance and bruised his well-fed flanks, he saw beneath him a comparatively slim camel passing through the eye of a needle and being woven into the robe of God. The Gospels all through couple stoutness and slowness. They point out what is perfectly obvious, yet seldom realized: that if you have a lot of things you cannot move about a lot, that furniture requires dusting, dusters require servants, servants require insurance stamps, and the whole tangle of them makes you think twice before you accept an invitation to dinner or go for a bathe in the Jordan. Sometimes the Gospels proceed further and say with Tolstoy that property is sinful; they approach the difficult ground of asceticism here, where I cannot follow them. But as to the immediate effects of property on people, they just show straightforward logic. It produces men of weight. Men of weight cannot, by definition, move like the lightning from the East unto the West, and the ascent of a fourteen-stone bishop into a pulpit is thus the exact antithesis of the coming of the Son of Man. My wood makes me feel heavy.

In the second place, it makes me feel it ought to be larger.   3

The other day I heard a twig snap in it. I was annoyed at first, for I   4 thought that someone was blackberrying, and depreciating the value of the undergrowth. On coming nearer, I saw it was not a man who had trodden on the twig and snapped it, but a bird, and I felt pleased. My bird. The bird was not equally pleased. Ignoring the relation between us, it took fright as soon as it saw the shape of my face, and flew straight over the boundary hedge into a field, the property of Mrs. Henessy, where it sat down with a loud squawk. It had become Mrs. Henessy's bird. Something seemed grossly amiss here, something that would not have occurred had the wood been larger. I could not afford to buy Mrs. Henessy out, I dared not murder her, and limitations of this sort beset me on every side. . . .

In the third place, property makes its owner feel that he ought to   5 do something to it. Yet he isn't sure what. A restlessness comes over him, a vague sense that he has a personality to express — the same sense which, without any vagueness, leads the artist to an act of creation. Sometimes I think I will cut down such trees as remain in the wood, at other times I want to fill up the gaps between them with new trees. Both impulses are pretentious and empty. They are not honest movements toward money-making or beauty. They spring from a foolish desire to express myself and from an inability to enjoy what I have got. Creation, property, enjoyment form a sinister trinity in the human mind. Creation and enjoyment are both very, very good, yet they are often unattainable without a material basis, and at such moments property pushes itself in as a substitute, saying, "Accept me instead — I'm good enough for all three." It is not enough. It is, as Shakespeare said of lust, "The expense of spirit in a waste of shame": it is "Before, a joy proposed; behind, a dream." Yet we don't know how to shun it. It is forced on us by our economic system as the alternative to starvation. It is also forced on us by an internal defect in the soul, by the feeling that in property may lie the germs of self-development and of exquisite or heroic deeds. Our life on earth is, and ought to be, material and carnal. But we have not yet learned to manage our materialism and carnality properly; they are still entangled with the desire for ownership, where (in the words of Dante) "Possession is one with loss."

And this brings us to our fourth and final point: the blackberries. 6

Blackberries are not plentiful in this meagre grove, but they are eas- 7 ily seen from the public footpath which traverses it, and all too easily gathered. Foxgloves, too — people will pull up the foxgloves, and ladies of an educational tendency even grub for toadstools to show them on the Monday in class. Other ladies, less educated, roll down the bracken in the arms of their gentlemen friends. There is paper, there are tins. Pray, does my wood belong to me or doesn't it? And, if it does, should I not own it best by allowing no one else to walk there? There is a wood near Lyme Regis, also cursed by a public footpath, where the owner has not hesitated on this point. He had built high stone walls each side of the path, and has spanned it by bridges, so that the public circulate like termites while he gorges on the blackberries unseen. He really does own his wood, this able chap. And perhaps I shall come to this in time. I shall wall in and fence out until I really taste the sweets of property. Enormously stout, endlessly avaricious, pseudo-creative, intensely selfish, I shall weave upon my forehead the quadruple crown of possession until those nasty Bolshies come and take it off again and thrust me aside into the outer darkness.

CONSIDERATIONS

1. In the second paragraph, the terms "heavy" and "weight" include non-literal meanings. Give a literal explanation of this first effect of property on Forster's character. What is added by Forster's figurative presentation?
2. In paragraph four, explain the effect of the short sentence: "My bird."
3. Explain Forster's somewhat difficult point about property becoming a substitute for creativity and enjoyment. From his viewpoint, how is that to be avoided?
4. The essay includes an abundance of references to history, literature, and religion and they occur without much introduction or clarification. What is their purpose? And what is the effect of their suddenness?
5. WRITING TOPIC. Forster uses concrete and personal details to discuss generalities; that is, he talks about his own experiences in order to explain "the effect of property upon the character." Reversing the method, write a 500-word essay that generalizes Forster's observations. What complicated attitudes and possible hypocrisies over property ownership does he draw attention to? In addition to himself, who holds mixed views about property? What does he mean when he talks about the moral effects of property ownership in our society?

Flannery O'Connor

THE KING
OF THE BIRDS

◊

FLANNERY O'CONNOR (1925–1964), who lived in Georgia and attended the Writers' Workshop at the University of Iowa, was one of America's finest short-story writers. Her fiction usually presents a disturbingly funny, grotesquely comic view of deep spiritual issues in her commonplace characters' lives. Her stories have been collected in *The Complete Stories* (1971) and her essays and other short nonfiction are assembled in *Mystery and Manners* (1969), from which the following essay is taken. Her passion for peacocks was clearly a lifelong test of her sense of humor and her reasonableness.

When I was five, I had an experience that marked me for life. 1
Pathé News sent a photographer from New York to Savannah to take a picture of a chicken of mine. This chicken, a buff Cochin Bantam, had the distinction of being able to walk either forward or backward. Her fame had spread through the press, and by the time she reached the attention of Pathé News, I suppose there was nowhere left for her to go — forward or backward. Shortly after that she died, as now seems fitting.

If I put this information in the beginning of an article on peacocks, 2
it is because I am always being asked why I raise them, and I have no short or reasonable answer.

From that day with the Pathé man I began to collect chickens. 3
What had been only a mild interest became a passion, a quest. I had to have more and more chickens. I favored those with one green eye and one orange or with overlong necks and crooked combs. I wanted one with three legs or three wings but nothing in that line turned up. I pondered over the picture in Robert Ripley's book, *Believe It or Not*, of a rooster that had survived for thirty days without his head; but I

did not have a scientific temperament. I could sew in a fashion and I began to make clothes for chickens. A gray bantam named Colonel Eggbert wore a white piqué coat with a lace collar and two buttons in the back. Apparently Pathé News never heard of any of these other chickens of mine; it never sent another photographer.

My quest, whatever it was actually for, ended with peacocks. In- 4 stinct, not knowledge, led me to them. I had never seen or heard one. Although I had a pen of pheasants and a pen of quail, a flock of turkeys, seventeen geese, a tribe of mallard ducks, three Japanese silky bantams, two Polish Crested ones, and several chickens of a cross between these last and the Rhode Island Red, I felt a lack. I knew that the peacock had been the bird of Hera, the wife of Zeus, but since that time it had probably come down in the world — the Florida *Market Bulletin* advertised three-year-old peafowl at sixty-five dollars a pair. I had been quietly reading these ads for some years when one day, seized, I circled an ad in the *Bulletin* and passed it to my mother. The ad was for a peacock and hen with four seven-week-old peabiddies. "I'm going to order me those," I said.

My mother read the ad. "Don't those things eat flowers?" she 5 asked.

"They'll eat Startena like the rest of them," I said. 6

The peafowl arrived by Railway Express from Eustis, Florida, on a 7 mild day in October. When my mother and I arrived at the station, the crate was on the platform and from one end of it protruded a long, royal-blue neck and crested head. A white line above and below each eye gave the investigating head an expression of alert composure. I wondered if this bird, accustomed to parade about in a Florida orange grove, would readily adjust himself to a Georgia dairy farm. I jumped out of the car and bounded forward. The head withdrew.

At home we uncrated the party in a pen with a top on it. The man 8 who sold me the birds had written that I should keep them penned up for a week or ten days and then let them out at dusk at the spot where I wanted them to roost; thereafter, they would return every night to the same roosting place. He had also warned me that the cock would not have his full complement of tail feathers when he arrived; the peacock sheds his tail in late summer and does not regain it fully until after Christmas.

As soon as the birds were out of the crate, I sat down on it and 9 began to look at them. I have been looking at them ever since, from one station or another, and always with the same awe as on that first occasion; though I have always, I feel, been able to keep a balanced view and an impartial attitude. The peacock I had bought had nothing whatsoever in the way of a tail, but he carried himself as if he not only had a train behind him but a retinue to attend it. On that first occasion, my problem was so greatly what to look at first that my gaze moved constantly from the cock to the hen to the four young pea-chickens, while they, except that they gave me as wide a berth as possible, did nothing to indicate they knew I was in the pen.

Over the years their attitude toward me has not grown more gener-   10
ous. If I appear with food, they condescend, when no other way can be found, to eat it from my hand; if I appear without food, I am just another object. If I refer to them as "my" peafowl, the pronoun is legal, nothing more. I am the menial, at the beck and squawk of any feathered worthy who wants service. When I first uncrated these birds, in my frenzy I said, "I want so many of them that every time I go out the door, I'll run into one." Now every time I go out the door, four or five run into me — and give me only the faintest recognition. Nine years have passed since my first peafowl arrived. I have forty beaks to feed. Necessity is the mother of several other things besides invention. . . .

Many people, I have found, are congenitally unable to appreciate   11
the sight of a peacock. Once or twice I have been asked what the peacock is "good for" — a question which gets no answer from me because it deserves none. The telephone company sent a lineman out one day to repair our telephone. After the job was finished, the man, a large fellow with a suspicious expression half hidden by a yellow helmet, continued to idle about, trying to coax a cock that had been watching him to strut. He wished to add this experience to a large number of others he had apparently had. "Come on now, bud," he said, "get the show on the road, upsy-daisy, come on now, snap it up, snap it up."

The peacock, of course, paid no attention to this.   12
"What ails him?" the man asked.   13
"Nothing ails him," I said. "He'll put it up terreckly. All you have   14
to do is wait."
The man trailed about after the cock for another fifteen minutes or   15

so; then, in disgust, he got back in his truck and started off. The bird shook himself and his tail rose around him.

"He's doing it!" I screamed. "Hey, wait! He's doing it!" 16

The man swerved the truck back around again just as the cock 17 turned and faced him with the spread tail. The display was perfect. The bird turned slightly to the right and the little planets above him hung in bronze, then he turned slightly to the left and they were hung in green. I went up to the truck to see how the man was affected by the sight.

He was staring at the peacock with rigid concentration, as if he 18 were trying to read fine print at a distance. In a second the cock lowered his tail and stalked off.

"Well, what did you think of that?" I asked. 19

"Never saw such long ugly legs," the man said. "I bet that rascal 20 could outrun a bus."

Some people are genuinely affected by the sight of a peacock, even 21 with his tail lowered, but do not care to admit it; others appear to be incensed by it. Perhaps they have the suspicion that the bird has formed some unfavorable opinion of them. The peacock himself is a careful and dignified investigator. Visitors to our place, instead of being barked at by dogs rushing from under the porch, are squalled at by peacocks whose blue necks and crested heads pop up from behind tufts of grass, peer out of bushes, and crane downward from the roof of the house, where the bird has flown, perhaps for the view. One of mine stepped from under the shrubbery one day and came forward to inspect a carful of people who had driven up to buy a calf. An old man and five or six white-haired, bare-footed children were piling out the back of the automobile as the bird approached. Catching sight of him they stopped in their tracks and stared, plainly hacked to find this superior figure blocking their path. There was silence as the bird regarded them, his head drawn back at its most majestic angle, his folded train glittering behind him in the sunlight.

"Whut is thet thang?" one of the small boys asked finally in a sul- 22 len voice.

The old man had got out of the car and was gazing at the peacock 23 with an astounded look of recognition. "I ain't seen one of them since my grandaddy's day," he said, respectfully removing his hat. "Folks used to have 'em, but they don't no more."

"Whut is it?" the child asked again in the same tone he had used 24
before.

"Churren," the old man said, "that's the king of the birds!" 25

The children received this information in silence. After a minute 26
they climbed back into the car and continued from there to stare at
the peacock, their expressions annoyed, as if they disliked catching the
old man in the truth. . . .

It is hard to tell the truth about this bird. The habits of any pea- 27
chicken left to himself would hardly be noticeable, but multiplied by
forty, they become a situation. I was correct that my peachickens
would all eat Startena; they also eat everything else. Particularly they
eat flowers. My mother's fears were all borne out. Peacocks not only
eat flowers, they eat them systematically, beginning at the head of a
row and going down it. If they are not hungry, they will pick the
flower anyway, if it is attractive, and let it drop. For general eating
they prefer chrysanthemums and roses. When they are not eating
flowers, they enjoy sitting on top of them, and where the peacock sits
he will eventually fashion a dusting hole. Any chicken's dusting hole
is out of place in a flower bed, but the peafowl's hole, being the size of
a small crater, is more so. When he dusts he all but obliterates the
sight of himself with sand. Usually when someone arrives at full gallop
with the leveled broom, he can see nothing through the cloud of dirt
and flying flowers but a few green feathers and a beady, pleasure-
taking eye.

From the beginning, relations between these birds and my mother 28
were strained. She was forced, at first, to get up early in the morning
and go out with her clippers to reach the Lady Bankshire and the
Herbert Hoover roses before some peafowl had breakfasted upon
them; now she has halfway solved her problem by erecting hundreds
of feet of twenty-four-inch-high wire to fence the flower beds. She
contends that peachickens do not have enough sense to jump over a
low fence. "If it were a high wire," she says, "they would jump onto it
and over, but they don't have sense enough to jump over a low wire."

It is useless to argue with her on this matter. "It's not a challenge," 29
I say to her; but she has made up her mind.

In addition to eating flowers, peafowl also eat fruit, a habit which 30
has created a lack of cordiality toward them on the part of my uncle,
who had the fig trees planted about the place because he has an appe-

tite for figs himself. "Get that scoundrel out of that fig bush!" he will roar, rising from his chair at the sound of a limb breaking, and someone will have to be dispatched with a broom to the fig trees.

Peafowl also enjoy flying into barn lofts and eating peanuts off peanut hay; this has not endeared them to our dairyman. And as they have a taste for fresh garden vegetables, they have often run afoul of the dairyman's wife. 31

The peacock likes to sit on gates or fence posts and allow his tail to hang down. A peacock on a fence post is a superb sight. Six or seven peacocks on a gate are beyond description; but it is not very good for the gate. Our fence posts tend to lean in one direction or another and all our gates open diagonally. 32

In short, I am the only person on the place who is willing to underwrite, with something more than tolerance, the presence of peafowl. In return, I am blessed with their rapid multiplication. The population figure I give out is forty, but for some time now I have not felt it wise to take a census. I had been told before I bought my birds that peafowl are difficult to raise. It is not so, alas. In May the peahen finds a nest in some fence corner and lays five or six large buff-colored eggs. Once a day, thereafter, she gives an abrupt *hee-haa-awww!* and shoots like a rocket from her nest. Then for half an hour, her neck ruffled and stretched forward, she parades around the premises, announcing what she is about. I listen with mixed emotions. 33

In twenty-eight days the hen comes off with five or six mothlike, murmuring peachicks. The cock ignores these unless one gets under his feet (then he pecks it over the head until it gets elsewhere), but the hen is a watchful mother and every year a good many of the young survive. Those that withstand illnesses and predators (the hawk, the fox, and the opossum) over the winter seem impossible to destroy, except by violence. 34

A man selling fence posts tarried at our place one day and told me that he had once had eighty peafowl on his farm. He cast a nervous eye at two of mine standing nearby. "In the spring, we couldn't hear ourselves think," he said. "As soon as you lifted your voice, they lifted their'n, if not before. All our fence posts wobbled. In the summer they ate all the tomatoes off the vines. Scuppernongs went the same way. My wife said she raised her flowers for herself and she was not going to have them eat up by a chicken no matter how long his tail was. And in the fall they shed them feathers all over the place anyway and it was 35 a job to clean up. My old grandmother was living with us then and she was eighty-five. She said, 'Either they go, or I go.' "

"Who went?" I asked.   36

"We still got twenty of them in the freezer," he said.   37

"And how," I asked, looking significantly at the two standing   38
nearby, "did they taste?"

"No better than any other chicken," he said, "but I'd a heap rather   39
eat them than hear them."

I have tried imagining that the single peacock I see before me is the   40
only one I have, but then one comes to join him; another flies off the
roof, four or five crash out of the crêpe-myrtle hedge; from the pond
one screams and from the barn I hear the dairyman denouncing another that has got into the cowfeed. My kin are given to such phrases
as, "Let's face it."

I do not like to let my thoughts linger in morbid channels, but   41
there are times when such facts as the price of wire fencing and the
price of Startena and the yearly gain in peafowl all run uncontrolled
through my head. Lately I have had a recurrent dream: I am five years
old and a peacock. A photographer has been sent from New York and
a long table is laid in celebration. The meal is to be an exceptional
one: myself. I scream, "Help! Help!" and awaken. Then from the
pond and the barn and the trees around the house, I hear that chorus
of jubilation begin:

> *Lee-yon lee-yon,*
> *Mee-yon mee-yon!*
> *Eee-e-yoy eee-e-yoy!*
> *Eee-e-yoy eee-e-yoy!*

I intend to stand firm and let the peacocks multiply, for I am sure   42
that, in the end, the last word will be theirs.

CONSIDERATIONS

1. How does the dialogue in paragraphs 4 to 6 and elsewhere characterize
   the young girl? What does the style of speaking add to our interest in her
   particular activity?

2. What first strikes the girl with awe over the peacocks? How does this trait of the birds introduce a central theme in the essay?

3. How does O'Connor emphasize the differences between the telephone repairman and the old man who comes to buy a calf? What do these contrasts contribute to the themes of the essay?

4. Explain the full significance of the dream that O'Connor recounts in Paragraph 41. What contradictory attitudes does it indicate?

5. WRITING TOPIC. As O'Connor's essay illustrates, our possessions can possess us — and they frequently do, sometimes delightfully, sometimes harmfully. Nearly everyone has sometimes felt that the essence of life was summed up for the moment by a record collection, or a pair of skis, or earrings, or a special pair of jeans. In 500 words, explain how your obsession with a special personal belonging arose, and clarify the ways it affected your life then or now. Be sure to give your reader a sense of the importance of this possession at the time you required it.

Matthew

THE LILIES OF
THE FIELD

◊

MATTHEW (first century A.D.), who was a tax collector for the Roman Empire in Galilee, became a disciple of Jesus and wrote one of the four Gospels that relate the life of Jesus in the New Testament. In this passage (Matthew 6:19–34) from the Sermon on the Mount, Jesus gives advice about righteous living and the pursuit of wealth. Matthew writes that when Jesus finished his sermon the people who had assembled on the mountainside to hear him "were astonished at his doctrine," because he spoke with such strong personal conviction about questions of holiness and virtue. This translation into English is from the Revised Standard Version.

"Do not lay up for yourselves treasures on earth, where moth and 19 rust consume and where thieves break in and steal,

but lay up for yourselves treasures in heaven, where neither moth 20 nor rust consumes and where thieves do not break in and steal.

For where your treasure is, there will your heart be also. 21

"The eye is the lamp of the body. So, if your eye is sound, your 22 whole body will be full of light;

but if your eye is not sound, your whole body will be full of dark- 23 ness. If then the light in you is darkness, how great is the darkness!

"No one can serve two masters; for either he will hate the one and 24 love the other, or he will be devoted to the one and despise the other. You cannot serve God and mammon.

"Therefore I tell you, do not be anxious about your life, what you 25 shall eat or what you shall drink, nor about your body, what you shall put on. Is not life more than food, and the body more than clothing?

Look at the birds of the air: they neither sow nor reap nor gather 26 into barns, and yet your heavenly Father feeds them. Are you not of more value than they?

And which of you by being anxious can add one cubit to his span of 27 life?

And why are you anxious about clothing? Consider the lilies of the 28 field, how they grow; they neither toil nor spin;

yet I tell you, even Solomon in all his glory was not arrayed like one 29 of these.

But if God so clothes the grass of the field, which today is alive and 30 tomorrow is thrown into the oven, will he not much more clothe you, O men of little faith?

Therefore do not be anxious, saying, 'What shall we eat?' or 'What 31 shall we drink?' or 'What shall we wear?'

For the Gentiles seek all these things; and your heavenly Father 32 knows that you need them all.

But seek first his kingdom and his righteousness, and all these 33 things shall be yours as well.

"Therefore do not be anxious about tomorrow, for tomorrow will 34 be anxious for itself. Let the day's own trouble be sufficient for the day.

CONSIDERATIONS

1. Biblical writing is loaded with repetitions of words and phrases. Underline and connect some of the repeated expressions in this passage. What effects would the repetition have on the people listening to this sermon?
2. What are the illustrations from nature meant to show?
3. What does Jesus advise people to do about the practical necessities of life? How do you suppose this sermon made the audience feel?
4. WRITING TOPIC. What connections between poverty and piety do you observe in the world around you? Are people more likely to be religious if they are not wealthy? Are people with security and some luxuries more grateful for life? Do material possessions diminish or increase one's reverence for spiritual values? In 500 words, support, refute, or modify the message in the Sermon on the Mount.

John Kenneth Galbraith

ACCOMMODATION
TO POVERTY

◊

JOHN KENNETH GALBRAITH (b. 1908) was raised on a farm in Canada, and after finishing agricultural college in Ontario he went on for a doctorate in agricultural economics at the University of California at Berkeley. His keen sense of the contrasts between agricultural and industrial societies is a theme in his copious writings through a varied career as a professor at Harvard University, a federal administrator, and a presidential adviser. He served as the American ambassador to India during the early 1960s. Among his widely read books are *The Affluent Society* (1958), *The New Industrial State* (1967), and *Money* (1975). This selection is from *The Nature of Mass Poverty* (1979) in which he examines reasons why poverty is a fixed condition of life in many nations of the world.

In the rich country a large proportion of the people have come to 1 expect a comfortable and also an increasing income. This is a circumstance to which they have accommodated their thoughts and expectations. An effort, general though by no means universal, to improve income is assumed. Most significantly, it is assumed by economists and other scholars. There is broad accommodation to the idea of increasing income.

It should not surprise us then, though it does, that the poor also ac- 2 commodate to their poverty. And especially so the rural poor. This tendency to accommodation is a fact of the greatest importance. . . .

. . . Nothing so reinforces [poverty] as the absence of aspiration — 3 the absence of effort to escape it. In the poor rural community such aspiration, in turn, is in conflict with one of the most profound and predictable elements of human behavior. That is the refusal to struggle against the impossible, the tendency to prefer acquiescence to frustration.

People who have lived for centuries in poverty in the relative isola- 4
tion of the rural village have come to terms with this existence. It
would be astonishing were it otherwise. People do not strive, generation after generation, century after century, against circumstances
that are so constituted as to defeat them. They accept. Nor is such
acceptance a sign of weakness of character. Rather, it is a profoundly
rational response. Given the formidable hold of the . . . poverty within
which they live, accommodation is the optimal solution. Poverty is
cruel. A continuing struggle to escape that is continuously frustrated
is more cruel. It is more civilized, more intelligent, as well as more
plausible, that people, out of the experience of centuries, should reconcile themselves to what has for so long been the inevitable.

The deeply rational character of accommodation lies back, at least 5
in part, of the central instruction of the principal world religions. All,
without exception, urge acquiescence, some in remarkably specific
form. The blessedness that Christianity accords to the meek is cate-
gorical. The pain of poverty is not denied, but its compensatory spiritual reward is very high. The poor pass through the eye of the needle
into Paradise; the rich remain outside with the camels. Acquiescence
is equally urged, or as in the case of Hinduism compelled, by the other
ancient faiths. There has long been a suspicion, notably enhanced by
Marx, that the contentment urged by religion is a design for diverting
attention from the realities of class and exploitation — it is the opiate
of the people. It is, more specifically, a formula for making the best of
a usually hopeless situation.

The ethical judgment of the affluent community, as well as its eco- 6
nomics, is thought appropriate to the poor. Accordingly and instinctively, the rich community reacts derogatorily to the accommodation
of the poor to their poverty; here are people who deserve no sympathy,
for they do not even try. This again reflects a serious failure of understanding, another example of the highly inappropriate transfer of the
highly conditioned attitudes of the rich country to the poor.

CONSIDERATIONS

1. Galbraith makes a number of general points without including much supporting evidence. What is his main point in this selection? What are the
   subpoints that follow?

2. What is the intended audience for this selection? What features of the writing suggest that this piece may be part of a lecture? To whom? And under what circumstances?

3. How does Galbraith see Christianity? Does the Sermon on the Mount (see the preceding selection) confirm or refute his view? Would Galbraith's perspective tend to undermine or to strengthen someone's religious belief?

4. What is mistaken in the view that rich nations hold toward poor nations?

5. WRITING TOPIC. In the first paragraph, Galbraith states that we make a special "accommodation" to increasing wealth. What are the signs around us that we regard economic gains as necessary or natural? In a 500-word essay, examine some social reinforcement of our expectation of increasing wealth. You may find interesting evidence within family life; or from community institutions, such as schools, churches, and clubs; or from advertising and entertainment.

Kennedy Fraser

MODESTY

◊

KENNEDY FRASER grew up in Coventry, England and earned an honors degree in literature at Oxford University. After writing book reviews and other short pieces for magazines, Fraser became the fashion editor for the *New Yorker*, in which the following essay first appeared. Her articles on clothing styles, fads, taste, and tastelessness have been collected in *The Fashionable Mind; Reflections on Fashion* (1981). Fraser now lives in New York City and Yorkshire, England.

Viewing the toplessness, scantiness, or outright jettisoning of women's bathing suits these days — particularly on the Mediterranean beaches — one wonders whether all idea of modesty has vanished. Definitions of propriety in hot-weather dress here in town are certainly laxer than ever. Women go bare-legged, bare-backed, and braless to the office and to restaurants, and after working hours they sometimes career around on roller skates in handkerchief-size shorts. If women are ever really men's social equals, will modesty survive in any way? Much of past modesty has been imposed by the code of menfolk who saw women as personal assets to be protected from corruption by outsiders. Women who are proud of their fitness and slimness do not *seem* to be particularly interested in modesty at the moment. That quality is most often found in people, of either sex, who are embarrassed by what they think is their own imperfect body compared to our culture's endless images of ideal nudity or semi-nudity. In mixed company and with lovers, it is men who are probably more inclined to cover themselves. Colette, in telling of a young bride who took only too exuberantly to honeymoon life without clothes, referred with reason to the "shadowy, delicate modesty of the male." And one version of the Adam and Eve story has it that when the pair adopted fig leaves he used his for the proper purpose while his flightier companion used hers to make herself a charming hat.

The beaches of the South of France, in particular, seem to bear 2 witness to a womankind brave, free, and pagan, which, after centuries of confinement by masculine rules, has finally thrown off the shackles of the brassiere. It is not just the dazzling young blondes on the decks of white yachts who go topless, either. So do the conservative middle-aged matrons who sit composedly under beach parasols, knitting and holding court for grandchildren and sons-in-law. Fashion has moved far and fast since the bikinis of the Brigitte Bardot era, twenty-odd years ago. To eyes accustomed to the string bikini, the early prototypes seem almost prim period pieces. Constructed in the armored-corsetry tradition of the fifties, they depend for titillation on the sight of the navel set in a comparatively narrow band of flesh. When Rudi Gernreich promoted his "monokini" in 1964, it was banned in France. Most of Gernreich's bare-breasted designs seem antiquated now but still quite indecent — especially a demure black bathing suit with built-up straps which just happens to be scooped to the waist in front. In 1967, Yves Saint Laurent introduced the braless look to the haute couture, and his gauzy, spangled semi-toplessness was briefly taken up by night-club habituées. But — like "hot pants," which were initially quite respectable, and which have emerged a decade later with the healthier name shorts — such toplessness was always toying with vulgarity and rapidly became part of the uniform of society's real underworld. (Ironically, this was all at a time when high fashion was reaching down to that underworld to reproduce the "hooker look" or some camp notion of it.)

The definition of what part of woman is too erotic to be decently 3 revealed has shifted around quite a bit. Traditional Arab mores decree that everything should be hidden from public view except the eyes. In the Middle Ages, it was the hair that was seen as a dangerous snare, something to be hidden away under coifs and plucked away from the brow. The ladies of ancient Crete, seventeenth-century Venice, and the Paris of the Directoire bared their breasts but had skirts or draperies, however flimsy, round their legs. And the patriarchal Victorians, taking the concept of modesty to unprecedented lengths, covered up the legs of pianos, referred to men's pants as "nether garments," and considered it unthinkable that upper- and middle-class women should be seen to have two legs. (Women working on farms and in factories, being beyond the social pale and the decree of modesty, could hitch up their skirts in order to work better.) Respectable women moved smoothly along in bell-like skirts as though on wheels. Shoulders, necks, and bosoms meanwhile rose white, soft, and vulnerable from above the rigidly corseted torso. Man was prevented from getting too close to this tempting display of upper flesh by the huge crinoline skirt, which kept him a flirtatious arm's length away.

The history of modesty and that of flirtation are hopelessly inter- 4 mingled. Imagination has traditionally played a great part in seduction, and the tantalizing glimpse of the unseen but guessed-at feature has often proved more enticing than the totally revealed. I noticed in France that only when women don their bikini tops, wrap a *pareo* round their hips, and sit down to lunch does it become safe for the atmosphere of flirtation between men and women to set in. While sun-bathing, the new Amazons are wrapped not only in suntans that are like a copper-colored body stocking but also in an invisible aura of untouchable innocence, childlike self-absorption, and defiant lack of sexuality. The current wave of nudity follows the general interest in sporty naturalness and health. It is in most cases studiously unprovocative. But, clearly, there is a narrow line between fashions that are simply healthy, spontaneous, and a feminist rejection of unnecessary garments and those fashions which seem to play on the taste for striptease. The minimal style of dress calls for just the same social instincts as any other style, the same fine distinctions. In an age of sexual emancipation, standards of modesty may be eroded. But women are still expected to have an understanding of what can only be called propriety. In the topless world of the Côte d'Azur, quite subtle rules have evolved about when it would strike a false note to take off a bikini top and when it would be almost impolite to leave it on. "Comfort" and "naturalness" remain small considerations in the fashion scene compared to the rules of society, questions of taste, and the sense of appropriate place and time. And people will never be induced to wear any sort of fashion if they see it being worn by people with whom they prefer not to be identified. Among other reasons, some people's perception that the "wrong" people are in exiguous two-piece suits may account for the current popularity — at least in this country — of the one-piece maillot.

Several factors have combined to make skimpy clothing more visu- 5 ally and socially acceptable than it was in the past. The passion for boyish slenderness has made for fewer distinctively feminine, hour-glass figures. But the current fashion in the female shape may not be the last. *Vogue* recently moved to redress the balance of androgynous, if not anorectic, youth with the image of classical womanliness. It published a photograph of a naked girl of what it called "appealing plumpness," and pointed out that for some bodies this was healthy and attractive. The popularity of suntans, which have also made it eas-ier for our eye to accept the sight of near-nakedness, may not be indef-inite, either. Limbs are transformed by a tan, made to look more plas-tic and more hygienic. The color evens things out — eliminates knobs, imperfections, and textures. But, like smoking, which was also chic in its day, deep tanning can be aging and dangerous, and may decline in favor. For the moment, though, tans go on getting darker and bathing suits get smaller. At the same time, sunglasses have been getting darker and growing in size. If there is no longer any modesty of the flesh, there is still the modesty of the eye. At present, sunglasses are modesty's last frontier, the masks behind which people protect their thoughts — a more intimate matter than sexual encounters. It's not our bodies we're interested in keeping hidden so much as our reac-tions to others, or our lack of reactions. Sunglasses are the perfect ac-cessory for that part of the modern sensibility which prides itself on being "cool." Sunglasses are worn over the modern eye — an organ that functions best in solitude and under cover of the dark. It's the eye for movie going and television watching and for going to the beach. If ever women are plump and white again and people all take off their sunglasses, there's a fair chance that old-style modesty will be revived.

CONSIDERATIONS

1. Fraser implies that modesty in clothing is a more fully accepted standard for men than for women. What evidence does she mention in the essay? Do you find this difference reflected in the styles and habits of dress among the young people you know?
2. Does Fraser stereotype the sexes? What images of women emerge from this article? To what audience is she writing?
3. According to Fraser, what has helped to make the fashion of skimpiness more acceptable nowadays? Can you add some additional explanations of this change in style?

4. Why does Fraser call sunglasses "modesty's last frontier"? Are there relevant connotations to the phrase "last frontier"? Is the sunglasses type of modesty also linked to flirtation?

5. WRITING TOPIC. When we wear certain fashionable clothes, or wear clothes in a certain fashionable way, are we communicating something real about ourselves, or something acknowledged to be purely an illusion? What is the purpose of "fashion" in the way we dress? Write a 500-word essay on a fashion, such as designer jeans or loose shirt tails, that you adopted for some deliberate effect.

Harry Crews

THE CAR

◊

HARRY CREWS (b. 1935), who was raised in Georgia, joined the Marine Corps after high school and became a sergeant before he left the
Corps to go to college. He was educated at the University of Florida,
where he now teaches writing. His novels include *CAR* (1972) and *A
Feast of Snakes* (1976). He often writes for such magazines as *Playboy*
and *Esquire*, in the second of which this essay first appeared.

The other day, there arrived in the mail a clipping sent by a friend 1
of mine. It had been cut from a Long Beach, California, newspaper
and dealt with a young man who had eluded police for fifty-five minutes while he raced over freeways and through city streets at speeds up
to 130 miles per hour. During the entire time, he ripped his clothes
off and threw them out the window bit by bit. It finally took twenty-
five patrol cars and a helicopter to catch him. When they did, he said
that God had given him the car, and that he had "found God."

I don't want to hit too hard on a young man who obviously has his 2
own troubles, maybe even is a little sick with it all, but when I read
that he had found God in the car, my response was: *So say we all.* We
have found God in cars, or if not the true God, one so satisfying, so
powerful, and awe-inspiring that the distinction is too fine to matter.
Except perhaps ultimately, but pray we must not think too much on
that.

The operative word in all this is *we.* It will not do for me to main- 3
tain that I have been above it all, that somehow I've managed to remain aloof from the national love affair with cars. It is true that I got a
late start. I did not learn to drive until I was twenty-one; my brother
was twenty-five before he learned. The reason is simple enough. In
Bacon County, Georgia, where I grew up, many families had nothing

with a motor in it. Ours was one such family. But starting as late as I did, I still had my share, and I've remembered them all, the cars I've owned. I remember them in just the concrete specific way you remember anything that changed your life. Especially I remember the early ones.

The first car I ever owned was a 1938 Ford coupe. It had no low 4 gear and the door on the passenger side wouldn't open. I eventually put a low gear in it, but I never did get the door to work. One hot summer night on a clay road a young lady whom I'll never forget had herself braced and ready with one foot on the rearview mirror and the other foot on the wind vent. In the first few lovely frantic moments, she pushed out the wing vent, broke off the rearview mirror and left her little footprints all over the ceiling. The memory of it was so affecting that I could never bring myself to repair the vent or replace the headliner she had walked all over upside down.

Eight months later I lost the car on a rain-slick road between Folk- 5 ston, Georgia, and Waycross. I'd just stopped to buy a stalk of bananas (to a boy raised in the hookworm and rickets belt of the South, bananas will always remain an incredibly exotic fruit, causing him to buy whole stalks at a time), and back on the road again I was only going about fifty in a misting rain when I looked over to say something to my buddy, whose nickname was Bonehead and who was half drunk in the seat beside me. For some reason I'll never understand, I felt the back end of the car get loose and start to come up on us in the other lane. Not having driven very long, I overcorrected and stepped on the brake. We turned over four times. Bonehead flew out of the car and shot down a muddy ditch about forty yards before he stopped, sober and unhurt. I ended up under the front seat, thinking I was covered with gouts of blood. As it turned out, I didn't have much wrong with me and what I was covered with was gouts of mashed banana.

The second car I had was a 1940 Buick, square, impossibly heavy, 6 built like a Sherman tank, but it had a '52 engine in it. Even though it took about ten miles to get her open full bore, she'd do over a hundred miles an hour on flat ground. It was so big inside that in an emergency it could sleep six. I tended to live in that Buick for almost a year and no telling how long I would have kept it if a boy who was not a friend of mine and who owned an International Harvester pickup truck hadn't said in mixed company that he could make the run from

New Lacy in Coffee County, Georgia, to Jacksonville, Florida, quicker than I could. He lost the bet, but I wrung the speedometer off the Buick, and also — since the run was made on a blistering day in July — melted four inner tubes, causing them to fuse with the tires, which were already slick when the run started. Four new tires and tubes cost more than I had or expected to have anytime soon, so I sadly put that old honey up on blocks until I could sell it to a boy who lived up toward Macon.

After the Buick, I owned a 1953 Mercury with three-inch lowering 7 blocks, fender skirts, twin aerials, and custom upholstering made of rolled Naugahyde. Staring into the bathroom mirror for long periods of time I practiced expressions to drive it with. It was that kind of car. It looked mean, and it was mean. Consequently, it had to be handled with a certain style. One-handing it through a ninety-degree turn on city streets in a power slide where you were in danger of losing your ass as well as the car, you were obligated to have your left arm hanging half out the window and a very *bored* expression on your face. That kind of thing.

Those were the sweetest cars I was ever to know because they were 8 my first. I remember them like people — like long-ago lovers — their idiosyncrasies, what they liked and what they didn't. With my hands deep in crankcases, I was initiated into their warm greasy mysteries. Nothing in the world was more satisfying than winching the front end up under the shade of a chinaberry tree and sliding under the chassis on a burlap sack with a few tools to see if the car would not yield to me and my expert ways.

The only thing that approached working on a car was talking about 9 one. We'd stand about for hours, hustling our balls and spitting, telling stories about how it had been somewhere, sometime, with the car we were driving. It gave our lives a little focus and our talk a little credibility, if only because we could point to the evidence.

"But, hell, don't it rain in with that wing vent broke out like that?" 10

"Don't mean nothing to me. Soon's Shirley kicked it out, I known 11 I was in love. I ain't about to put it back."

Usually we met to talk at night behind the A&W Root Beer stand, 12 with the air heavy with the smell of grease and just a hint of burned French fries and burned hamburgers and burned hot dogs. It remains one of the most sensuous, erotic smells in my memory because through it, their tight little asses ticking like clocks, walked the sweetest softest short-skirted carhops in the world. I knew what it was to stand for hours with my buddies, leaning nonchalant as hell on a fender, pretending not to look at the carhops, and saying things like: "This little baby don't look like much, but she'll git rubber in three gears." And when I said it, it was somehow my own body I was talking about. It was *my* speed and *my* strength that got rubber in three gears. In the mystery of that love affair, the car and I merged.

But, like many another love affair, it has soured considerably. 13 Maybe it would have been different if I had known cars sooner. I was already out of the Marine Corps and twenty-two years old before I could stand behind the A&W Root Beer and lean on the fender of a 1938 coupe. That seems pretty old to me to be talking about getting rubber in three gears, and I'm certain it is *very* old to feel your own muscle tingle and flush with blood when you say it. As is obvious, I was what used to be charitably called a late bloomer. But at some point I did become just perceptive enough to recognize bullshit when I was neck deep in it.

The 1953 Mercury was responsible for my ultimate disenchant- 14 ment with cars. I had already bored and stroked the engine and contrived to place a six-speaker sound system in it when I finally started to paint it. I spent the better half of a year painting that car. A friend of mine owned a body shop and he let me use the shop on weekends. I sanded the Mercury down to raw metal, primed it, and painted it. Then I painted it again. And again. And then again. I went a little nuts, as I am prone to do, because I'm the kind of guy who if he can't have too much of a thing doesn't want any at all. So one day I came out of the house (I was in college then) and saw it, the '53 Mercury, the car upon which I had heaped more attention and time and love than I had ever given a human being. It sat at the curb, its black surface a shimmering of the air, like hundreds of mirrors turned to catch the sun. It had twenty-seven coats of paint, each coat laboriously hand-rubbed. It seemed to glow, not with reflected light, but with some internal light of its own.

I stood staring, and it turned into one of those great scary rare mo- 15 ments when you are privileged to see into your own predicament. Clearly, there were two ways I could go. I could sell the car, or I could keep on painting it for the rest of my life. If twenty-seven coats of paint, why not a hundred and twenty-seven? The moment was brief and I understand it better now than I did then, but I did realize, if imperfectly, that something was dreadfully wrong, that the car owned me much more than I would ever own the car, no matter how long I kept it. The next day I drove to Jacksonville and left the Mercury on a used-car lot. It was an easy thing to do.

Since that day, I've never confused myself with a car, a confusion common everywhere about us — or so it seems to me. I have a car now, but I use it like a beast, the way I've used all cars since the Mercury, like a beast unlovely and unlikable but necessary. True as all that is, though, God knows I'm in the car's debt for that blistering winning July run to Jacksonville, and the pushed-out wing vent, and finally for that greasy air heavy with the odor of burned meat and potatoes there behind the A&W Root Beer. I'll never smell anything that good again.

CONSIDERATIONS

1. What does Crews mean in saying that "We have found God in cars"? Why does the thought lead him immediately to say, in almost the same breath, "pray we must not think too much on that"?
2. Crews seems to be exaggerating some details in his descriptions of his car and in his accounts of his experiences. What kind of exaggerations does he lard into his essay and what effects do they have on our response to him as a writer? What qualities of his might be objectionable? What qualities might be thought of as attractive?
3. At what point did Crews first begin to realize that he was identifying himself too closely with his cars? What other realization is it linked with?
4. In the final paragraph Crews says that people around him seem to be confusing themselves with their cars. In what ways? What features of common American life is he alluding to in that observation?
5. The tone of the essay includes some nostalgia — over what, precisely? What broader theme is included in his treatment of the main topic?
6. WRITING TOPIC. In 300 words, describe an object that you would like to own — that is, something such as a musical instrument, sports equipment, a vehicle, a collection, or some other specially personal object that you enjoy imagining in your possession. Include enough concrete details to make it appear real to your reader and indicate why it would have particular value for you.

John Ciardi

A CADILLAC
FULL OF DIAMONDS

◊

JOHN CIARDI (b. 1916), a poet and critic, grew up in an immigrant family in Boston and was graduated from Tufts University. He has been a professor of English at Rutgers University and the poetry editor of the *Saturday Review of Literature* for which he also wrote far-ranging personal essays and fictional sketches, such as this whimsical story about a man who won the ultimate jackpot and whose winnings grind him down. Many of Ciardi's writings have been collected in *Dialogue with an Audience* (1963) and *Manner of Speaking* (1972). His widely read book *How Does a Poem Mean?* (1960; second edition, 1975) is an excellent aid to enjoying poetry.

One day I did pull the right lever at the right time and I was rich! 1

I filled the car with diamonds as fast as they poured down the 2 chute. I threw away the spare tire and the jack and crammed the trunk full. Then I yanked out the back seat. Then the right front seat. Then even the driver's seat. Then I crammed my pockets, throwing my money away to make room. Then I tied the bottoms of my pants and stuffed my pants legs. Then my shirt.

That about did it, but I still had to get into the car, and I couldn't 3 open the door without starting an avalanche. Luckily I had left the left front window open, though I don't suppose I can take credit for that: I had had to pour them into the car through *some* opening.

But stuffed as I was, I could never wriggle through the window. 4 There was no help for it: I had to unbutton my shirt, untie my pants legs, and let them spill. Then I had to empty my pockets. I was excited — who wouldn't be? — but I kept my head and took the time to bury them carefully. Waste not, want not.

And even then I couldn't make it through the window. I had, fi- 5 nally, to take my clothes off. Naked, I was just able to scrape through — and "scrape" is exactly the word: I was half way in, my hips ripped and raw, when I realized I had no driver's seat. It was an agony, but I forced my way out, retrieved the money I had thrown away, and made a padding out of it, pushing the stones around to make a little shelf. It was, to be sure, an improvisation, but it looked reasonably comfortable with the money smoothed out flat. Thank God I had just cashed a check!

So, finally, I managed to wriggle in and be seated. I was naked, 6 scraped raw, and panting with exertion, but not seriously injured. Inevitably, some of the diamonds spilled out as I wiggled about to make room behind the wheel. I even thought for a fraction of an instant of getting out and burying them with the others, but that thought was immediately supplanted by the realization that in my excitement I had already forgotten where I had buried them.

I began to see I should have to develop a new attitude. Forcing 7 myself to be calm, I concentrated on how to work the controls. Thank God I had an automatic shift: I could never have worked a stick shift in all that gravel. Even so, some of the rocks were jamming the brake and the accelerator. I had to keep poking around with my feet until I felt a little play in the pedals. It was going to be tricky — no doubt about that — but I could make it with a little luck. It wasn't much of a drive to my house.

But when I had made it at last — at what seemed to be a mile a 8 week — there was no way to get out. A truck was blocking my driveway and when I looked closer, I saw it was bedded down in the macadam right to the axles. Don't ask me to explain. It's the sort of thing that just seems to keep happening. The truck had become a monument to all the world's past deliveries and was now no more movable than Grant's Tomb.

So the driveway was out. And every place at the curb was taken by 9 cars that seemed to be made of girders pile-driven into the pavement and rusted together. Don't ask me to explain that either: every monument needs some sort of approach to it. I drove around the block twenty times, then around the next block and the next. There wasn't a place to park short of the last few farms, up there on the ridges.

And suppose I did get a farmer to rent me a field: could I just crawl 10 out the window and ask it to crank itself shut from the inside? I had to unload. Sooner or later, too, I had to pick up some clothes. It was cold and some of these diamonds had sharp edges.

I drove back home and circled and circled until I honked my wife 11 up. "Whatta ya want?" she yelled from the bedroom window. "Bring a bucket!" I shouted. But there were cars honking behind me, backed up for half a mile. I moved on and circled the block twelve times before she made it to the curb.

Without the bucket. 12

And another line of cars honking behind me. 13

"Here!" I said and tossed her a handful as I went by. I had to reach 14 up and throw them over the top of the car from the left, and naturally they scattered all over the place.

I'll say this for her: she seemed to know the stuff was real even 15 while it was still in the air. "Lemme get in!" she shrieked the next time around. "In where?" I shrieked back, tossing out another handful. "Stop it!" she shrieked, "I haven't any pockets!" Now, wasn't that just like her! "Get the damn bucket!" I bellowed back.

It went on that way all night and all day, and all the next night and 16 the next day, too. By the third night we were both worn out, but she let me snatch some sandwiches as I went by, and then my service .45, and on the last lap, as I crawled along, she managed to get some gas into the tank by running behind me. She still hadn't focused enough to get the bucket, but I passed out a double handful of gravel, waved her off, and drove out to the country to get some sleep, the .45 on my lap.

I had hardly dozed off, of course, before the farmer was tapping at 17 my window and shining his light in. But he wasn't any trouble. For half a million from my padding and a look at my .45, he sold me the field and threw in some boards to box in the gas pedal and the brake and even drilled holes in the two top boards for me. By pushing a stick through the holes in each box I could work the pedals fine, except that I hadn't room for two sticks, so I had to keep fishing for the right knot hole as occasion demanded, and there was every chance that occasion might keep demanding it a bit faster than I could fish.

But he fixed me up as well as he could and he even brought me 18 some coffee. He really turned out to be a pleasant sort. "I've tried those levers myself," he said. "It gives me heart to know someone has made it."

That was a long time ago.   19

We have it pretty well worked out by now, except that she has 20
some sort of block about the bucket and never remembers to bring it
out. I drive around more-or-less on schedule, depending on the traffic,
and she's out there waiting. She holds the kid up so I can wave, and I
toss them another handful of marbles. She has box lunches ready and
a thermos and the receipted bills. We're trying to buy the house next
door so we can tear it down for me to park there, if the dynamiters
ever clear the cars parked in front of it. But the old buzzard won't sell,
and none of the crews we have working has been able to budge the
truck in front of my driveway.

It's no way to live. Many a time I've thought that if I had to make 21
just one more circle, I'd just put the .45 to my head and pull the trigger. But I've got to hold on for my wife's sake and for the kids. It's
even possible the buzzard next door will finally croak, though his kind
never does. *Something* has to give. I almost wish it could be me, but
I'm in no position to think just of myself. I have responsibilities. I've
got to hold on.

CONSIDERATIONS

1. In the second paragraph what indicates the narrator's feverish excitement?
2. What realistic details are intermixed with the fantasy? How do they add
   to the humor? What do the realistic details draw our attention to?
3. What are the narrator's relations with his family? How are they indicated
   in the story?
4. When the diamonds become burdensome, how does the narrator see
   himself? What are the indications of his attitude?
5. How do Ciardi and Forster (see "My Wood," p. 230) agree and differ in
   their views about the effects of wealth on the character? Do all or only
   some of Forster's observations about himself apply also to Ciardi's narrator?
6. WRITING TOPIC. In a 500-word essay explain how something that you
   once proudly owned turned into an unwelcome responsibility. What were
   the unexpected or unpleasant effects of owning that particular thing?

Jack Matthews

A REASONABLE MADNESS

◊

JACK MATTHEWS (b. 1925) was born in Columbus, Ohio, educated at
Ohio State University, and now teaches English at Ohio University.
He is a poet, fiction writer, and bibliophile whose works include a collection of short stories, *Bitter Knowledge* (1964), a novel, *The Cha-
risma Campaigns* (1972), and a guide for book-lovers, *Collecting Rare
Books for Pleasure and Profit* (1977, revised 1981). In this excerpt from
the last work, Matthews argues that the obsession to possess old books
is not as crazy as it may appear.

Buying first editions of contemporary, or temporarily neglected, 1
writers with the conviction their work will appreciate [in monetary
value] is an exciting game; but it is only part of the fun. The average
antique, used furniture, or junk dealer is not likely to know very much
about book values, and their establishments are fair game to the energetic collector. Do not feel sorry for these dealers, for they are willing
to play for keeps or they would not be in the business; and if they are
gullible and ignorant in negotiating with you, they will get even in another context, buying crystal goblets at the cost of Orange Crush bottles and fine china for the price of Dixie cups. They are not likely to
resent your outsmarting them, providing you have the minimal grace
of not gloating over some bargain you have gotten through their ignorance. And in spite of all the fine bargains I have gotten through the
years, I think it is certain that the seller has seldom, if ever, taken
much of a loss.

Needless to say, book dealers themselves — all of them — occa- 2
sionally miss great opportunities, for no one can know enough about
books, about their prices, their points, the pen names of authors, the
desiderata of countless anonymous collectors throughout the world.
Several years ago, in an antique and book shop in New Bedford, Mas-

261

sachusetts, I was informed by the proprietor that "ten New York dealers" had gone through his lofts recently and that no real finds could possibly remain. I thanked him for his courtesy, but climbed up into the lofts anyway, to descend some two hours later with a stack of dirty books in my dirty hands. Included in the stack was the first printing of Thomas Bailey Aldrich's *The Story of a Bad Boy* (1870), which I purchased for three dollars. Next month, Goodspeed's of Boston advertised a copy of this book for five hundred dollars, although the Goodspeed copy was described as mint, whereas mine was only good.* Still, I traded my copy to another dealer for some Mark Twain first editions, along with several other more desirable books (in my opinion), adding up to at least fifty or sixty, or perhaps one hundred, times the money I had invested in the Aldrich volume.

Every collector has such stories to tell, and it is a happy and rela- 3 tively innocent form of boasting to tell them, bringing back to the teller himself the memory of that unique thrill of seeing a rare and highly desirable book stuck unknowingly on the twenty-five or fifty-cent shelf, along with the despised and musty detritus from past years. The joy is complete when you reach for it and discover that it has the right points, that it is indeed the real thing. I picked up such a book in a junk store in Zanesville, Ohio, once; it was a first edition of F. Scott Fitzgerald's *Tender Is the Night*, and I paid forty cents for it. At a similar store in Columbus, I came upon the first edition of William Butler Yeats' *Fairy and Folk Tales of the Irish Peasantry*, which I paid thirty-five cents for. The Yeats volume is rare, for it is only his second published book; it is also a beautiful and desirable copy (with the spine only slightly faded) that I found lying at the bottom of a cardboard box, with junk of all sorts piled on top. Later, in checking the book out, I found that a similar copy had sold at auction in 1965 for $225.

Unlike that of corn and wheat, the harvest of good books is gratify- 4 ingly consistent to anyone who cares enough about them simply to keep looking. Years ago, I tried my hand at various kinds of door-to-door selling, and it was an axiom common to all that if you knock on enough doors, you'll be sure to make a sale. Maybe you'd have to knock on fifteen doors, maybe twenty, but, as the saying went, the sale had to be getting closer. Generally, I've found this a more valid prin-

---

* "Mint" and "good" describe the condition of the volumes.

ciple in book scouting than in selling during those hard old days. But, of course, one is often discouraged, and one can often hear the voice of the Devil whispering in his ear, "What in the hell are you doing wasting all this *time?*"

As a matter of fact, that voice was becoming more and more audi- 5 ble to me recently on a cold Saturday morning, when I drove to a moving sale held by some hardy movers in an open, unheated garage. The temperature was five above zero, and after shuffling through several boxes of some twenty or thirty books each, my bare hands were so cold they were beginning to feel like big wooden spoons. The books were a dreary lot — drab school texts, mostly — and stuffed under various tables and behind dusty picture frames along with an old lawn mower for the sake of maximum inconvenience. The owner, obviously insensitive to most human values, was jovial, and asked me a question of some sort (I couldn't hear, because the Devil's voice was too loud by now). I think he was asking what sort of books I collected, and I think I answered evasively, not particularly interested in starting up a conversation. He then told me he had a complete set of Shakespeare that was very old — published way back around 1918, which made me feel worse, because that wasn't a hell of a long time before I was born. I was about to point out that his index of age in books was a trifle screwed up, when I saw what might have appeared to be a geography text lying there among the school books. It was titled *Geography and Plays*. It had been printed in Boston, at the Four Seas Company; the single date on the copyright page was 1922; and the author was Gertrude Stein. In excellent condition, this copy was nevertheless in a basket of books that were being sold for a nickel apiece. Five cents, or half a dime.

By the time I left with my prize, I was pumping this insensitive fel- 6 low's hand most heartily, and blessing him in all his future dwellings. Returning home and warming myself I consulted a catalogue I had gotten only two days before, and saw a copy of this very book (like mine in excellent condition but lacking the dust jacket) advertised for $95. Not really a bad price even at that, for the book is very rare and very important, representing the work of a genuinely significant modern author. It is in this book that Ms. Stein delivered herself of the Rose is a Rose is a Rose sermon.

These stories are of course the good stories, the successes. I will re- 7 main silent about all the errors I have made in judgment, trading more expensive books for less valuable ones (which is always defensible, of course, if one knows what he's doing and simply desires the less expensive one), paying too much, or buying books that were not what I thought they were. I don't regret these lapses, however, any more than I resent those who knew more than I; if I was not deliberately lied to or misled, I have no justifiable complaint. When you enter the arena, for *this* contest, you're sure to get hit sooner or later. And indeed this is part of the game, part of the adventure.

Often people quite reasonably ask why a collector should covet first 8 editions, and — as in trying to define any passion — the answer is not easy. And yet, there are several important qualities inherent in the first edition of a rare book that can be explained. First of all, it is simply human to want to possess what others desire. If that sounds too ugly, let me suggest that the desire to possess is not necessarily conversely a desire to deprive others: it is to own that which is acknowledged to be worth owning. There is, of course, a certain arbitrariness in this, and indeed if great numbers of people — for whatever inscrutable reason — started to collect jelly glasses or empty cereal boxes, many of us would be tempted to join in the madness. This is really not so strange, nor is it a particularly grubby human quality. Possibly half the people in a football stadium don't really have a clear idea of what's happening on the field, but their enjoyment is genuine, for they are participating in a ceremony of enthusiasm. In very much the same way, a collector of first editions — whose hearing is preternaturally acute in such matters — can hear the cheering when he makes a great play and buys a first edition of *Innocents Abroad* or *The Spoils of Poynton* for only five dollars.*

But there is more than this, of course. It is almost an understate- 9 ment to remind ourselves that a book is a visible act of communication and not just a thing. To read a novel by Anthony Trollope, for example, is to gain familiarity with a remarkable man and to understand through the words he wrote something of the world as he uniquely experienced and conceived of it; it is to "see things through his eyes" and to take on some of the shrewdness and wisdom that were the particular signature of this fascinating writer. But if one can

---

* *The Innocents Abroad* (1869) is by Mark Twain; *The Spoils of Poynton* (1897) is by Henry James.

read his novel in the first edition, he is given a still closer access to his world, for the style of Trollope's time, as well as that of the man himself, is expressed in the physical book — the paper, the binding, the illustrations, the type. The first edition possesses its own signature; it is the book as Trollope first knew it, and it thus possesses a validity that later editions — even skillfully produced facsimiles, and even those that followed almost immediately — do not possess symbolically. For the collector of Trollope, a complete collection of his first editions is not a shrine, but an abiding statement of the man, symbolically and — in the form of these symbols — tangibly present.

But this still does not exhaust the matter. Like all first editions, that of *Huckleberry Finn* (which in only fair to good condition is not extraordinarily expensive in view of its stature as a classic) carries with it the signature of the time, the author, and the occasion. But also it is *original* and possesses the singular appeal of the original. There is something in our human need for truth that wants to know the origin of a thing in order to understand its nature. In fact, the word *nature* originally (OED) signified the birth or origin of something as the key to what it "naturally" is. And so it is with the word *genuine*, having to do with the original form of something, that which is not vitiated or changed and thus of a pristine worth. The collector of first editions is therefore concerned with the genuine and natural state, in both these old-fashioned conceptions, of the books he honors and desires to own. This is one aspect of the reality he desires. . . . 10

Of course, the rare find is indeed rare, and if one is intent upon scouting for his finds, he must be willing to spend a lot of time and energy, often with negligible or invisible results, for the occasional kiss of luck. But like the prospectors for gold in the Old West, the true book collector is never defeated or discouraged; and failure only goads him on to more passionate efforts and to more intense visions of the Great Reward. 11

Just as the collector who doesn't read his acquisitions mocks the very things he professes to admire, so does the bibliophilic serendipper fail grievously if he does not respond fully to the accidents that befall him. A book is, after all, part of a message: it is the transmitting part that does not become a full message until it is received or read. Consider a used-book store, with shelves crowded to groaning under their 12 thousands of books; then consider how many of these books are being read now, or have been read within the past year, or even the past decade, by anyone.

In short, it can be an adventure and an excitement to read from an   13 old, forgotten book and thus receive a message no one else today is taking in, or no one else remembers clearly. It is an act of liberation, of freedom, to pick up a volume on impulse, give it a few minutes and listen to the message it is sending out. No doubt most of the books you pick up will prove worthless to you at that time; still you have given them another chance, and you haven't *really* wasted your time.

But of course it is possible to discover gold in the unknown book: to   14 read authors who are not read today — who are not even remembered. Surely some of these are worth our attention! Several years ago, I went into an antique shop in Parkesburg, West Virginia, and bought two things that were wonderfully unexpected. The first was a framed letter in Henry George's handwriting whose first sentence reads: "I think Count Tolstoy has never read my book, though I am inclined to think one has been sent to him." The letterhead is that of George's paper, *The Standard*, and the date is April 2, 1888. When I asked the price, the lady proprietor asked how much I would be willing to give. I told her five dollars, and she consented willingly. This letter still hangs on the wall of my study.

My other purchase from this shop was a book I had not heard of,   15 and it was priced two dollars, a price I promptly and happily paid, for the book was an 1870 edition (a first, probably, since this was also the copyright date) of *Belden, The White Chief. Or*, as the title page goes on in that gabbiness of old-fashioned title pages, *Twelve Years among the Wild Indians of the Plains. From the Diaries and Manuscripts of George P. Belden, the Adventurous White Chief, Soldier, Hunter, Trapper, and Guide. Edited by Gen. James S. Brisbin, U.S.A.*

Who could resist a book with such a title? Never mind the fact that   16 almost *any* book of this date, having to do with the western Indians or the frontier (and in decent condition) is going to prove a nifty bargain at two dollars. Wright Howes' *U.S.-iana* — possibly the most dependable price index for books about America's past, even though the prices are almost all far too cheap, since the second and last edition was published in 1962 — lists the first edition of Belden as an "a" item, which is Howes' code for books in the ten- to twenty-five-dollar class.

But the Belden volume was not simply a good find in terms of its 17
resale value, should I choose to dispose of it (which I won't). When I
started reading it, I was immediately fascinated. Belden was a natural
egotist, a natural braggart, a natural adventurer, a natural writer. He
had a clear, vivid, focused mind; and his brief life was filled with extraordinary events. His flamboyant style, along with a habit of being
somewhat casual with regard to historical fact, quickly earned him the
distrust and even disdain of historians. As Colton Storm, in his monumental compilation of the *Catalogue of the Everett D. Graff Collection of Western Americana*, says with austere and understated disap-
proval: "Belden's veracity has often been questioned."

Nevertheless, the book itself is so lively and so informative in re- 18
gard to the folkways, mentality, and daily life of the Sioux (among
whom Belden lived for several years) that it is immensely readable, interesting, and valuable. My enthusiasm proved irresistible, in fact, and
eventually I edited and wrote the Introduction for a facsimile edition
published by the Ohio University Press in 1974, a few parts of which
Introduction I have just now repeated and paraphrased.

I have come upon many other interesting and powerful writers in 19
this way — writers who may not all be "unknown," but certainly people who are not found in today's canon of important or even worthwhile writers. Elias Canetti, Mason Weems, Jake Falstaff, O. E.
Rölvaag, John Cowper Powys, Janet Lewis, H. M. Brackenridge, and
Norman Douglas (still a famous name in England, but almost unknown to the large American reading public), are only a few of the
writers whose work, in the form of old or first editions or rare bind-
ings, I came upon via the antiquarian book dealer or dusty used-book
pile; and the richness and diversity of their testaments is, although
only a sample, nothing short of marvelous. To receive a message that
all other people conspire tacitly in ignoring is to focus one more area
of the infinite human spectrum, one of whose names is "reality."

Man finds and creates maps for this reality everywhere. His games, 20
whether of book collecting, poker, or chess, are microcosmic, for they
present symbolically those varieties of occasion for skill, along with
those disruptions of chance, that characterize the macrocosm, or the
world beyond. The game of collecting shares this symbolic intensifi-
cation. Who knows what book I will come on tomorrow, and how it
may broaden the horizon of my mind, or introduce an enzymic idea
into the compounds of my emotions, and enrich my sense of life!

Whatever it is, if I feel its power, I will want to own it and let it find its place in that little world of my library, whose cultivation is a human and vital act.

By now it must be firmly established that the collecting of   21 books — particularly first editions — is the most reasonable, moral, and spiritually therapeutic activity in all the world; it may in addition — with the help of shrewdness, passion, industry, and good breath — prove to be financially profitable. But it must also be admitted that to become a true book collector it helps if you are benignly and a little — *just* a little — mad.

CONSIDERATIONS

1. The first seven paragraphs recount the author's successes in buying books at "a steal," so to speak. Does Matthews appear greedy or unfair? Describe his personality in this section of the essay. What seems to motivate him? What guides his behavior?

2. In paragraphs 8 through 10, Matthews develops three reasons "why a collector should covet first editions." Which reason do you find most appealing or persuasive? That is, which of his reasons is most interestingly explained?

3. What is the special pleasure of reading forgotten, unknown books? Why does their oblivion increase his enjoyment in reading them?

4. Does Matthews always manage to address an audience of book-lovers without neglecting or patronizing a broader audience? Show how you would add or delete information in one or two places without changing the author's overall tone.

5. WRITING TOPIC. You have probably been seized at least once by a passion for collecting something — stamps, comic books, records, stuffed animals, Matchbox cars, or art prints. Write a 750-word essay about the joys (and the tinge of madness) of collecting. Include some explanation of how you got started, how you developed your collection, and what makes it interesting to pursue or to remember.

IMAGES

Norman Sanders, Andrew.

Jeff Albertson, Rolls-Royce. (*Stock, Boston*)

Linda G. Rich, Miss May, *1979.*

ADDITIONAL
WRITING TOPICS

◊

POSSESSIONS

1. Everyone has felt the hope of winning big money in a lottery, a contest, or a bet on a long shot. The lure of Las Vegas and other gambling casinos is part of popular entertainment in movies and television; many states now conduct public lotteries and offer daily gambling on the numbers game; breakfast-food and fast-food companies sponsor nationwide contests with labels or matching tickets; horse races and many other sports events include the possibility of big payoffs. Write a 750-word essay on the many ways and reasons why we are stimulated to keep expecting to win sudden riches.

2. In many households there happens to be some specially treasured object that is associated with earlier generations or with an important period in the recent family past. Perhaps it is a vase or lamp or a Bible or jewelry or a piece of furniture or a rug. The object comes to be treated as something precious and irreplaceable — even though it may be a fairly common thing — because it embodies certain ideals or sentimental associations. Select some object that holds this special status, and write a 500-word extended description of it that conveys its physical appearance and its meaningfulness as a possession.

3. People often express themselves in the way they furnish and decorate their own rooms or apartments. In 500 words — or more if you wish — describe one room that suggests the character of someone outside your immediate family. Consider colors and textures as well as objects. Give concrete, precise details, and organize your description so your reader can acquire a sense of the whole room as well as vivid impressions of its particular features. Or, if you prefer, explain what you find expressed in the young man's room in the photograph on page 269.

4. The photograph of the man with his Rolls-Royce on page 270 illustrates a kind of symbolism in possessions that is evident also in the photograph of the man on his motorcycle, which is at the beginning of this section, on page 220. For each man what are the satisfactions and effects of possessing these particular vehicles? What do the car and motorcycle signify

to them, and how do the photographs convey this meaning? What does the presence or absence of other people suggest? What do the backgrounds contribute? Are the photographs critical or ironical about the men's involvements with their machines? In a 500–700 word essay, compare and contrast these two views of personal identification with a set of wheels.

5. The photograph on page 271 shows a woman with a collection of dolls that appear well-made and possibly costly. They could be productions by a notable dollmaker, or they could be handmade by the woman herself. Consider the room, its furnishings, her appearance, the arrangement of the collection, and the perspective from which the photographer views them. What is the photographer's implied attitude toward the subject? Is the woman the object of criticism? pity? admiration? ridicule? affection? or some mixed response? What is your own response? In a 500-word essay, analyze this photograph's viewpoint, and explain how it affects your own.

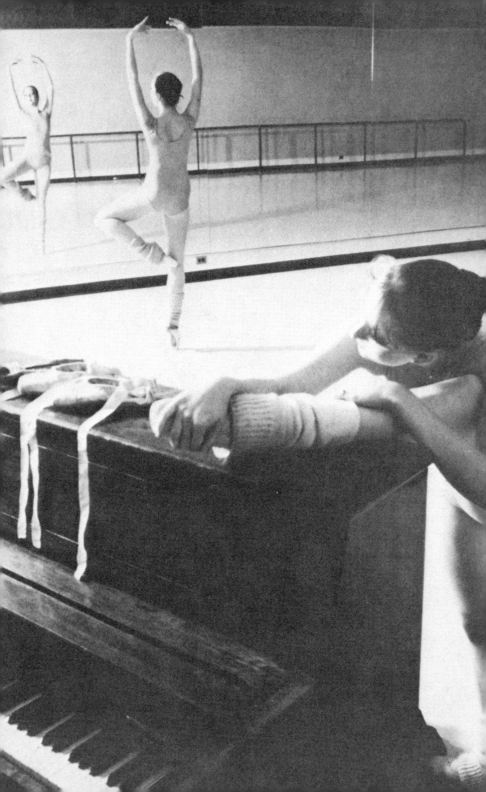

5

AMBITIONS

INSIGHTS

Ah, but a man's reach should exceed his grasp,
Or what's a heaven for?

– ROBERT BROWNING

Winning is not the most important thing; it's everything.

– VINCE LOMBARDI

If you hear a voice within you saying, "You are not a painter," *then by all means paint,* boy, and that voice will be silenced, but only by working. He who goes to friends and tells his troubles when he feels like that loses part of his manliness, part of the best that's in him; your friends can only be those who themselves struggle against it, who raise your activity by their own example of action. One must undertake it with confidence, with a certain assurance that one is doing a reasonable thing, like the farmer drives his plow, or like our friend in the scratch below, who is harrowing, and even drags the harrow himself. If one hasn't a horse, one is one's own horse — many people do so here.

– VINCENT VAN GOGH

I think that I shall be among the English poets after my death.

– JOHN KEATS

Joseph Epstein

THE VIRTUES OF AMBITION

◊

JOSEPH EPSTEIN (b. 1937) is a professor of English at Northwestern University and the editor of *The American Scholar*, a quarterly journal of essays published by the Phi Beta Kappa society. His own essays have been collected in *Familiar Territory* (1979). His observations in this essay about the good features of ambition are included in his study of *Ambition: The Secret Passion* (1980).

Ambition is one of those Rorschach words: define it and you in- 1
stantly reveal a great deal about yourself. Even that most neutral of works, *Webster's*, in its Seventh New Collegiate Edition, gives itself away, defining ambition first and foremost as "an ardent desire for rank, fame, or power." Ardent immediately assumes a heat incommensurate with good sense and stability, and rank, fame, and power have come under fairly heavy attack for at least a century. One can, after all, be ambitious for the public good, for the alleviation of suffering, for the enlightenment of mankind, though there are some who say that these are precisely the ambitious people most to be distrusted.

Surely ambition is behind dreams of glory, of wealth, of love, of 2
distinction, of accomplishment, of pleasure, of goodness. What life does with our dreams and expectations cannot, of course, be predicted. Some dreams, begun in selflessness, end in rancor; other dreams, begun in selfishness, end in large-heartedness. The unpredictability of the outcome of dreams is no reason to cease dreaming.

To be sure, ambition, the sheer thing unalloyed by some larger 3
purpose than merely clambering up, is never a pretty prospect to ponder. As drunks have done to alcohol, the single-minded have done to ambition — given it a bad name. Like a taste for alcohol, too, ambition does not always allow for easy satiation. Some people cannot

handle it; it has brought grief to others, and not merely the ambitious alone. Still, none of this seems sufficient cause for driving ambition under the counter.

What is the worst that can be said — that has been said — about 4 ambition? Here is a (surely) partial list:

To begin with, it, ambition, is often antisocial, and indeed is now 5 outmoded, belonging to an age when individualism was more valued and useful than it is today. The person strongly imbued with ambition ignores the collectivity; socially detached, he is on his own and out for his own. Individuality and ambition are firmly linked. The ambitious individual, far from identifying himself and his fortunes with the group, wishes to rise above it. The ambitious man or woman sees the world as a battle; rivalrousness is his or her principal emotion: the world has limited prizes to offer, and he or she is determined to get his or hers. Ambition is, moreover, jesuitical; it can argue those possessed by it into believing that what they want for themselves is good for everyone — that the satisfaction of their own desires is best for the commonweal. The truly ambitious believe that it is a dog-eat-dog world, and they are distinguished by wanting to be the dogs that do the eating.

From here it is but a short hop to believe that those who have 6 achieved the common goals of ambition — money, fame, power — have achieved them through corruption of a greater or lesser degree, mostly a greater. Thus all politicians in high places, thought to be ambitious, are understood to be, ipso facto, without moral scruples. How could they have such scruples — a weighty burden in a high climb — and still have risen as they have?

If ambition is to be well regarded, the rewards of ambition — 7 wealth, distinction, control over one's destiny — must be deemed worthy of the sacrifices made on ambition's behalf. If the tradition of ambition is to have vitality, it must be widely shared; and it especially must be esteemed by people who are themselves admired, the educated not least among them. The educated not least because, nowadays more than ever before, it is they who have usurped the platforms of public discussion and wield the power of the spoken and written word in newspapers, in magazines, on television. In an odd way, it is the educated who have claimed to have given up on ambition as an ideal. What is odd is that they have perhaps most benefited from ambition — if not always their own then that of their parents and grandparents. There is a heavy note of hypocrisy in this; a case of closing the barn door after the horses have escaped — with the educated themselves astride them.

Certainly people do not seem less interested in success and its ac- 8 coutrements now than formerly. Summer homes, European travel, BMWs — the locations, place names and name brands may change, but such items do not seem less in demand today than a decade or two years ago. What has happened is that people cannot own up to their dreams, as easily and openly as once they could, lest they be thought pushing, acquisitive, vulgar. Instead we are treated to fine pharisaical spectacles, which now more than ever seem in ample supply: the revolutionary lawyer quartered in the $250,000 Manhattan condominium; the critic of American materialism with a Southampton summer home; the publisher of radical books who takes his meals in three-star restaurants; the journalist advocating participatory democracy in all phases of life, whose own children are enrolled in private schools. For such people and many more perhaps not so egregious, the proper formulation is, "Succeed at all costs but refrain from *appearing* ambitious."

The attacks on ambition are many and come from various angles; 9 its public defenders are few and unimpressive, where they are not extremely unattractive. As a result, the support for ambition as a healthy impulse, a quality to be admired and inculcated in the young, is probably lower than it has ever been in the United States. This does not mean that ambition is at an end, that people no longer feel its stirrings and promptings, but only that, no longer openly honored, it is less often openly professed. Consequences follow from this, of course, some of which are that ambition is driven underground, or made sly, or perverse. It can also be forced into vulgarity, as witness the blatant pratings of its contemporary promoters. Such, then, is the way things stand: on the left angry critics, on the right obtuse supporters, and in the middle, as usual, the majority of earnest people trying to get on in life.

Many people are naturally distrustful of ambition, feeling that it 10 represents something intractable in human nature. Thus John Dean entitled his book about his involvement in the Watergate affair during the Nixon administration *Blind Ambition*, as if ambition were to blame for his ignoble actions, and not the constellation of qualities that make up his rather shabby character. Ambition, it must once again be underscored, is morally a two-sided street. Place next to John Dean Andrew Carnegie, who, among other philanthropic acts, bought the library of Lord Acton, at a time when Acton was in financial distress, and assigned its custodianship to Acton, who never was told who his benefactor was. Need much more be said on the subject than that, important though ambition is, there are some things that one must not sacrifice to it?

But going at things the other way, sacrificing ambition so as to 11 guard against its potential excesses, is to go at things wrongly. To discourage ambition is to discourage dreams of grandeur and greatness. All men and women are born, live, suffer, and die; what distinguishes us one from another is our dreams, whether they be dreams about worldly or unworldly things, and what we do to make them come about.

It may seem an exaggeration to say that ambition is the linchpin of 12 society, holding many of its disparate elements together, but it is not an exaggeration by much. Remove ambition and the essential elements of society seem to fly apart. Ambition, as opposed to mere fantasizing about desires, implies work and discipline to achieve goals, personal and social, of a kind society cannot survive without. Ambition is intimately connected with family, for men and women not only work partly for their families; husbands and wives are often ambitious for each other, but harbor some of their most ardent ambitions for their children. Yet to have a family nowadays — with birth control readily available, and inflation a good economic argument against having children — is nearly an expression of ambition in itself. Finally, though ambition was once the domain chiefly of monarchs and aristocrats, it has, in more recent times, increasingly become the domain of the middle classes. Ambition and futurity — a sense of building for tomorrow — are inextricable. Working, saving, planning — these, the daily aspects of ambition — have always been the distinguishing marks of a rising middle class. The attack against ambition is not incidentally an attack on the middle class and what it stands for. Like it or not, the middle class has done much of society's work in America; and it, the middle class, has from the beginning run on ambition.

It is not difficult to imagine a world shorn of ambition. It would 13 probably be a kinder world: without demands, without abrasions, without disappointments. People would have time for reflection. Such work as they did would not be for themselves but for the collectivity. Competition would never enter in. Conflict would be eliminated, tension become a thing of the past. The stress of creation would be at an end. Art would no longer be troubling, but purely celebratory in its functions. The family would become superfluous as a social unit, with all its former power for bringing about neurosis drained away. Longevity would be increased, for fewer people would die of heart attack or stroke caused by tumultuous endeavor. Anxiety would be extinct. Time would stretch on and on, with ambition long departed from the human heart.

Ah, how unrelievedly boring life would be!   14

There is a strong view that holds that success is a myth, and ambi-   15 tion therefore a sham. Does this mean that success does not really exist? That achievement is at bottom empty? That the efforts of men and women are of no significance alongside the force of movements and events? Now not all success, obviously, is worth esteeming, nor all ambition worth cultivating. Which are and which are not is something one soon enough learns on one's own. But even the most cynical secretly admit that success exists; that achievement counts for a great deal; and that the true myth is that the actions of men and women are useless. To believe otherwise is to take on a point of view that is likely to be deranging. It is, in its implications, to remove all motive for competence, interest in attainment, and regard for posterity.

We do not choose to be born. We do not choose our parents. We   16 do not choose our historical epoch, the country of our birth or the immediate circumstances of our upbringing. We do not, most of us, choose to die; nor do we choose the time or conditions of our death. But within all this realm of choicelessness, we do choose how we shall live: courageously or in cowardice, honorably or dishonorably, with purpose or in drift. We decide what is important and what is trivial in life. We decide that what makes us significant is either what we do or what we refuse to do. But no matter how indifferent the universe may be to our choices and decisions, these choices and decisions are ours to make. We decide. We choose. And as we decide and choose, so are our lives formed. In the end, forming our own destiny is what ambition is about.

CONSIDERATIONS

1. What does Epstein find wrong with the dictionary definition of ambition? What other assumptions about ambition does he expose in the first six paragraphs? What does Epstein accomplish by beginning his essay in this negative way?
2. Why are people hypocritical about ambition? What is a "pharisaical spectacle"?
3. According to Epstein, how does ambition hold society together? What might the world be like if nobody had ambitions?
4. Is Epstein claiming too much importance for the role of ambition in life? Is ambition really the main way we choose how we shall live?
5. WRITING TOPIC. In a 750-word essay, examine the various attitudes among college students and their families toward earning high grades. How openly are achievements pursued and displayed? What hypocrisies are generally accepted? What happens when kindness, loyalty, and generosity come into conflict with ambitions? How do they sometimes fuel ambitions? Examine the problem closely and come to a specific conclusion about the way ambition for high grades can affect a student's character for better or worse.

Andrew Carnegie

HOW I SERVED
MY APPRENTICESHIP

◊

ANDREW CARNEGIE (1835–1919), one of the most prominent of America's self-made millionaires of the late nineteenth century (who were widely denounced as "robber barons"), expounded the ethics of business ambition with unjaundiced idealism and a sense of *noblesse oblige*, or responsibility for the rest of society. With the immense fortune he made in the steel industry he established public libraries around the country and he endowed the philanthropic Carnegie Foundation. He said that it was a disgrace to die rich, but that was the one failure he chose not to avoid. His widely read book *The Gospel of Wealth* (1900) upheld the individual accumulation of riches as a stewardship that ultimately benefits humanity. In this excerpt from the opening chapter, he recalls the earliest satisfactions of his apprenticeship in business.

It is a great pleasure to tell how I served my apprenticeship as a 1 business man. But there seems to be a question preceding this: Why did I become a business man? I am sure that I should never have selected a business career if I had been permitted to choose.

The eldest son of parents who were themselves poor, I had, fortu- 2 nately, to begin to perform some useful work in the world while still very young in order to earn an honest livelihood, and was thus shown even in early boyhood that my duty was to assist my parents and, like them, become, as soon as possible, a bread-winner in the family. What I could get to do, not what I desired, was the question.

When I was born my father was a well-to-do master weaver in 3 Dunfermline, Scotland. He owned no less than four damask-looms and employed apprentices. This was before the days of steam-factories for the manufacture of linen. A few large merchants took orders, and employed master weavers, such as my father, to weave the cloth, the merchants supplying the materials.

As the factory system developed, hand-loom weaving naturally de- 4 clined, and my father was one of the sufferers by the change. The first serious lesson of my life came to me one day when he had taken in the last of his work to the merchant, and returned to our little home greatly distressed because there was no more work for him to do. I was then just about ten years of age, but the lesson burned into my heart, and I resolved then that the wolf of poverty should be driven from our door some day, if I could do it.

The question of selling the old looms and starting for the United 5 States came up in the family council, and I heard it discussed from day to day. It was finally resolved to take the plunge and join relatives already in Pittsburg. I well remember that neither father nor mother thought the change would be otherwise than a great sacrifice for them, but that "it would be better for the two boys."

In after life, if you can look back as I do and wonder at the com- 6 plete surrender of their own desires which parents make for the good of their children, you must reverence their memories with feelings akin to worship.

On arriving in Allegheny City (there were four of us: father, 7 mother, my younger brother, and myself), my father entered a cotton factory. I soon followed, and served as a "bobbin-boy," and this is how I began my preparation for subsequent apprenticeship as a business man. I received one dollar and twenty cents a week, and was then just about twelve years old.

I cannot tell you how proud I was when I received my first week's 8 own earnings. One dollar and twenty cents made by myself and given to me because I had been of some use in the world! No longer entirely dependent upon my parents, but at last admitted to the family part- nership as a contributing member and able to help them! I think this makes a man out of a boy sooner than almost anything else, and a real man, too, if there be any germ of true manhood in him. It is every- thing to feel that you are useful.

I have had to deal with great sums. Many millions of dollars have 9 since passed through my hands. But the genuine satisfaction I had from that one dollar and twenty cents outweighs any subsequent pleasure in money-getting. It was the direct reward of honest, manual labor; it represented a week of very hard work — so hard that, but for the aim and end which sanctified it, slavery might not be much too strong a term to describe it.

For a lad of twelve to rise and breakfast every morning, except the 10 blessed Sunday morning, and go into the streets and find his way to the factory and begin to work while it was still dark outside, and not be released until after darkness came again in the evening, forty minutes' interval only being allowed at noon, was a terrible task.

But I was young and had my dreams, and something within always 11 told me that this would not, could not, should not last — I should some day get into a better position. Besides this, I felt myself no longer a mere boy, but quite a little man, and this made me happy.

A change soon came, for a kind old Scotsman, who knew some of 12 our relatives, made bobbins, and took me into his factory before I was thirteen. But here for a time it was even worse than in the cotton factory, because I was set to fire a boiler in the cellar, and actually to run the small steam-engine which drove the machinery. The firing of the boiler was all right, for fortunately we did not use coal, but the refuse wooden chips; and I always liked to work in wood. But the responsibility of keeping the water right and of running the engine, and the danger of my making a mistake and blowing the whole factory to pieces, caused too great a strain, and I often awoke and found myself sitting up in bed through the night, trying the steam-gauges. But I never told them at home that I was having a hard tussle. No, no! everything must be bright to them.

This was a point of honor, for every member of the family was 13 working hard, except, of course, my little brother, who was then a child, and we were telling each other only all the bright things. Besides this, no man would whine and give up — he would die first.

There was no servant in our family, and several dollars per week 14 were earned by the mother by binding shoes after her daily work was done! Father was also hard at work in the factory. And could I complain?

My kind employer, John Hay — peace to his ashes! — soon re- 15 lieved me of the undue strain, for he needed some one to make out bills and keep his accounts, and finding that I could write a plain school-boy hand and could "cipher," he made me his only clerk. But still I had to work hard upstairs in the factory, for the clerking took but little time.

You know how people moan about poverty as being a great evil, 16 and it seems to be accepted that if people had only plenty of money and were rich, they would be happy and more useful, and get more out of life.

As a rule, there is more genuine satisfaction, a truer life, and more 17 obtained from life in the humble cottages of the poor than in the palaces of the rich. I always pity the sons and daughters of rich men, who are attended by servants, and have governesses at a later age, but am glad to remember that they do not know what they have missed.

They have kind fathers and mothers, too, and think that they enjoy 18 the sweetness of these blessings to the fullest: but this they cannot do; for the poor boy who has in his father his constant companion, tutor, and model, and in his mother — holy name! — his nurse, teacher, guardian angel, saint, all in one, has a richer, more precious fortune in life than any rich man's son who is not so favored can possibly know, and compared with which all other fortunes count for little.

It is because I know how sweet and happy and pure the home of 19 honest poverty is, how free from perplexing care, from social envies and emulations, how loving and how united its members may be in the common interest of supporting the family, that I sympathize with the rich man's boy and congratulate the poor man's boy; and it is for these reasons that from the ranks of the poor so many strong, eminent, self-reliant men have always sprung and always must spring.

If you will read the list of the immortals who "were not born to 20 die," you will find that most of them have been born to the precious heritage of poverty.

It seems, nowadays, a matter of universal desire that poverty should 21 be abolished. We should be quite willing to abolish luxury, but to abolish honest, industrious, self-denying poverty would be to destroy the soil upon which mankind produces the virtues which enable our race to reach a still higher civilization than it now possesses.

CONSIDERATIONS

1. How was young Carnegie deprived of the freedom to choose his career? How did the circumstances affect him at the time?
2. How does he express the satisfactions of earning his first wages? How did the earnings change his view of himself?

3. How do you regard the parents whom he reveres and the factory owner to whom he is grateful?
4. Why does he have "pity" and "sympathy" for the sons of wealthy fathers?
5. What are the specific benefits of poverty? Is Carnegie writing a snow job for poor young men? Is there any truth to his idealization of poverty?
6. In the preceding selection, Joseph Epstein mentions Carnegie's special generosity toward Lord Acton. How does Carnegie's account of his early life help us to understand that particular act of philanthropy?
7. WRITING TOPIC. In a 500-word essay, analyze the family origins of Carnegie's drive for success. What was the carrot-and-stick stimulus to his ambitions?

Pauline Newman

WORKING FOR THE UNION

◊

PAULINE NEWMAN (b. 1893) came to America from Lithuania at the
age of eight and went to work in a sweatshop in New York City. She
left the Triangle Shirtwaist Factory shortly before the calamitous fire
there in 1911 that killed 146 women and girls who were trapped in the
workroom. Newman became a union organizer and later an executive
of the newly formed International Ladies Garment Workers' Union.
At the age of eighty-six, when this interview took place, she was still
actively involved as the union's educational director. This life story,
along with others, appeared first in *American Mosaic: The Immigrant
Experience in the Words of Those Who Lived It* (1980).

The village I came from was very small. One department store, one 1
synagogue, and one church. There was a little square where the peasants would bring their produce, you know, for sale. And there was one
teahouse where you could have a glass of tea for a penny and sit all
day long and play checkers if you wanted.

In the winter we would skate down the hilltop toward the lake, and 2
in the summer we'd walk to the woods and get mushrooms, raspberries. The peasants lived on one side of the lake, and the Jewish people
on the other, in little square, thatched-roofed houses. In order to go to
school you had to own land and we didn't own land, of course. Very
few Jews did. But we were allowed to go to Sunday School and I never
missed going to Sunday School. They would sing Russian folk songs
and recite poetry. I liked it very much. It was a narrow life, but you
didn't miss anything because you didn't know what you were missing.

That was the time, you see, when America was known to foreigners 3
as the land where you'd get rich. There's gold on the sidewalk — all
you have to do is pick it up. So people left that little village and went
to America. My brother first and then he sent for one sister, and after

that, a few years after that, my father died and they sent for my mother and my other two sisters and me. I was seven or eight at the time. I'm not sure exactly how old, because the village I came from had no registration of birth, and we lost the family Bible on the ship and that was where the records were.

Of course we came steerage. That's the bottom of the ship and 4 three layers of bunks. One, two, three, one above the other. If you were lucky, you got the first bunk. Of course you can understand that it wasn't all that pleasant when the people on the second bunk or the third bunk were ill. You had to suffer and endure not only your own misery, but the misery from the people above you.

My mother baked rolls and things like that for us to take along, be- 5 cause all you got on the boat was water, boiled water. If you had tea, you could make tea, but otherwise you just had the hot water. Sometimes they gave you a watery soup, more like a mud puddle than soup. It was stormy, cold, uncomfortable. I wasn't sick, but the other members of my family were.

When we landed at Ellis Island our luggage was lost. We inquired 6 for it and they said, "Come another time. Come another time. You'll find it. We haven't got time now." So we left and we never saw our luggage again. We had bedding, linen, beautiful copper utensils, that sort of thing.

From Ellis Island we went by wagon to my brother's apartment on 7 Hester Street. Hester Street and Essex on the Lower East Side. We were all bewildered to see so many people. Remember we were from a little village. And here you had people coming and going and shouting. Peddlers, people on the streets. Everything was new, you know.

At first we stayed in a tiny apartment with my brother and then, 8 finally, we got one of our own. Two rooms. The bedroom had no windows. The toilets were in the yard. Just a coal stove for heat. The rent was ten dollars a month.

A cousin of mine worked for the Triangle Shirtwaist Company and 9 she got me on there in October of 1901. It was probably the largest shirtwaist factory in the city of New York then. They had more than two hundred operators, cutters, examiners, finishers. Altogether more than four hundred people on two floors. The fire took place on one floor, the floor where we worked. You've probably heard about that. But that was years later.

We started work at seven-thirty in the morning, and during the 10 busy season we worked until nine in the evening. They didn't pay you any overtime and they didn't give you anything for supper money. Sometimes they'd give you a little apple pie if you had to work very late. That was all. Very generous.

What I had to do was not really very difficult. It was just monoto- 11 nous. When the shirtwaists were finished at the machine there were some threads that were left, and all the youngsters — we had a corner on the floor that resembled a kindergarten — we were given little scissors to cut the threads off. It wasn't heavy work, but it was monotonous, because you did the same thing from seven-thirty in the morning till nine at night.

What about the child labor laws?

Well, of course, there were laws on the books, but no one bothered 12 to enforce them. The employers were always tipped off if there was going to be an inspection. "Quick," they'd say, "into the boxes!" And we children would climb into the big boxes the finished shirts were stored in. Then some shirts were piled on top of us, and when the inspector came — no children. The factory always got an okay from the inspector, and I suppose someone at City Hall got a little something, too.

The employers didn't recognize anyone working for them as a 13 human being. You were not allowed to sing. Operators would have liked to have sung, because they, too, had the same thing to do and weren't allowed to sing. We weren't allowed to talk to each other. Oh, no, they would sneak up behind if you were found talking to your next colleague. You were admonished: "If you keep on you'll be fired." If you went to the toilet and you were there longer than the floor lady thought you should be, you would be laid off for half a day and sent home. And, of course, that meant no pay. You were not allowed to have your lunch on the fire escape in the summertime. The door was locked to keep us in. That's why so many people were trapped when the fire broke out.

My pay was $1.50 a week no matter how many hours I worked. My 14 sisters made $6.00 a week; and the cutters, they were the skilled workers, they might get as much as $12.00. The employers had a sign in the elevator that said: "If you don't come in on Sunday, don't come in on Monday." You were expected to work every day if they needed you and the pay was the same whether you worked extra or not. You had to be there at seven-thirty, so you got up at five-thirty, took the horse car, then the electric trolley to Greene Street, to be there on time.

At first I tried to get somebody who could teach me English in the 15 evening, but that didn't work out because I don't think he was a very good teacher, and, anyhow, the overtime interfered with private lessons. But I mingled with people. I joined the Socialist Literary Society. Young as I was and not very able to express myself, I decided that it wouldn't hurt if I listened. There was a Dr. Newman, no relation of mine, who was teaching in City College. He would come down to the Literary Society twice a week and teach us literature, English literature. He was very helpful. He gave me a list of books to read, and, as I said, if there is a will you can learn. We read Dickens, George Eliot, the poets. I remember when we first heard Thomas Hood's "Song of the Shirt." I figured that it was written for us. You know, because it told the long hours of "stitch, stitch, stitch." I remember one of the girls said, "He didn't know us, did he?" And I said, "No, he didn't." But it had an impact on us. Later on, of course, we got to know Shelley. Shelley's known for his lyrics, but very few people know his poem dealing with slavery, called "The Masque of Anarchy." It appealed to us, too, because it was a time when we were ready to rise and that helped us a great deal. [*Recites:* "Rise like Lions after slumber."]

I regretted that I couldn't go even to evening school, let alone 16 going to day school; but it didn't prevent me from trying to learn and it doesn't have to prevent anybody who wants to. I was then and still am an avid reader. Even if I didn't go to school I think I can hold my own with anyone, as far as literature is concerned.

Conditions were dreadful in those days. We didn't have anything. 17 If the season was over, we were told, "You're laid off. Shift for yourself." How did you live? After all, you didn't earn enough to save any money. Well, the butcher trusted you. He knew you'd pay him when you started work again. Your landlord, he couldn't do anything but wait, you know. Sometimes relatives helped out. There was no welfare, no pension, no unemployment insurance. There was nothing. We were much worse off than the poor are today because we had nothing to lean on; nothing to hope for except to hope that the shop would open again and that we'd have work.

But despite that, we had good times. In the summer we'd go to 18 Central Park and stay out and watch the moon arise; go to the Palisades and spend the day. We went to meetings, too, of course. We had friends and we enjoyed what we were doing. We had picnics. And, remember, in that time you could go and hear Caruso for twenty-five cents. We heard all the giants of the artistic world — Kreisler, Pavlova. We only had to pay twenty-five cents. Of course, we went upstairs, but we heard the greatest soloists, all for a quarter, and we enjoyed it immensely. We loved it. We'd go Saturday night and stand in line no matter what the weather. In the winter we'd bring blankets along. Just imagine, the greatest artists in the world, from here and abroad, available to you for twenty-five cents. The first English play I went to was *Peer Gynt.* The actor's name was Mansfield. I remember it very well. So, in spite of everything, we had fun and we enjoyed what we learned and what we saw and what we heard.

I stopped working at the Triangle Factory during the strike in 1909 19 and I didn't go back. The union sent me out to raise money for the strikers. I apparently was able to articulate my feelings and opinions about the criminal conditions, and they didn't have anyone else who could do better, so they assigned me. And I was successful getting money. After my first speech before the Central Trade and Labor Council I got front-page publicity, including my picture. I was only about fifteen then. Everybody saw it. Wealthy women were curious and they asked me if I would speak to them in their homes. I said I would if they would contribute to the strike, and they agreed. So I spent my time from November to the end of March upstate in New York, speaking to the ladies of the Four Hundred [the elite of New York's society] and sending money back.

Those ladies were very kind and generous. I had never seen or 20 dreamed of such wealth. One Sunday, after I had spoken, one of the women asked me to come to dinner. And we were sitting in the living room in front of a fireplace; remember it was winter. A beautiful library and comfort that I'd never seen before and I'm sure the likes of me had never seen anything like it either. And the butler announced that dinner was ready and we went into the dining room and for the first time I saw the silver and the crystal and the china and the beautiful tablecloth and vases — beautiful vases, you know. At that moment I didn't know what the hell I was doing there. The butler had probably never seen anything like me before. After the day was over, a beautiful limousine took me back to the YWCA where I stayed.

In Buffalo, in Rochester, it was the same thing. The wealthy ladies 21 all asked me to speak, and they would invite me into their homes and contribute money to the strike. I told them what the conditions were that made us get up: the living conditions, the wages, the shop conditions. They'd probably never heard anything like this. I didn't exaggerate. I didn't have to. I remember one time in Syracuse a young woman sitting in front of me wept.

We didn't gain very much at the end of the strike. I think the hours 22 were reduced to fifty-six a week or something like that. We got a 10 percent increase in wages. I think that the best thing that the strike did was to lay a foundation on which to build a union. There was so much feeling against unions then. The judge, when one of our girls came before him, said to her: "You're not striking against your employer, you know, young lady. You're striking against God," and sentenced her to two weeks on Blackwell's Island, which is now Welfare Island. And a lot of them got a taste of the club.

I can look back and find that there were some members of the 23 union who might very well be compared to the unknown soldier. I'll never forget one member in the Philadelphia union. She was an immigrant, a beautiful young woman from Russia, and she was very devoted to the local union. And one Friday we were going to distribute leaflets to a shop that was not organized. They had refused to sign any agreement and we tried to work it that way to get the girls to join. But that particular day — God, I'll never forget the weather. Hail, snow, rain, cold. It was no weather for any human being to be out in, but she came into my office. I'd decided not to go home because of the weather and I'd stayed in the office. She came in and I said, "You're not going out tonight. I wouldn't send a dog out in weather like this." And I went to the window and I said, "Look." And while my back was turned, she grabbed a batch of leaflets and left the office. And she went out. And the next thing I heard was that she had pneumonia and she went to the hospital and in four days she was gone. I can't ever forget her. Of course, perhaps it was a bit unrealistic on her part, but on the other hand, I can't do anything but think of her with admiration. She had the faith and the will to help build the organization and, as I often tell other people, she was really one of the unknown soldiers.

After the 1909 strike I worked with the union, organizing in Phila- 24 delphia and Cleveland and other places, so I wasn't at the Triangle Shirtwaist Factory when the fire broke out, but a lot of my friends were. I was in Philadelphia for the union and, of course, someone from here called me immediately and I came back. It's very difficult to describe the feeling because I knew the place and I knew so many of the girls. The thing that bothered me was the employers got a lawyer. How anyone could have *defended* them! — because I'm quite sure that the fire was planned for insurance purposes. And no one is going to convince me otherwise. And when they testified that the door to the fire escape was open, it was a lie! It was never open. Locked all the time. One hundred and forty-six people were sacrificed, and the judge fined Blank and Harris seventy-five dollars!

Conditions were dreadful in those days. But there was something 25 that is lacking today and I think it was the devotion and the belief. We *believed* in what we were doing. We fought and we bled and we died. Today they don't have to.

You sit down at the table, you negotiate with the employers, you 26 ask for 20 percent, they say 15, but the girls are working. People are working. They're not disturbed, and when the negotiations are over they get the increases. They don't really have to fight. Of course, they'll belong to the union and they'll go on strike if you tell them to, but it's the inner faith that people had in those days that I don't see today. It was a terrible time, but it was interesting. I'm glad I lived then.

Even when things were terrible, I always had that faith. . . . Only 27 now, I'm a little discouraged sometimes when I see the workers spending their free hours watching television — trash. We fought so hard for those hours and they waste them. We used to read Tolstoy, Dickens, Shelley, by candlelight, and they watch the "Hollywood Squares." Well, they're free to do what they want. That's what we fought for.

CONSIDERATIONS

1. How did Newman's whole family get to America? What outlook and values in the family are indicated by that experience?
2. What were the immigrants' expectations of America and what were their first impressions of the actuality?
3. What pleasures of life does Newman recall from her childhood on the

Lower East Side of New York City? How do we know that this enjoyment helped give direction and meaning to her life?

4. What are her present attitudes toward rich people, and what conveys that impression to the reader?

5. Is Newman satisfied with the outcome of her lifelong work in the union? What does she think of as the main accomplishment of her efforts?

6. WRITING TOPIC. In four or five pages, write a dialogue between Andrew Carnegie (see the preceding selection) and Pauline Newman that deals with experiences and interests that they have in common, such as immigration, child labor, the influence of poverty on character, the determination to succeed, and their sense of the fullest promises of life. Vary the interchange between them to include both lengthy comments and short responses, and allow yourself the freedom to imagine what these two very ambitious old people might have had to say to each other or even to argue about. Invent plausible details when you need to add material that is not available from the selections.

Richard Rodriguez

READING FOR SUCCESS

◊

RICHARD RODRIGUEZ (b. 1944) grew up in San Francisco, where as the child of Spanish-speaking Mexican Americans he received his education in a language that was not spoken at home. His attraction to English and to English-speaking culture became his avenue to a promising future but he felt torn away from the people he loved. He received a Ph.D. in English from the University of California at Berkeley and remained there as a teacher, until he decided to write about the conflicting aspirations that divided him between two worlds. This selection from his autobiography, *Hunger of Memory* (1982), recalls the origin of his passion for reading.

From an early age I knew that my mother and father could read 1 and write both Spanish and English. I had observed my father making his way through what, I now suppose, must have been income tax forms. On other occasions I waited apprehensively while my mother read onion-paper letters air-mailed from Mexico with news of a relative's illness or death. For both my parents, however, reading was something done out of necessity and as quickly as possible. Never did I see either of them read an entire book. Nor did I see them read for pleasure. Their reading consisted of work manuals, prayer books, newspapers, recipes. . . .

In our house each school year would begin with my mother's care- 2 ful instruction: "Don't write in your books so we can sell them at the end of the year." The remark was echoed in public by my teachers, but only in part: "Boys and girls, don't write in your books. You must learn to treat them with great care and respect."

OPEN THE DOORS OF YOUR MIND WITH BOOKS, read the red and 3 white poster over the nun's desk in early September. It soon was apparent to me that reading was the classroom's central activity. Each course had its own book. And the information gathered from a book was unquestioned. READ TO LEARN, the sign on the wall advised in December. I privately wondered: What was the connection between reading and learning? Did one learn something only by reading it? Was an idea only an idea if it could be written down? In June, CONSIDER BOOKS YOUR BEST FRIENDS. Friends? Reading was, at best, only a chore. I needed to look up whole paragraphs of words in a dictionary. Lines of type were dizzying, the eye having to move slowly across the page, then down, and across. . . . The sentences of the first books I read were coolly impersonal. Toned hard. What most bothered me, however, was the isolation reading required. To console myself for the loneliness I'd feel when I read, I tried reading in a very soft voice. Until: "Who is doing all that talking to his neighbor?" Shortly after, remedial reading classes were arranged for me with a very old nun.

At the end of each school day, for nearly six months, I would meet 4 with her in the tiny room that served as the school's library but was actually only a storeroom for used textbooks and a vast collection of *National Geographics.* Everything about our sessions pleased me: the smallness of the room; the noise of the janitor's broom hitting the edge of the long hallway outside the door; the green of the sun, lighting the wall; and the old woman's face blurred white with a beard. Most of the time we took turns. I began with my elementary text. Sentences of astonishing simplicity seemed to me lifeless and drab: "The boys ran from the rain. . . . She wanted to sing. . . . The kite rose in the blue." Then the old nun would read from her favorite books, usually biographies of early American presidents. Playfully she ran through complex sentences, calling the words alive with her voice, making it seem that the author somehow was speaking directly to me. I smiled just to listen to her. I sat there and sensed for the very first time some possibility of fellowship between a reader and a writer, a communication, never *intimate* like that I heard spoken words at home convey, but one nonetheless *personal.*

One day the nun concluded a session by asking me why I was so 5 reluctant to read by myself. I tried to explain; said something about the way written words made me feel all alone — almost, I wanted to add but didn't, as when I spoke to myself in a room just emptied of furniture. She studied my face as I spoke; she seemed to be watching more than listening. In an uneventful voice she replied that I had nothing to fear. Didn't I realize that reading would open up whole new worlds? A book could open doors for me. It could introduce me to people and show me places I never imagined existed. She gestured toward the bookshelves. (Bare-breasted African women danced, and the shiny hubcaps of automobiles on the back covers of the *Geographic* gleamed in my mind.) I listened with respect. But her words were not very influential. I was thinking then of another consequence of literacy, one I was too shy to admit but nonetheless trusted. Books were going to make me "educated." *That* confidence enabled me, several months later, to overcome my fear of the silence.

In fourth grade I embarked upon a grandiose reading program. 6 "Give me the names of important books," I would say to startled teachers. They soon found out that I had in mind "adult books." I ignored their suggestion of anything I suspected was written for children. (Not until I was in college, as a result, did I read *Huckleberry Finn* or *Alice's Adventures in Wonderland.*) Instead, I read *The Scarlet Letter* and Franklin's *Autobiography.* And whatever I read I read for extra credit. Each time I finished a book, I reported the achievement to a teacher and basked in the praise my effort earned. Despite my best efforts, however, there seemed to be more and more books I needed to read. At the library I would literally tremble as I came upon whole shelves of books I hadn't read. So I read and I read and I read: *Great Expectations;* all the short stories of Kipling; *The Babe Ruth Story;* the entire first volume of the *Encyclopaedia Britanica* (A–ANSTEY); the *Iliad; Moby Dick; Gone with the Wind; The Good Earth; Ramona; Forever Amber; The Lives of the Saints; Crime and Punishment; The Pearl.* . . . Librarians who initially frowned when I checked out the maximum ten books at a time started saving books they thought I might like. Teachers would say to the rest of the class, "I only wish the rest of you took reading as seriously as Richard obviously does."

But at home I would hear my mother wondering, "What do you 7 see in your books?" (Was reading a hobby like her knitting? Was so much reading even healthy for a boy? Was it the sign of "brains"? Or was it just a convenient excuse for not helping around the house on Saturday mornings?) Always, "What do you see . . . ?"

What *did* I see in my books? I had the idea that they were crucial 8 for my academic success, though I couldn't have said exactly how or why. In the sixth grade I simply concluded that what gave a book its value was some major idea or theme it contained. If that core essence could be mined and memorized, I would become learned like my teachers. I decided to record in a notebook the themes of the books that I read. After reading *Robinson Crusoe*, I wrote that its theme was "the value of learning to live by oneself." When I completed *Wuthering Heights*, I noted the danger of "letting emotions get out of control." Rereading these brief moralistic appraisals usually left me disheartened. I couldn't believe that they were really the source of reading's value. But for many more years, they constituted the only means I had of describing to myself the educational value of books.

In spite of my earnestness, I found reading a pleasurable activity. I 9 came to enjoy the lonely good company of books. Early on weekday mornings, I'd read in my bed. I'd feel a mysterious comfort then, reading in the dawn quiet — the blue-gray silence interrupted by the occasional churning of the refrigerator motor a few rooms away or the more distant sounds of a city bus beginning its run. On weekends I'd go to the public library to read, surrounded by old men and women. Or, if the weather was fine, I would take my books to the park and read in the shade of a tree. A warm summer evening was my favorite reading time. Neighbors would leave for vacation and I would water their lawns. I would sit through the twilight on the front porches or in backyards, reading to the cool, whirling sounds of the sprinklers.

I also had favorite writers. But often those writers I enjoyed most I 10 was least able to value. When I read William Saroyan's *The Human Comedy*, I was immediately pleased by the narrator's warmth and the charm of his story. But as quickly I became suspicious. A book so enjoyable to read couldn't be very "important." Another summer I determined to read all the novels of Dickens. Reading his fat novels, I loved the feeling I got — after the first hundred pages — of being at home in a fictional world where I knew the names of the characters and cared about what was going to happen to them. And it bothered me that I was forced away at the conclusion, when the fiction closed tight, like a fortune-teller's fist — the futures of all the major characters neatly resolved. I never knew how to take such feelings seriously, however. Nor did I suspect that these experiences could be part of a novel's meaning. Still, there were pleasures to sustain me after I'd finish my books. Carrying a volume back to the library, I would be pleased by its weight. I'd run my fingers along the edge of the pages and marvel at the breadth of my achievement. Around my room, growing stacks of paperback books reinforced my assurance.

I entered high school having read hundreds of books. My habit of 11
reading made me a confident speaker and writer of English. Reading also enabled me to sense something of the shape, the major concerns, of Western thought. (I was able to say something about Dante and Descartes and Engels and James Baldwin in my high school term papers.) In these various ways, books brought me academic success as I hoped that they would. But I was not a good reader. Merely bookish, I lacked a point of view when I read. Rather, I read in order to acquire a point of view. I vacuumed books for epigrams, scraps of information, ideas, themes — anything to fill the hollow within me and make me feel educated. When one of my teachers suggested to his drowsy tenth-grade English class that a person could not have a "complicated idea" until he had read at least two thousand books, I heard the re-mark without detecting either its irony or its very complicated truth. I merely determined to compile a list of all the books I had ever read. Harsh with myself, I included only once a title I might have read sev-eral times. (How, after all, could one read a book more than once?) And I included only those books over a hundred pages in length. (Could anything shorter be a book?)

There was yet another high school list I compiled. One day I came 12
across a newspaper article about the retirement of an English profes-sor at a nearby state college. The article was accompanied by a list of the "hundred most important books of Western Civilization." "More than anything else in my life," the professor told the reporter with fi-nality, "these books have made me all that I am." That was the kind of remark I couldn't ignore. I clipped out the list and kept it for the several months it took me to read all of the titles. Most books, of course, I barely understood. While reading Plato's *Republic*, for in-stance, I needed to keep looking at the book jacket comments to re-mind myself what the text was about. Nevertheless, with the special patience and superstition of a scholarship boy, I looked at every word of the text. And by the time I reached the last word, relieved, I con-vinced myself that I had read *The Republic*. In a ceremony of great pride, I solemnly crossed Plato off my list.

CONSIDERATIONS

1. What were the reasons why Rodriguez did not enjoy his early reading? What do you think was the greatest single barrier to his enjoyment? What leads you to this conclusion?
2. Do you agree with his remark that "I was not a good reader"? What does he think was wrong? Is his self-criticism justified?
3. Rodriguez implies that early reading experiences would be different for a child in a middle-class, English-speaking family. What specific matters do you think might be just the same?
4. WRITING TOPIC. In a 500-word essay, reconsider a book that for a while was your favorite reading. What were you finding in it that appealed strongly to you at that time? What was its main contrast or similarity with your actual life? To what extent did the book stimulate dreams about yourself?

Seymour Wishman

A LAWYER'S GUILTY
SECRETS

◇

SEYMOUR WISHMAN (b. 1942) grew up in New Jersey and was educated at Rutgers University. He has been a practicing lawyer in New
York City and a presidential advisor in Washington, D.C., and he now
devotes himself mainly to writing. His memoir, *Confessions of a Criminal Lawyer* (1981), recalls notable cases and clients. He has also written a novel, *Nothing Personal* (1978), and is at work on a book about
juries. The following article, which first appeared in *Newsweek*, suggests that our great ambitions include unconscious goals, making it
impossible to explain exactly why we are doing what we do.

During my sixteen years as a criminal lawyer I have represented 1
hundreds of people accused of crimes, and not only have most of
them been guilty, many have been guilty of atrocities. I have represented sons who hatcheted fathers, strangers who shot strangers,
lovers who knifed lovers — killings out of rage, passion, revenge, or for
no "good" reason.

It is a fundamental principle of our system of justice that every 2
criminal defendant is entitled to a lawyer, but too much of what I've
done in the courtroom is beyond justifying by that abstract principle.
I've humiliated pathetic victims of crimes by making liars out of them
to gain the acquittal of criminals; I've struggled to win for clients who
would go out and commit new outrages. This is not what I had in
mind when I entered law school.

One of the reasons I became a criminal lawyer was to defend the 3
innocent, but I haven't had much opportunity to do that. Instead, I
find myself facing a difficult question: why have I fought so hard for
the interests of the guilty?

The answers I come up with are disturbing. Much of the satisfac- 4
tion I get from my work is connected to a lifelong emotional identification with the underdog, even a despicable underdog, against authority. Although I do enjoy, for its own sake, performing well during
a trial, my courtroom performances more than anything else express a
need for power and admiration.

. . . In trying to figure out the rewards of my work, I've received lit- 5
tle guidance from my colleagues. Most criminal lawyers I've met are
extraordinarily perceptive about the personalities of others, but when
it comes to their own behavior, the level of self-analysis usually
doesn't get much beyond: "When I'm trying a case, standing in front
of a jury, I feel totally alive."

The sense of aliveness comes, in part, from the fact that the court- 6
room is an acceptable forum in which to act out a whole range of intense emotions. On one level these displays of emotions are fake because they are controlled and purposeful. (I'm sure I'm not the first
trial lawyer who knew exactly when he was going to "lose" his temper,
what he would do while his temper was "lost," and how long it would
be before he recovered it.) Yet on another level these contrived emotions are as real and intense as anything else in my life. I have felt
genuine rage during an outburst when I had trapped a cop lying: I've
had real tears in my eyes when describing a horrible wound.

All the lawyer's emotions and skills are deployed for one pur- 7
pose — winning. During a cross-examination, all energy is spent on
beating the witness. With a tough witness, the duel can be thrilling.
Few lawyers would admit that anything other than the pleasure of
craftsmanship had been involved in subduing a witness. And yet I
have seen lawyers work a witness over, control him, dominate and
beat him — and then continue to torment him. Deriving enjoyment
from inflicting that unnecessary measure of pain might be rare, but
not that rare. If the witness is a woman, there might even be sexual
overtones to the encounter. Half joking, a colleague once told me,
"It's better than going home and hitting my wife."

Such sadism notwithstanding, most criminal lawyers are different 8
from their clients. Through mine I have become familiar with a world
that would have otherwise remained hidden from me — an intrigu-
ing, seductive, dark world. With little prompting, my clients would
describe their lives in lurid detail — passionate, desperate lives filled
with violence, drugs, and sex. I must confess I have sometimes felt a

vicarious excitement on hearing the exploits of these people so unfettered by normal restraints.

I haven't been the only one titillated by the stories. Judges, prosecutors, detectives, jurors — virtually all those connected with the administration of criminal justice — experience at one time or another this voyeurism. 9

But I have other, perhaps less neurotic reasons for finding my work satisfying. Sometimes a trial has made me feel wonderful. I've experienced a sense of power and control over events and people that is lacking in most jobs. I could decide to make heroes or villains of people, to make them fear me or like me or respect me, and go ahead and do it. I could want to move a jury to tears, and go ahead and do it. 10

. . . The lawyer's performance is in front of an audience. All eyes are focused on me. The jury is composed of twelve critics to be persuaded; they watch my every movement. Spectators fill the courtroom to cheer their favorites. The witness, the client, the court attendants, the court reporter taking down every word — all are there to see and appreciate. One can feel very special. 11

Looking down on the whole drama, watching me perform with skill, maybe even elegance, is this fatherlike authority — the robed judge. I may be impressing him, and his approval can be inordinately reassuring to me. But if he becomes an adversary during the trial, the experience of standing up to him, defying him, outmaneuvering him can provide a sense of liberation far beyond the agreeable sensation of simply helping a client. 12

Viewed another way, the trial is a battle between adversaries in which the trial lawyers are competitors. Winning the case means beating the other guy, beating your brother lawyer, just as it sometimes means beating your father, the judge. The verdict is clear and unequivocal, and it is announced in front of all those observers. A victory can provide an exhilaration like no other. 13

The trial is also a contest for high stakes. The lawyer is playing for a life. A belief in the justness of the cause, if this is possible in a given case, carries its own rewards, but rescuing anyone — even a guilty client — can be very gratifying. A client's life, or years of it, can depend on his lawyer's efforts, and those efforts can arouse the same messianic illusions in the lawyer's head whether the client is a hero or villain. 14

In trying to understand myself and my work, I am led ineluctably to the murky and subjective realm of what I brought with me when I 15 first stepped into a courtroom. It was clearly not just the belief that every criminal defendant has a right to counsel.

CONSIDERATIONS

1. What is Wishman's strongest incentive to win a case? What motives does he find generally in lawyers? What motives does he observe only in *other* lawyers?
2. How do lawyers perceive the judge? How do they react to him?
3. How appropriate is the title of the article? Perfect? Overstated? Or misleading?
4. In the final paragraph Wishman says that he is trying to recognize "what I brought with me when I first stepped into a courtroom." Summarize his article by defining the ambitions that he brings to his work.
5. WRITING TOPIC. What is the most competitive activity that you have been seriously engaged in? What made it intense? In a 500-word essay, explain the aims and some of the unexpected satisfactions of winning, or the special burdens of losing. Be specific and precise; avoid drifting into generalities and vagueness about your responses.

Fran Lebowitz

THE LAST LAUGH

FRAN LEBOWITZ (b. 1951) comes from a family of furniture store pro-
prietors in New Jersey, a fact of life that she takes into account in this
explanation of her work as a humorist. Before finding her niche, she
says that she worked at other "glamorous" jobs in New York City, such
as bulk mailing, taxi driving, and apartment cleaning. Now she satirizes
the affectations of stylish living, such as the excesses of indoor plants in
city apartments and the intrusions everywhere of music, and in general
she exudes crankiness and malice wherever she can. Her pieces have
been collected in *Metropolitan Life* (1978) and *Social Studies* (1981)
from which this selection is taken.

Coming from a family where literary tradition runs largely toward 1
the picture postcard, it is not surprising that I have never really succeeded in explaining to my grandmother exactly what it is that I do. It
is not that my grandmother is unintelligent; quite the contrary. It is
simply that so firmly implanted are her roots in retail furniture that
she cannot help but view all other occupations from this rather limited vantage point. Therefore, every time I see my grandmother I am
fully prepared for the following exchange:

"So, how are you?" 2

"Fine, Grandma. How are you?" 3

"Fine. So how's business, good?" 4

"Very good, Grandma." 5

"You busy this time of year? Is this a good season for you?" 6

"Very good, Grandma." 7

"Good. It's good to be busy." 8

"Yes, Grandma." 9

Satisfied with my responses, my grandmother will then turn to my 10
father and ask the very same questions, a dialogue a bit more firmly

grounded in reality, since he has not deviated from the Lebowitz custom of fine upholstered furniture.

The lack of understanding between my grandmother and myself 11 has long troubled me, and in honor of her recently celebrated ninety-fifth birthday I have prepared the following business history in order that she might have a clearer vision of my life and work.

My beginnings were humble, of course, but I am not ashamed of 12 them. I started with a humor pushcart on Delancey Street — comic essays, forty cents apiece, four for a dollar. It was tough out there on the street; competition was cutthroat, but it was the best education in the world because on Delancey "mildly amusing" was not enough — you had to be *funny.* I worked ten-hour days, six days a week, and soon I had a nice little following. Not exactly a cult, maybe, but I was doing okay. It was a living. I was able to put aside some money, and things looked pretty good for a store of my own in the not too distant future. Oh sure, I had my troubles, who doesn't? The housewives browsing through every essay on the cart, trying to contain their glee in the hope that I'd come down a little in price. The kids snitching a couple of paragraphs when my back was turned. And Mike the cop with his hand out all the time looking for a free laugh. But I persevered, never losing sight of my objective, and after years of struggle I was ready to take the plunge.

I went down to Canal Street to look for a store, a store of my own. 13 Not being one to do things halfway, I was thorough and finally found a good location. Lots of foot traffic, surgical supplies on one side, maternity clothes on the other — these were people who could use a good laugh. I worked like a dog getting ready for that opening. I put in a very reasonable ready-to-hear line, an amusing notions counter, a full stock of epigrams, aphorisms, and the latest in wit and irony. At last I was ready; Fran's Humor Heaven: Home of the Devastating Double Entendre was open for business. It was tough going at first, but my overhead was low. I wrote all my own stock. And eventually I began to show a nice healthy gross and a net I could live with.

I don't know when it all began to go sour — who can tell about 14 these things, I'm a humorist, not a fortuneteller — but business began to slip. First I took a bath with some barbed comments I was trying out, and then I got stuck with a lot of entertaining anecdotes. I hoped it was just an off season, but it didn't let up, and before I knew it I was in really big trouble. I tried everything, believe you me. I ran big sales — "Buy one epigram, get one free," "Twenty percent off all phrases." I even instituted a "Buy now, say later" plan. But nothing worked. I was at my wits' end; I owed everybody and was in hock up to my ears. So one day, pen in hand, I went to Morris "The Thesaurus" Pincus — a shy on East Houston who lent money to humorists in a jam. The interest rates were exorbitant but I signed my life away. What else could I do?

But it wasn't enough, and I was forced to take in a collaborator. At 15 first he seemed to be working out. He specialized in parodies and they were moving pretty good, but before too long I began to get suspicious of him. I mean, I could barely put food on my table, and there he was, riding around in a Cadillac a block long. One night after dinner I went back to the store and went over the books with a fine-tooth comb. Just as I thought, there it was in black and white: the guy was a thief. He'd been stealing my lines all along. I confronted him with the evidence and what could he do? He promised to pay me back a few pages a week, but I knew that was one joker I'd never see again.

I kicked him out and worked even harder. Eighty-hour weeks, open 16 every night until ten, but it was a losing battle. With the big humor chains moving in, what chance did an independent like me have? Then the day came when I knew all was lost. Sol's Discount Satire opened up right across the street. He wrote in bulk; I couldn't meet his prices. I, of course, was wittier, but nobody cared about quality anymore. Their attitude was "So it's a little broad, but at forty percent below list we'll forsake a little subtlety." I went in the back of the store and sat down, trying desperately to figure something out. There was a sharp rap at the door, and in walked Morris, a goon on either side, ready to collect. I told him I didn't have it. I begged for more time. I was pleading for my life. Morris stared at me coolly, a hard glint in his eye as he cleaned his nails with a lethal-looking fountain pen.

"Look, Fran," he said, "you're breaking my heart. Either you pay 17 up by next Monday, or I'm gonna spread it around that you're mixing your metaphors."

With that he turned on his heel and walked out the door followed 18 by the two gorillas. I was sweating bullets. If Morris spread that around, I'd never get another laugh as long as I lived. My head swam with crazy plans, and when I realized what I had to do, my heart thumped like a jackhammer.

Late that night I went back to the store. I let myself in through the 19 side door and set to work. I poured a lot of gasoline around, took a last look, threw in a match and beat it the hell out of there. I was twenty blocks away when the full realization of what I'd done hit me. Overcome by remorse, I ran all the way back, but it was too late. The deed was done; I'd burned my comic essays for the insurance money.

The next day I met with the adjuster from That's Life, and thank 20 God he bought the fire and paid me off. It was just enough to settle with Morris, and then I was broke again.

I started to free-lance for other stores, writing under a pseudonym, 21 of course. My heart wasn't in it, but I needed the cash. I was grinding it out like hamburger meat, trying to build up some capital. The stuff was too facile, I knew that, but there was a market for it, so I made the best of it.

The years went by and I was just getting to the point where I could 22 take it a little easy, when I was struck by an idea that was to change not only my own life but that of everyone in the entire humor business. The idea? Fast humor. After all, the pace had picked up a lot since my days on Delancey Street. The world was a different place; humor habits had changed. Everyone was in a hurry. Who had time anymore for a long comic essay, a slow build, a good long laugh? Everything was rush, rush, rush. Fast humor was an idea whose time had come.

Once again I started small, just a little place out on Queens Boule- 23 vard. I called it Rapid Repartee and used every modern design technique available. All chrome and glass, everything sleek and clean. Known in the business for my cunning and waggish ways, I couldn't resist a little joke and so used as my trademark a golden arch. No one got it. So I added another one, and got a great reaction. You really have to hit people over the head, don't you? Be that as it may, the place caught on like wildfire. I couldn't keep Quick Comebacks in stock, and the Big Crack was the hit of the century. I began to franchise, but refused to relinquish quality control. Business boomed and today I can tell you I'm sitting pretty. I've got it all: a penthouse on Park, a yacht the size of the *Queen Mary*, and a Rolls you could live in. But still, every once in a while I get that old creative itch. When this happens I slip on an apron and cap, step behind one of my thousands of counters, smile pleasantly at the customer and say, "Good morning. Something nice in a Stinging Barb?" If I'm recognized, it's always good for a laugh, because, believe you me, in this business unless you have a sense of humor you're dead.

CONSIDERATIONS

1. Most of Lebowitz's humor comes from recycling trite details about commerce in a new, bizarre, and unlikely context. Which of the many clichés that she employs are especially surprising and funny? Which ones remain pretty flat? How densely are the jokes paced, or distributed, through the piece?
2. What is the effect of her starting with an anecdote about her grandmother?
3. This piece doesn't say anything directly about working as a writer, but what do you think it may be seriously saying, at least by implication, about being a humorist?
4. WRITING TOPIC. If you have ever been confronted by someone's total failure to understand your intentions or activities (and who has not?), reconsider the situation from the other person's perspective. In a 500-word essay, explain to that person what you feel was previously not understood about your aims.

Sherwood Anderson

THE EGG

◊

SHERWOOD ANDERSON (1876–1941), whose prophetic nickname as a child was "Jobby," grew up to become an aggressive, successful paint manufacturer in Elyria, Ohio, before he abruptly abandoned his business career in order to become a writer. His first important book, *Winesburg, Ohio* (1919), sketches the isolated inhabitants of a small town in which loneliness drives people to the brink of madness. In other fiction about conventional middle-class life, such as *Many Marriages* (1923), Anderson portrays the drive for success as an emotionally deadening ambition; and in all his works he sympathizes deeply with the world's obvious failures. His compassion is mixed with folksy humor and a flair for deliciously absurd circumstances in this short story about the ultimate frustrations of pursuing success.

My father was, I am sure, intended by nature to be a cheerful, 1 kindly man. Until he was thirty-four years old he worked as a farmhand for a man named Thomas Butterworth whose place lay near the town of Bidwell, Ohio. He had then a horse of his own, and on Saturday evenings drove into town to spend a few hours in social intercourse with other farmhands. In town he drank several glasses of beer and stood about in Ben Head's saloon — crowded on Saturday evenings with visiting farmhands. Songs were sung and glasses thumped on the bar. At ten o'clock father drove home along a lonely country road, made his horse comfortable for the night, and himself went to bed, quite happy in his position in life. He had at that time no notion of trying to rise in the world.

It was in the spring of his thirty-fifth year that father married my 2 mother, then a country school-teacher, and in the following spring I came wriggling and crying into the world. Something happened to the

311

two people. They became ambitious. The American passion for getting up in the world took possession of them.

It may have been that mother was responsible. Being a school- 3
teacher she had no doubt read books and magazines. She had, I presume, read of how Garfield, Lincoln, and other Americans rose from poverty to fame and greatness, and as I lay beside her — in the days of her lying-in — she may have dreamed that I would some day rule men and cities. At any rate she induced father to give up his place as a farmhand, sell his horse, and embark on an independent enterprise of his own. She was a tall silent woman with a long nose and troubled gray eyes. For herself she wanted nothing. For father and myself she was incurably ambitious.

The first venture into which the two people went turned out badly. 4
They rented ten acres of poor stony land on Grigg's Road, eight miles from Bidwell, and launched into chicken-raising. I grew into boyhood on the place and got my first impressions of life there. From the beginning they were impressions of disaster, and if, in my turn, I am a gloomy man inclined to see the darker side of life, I attribute it to the fact that what should have been for me the happy joyous days of childhood were spent on a chicken farm.

One unversed in such matters can have no notion of the many and 5
tragic things that can happen to a chicken. It is born out of an egg, lives for a few weeks as a tiny fluffy thing such as you will see pictured on Easter cards, then becomes hideously naked, eats quantities of corn and meal bought by the sweat of your father's brow, gets diseases called pip, cholera, and other names, stands looking with stupid eyes at the sun, becomes sick and dies. A few hens and now and then a rooster, intended to serve God's mysterious ends, struggle through to maturity. The hens lay eggs out of which come other chickens and the dreadful cycle is thus made complete. It is all unbelievably complex. Most philosophers must have been raised on chicken farms. One hopes for so much from a chicken and is so dreadfully disillusioned. Small chickens, just setting out on the journey of life, look so bright and alert and they are in fact so dreadfully stupid. They are so much like people they mix one up in one's judgments of life. If disease does not kill them, they wait until your expectations are thoroughly aroused and then walk under the wheels of a wagon — to go squashed and dead back to their maker. Vermin infest their youth, and fortunes must be spent for curative powders. In later life I have seen how a lit-

erature has been built up on the subject of fortunes to be made out of the raising of chickens. It is intended to be read by the gods who have just eaten of the tree of the knowledge of good and evil. It is a hopeful literature and declares that much may be done by simple ambitious people who own a few hens. Do not be led astray by it. It was not written for you. Go hunt for gold on the frozen hills of Alaska, put your faith in the honesty of a politician, believe if you will that the world is daily growing better and that good will triumph over evil, but do not read and believe the literature that is written concerning the hen. It was not written for you.

I, however, digress. My tale does not primarily concern itself with 6 the hen. If correctly told it will center on the egg. For ten years my father and mother struggled to make our chicken farm pay and then they gave up their struggle and began another. They moved into the town of Bidwell, Ohio, and embarked in the restaurant business. After ten years of worry with incubators that did not hatch, and with tiny — and in their own way lovely — balls of fluff that passed on into semi-naked pullethood and from that into dead henhood, we threw all aside and, packing our belongings on a wagon, drove down Grigg's Road toward Bidwell, a tiny caravan of hope looking for a new place from which to start on our upward journey through life.

We must have been a sad-looking lot, not, I fancy, unlike refugees 7 fleeing from a battlefield. Mother and I walked in the road. The wagon that contained our goods had been borrowed for the day from Mr. Albert Griggs, a neighbor. Out of its side stuck the legs of cheap chairs, and at the back of the pile of beds, tables, and boxes filled with kitchen utensils was a crate of live chickens, and on top of that the baby carriage in which I had been wheeled about in my infancy. Why we stuck to the baby carriage I don't know. It was unlikely other children would be born and the wheels were broken. People who have few possessions cling tightly to those they have. That is one of the facts that make life so discouraging.

Father rode on top of the wagon. He was then a bald-headed man 8 of forty-five, a little fat, and from long association with mother and the chickens he had become habitually silent and discouraged. All during our ten years on the chicken farm he had worked as a laborer on neighboring farms and most of the money he had earned had been spent for remedies to cure chicken diseases, on Wilmer's White Wonder Cholera Cure or Professor Bidlow's Egg Producer or some other preparations that mother found advertised in the poultry papers. There were two little patches of hair on father's head just above his ears. I remember that as a child I used to sit looking at him when he had gone to sleep in a chair before the stove on Sunday afternoons in the winter. I had at that time already begun to read books and have notions of my own, and the bald path that led over the top of his head was, I fancied, something like a broad road, such a road as Caesar might have made on which to lead his legions out of Rome and into the wonders of an unknown world. The tufts of hair that grew above father's ears were, I thought, like forests. I fell into a half-sleeping, half-waking state and dreamed I was a tiny thing going along the road into a far beautiful place where there were no chicken farms and where life was a happy eggless affair.

One might write a book concerning our flight from the chicken 9 farm into town. Mother and I walked the entire eight miles — she to be sure that nothing fell from the wagon and I to see the wonders of the world. On the seat of the wagon beside father was his greatest treasure. I will tell you of that.

On a chicken farm, where hundreds and even thousands of 10 chickens come out of eggs, surprising things sometimes happen. Grotesques are born out of eggs as out of people. The accident does not often occur — perhaps once in a thousand births. A chicken is, you see, born that has four legs, two pairs of wings, two heads, or what not. The things do not live. They go quickly back to the hand of their maker that has for a moment trembled. The fact that the poor little things could not live was one of the tragedies of life to father. He had some sort of notion that if he could but bring into henhood or rooster-hood a five-legged hen or a two-headed rooster his fortune would be made. He dreamed of taking the wonder about the county fairs and of growing rich by exhibiting it to other farmhands.

At any rate, he saved all the little monstrous things that had been 11 born on our chicken farm. They were preserved in alcohol and put each in its own glass bottle. These he had carefully put into a box, and on our journey into town it was carried on the wagon seat beside him. He drove the horses with one hand and with the other clung to the box. When we got to our destination, the box was taken down at once and the bottles removed. All during our days as keepers of a restaurant in the town of Bidwell, Ohio, the grotesques in their little glass bottles sat on a shelf back of the counter. Mother sometimes protested, but father was a rock on the subject of his treasure. The grotesques were, he declared, valuable. People, he said, liked to look at strange and wonderful things.

Did I say that we embarked in the restaurant business in the town 12 of Bidwell, Ohio? I exaggerated a little. The town itself lay at the foot of a low hill and on the shore of a small river. The railroad did not run through the town and the station was a mile away to the north at a place called Pickleville. There had been a cider mill and pickle factory at the station, but before the time of our coming they had both gone out of business. In the morning and in the evening busses came down to the station along a road called Turner's Pike from the hotel on the main street of Bidwell. Our going to the out-of-the-way place to embark in the restaurant business was mother's idea. She talked of it for a year and then one day went off and rented an empty store building opposite the railroad station. It was her idea that the restaurant would be profitable. Traveling men, she said, would be always waiting around to take trains out of town and town people would come to the station to await incoming trains. They would come to the restaurant to buy pieces of pie and drink coffee. Now that I am older I know that she had another motive in going. She was ambitious for me. She wanted me to rise in the world, to get into a town school and become a man of the towns.

At Pickleville father and mother worked hard, as they always had 13 done. At first there was the necessity of putting our place into shape to be a restaurant. That took a month. Father built a shelf on which he put tins of vegetables. He painted a sign on which he put his name in large red letters. Below his name was the sharp command — "EAT HERE" — that was so seldom obeyed. A showcase was bought and filled with cigars and tobacco. Mother scrubbed the floors and the walls of the room. I went to school in the town and was glad to be away from the farm, from the presence of the discouraged, sad-looking chickens. Still I was not very joyous. In the evening I walked home from school along Turner's Pike and remembered the children I had seen playing in the town school yard. A troop of little girls had gone hopping about and singing. I tried that. Down along the frozen road I went hopping solemnly on one leg. "Hippity Hop To The Barber Shop," I sang shrilly. Then I stopped and looked doubtfully about. I was afraid of being seen in my gay mood. It must have seemed to me that I was doing a thing that should not be done by one who, like myself, had been raised on a chicken farm where death was a daily visitor.

Mother decided that our restaurant should remain open at night.   14
At ten in the evening a passenger train went north past our door followed by a local freight. The freight crew had switching to do in Pickleville, and when the work was done they came to our restaurant for
hot coffee and food. Sometimes one of them ordered a fried egg. In
the morning at four they returned north-bound and again visited us. A
little trade began to grow up. Mother slept at night and during the
day tended the restaurant and fed our boarders while father slept. He
slept in the same bed mother had occupied during the night and I
went off to the town of Bidwell and to school. During the long nights,
while mother and I slept, father cooked meats that were to go into
sandwiches for the lunch baskets of our boarders. Then an idea in regard to getting up in the world came into his head. The American
spirit took hold of him. He also became ambitious.

In the long nights when there was little to do, father had time to   15
think. That was his undoing. He decided that he had in the past been
an unsuccessful man because he had not been cheerful enough and
that in the future he would adopt a cheerful outlook on life. In the
early morning he came upstairs and got into bed with mother. She
woke and the two talked. From my bed in the corner I listened.

It was father's idea that both he and mother should try to entertain   16
the people who came to eat at our restaurant. I cannot now remember
his words, but he gave the impression of one about to become in some
obscure way a kind of public entertainer. When people, particularly
young people from the town of Bidwell, came into our place, as on
very rare occasions they did, bright entertaining conversation was to
be made. From father's words I gathered that something of the jolly
innkeeper effect was to be sought. Mother must have been doubtful
from the first, but she said nothing discouraging. It was father's notion
that a passion for the company of himself and mother would spring up
in the breasts of the younger people of the town of Bidwell. In the evening bright happy groups would come singing down Turner's Pike.
They would troop shouting with joy and laughter into our place.
There would be song and festivity. I do not mean to give the impression that father spoke so elaborately of the matter. He was, as I
have said, an uncommunicative man. "They want some place to go. I
tell you they want some place to go," he said over and over. That was
as far as he got. My own imagination has filled in the blanks.

For two or three weeks this notion of father's invaded our house. 17 We did not talk much, but in our daily lives tried earnestly to make smiles take the place of glum looks. Mother smiled at the boarders and I, catching the infection, smiled at our cat. Father became a little feverish in his anxiety to please. There was, no doubt, lurking somewhere in him, a touch of the spirit of the showman. He did not waste much of his ammunition on the railroad men he served at night, but seemed to be waiting for a young man or woman from Bidwell to come in to show what he could do. On the counter in the restaurant there was a wire basket kept always filled with eggs, and it must have been before his eyes when the idea of being entertaining was born in his brain. There was something pre-natal about the way eggs kept themselves connected with the development of his idea. At any rate, an egg ruined his new impulse in life. Late one night I was awakened by a roar of anger coming from father's throat. Both mother and I sat upright in our beds. With trembling hands she lighted a lamp that stood on a table by her head. Downstairs the front door of our restaurant went shut with a bang and in a few minutes father tramped up the stairs. He held an egg in his hand and his hand trembled as though he were having a chill. There was a half-insane light in his eyes. As he stood glaring at us I was sure he intended throwing the egg at either mother or me. Then he laid it gently on the table beside the lamp and dropped on his knees beside mother's bed. He began to cry like a boy, and I, carried away by his grief, cried with him. The two of us filled the little upstairs room with our wailing voices. It is ridiculous, but of the picture we made I can remember only the fact that mother's hand continually stroked the bald path that ran across the top of his head. I have forgotten what mother said to him and how she induced him to tell her of what had happened downstairs. His explanation also has gone out of my mind. I remember only my own grief and fright and the shiny path over father's head glowing in the lamplight as he knelt by the bed.

As to what happened downstairs. For some unexplainable reason I 18 know the story as well as though I had been a witness to my father's discomfiture. One in time gets to know many unexplainable things. On that evening young Joe Kane, son of a merchant of Bidwell, came to Pickleville to meet his father, who was expected on the ten-o'clock evening train from the South. The train was three hours late and Joe came into our place to loaf about and to wait for its arrival. The local freight train came in and the freight crew were fed. Joe was left alone in the restaurant with father.

From the moment he came into our place the Bidwell young man   19
must have been puzzled by my father's actions. It was his notion that father was angry at him for hanging around. He noticed that the restaurant-keeper was apparently disturbed by his presence and he thought of going out. However, it began to rain and he did not fancy the long walk to town and back. He bought a five-cent cigar and ordered a cup of coffee. He had a newspaper in his pocket and took it out and began to read. "I'm waiting for the evening train. It's late," he said apologetically.

For a long time father, whom Joe Kane had never seen before, re-   20
mained silently gazing at his visitor. He was no doubt suffering from an attack of stage fright. As so often happens in life he had thought so much and so often of the situation that now confronted him that he was somewhat nervous in its presence.

For one thing, he did not know what to do with his hands. He   21
thrust one of them nervously over the counter and shook hands with Joe Kane. "How-de-do," he said. Joe Kane put his newspaper down and stared at him. Father's eyes lighted on the basket of eggs that sat on the counter and he began to talk. "Well," he began hesitatingly, "well, you have heard of Christopher Columbus, eh?" He seemed to be angry. "That Christopher Columbus was a cheat," he declared emphatically. "He talked of making an egg stand on its end. He talked, he did, and then he went and broke the end of the egg."

My father seemed to his visitor to be beside himself at the duplicity   22
of Christopher Columbus. He muttered and swore. He declared it was wrong to teach children that Christopher Columbus was a great man when, after all, he cheated at the critical moment. He had declared he would make an egg stand on end and then, when his bluff had been called, he had done a trick. Still grumbling at Columbus, father took an egg from the basket on the counter and began to walk up and down. He rolled the egg between the palms of his hands. He smiled genially. He began to mumble words regarding the effect to be produced on an egg by the electricity that comes out of the human body. He declared that, without breaking its shell and by virtue of rolling it back and forth in his hands, he could stand the egg on its end. He explained that the warmth of his hands and the gentle rolling movement

he gave the egg created a new center of gravity, and Joe Kane was mildly interested. "I have handled thousands of eggs," father said. "No one knows more about eggs than I do."

He stood the egg on the counter and it fell on its side. He tried the 23 trick again and again, each time rolling the egg between the palms of his hands and saying the words regarding the wonders of electricity and the laws of gravity. When after a half-hour's effort he did succeed in making the egg stand for a moment, he looked up to find that his visitor was no longer watching. By the time he had succeeded in calling Joe Kane's attention to the success of his effort, the egg had again rolled over and lay on its side.

Afire with the showman's passion and at the same time a good deal 24 disconcerted by the failure of his first effort, father now took the bottles containing the poultry monstrosities down from their place on the shelf and began to show them to his visitor. "How would you like to have seven legs and two heads like this fellow?" he asked, exhibiting the most remarkable of his treasures. A cheerful smile played over his face. He reached over the counter and tried to slap Joe Kane on the shoulder as he had seen men do in Ben Head's saloon when he was a young farmhand and drove to town on Saturday evenings. His visitor was made a little ill by the sight of the body of the terribly deformed bird floating in the alcohol in the bottle and got up to go. Coming from behind the counter, father took hold of the young man's arm and led him back to his seat. He grew a little angry and for a moment had to turn his face away and force himself to smile. Then he put the bottles back on the shelf. In an outburst of generosity he fairly compelled Joe Kane to have a fresh cup of coffee and another cigar at his expense. Then he took a pan and filling it with vinegar, taken from a jug that sat beneath the counter, he declared himself about to do a new trick. "I will heat this egg in this pan of vinegar," he said. "Then I will put it through the neck of a bottle without breaking the shell. When the egg is inside the bottle it will resume its normal shape and the shell will become hard again. Then I will give the bottle with the egg in it to you. You can take it about with you wherever you go. People will want to know how you got the egg in the bottle. Don't tell them. Keep them guessing. That is the way to have fun with this trick."

Father grinned and winked at his visitor. Joe Kane decided that the 25

man who confronted him was mildly insane but harmless. He drank
the cup of coffee that had been given him and began to read his paper
again. When the egg had been heated in vinegar, father carried it on a
spoon to the counter and going into a back room got an empty bottle.
He was angry because his visitor did not watch him as he began to do
his trick, but nevertheless went cheerfully to work. For a long time he
struggled, trying to get the egg to go through the neck of the bottle.
He put the pan of vinegar back on the stove, intending to reheat the
egg, then picked it up and burned his fingers. After a second bath in
the hot vinegar, the shell of the egg had been softened a little, but not
enough for his purpose. He worked and worked and a spirit of desperate determination took possession of him. When he thought that
at last the trick was about to be consummated, the delayed train came
in at the station and Joe Kane started to go nonchalantly out at the
door. Father made a last desperate effort to conquer the egg and make
it do the thing that would establish his reputation as one who knew
how to entertain guests who came into his restaurant. He worried the
egg. He attempted to be somewhat rough with it. He swore and the
sweat stood out on his forehead. The egg broke under his hand. When
the contents spurted over his clothes, Joe Kane, who had stopped at
the door, turned and laughed.

A roar of anger rose from my father's throat. He danced and 26
shouted a string of inarticulate words. Grabbing another egg from the
basket on the counter, he threw it, just missing the head of the young
man as he dodged through the door and escaped.

Father came upstairs to mother and me with an egg in his hand. I 27
do not know what he intended to do. I imagine he had some idea of
destroying it, of destroying all eggs, and that he intended to let
mother and me see him begin. When, however, he got into the presence of mother, something happened to him. He laid the egg gently
on the table and dropped on his knees by the bed as I have already
explained. He later decided to close the restaurant for the night and to
come upstairs and get into bed. When he did so, he blew out the light
and after much muttered conversation both he and mother went to
sleep. I suppose I went to sleep also, but my sleep was troubled. I
awoke at dawn and for a long time looked at the egg that lay on the
table. I wondered why eggs had to be and why from the egg came the
hen who again laid the egg. The question got into my blood. It has
stayed there, I imagine, because I am the son of my father. At any

rate, the problem remains unsolved in my mind. And that, I conclude, is but another evidence of the complete and final triumph of the egg — at least as far as my family is concerned.

CONSIDERATIONS

1. What does the first sentence imply about the relationship between father and son, and what precisely implies it?
2. In the fifth paragraph how does Anderson inflate the difficulties of chicken farming? What theme unifies his humor in this paragraph?
3. Anderson takes many elements of a conventional success story and treats them ironically. What general facts of character, setting, and plot in the story are often associated with "the American passion" for getting ahead in the world? How are the particular details different in this story?
4. The narrator says about his story, "If correctly told it will center on the egg" (paragraph 6). Does the story, title and all, succeed in centering on the egg? What meaning and value does the egg come to have in this story?
5. How do Anderson and Lebowitz (in the preceding selection) compare as humorous critics of America's commercial values?
6. WRITING TOPIC. In a 500-word essay, clarify Anderson's satire of the American dream of business success. What are the main features of the nightmare that the author perceives underlying the dream? What sympathies and alternative values are implicit in the story?

Ecclesiastes

ALL IS VANITY

◊

THE PREACHER (fourth century? B.C.) is the author of the Book of Ecclesiastes in the Old Testament. He compiled traditional Hebrew sayings that convey a predominantly skeptical and world-weary attitude; these observations are presented as the wisdom of King Solomon in his old age. To the Preacher, most people's serious concerns in life appear to be mere delusions, or "vanities." In the twentieth century many of the Preacher's sayings have reappeared in secular literature — as in the titles of Henry James's *The Golden Bowl* and Ernest Hemingway's *The Sun Also Rises* — and his words have been set to a popular folk song, "Turn, Turn, Turn." This selection consists of the King James Version of Ecclesiastes 1:1–18 and 9:11.

The words of the Preacher, the son of David, king in Jerusalem. 1

Vanity of vanities, saith the Preacher, vanity of vanities; all *is* vanity. 2

What profit hath a man of all his labour which he taketh under the sun? 3

One generation passeth away, and *another* generation cometh: but the earth abideth for ever. 4

The sun also ariseth, and the sun goeth down, and hasteth to his place where he arose. 5

The wind goeth toward the south, and turneth about unto the north; it whirleth about continually, and the wind returneth again according to his circuits. 6

All the rivers run into the sea; yet the sea *is* not full; unto the place from whence the rivers come, thither they return again. 7

All things *are* full of labour; man cannot utter *it:* the eye is not satisfied with seeing, nor the ear filled with hearing. 8

The thing that hath been, it *is that* which shall be; and that which 9 is done *is* that which shall be done: and *there is* no new *thing* under the sun.

Is there *any* thing whereof it may be said, See, this *is* new? it hath 10 been already of old time, which was before us.

There is no remembrance of former *things*; neither shall there be 11 *any* remembrance of *things* that are to come with *those* that shall come after.

I the Preacher was king over Israel in Jerusalem. 12

And I gave my heart to seek and search out by wisdom concerning 13 all *things* that are done under heaven: this sore travail hath God given to the sons of man to be exercised therewith.

I have seen all the works that are done under the sun; and, behold, 14 all *is* vanity and vexation of spirit.

That which is crooked cannot be made straight: and that which is 15 wanting cannot be numbered.

I communed with mine own heart, saying, Lo, I am come to great 16 estate, and have gotten more wisdom than all *they* that have been before me in Jerusalem: yea, my heart had great experience of wisdom and knowledge.

And I gave my heart to know wisdom, and to know madness and 17 folly: I perceived that this also is vexation of spirit.

For in much wisdom *is* much grief: and he that increaseth knowl- 18 edge increaseth sorrow. . . .

I returned, and saw under the sun, that the race *is* not to the swift, 19 nor the battle to the strong, neither yet bread to the wise, nor yet riches to men of understanding, nor yet favour to men of skill; but time and chance happeneth to them all.

CONSIDERATIONS

1. What different aspects of the sun, wind, and sea does the Preacher bring to attention?
2. What specific aspects of culture does the Preacher observe?
3. What could he be referring to in verse 15? What sort of an audience could he be addressing?
4. What do you think is a probable cause of his feelings of futility?

5. WRITING TOPIC. Do the movies, television, or currently popular fiction express a viewpoint similar to the Preacher's despair over all goals and pleasures in life? Is his feeling of disenchantment with the world too painful to be enjoyable? Or too depressing to be beneficial? In a 500-word essay, argue for or against an increase in the expression of "negative ambition" in our society.

Henry David Thoreau

WHERE I LIVED,
AND WHAT I LIVED FOR

◊

HENRY DAVID THOREAU (1817–1862), one of America's greatest writers, was graduated from Harvard and went home to Concord, Massachusetts, to consider what to do in life, since he did not care to enter business or the professions, and, despite the pressures from his family and the townspeople who saw him as a drifter, he strongly resisted following any career. For a few years he and his brother tried to run a school, and Thoreau sometimes helped his father who manufactured pencils, or he took odd jobs as a surveyor. His main activity was keeping a daily journal in which he wrote probing, meticulous observations of nature around him and human nature within him. He was an intellectual rebel who condemned the shams of political democracy in his essay on "Civil Disobedience"(1849) just as he condemned slavery, which was still upheld in the United States throughout his life. He tested his ideas about self-reliance when he lived for two years in the woods at Walden Pond. This excerpt from his account of the experience, *Walden* (1854), explains that he was searching for "simplicity of life and elevation of purpose."

I went to the woods because I wished to live deliberately, to front 1
only the essential facts of life, and see if I could not learn what it had
to teach, and not, when I came to die, discover that I had not lived. I
did not wish to live what was not life, living is so dear; nor did I wish
to practise resignation, unless it was quite necessary. I wanted to live
deep and suck out all the marrow of life, to live so sturdily and Spartan-like as to put to rout all that was not life, to cut a broad swath
and shave close, to drive life into a corner, and reduce it to its lowest
terms, and, if it proved to be mean, why then to get the whole and
genuine meanness of it, and publish its meanness to the world; or if it

were sublime, to know it by experience, and be able to give a true account of it in my next excursion. For most men, it appears to me, are in a strange uncertainty about it, whether it is of the devil or of God, and have *somewhat hastily* concluded that it is the chief end of man here to "glorify God and enjoy him forever."

Still we live meanly, like ants; though the fable tells us that we were 2 long ago changed into men; like pygmies we fight with cranes; it is error upon error, and clout upon clout, and our best virtue has for its occasion a superfluous and evitable wretchedness. Our life is frittered away by detail. An honest man has hardly need to count more than his ten fingers, or in extreme cases he may add his ten toes, and lump the rest. Simplicity, simplicity, simplicity! I say, let your affairs be as two or three, and not a hundred or a thousand; instead of a million count half a dozen, and keep your accounts on your thumb-nail. In the midst of this chopping sea of civilized life, such are the clouds and storms and quicksands and thousand-and-one items to be allowed for, that a man has to live, if he would not founder and go to the bottom and not make his port at all, by dead reckoning, and he must be a great calculator indeed who succeeds. Simplify, simplify. Instead of three meals a day, if it be necessary eat but one; instead of a hundred dishes, five; and reduce other things in proportion. Our life is like a German Confederacy, made up of petty states, with its boundary forever fluctuating, so that even a German cannot tell you how it is bounded at any moment. The nation itself, with all its so-called internal improvements, which, by the way, are all external and superficial, is just such an unwieldy and overgrown establishment, cluttered with furniture and tripped up by its own traps, ruined by luxury and heedless expense, by want of calculation and a worthy aim, as the million households in the land; and the only cure for it, as for them, is in a rigid economy, a stern and more than Spartan simplicity of life and elevation of purpose. It lives too fast. Men think that it is essential that the *Nation* have commerce, and export ice, and talk through a telegraph, and ride thirty miles an hour, without a doubt, whether *they* do or not; but whether we should live like baboons or like men, is a little uncertain. If we do not get out sleepers, and forge rails, and devote days and nights to the work, but go to tinkering upon our *lives* to improve *them,* who will build railroads? And if railroads are not built, how shall we get to Heaven in season? But if we stay at home and mind our business, who will want railroads? We do not ride on the railroad; it rides upon us. Did you ever think what those sleepers are that underlie the railroad? Each one is a man, an Irishman, or a Yankee man. The rails are laid on them, and they are covered with sand, and the cars run smoothly over them. They are sound sleepers, I assure you. And every few years a new lot is laid down and run over; so that, if some have the pleasure of riding on a rail, others have the misfortune to be ridden upon. And when they run over a man that is walking in his sleep, a supernumerary sleeper in the wrong position, and wake him up, they suddenly stop the cars, and make a hue and cry about it, as if this were an exception. I am glad to know that it takes a gang of men for every five miles to keep the sleepers down and level in their beds as it is, for this is a sign that they may sometime get up again. . . .

Let us spend one day as deliberately as Nature, and not be thrown 3 off the track by every nutshell and mosquito's wing that falls on the rails. Let us rise early and fast, or break fast, gently and without perturbation; let company come and let company go, let the bells ring and the children cry — determined to make a day of it. Why should we knock under and go with the stream? Let us not be upset and overwhelmed in that terrible rapid and whirlpool called a dinner, situated in the meridian shallows. Weather this danger and you are safe, for the rest of the way is down hill. With unrelaxed nerves, with morning vigor, sail by it, looking another way, tied to the mast like Ulysses. If the engine whistles, let it whistle till it is hoarse for its pains. If the bell rings, why should we run? We will consider what kind of music they are like. Let us settle ourselves, and work and wedge our feet downward through the mud and slush of opinion, and prejudice, and tradition, and delusion, and appearance, that alluvion which covers the globe, through Paris and London, through New York and Boston and Concord, through Church and State, through poetry and philosophy and religion, till we come to a hard bottom and rocks in place, which we can call *reality*, and say, This is, and no mistake; and then begin, having a *point d'appui*, below freshet and frost and fire, a place where you might found a wall or a state, or set a lamp-post safely, or perhaps a gauge, not a Nilometer, but a Realometer, that future ages might know how deep a freshet of shams and appearances had gathered from time to time. If you stand right fronting and face to face to a fact, you will see the sun glimmer on both its surfaces, as if it were a cimeter, and feel its sweet edge dividing you through the heart and marrow, and so you will happily conclude your mortal career. Be it life or death, we crave only reality. If we are really dying, let us hear the rattle in our throats and feel cold in the extremities; if we are alive, let us go about our business.

CONSIDERATIONS

1. What would be the opposite of living "deliberately"? Think of two or three adverbs that clarify the contrast Thoreau has in mind in the first paragraph between living "life" and living "not life."
2. What is the literal meaning of "dead reckoning" in the second paragraph? How does this term fit into his surrounding figures of speech? What kind of action does Thoreau mean by this term?
3. What is the point of Thoreau's puns about railroad ties? Is he condemning the exploitation of cheap labor, or is he criticizing something else?
4. What does Thoreau say needs to be cleared away in order to reach bedrock reality?
5. In the third sentence from the end, what analogy does Thoreau use for the direct perception of truth? What emotional state does it suggest?
6. What is the argumentative purpose, or the effect on the reader, of Thoreau's abundance of puns, figures of speech, and allusions to legends and history?
7. WRITING TOPIC. If Thoreau were a college friend of yours, how would you argue with him over his insistence that you should simplify your life and your ambitions? In a 500-word response directly to Thoreau, tell him why his point of view does or does not measure up on your own Realometer.

Virginia Woolf

PROFESSIONS FOR WOMEN

VIRGINIA WOOLF (1882–1941) was an important British novelist noted for her emphasis on the subjective meaning of events rather than the outward circumstances of plot and appearance. Her novels include *Mrs. Dalloway* (1925) and *To the Lighthouse* (1927). Born into a distinguished literary family, she was educated at home, and began her writing career as a book reviewer for the London *Times Literary Supplement*. With her husband she lived among a group of artists and intellectuals known as the Bloomsbury group — a group that included E. M. Forster, John Maynard Keynes, Bertrand Russell, and Lytton Strachey. She spoke out consistently for freedom and equality for women in such works as *A Room of One's Own* (1929) and the following address to the Women's Service League. Her essays are collected in four volumes of *Collected Essays* (1967).

When your secretary invited me to come here, she told me that 1
your Society is concerned with the employment of women and she suggested that I might tell you something about my own professional experiences. It is true I am a woman; it is true I am employed; but what professional experiences have I had? It is difficult to say. My profession is literature; and in that profession there are fewer experiences for women than in any other, with the exception of the stage — fewer, I mean, that are peculiar to women. For the road was cut many years ago — by Fanny Burney, by Aphra Behn, by Harriet Martineau, by Jane Austen, by George Eliot* — many famous women, and many more unknown and forgotten, have been before me, making the path smooth, and regulating my steps. Thus, when I came to write, there were very few material obstacles in my way. Writing was a reputable and harmless occupation. The family peace was not broken by the

---

* British women novelists of the eighteenth and nineteenth centuries.

scratching of a pen. No demand was made upon the family purse. For ten and sixpence one can buy paper enough to write all the plays of Shakespeare — if one has a mind that way. Pianos and models, Paris, Vienna and Berlin, masters and mistresses, are not needed by a writer. The cheapness of writing paper is, of course, the reason why women have succeeded as writers before they have succeeded in the other professions.

But to tell you my story — it is a simple one. You have only got to 2 figure to yourselves a girl in a bedroom with a pen in her hand. She had only to move that pen from left to right — from ten o'clock to one. Then it occurred to her to do what is simple and cheap enough after all — to slip a few of those pages into an envelope, fix a penny stamp in the corner, and drop the envelope into the red box at the corner. It was thus that I became a journalist; and my effort was rewarded on the first day of the following month — a very glorious day it was for me — by a letter from an editor containing a cheque for one pound ten shillings and sixpence. But to show you how little I deserve to be called a professional woman, how little I know of the struggles and difficulties of such lives, I have to admit that instead of spending that sum upon bread and butter, rent, shoes and stockings, or butcher's bills, I went out and bought a cat — a beautiful cat, a Persian cat, which very soon involved me in bitter disputes with my neighbours.

What could be easier than to write articles and to buy Persian cats 3 with the profits? But wait a moment. Articles have to be about something. Mine, I seem to remember, was about a novel by a famous man. And while I was writing this review I discovered that if I were going to review books I should need to do battle with a certain phantom. And the phantom was a woman, and when I came to know her better I called her after the heroine of a famous poem, The Angel in the House. It was she who used to come between me and my paper when I was writing reviews. It was she who bothered me and wasted my time and so tormented me that at last I killed her. You who come of a younger and happier generation may not have heard of her — you may not know what I mean by the Angel in the House. I will describe her as shortly as I can. She was intensely sympathetic. She was immensely charming. She was utterly unselfish. She excelled in the difficult arts of family life. She sacrificed herself daily. If there was chicken, she took the leg; if there was a draught she sat in it — in short she was so constituted that she never had a mind or a wish of her own, but preferred to sympathize always with the minds and wishes of others. Above all — I need not say it — she was pure. Her purity was supposed to be her chief beauty — her blushes, her great grace. In those days — the last of Queen Victoria — every house had its Angel. And when I came to write I encountered her with the very first words. The shadow of her wings fell on my page; I heard the rustling of her skirts in the room. Directly, that is to say, I took my pen in hand to review that novel by a famous man, she slipped behind me and whispered: "My dear, you are a young woman. You are writing about a book that has been written by a man. Be sympathetic; be tender; flatter; deceive; use all the arts and wiles of our sex. Never let anybody guess that you have a mind of your own. Above all, be pure." And she made as if to guide my pen. I now record the one act for which I take some credit to myself, though the credit rightly belongs to some excellent ancestors of mine who left me a certain sum of money — shall we say five hundred pounds a year? — so that it was not necessary for me to depend solely on charm for my living. I turned upon her and caught her by the throat. I did my best to kill her. My excuse, if I were to be had up in a court of law, would be that I acted in self-defense. Had I not killed her she would have killed me. She would have plucked the heart out of my writing. For, as I found, directly I put pen to paper, you cannot review even a novel without having a mind of your own, without expressing what you think to be the truth about human relations, morality, sex. And all these questions, according to the Angel in the House, cannot be dealt with freely and openly by women; they must charm, they must conciliate, they must — to put it bluntly — tell lies if they are to succeed. Thus, whenever I felt the shadow of her wing or the radiance of her halo upon my page, I took up the inkpot and flung it at her. She died hard. Her fictitious nature was of great assistance to her. It is far harder to kill a phantom than a reality. She was always creeping back when I thought I had despatched her. Though I flatter myself that I killed her in the end, the struggle was severe; it took much time that had better have been spent upon learning Greek grammar; or in roaming the world in search of adventures. But it was a real experience; it was an experience that was bound to befall all women writers at that time. Killing the Angel in the House was part of the occupation of a woman writer.

But to continue my story. The Angel was dead; what then remained? You may say that what remained was a simple and common object — a young woman in a bedroom with an inkpot. In other words, now that she had rid herself of falsehood, that young woman had only to be herself. Ah, but what is "herself"? I mean, what is a woman? I assure you, I do not know. I do not believe that you know. I do not believe that anybody can know until she has expressed herself in all the arts and professions open to human skill. That indeed is one of the reasons why I have come here — out of respect for you, who are in process of showing us by your experiments what a woman is, who are in process of providing us, by your failures and successes, with that extremely important piece of information.

But to continue the story of my professional experiences. I made 5 one pound ten and six by my first review; and I bought a Persian cat with the proceeds. Then I grew ambitious. A Persian cat is all very well, I said; but a Persian cat is not enough. I must have a motor car. And it was thus that I became a novelist — for it is a very strange thing that people will give you a motor car if you will tell them a story. It is a still stranger thing that there is nothing so delightful in the world as telling stories. It is far pleasanter than writing reviews of famous novels. And yet, if I am to obey your secretary and tell you my professional experiences as a novelist, I must tell you about a very strange experience that befell me as a novelist. And to understand it you must try first to imagine a novelist's state of mind. I hope I am not giving away professional secrets if I say that a novelist's chief desire is to be as unconscious as possible. He has to induce in himself a state of perpetual lethargy. He wants life to proceed with the utmost quiet and regularity. He wants to see the same faces, to read the same books, to do the same things day after day, month after month, while he is writing, so that nothing may break the illusion in which he is living — so that nothing may disturb or disquiet the mysterious nosings about, feelings round, darts, dashes and sudden discoveries of that very shy and illusive spirit, the imagination. I suspect that this state is the same both for men and women. Be that as it may, I want you to imagine me writing a novel in a state of trance. I want you to figure to yourselves a girl sitting with a pen in her hand, which for minutes, and indeed for hours, she never dips into the inkpot. The image that comes to my mind when I think of this girl is the image of a fisherman lying sunk in dreams on the verge of a deep lake with a rod held out over the water. She was letting her imagination sweep unchecked round every rock and cranny of the world that lies submerged in the depths of our unconscious being. Now came the experience, the experience that I believe to be far commoner with women writers than with men. The line raced through the girl's fingers. Her imagination had rushed away. It had sought the pools, the depths, the dark places where the largest fish slumber. And then there was a smash. There was an explosion. There was foam and confusion. The imagination had dashed itself against something hard. The girl was roused from her dream. She was indeed in a state of the most acute and difficult distress. To speak without figure she had thought of something, something about the body, about the passions which it was unfitting for her as a woman to say. Men, her reason told her, would be shocked. The consciousness of what men will say of a woman who speaks the truth about her passions had roused her from her artist's state of unconsciousness. She could write no more. The trance was over. Her imagination could work no longer. This I believe to be a very common experience with women writers — they are impeded by the extreme conventionality of the other sex. For though men sensibly allow themselves great freedom in these respects, I doubt that they realize or can control the extreme severity with which they condemn such freedom in women.

These then were two very genuine experiences of my own. These 6 were two of the adventures of my professional life. The first — killing the Angel in the House — I think I solved. She died. But the second, telling the truth about my own experiences as a body, I do not think I solved. I doubt that any woman has solved it yet. The obstacles against her are still immensely powerful — and yet they are very difficult to define. Outwardly, what is simpler than to write books? Outwardly, what obstacles are there for a woman rather than for a man? Inwardly, I think, the case is very different; she has still many ghosts to fight, many prejudices to overcome. Indeed it will be a long time still, I think, before a woman can sit down to write a book without finding a phantom to be slain, a rock to be dashed against. And if this is so in literature, the freest of all professions for women, how is it in the new professions which you are now for the first time entering?

Those are the questions that I should like, had I time, to ask you. 7 And indeed, if I have laid stress upon these professional experiences of mine, it is because I believe that they are, though in different forms, yours also. Even when the path is nominally open — when there is nothing to prevent a woman from being a doctor, a lawyer, a civil servant — there are many phantoms and obstacles, as I believe, looming in her way. To discuss and define them is I think of great value and importance; for thus only can the labour be shared, the difficulties be solved. But besides this, it is necessary also to discuss the ends and the aims for which we are fighting, for which we are doing battle with these formidable obstacles. Those aims cannot be taken for granted; they must be perpetually questioned and examined. The whole position, as I see it — here in this hall surrounded by women practising for the first time in history I know not how many different professions — is one of extraordinary interest and importance. You have won rooms of your own in the house hitherto exclusively owned by men. You are able, though not without great labor and effort, to pay the rent. You are earning your five hundred pounds a year. But this freedom is only a beginning; the room is your own, but it is still bare. It has to be furnished; it has to be decorated; it has to be shared. How are you going to furnish it, how are you going to decorate it? With whom are you going to share it, and upon what terms? These, I think are questions of the utmost importance and interest. For the first time in history you are able to ask them; for the first time you are able to decide for yourselves what the answers should be. Willingly would I stay and discuss those questions and answers — but not tonight. My time is up; and I must cease.

CONSIDERATIONS

1. In the first two paragraphs, what relation does Woolf establish with her audience? What details make her appear ingratiating? Condescending? Earnest?

2. Does the Angel in the House still exist? What has changed, and what remains the same, in present-day expectations of women?

3. Does Woolf assume that men writers encounter no difficulties or conflicts in thinking independently and expressing themselves? Is Woolf a female sexist in some of her observations? How would you explain her views to an audience of men?

4. What relationships between men and women are implied in Woolf's many references to women in a house and a room? What changes in the future are suggested by the metaphorical use of "house" in the final paragraph?

5. WRITING TOPIC. In 700 words, consider the obstacles between you and an appealing but unlikely choice of profession. Freely imagine yourself in any role fifteen years from now and explain why it is genuinely attractive to you. Differentiate between limitations or conflicts that would be particularly your own and hurdles in the profession itself. How would you or the world need to be different for you to pursue that course?

IMAGES

Donald Patterson, Campaigning. (*Stock, Boston*)

David S. Strickler, Showing Little Brother the
Trophies Won as a Track Star in High School.
(*The Picture Cube*)

Peter Vandermark, Piano Recital.

ADDITIONAL
WRITING TOPICS

◊

AMBITIONS

1. Write a 750-word essay on golf or some other participant sport as a form of entertainment that embodies high ideals of workmanship that most people do not find in their jobs. Consider the sport from the viewpoint of a sociologist who is trying to find the values and stresses of a society as expressed in its recreational activities.

2. "What do you want to be when you grow up?" Children's answers to this universal question rarely express their *ambitions*. To children, any form of being adult means being more able to have what they presently want, not what they hope to achieve in the future. Their answers tell us about their likes and dislikes, which are often mixed together. In a 500-word essay, closely examine the meaning of a particular response of a child you know (or recall one of your own) when asked this question.

3. In 700 words, compare Joseph Epstein and Henry David Thoreau on the topic of ambition. Consider the issues of free choice, motivation, and the nature of failure that are part of each writer's consideration of the goals of life.

4. The photograph of the political candidate on page 335 adopts the unusual perspective of viewing the principal figures from behind. The changed effects of the lighting, the reversed stances and gestures, the disclosed details of the podium, and the faces in the audience all present the situation to the viewer in a special way. Does this perspective improve or hurt the candidate's political image? What details in the photograph make him more or less appealing to possible voters? What does the photograph imply about the campaign? In a 500-word essay, analyze the photograph's statements and suggestions about this man's political ambition.

5. The younger boy in the photograph on page 336 might or might not want to become a track star like his older brother. The older brother, on the other hand, might or might not like to see his achievements matched or surpassed. Write 500 words on the mixed attitudes toward ambition, including attitudes toward someone else's ambition, that are suggested by details of expression, stance, and the objects in this photograph.

6. Every child is sometimes asked to demonstrate a particular skill, as in the piano performance shown in the photograph on page 337. What kinds of encouragement and hindrance from other people are suggested in this picture? What details express the girl's feelings and the various attitudes in the audience? Was the event spontaneous or planned? What people are not in attendance? In 700 words, analyze the photograph and give it a title that fits your interpretation of the scene.

6

LOVE AND LONGINGS

INSIGHTS

All love is self-love.
— LAROCHEFOUCAULD

◊

God is love.
— ST. JOHN

◊

Christ, here's my discovery. You have got hold of the wrong absolutes and infinities. God as absolute? God as infinity? I don't even understand the words. I'll tell you what's absolute and infinite. Loving a woman. But how would you know? You see, your church knows what it's doing: rule out one absolute so you have to look for another.

Do you know what it's like to be a self-centered not unhappy man who leads a tolerable finite life, works, eats, drinks, hunts, sleeps, then one fine day discovers that the great starry heavens have opened to him and that his heart is bursting with it. It? She. Her. Woman. Not a category, not a sex, not one of two sexes, a human female creature, but an infinity. = ∞. What else is infinity but a woman become meat and drink to you, life and your heart's own music, the air you breathe? Just to be near her is to live and have your soul's own self. Just to open your mouth on the skin of her back. What joy just to wake up with her beside you in the morning. I didn't know there was such happiness.

But there is the dark converse: not having her is not breathing. I'm not kidding: I couldn't get my breath without her.

What else is man made for but this? I can see you agree about love but you look somewhat ironic. Are we talking about two different things? In any case, there's a catch. Love is infinite happiness. Losing it is infinite unhappiness.

— WALKER PERCY

◊

All's fair in love and war.
— ANONYMOUS

◊

During the first six months, the baby has the rudiments of a love language available to him. There is the language of the embrace, the language of the eyes, the language of the smile, vocal communications of pleasure and distress. It is the essential vocabulary of love before we can speak of love. Eighteen years later, when this baby is full grown and "falls in love" for the first time, he will woo his partner through the language of the eyes, the language of the smile, through the utterance of endearments, and the joy of the embrace. In his declarations of love he will use such phrases as "When I first looked into your eyes," "When you smiled at me," "When I held you in my arms." And naturally, in his exalted state, he will believe that he invented this love song.

— SELMA FRAIBERG

Susan Allen Toth

THE BOYFRIEND

◊

SUSAN ALLEN TOTH (b. 1940) grew up in Ames, Iowa, and was graduated from Smith College before she returned to the Midwest for a Ph.D. in English and a college teaching career. Toth writes for such magazines as *Redbook* and *Harper's*, and her scholarly articles have appeared in professional journals. She recounts her precollege years in *Blooming: A Small Town Girlhood* (1981), from which this excerpt is taken. In regard to boyfriends generally, she writes "I can't remember when I didn't want one."

Just when I was approaching sixteen, I found Peter Stone. Or did 1 he find me? Perhaps I magicked him into existence out of sheer need. I was spooked by the boys who teased us nice girls about being sweet-sixteen-and-never-been-kissed. I felt that next to being an old maid forever, it probably was most demeaning to reach sixteen and not to have experienced the kind of ardent embrace Gordon MacRae periodically bestowed on Kathryn Grayson between choruses of "Desert Song." I was afraid I would never have a real boyfriend, never go parking, never know true love. So when Peter Stone asked his friend Ted to ask Ted's girlfriend Emily who asked me if I would ever neck with anyone, I held my breath until Emily told me she had said to Ted to tell Peter that maybe I would.

Not that Peter Stone had ever necked with anyone either. But I 2 didn't realize that for a long time. High-school courtship usually was meticulously slow, progressing through inquiry, phone calls, planned encounters in public places, double or triple dates, single dates, hand-holding, and finally a good-night kiss. I assumed it probably stopped there, but I didn't know. I had never gotten that far. I had lots of time to learn about Peter Stone. What I knew at the beginning already attracted me: he was a year ahead of me, vice-president of Hi-Y, a shot-putter who had just managed to earn a letter sweater. An older man, *and* an athlete. Tall, heavy, and broad-shouldered, Peter had a sweet slow smile. Even at a distance there was something endearing about the way he would blink nearsightedly through his glasses and light up with pleased recognition when he saw me coming toward him down the hall.

For a long while I didn't come too close. Whenever I saw Peter he 3 was in the midst of his gang, a group of five boys as close and as self-protective as any clique we girls had. They were an odd mixture: Jim, an introspective son of a lawyer; Brad, a sullen hot-rodder; Ted, an unambitious and gentle boy from a poor family; Andy, a chubby comedian; and Peter. I was a little afraid of all of them, and they scrutinized me carefully before opening their circle to admit me, tentatively, as I held tight to Peter's hand. The lawyer's son had a steady girl, a fast number who was only in eighth grade but looked eighteen; the hot-rodder was reputed to have "gone all the way" with his adoring girl, a coarse brunette with plucked eyebrows; gentle Ted pursued my friend Emily with hangdog tenacity; but Peter had never shown real interest in a girlfriend before.

Although I had decided to go after Peter, I was hesitant about how 4 to plot my way into the interior of his world. It was a thicket of strange shrubs and tangled branches. Perhaps I see it that way because I remember the day Peter took me to a wild ravine to shoot his gun. Girls who went with one of "the guys" commiserated with each other that their boyfriends all preferred two other things to them: their cars and their guns. Although Peter didn't hunt and seldom went to practice at the target range, still he valued his gun. Without permits, "the guys" drove outside of town to fire their guns illegally. I had read enough in my *Seventeen* about how to attract boys to know I needed to show enthusiasm about Peter's hobbies, so I asked him if some day he would take me someplace and teach me how to shoot.

One sunny fall afternoon he did. I remember rattling over gravel 5 roads into a rambling countryside that had surprising valleys and woods around cultivated farmland. Eventually we stopped before a barred gate that led to an abandoned bridge, once a railroad trestle, now a splintering wreck. We had to push our way through knee-high weeds to get past the gate. I was afraid of snakes. Peter took my hand; it was the first time he had ever held it, and my knees weakened a little. I was also scared of walking onto the bridge, which had broken boards and sudden gaps that let you look some fifty feet down into the golden and rust-colored brush below. But I didn't mind being a little scared as long as Peter was there to take care of me.

I don't think I had ever held a gun until Peter handed me his pistol, 6 a heavy metal weapon that looked something like the ones movie sheriffs carried in their holsters. I was impressed by its weight and power. Peter fired it twice to show me how and then stood close to me, watching carefully, while I aimed at an empty beer can he tossed into the air. I didn't hit it. The noise of the gun going off was terrifying. I hoped nobody was walking in the woods where I had aimed. Peter said nobody was, nobody ever came here. When I put the gun down, he put his arm around me, very carefully. He had never done that before, either. We both just stood there, looking off into the distance, staring at the glowing maples and elms, dark red patches of sumac, brown heaps of leaves. The late afternoon sun beat down on us. It was hot, and after a few minutes Peter shifted uncomfortably. I moved away, laughing nervously, and we walked back to the car, watching the gaping boards at our feet.

What Peter and I did with our time together is a mystery. I try to 7 picture us at movies or parties or somebody's house, but all I can see is the two of us in Peter's car. "Going for a drive!" I'd fling at my mother as I rushed out of the house; "rinking" was our high-school term for it, drawn from someone's contempt for the greasy "hoods" who hung out around the roller-skating rink and skidded around corners on two wheels of their souped-up cars. Peter's car barely made it around a corner on all four wheels. Though he had learned something about how to keep his huge square Ford running, he wasn't much of a mechanic. He could make jokes about the Ford, but he didn't like anyone else, including me, to say it looked like an old black hearse or remind him it could scarcely do forty miles an hour on an open stretch of highway. Highways were not where we drove, anyway, nor was speed a necessity unless you were trying to catch up with someone who hadn't seen you. "Rinking" meant cruising aimlessly around town, looking for friends in *their* cars, stopping for conversations shouted out of windows, maybe parking somewhere for a while, ending up at the A&W Root Beer Stand or the pizza parlor or the Rainbow Cafe.

Our parents were often puzzled about why we didn't spend time in 8 each other's homes. "Why don't you invite Peter in?" my mother would ask a little wistfully, as I grabbed my billfold and cardigan and headed toward the door. Sometimes Peter would just pause in front of the house and honk; if I didn't come out quickly, he assumed I wasn't home and drove away. Mother finally made me tell him at least to come to the door and knock. I couldn't explain to her why we didn't want to sit in the living room, or go down to the pine-paneled basement at the Harbingers', or swing on the Harrises' front porch. We might not have been bothered at any of those places, but we really wouldn't have been alone. Cars were our private space, a rolling parlor, the only place we could relax and be ourselves. We could talk, fiddle with the radio if we didn't have much to say, look out the window, watch for friends passing by. Driving gave us a feeling of freedom.

Most of my memories of important moments with Peter center in 9 that old black Ford. One balmy summer evening I remember particularly because my friend Emily said I would. Emily and Ted were out cruising in his rusty two-tone Chevy, the lawyer's son Jim and his girl had his father's shiny Buick, and Peter and I were out driving in the Ford. As we rumbled slowly down Main Street, quiet and dark at night, Peter saw Ted's car approaching. We stopped in the middle of the street so the boys could exchange a few laconic grunts while Emily and I smiled confidentially at each other. We were all in a holiday mood, lazy and happy in the warm breezes that swept through the open windows. One of us suggested that we all meet later at Camp Canwita, a wooded park a few miles north of town. Whoever saw Jim would tell him to join us too. We weren't sure what we would do there, but it sounded like an adventure. An hour or so later, Peter and I bumped over the potholes in the road that twisted through the woods to the parking lot. We were the first ones there. When Peter turned off the motor, we could hear grasshoppers thrumming on all sides of us and leaves rustling in the dark. It was so quiet, so remote, I was a little frightened, remembering one of my mother's unnerving warnings about the dangerous men who sometimes preyed upon couples who parked in secluded places. We didn't have long to wait, though, before Ted's car coughed and sputtered down the drive. Soon Jim arrived too, and then we all pulled our cars close together in a kind of circle so we could talk easily out the windows. Someone's radio was turned on, and Frank Sinatra's mournful voice began to sing softly of passing days and lost love. Someone suggested that we get out of the cars and dance. It wouldn't have been Peter, who was seldom romantic. Ted opened his door so the overhead light cast a dim glow over the tiny area between the cars. Solemnly, a little self-consciously, we began the shuffling steps that were all we knew of what we called "slow dancing." Peter was not a good dancer, nor was I, though I liked putting my head on his bulky shoulder. But he moved me around the small lighted area as best he could, trying not to bump into Ted and Emily or Jim and his girl. I tried not to step on his toes. While Sinatra, Patti Page, and the Four Freshmen sang to us about moments to remember and Cape Cod, we all danced, one-two back, one-two back. Finally Emily, who was passing by my elbow, looked significantly at me and said, "This is something we'll be able to tell our grandchildren." Yes, I nodded, but I wasn't so sure. The mosquitoes were biting my legs and arms, my toes hurt, and I was getting a little bored. I think the others were too, because before long we all got into our cars and drove away.

Not all the time we spent in Peter's car was in motion. After several 10
months, we did begin parking on deserted country roads, side streets, even sometimes my driveway, if my mother had heeded my fierce instructions to leave the light turned off. For a while we simply sat and talked, with Peter's arm draped casually on the back of the seat. Gradually I moved a little closer. Soon he had his arm around me, but even then it was a long time before he managed to kiss me good-night. Boys must have been as scared as we girls were, though we always thought of them as having much more experience. We all compared notes, shyly, about how far our boyfriends had gone; was he holding your hand yet, or taking you parking, or . . . ? When a girl finally got kissed, telephone lines burned with the news next day. I was getting a little embarrassed about how long it was taking Peter to get around to it. My sixteenth birthday was only a few weeks away, and so far I had nothing substantial to report. I was increasingly nervous too because I still didn't know quite how I was going to behave. We girls joked about wondering where your teeth went and did glasses get in the way, but no one could give a convincing description. For many years I never told anyone about what *did* happen to me that first time. I was too ashamed. Peter and I were parked down the street from my house, talking, snuggling, listening to the radio. During a silence I turned my face toward him, and then he kissed me, tentatively and quickly. I was exhilarated but frightened. I wanted to respond in an adequate way,

but my instincts did not entirely cooperate. I leaned towards Peter, but at the last moment I panicked. Instead of kissing him, I gave him a sudden lick on the cheek. He didn't know what to say. Neither did I.

Next morning I was relieved that it was all over. I dutifully reported 11 my news to a few key girlfriends who could pass it on to others. I left out the part about the lick. That was my last bulletin. After a first kiss, we girls also respected each other's privacy. What more was there to know? We assumed that couples sat in their cars and necked, but nice girls, we also assumed, went no farther. We knew the girls who did. Their names got around. We marveled at them, uncomprehending as much as disapproving. Usually they talked about getting married to their boyfriends, and eventually some of them did. A lot of "nice" girls suffered under this distinction. One of them told me years later how she and her steady boyfriend had yearned and held back, stopped just short, petted and clutched and gritted their teeth. "When we went together to see the movie *Splendor in the Grass*, we had to leave the theatre," she said ruefully. "The part about how Natalie Wood and Warren Beatty wanted to make love so desperately and couldn't. . . . Well, that was just how we felt."

My mother worried about what was going on in the car during 12 those long evenings when Peter and I went "out driving." She needn't have. Amazing as it seems now, when courting has speeded up to a freeway pace, when I wonder if a man who doesn't try to get me to bed immediately might possibly be gay, Peter and I gave each other hours of affection without ever crossing the invisible line. We sat in his car and necked, a word that was anatomically correct. We hugged and kissed, nuzzling ears and noses and hairlines. But Peter never put a hand on my breast, and I wouldn't have known whether Peter had an erection if it had risen up and thwapped me in the face. I never got that close. Although we probably should have perished from frustration, in fact I reveled in all that holding and touching. Peter seemed pleased too, and he never demanded more. Later, I suppose, he learned quickly with someone else about what he had been missing. But I remember with gratitude Peter's awkward tenderness and the absolute faith I had in his inability to hurt me.

After Peter graduated and entered the university, our relationship 13 changed. Few high-school girls I knew went out with college men; it was considered risky, like dating someone not quite in your social set or from another town. You were cut off. At the few fraternity functions Peter took me to, I didn't know anyone there. I had no idea what to talk about or how to act. So I refused to go, and I stopped asking Peter to come with me to parties or dances at the high school. I thought he didn't fit in there either. When I was honest with myself, I admitted that romance had gone. Already planning to go away to college, I could sense new vistas opening before me, glowing horizons whose light completely eclipsed a boyfriend like Peter. When I got on the Chicago & Northwestern train to go east to Smith, I felt with relief that the train trip was erasing one problem for me. I simply rode away from Peter.

On my sixteenth birthday, Peter gave me a small cross on a chain. 14
All the guys had decided that year to give their girlfriends crosses on chains, even though none of them was especially religious. It was a perfect gift, they thought, intimate without being soppy. Everyone's cross cost ten dollars, a lot of money, because it was real sterling silver. Long after Peter and I stopped seeing each other, I kept my cross around my neck, not taking it off even when I was in the bathtub. Like my two wooden dolls from years before, I clung to that cross as a superstitious token. It meant that someone I had once cared for had cared for me in return. Once I had had a boyfriend.

CONSIDERATIONS

1. What moved Toth into her first romance? What was apparently *not* part of the impetus?
2. Where did Toth learn the appropriate way for her to interest Peter? What indicates her present attitude toward the episode with the gun?
3. Why didn't they ever come into each other's houses? What were the reasons for being in cars all the time?
4. Is there any part of this account that strikes you as probably oversimplified or idealized? What additions might make it more true to life without changing the main points of her memoir?
5. What was the lasting effect of this romance after it ended? Was it different from what she sought or expected?
6. WRITING TOPIC. From your own insights about friendship and early dating, explain how a group of friends of your own sex affects the progress of a romantic interest. What do friends provide? And what confusions or complications do they sometimes cause? In a 500-word essay, come to a

specific conclusion about the role of a group of friends in the context of high school dating.

7. WRITING TOPIC. Consider the photograph on page 406. In 500 words, discuss the harmony of details that contribute to its unified impression of the moment. Comment on the placement of the figures, their posture and suggestions of movement, the implications of the setting, and any other details that make this picture vividly expressive of the awkwardness of first romance.

Wendell Berry

GETTING MARRIED

◊

WENDELL BERRY (b. 1934) has made his native state of Kentucky the setting and also the subject of much of his writing. In poems, novels, and essays Berry presents ordinary life with reference to the meaning and value of nature. His sense of connection between the order of nature and the morality of human experience surfaces even in the titles of his books, such as *Essays Cultural and Agricultural* (1972); a book of poems, *The Country of Marriage* (1973); and *The Unsettling of America* (1977). This excerpt from an earlier collection of essays, *The Long-legged House* (1969), recalls the first months of his marriage, which were spent at his rustic house in the woods.

My student career was over in the spring of 1957, and I was glad 1 enough to be done with it. My wife and I were married in May of that year. In the fall I was to take my first teaching job. We decided to stay through the summer at the Camp. For me, that was a happy return. For Tanya, who was hardly a country girl, it was a new kind of place, confronting her with hardships she could not have expected. We were starting a long way from the all-electric marriage that the average modern American girl supposedly takes for granted. If Tanya had been the average modern American girl, she probably would have returned me to bachelorhood within a week — but then, of course, she would have had no interest in such a life, or in such a marriage, in the first place. As it was, she came as a stranger into the country where I had spent my life, and made me feel more free and comfortable in it than I had ever felt before. That is the most graceful generosity that I know.

For weeks before the wedding I spent every spare minute at the 2 Camp, getting it ready to live in. I mowed around it, and cleaned it out, and patched the roof. I replaced the broken windowpanes, and put on new screens, and whitewashed the walls, and scrounged furniture out of various family attics and back rooms. As a special wedding gift to Tanya I built a new privy — which never aspired so high as to have a door, but did sport a real toilet seat.

All this, I think, was more meaningful and proper than I knew at 3 the time. To a greater extent than is now common, or even possible for most men, I had by my own doing prepared the house I was to bring my wife to, and in preparing the house I prepared myself. This was the place that was more my own than any other in the world. In it, I had made of loneliness a good thing. I had lived days and days of solitary happiness there. And now I changed it, to make it the place of my marriage. A complex love went into those preparations — for Tanya, and for the place too. Working through those bright May days, the foliage fresh and full around me, the river running swift and high after rain, was an act of realization: as I worked, getting ready for the time when Tanya would come to live there with me, I understood more and more what the possible meanings were. If it had gone differently — if it had followed, say, the prescription of caution: first "enough" money, and then the "right" sort of house in the "right" sort of place — I think I would have been a poorer husband. And my life, I know, would have been poorer. It wasn't, to be sure, a pemanent place that I had prepared; we were going to be there only for the one summer. It was, maybe one ought to say, no more than a ritual. But it was a meaningful and useful ritual.

In the sense that is most meaningful, our wedding did not begin 4 until the ceremony was over. It began, it seems to me, the next morning when we went together to the Camp for the first time since I started work on it. I hesitate to try to represent here the pleasure Tanya may have felt on this first arrival at our house, or the pride that I felt — those feelings were innocent enough, and probably had no more foundation than innocence needs. The point is that, for us, these feelings were substantiated by the Camp; they had its atmosphere and flavor, and partook of its history. That morning when Tanya first came to it as my wife, its long involvement in my life was transformed, given a richness and significance it had not had before. It had come to a suddenly illuminating promise. A new life had been added to it, as a new life had been added to my life. The ramshackle old house and my renewal of it particularized a good deal more for us than we could have realized then. We began there.

It would be a mistake to imply that two lives can unite and make a life between them without discord and pain. Marriage is a perilous and fearful effort, it seems to me. There can't be enough knowledge at the beginning. It must endure the blundering of ignorance. It is both the cause and the effect of what happens to it. It creates pain that it is the only cure for. It is the only comfort for its hardships. In a time when divorce is as accepted and conventionalized as marriage, a marriage that lasts must look a little like a miracle. That ours lasts — and in its own right and its own way, not in pathetic and hopeless parody of some "expert" notion — is largely, I believe, owing to the way it began, to the Camp and what it meant and came to mean. In coming there, we avoided either suspending ourselves in some honeymoon resort or sinking ourselves into the stampede for "success." In the life we lived that summer we represented to ourselves what we wanted — and it was *not* the headlong pilgrimage after money and comfort and prestige. We were spared that stress from the beginning. And there at the Camp we had around us the elemental world of water and light and earth and air. We felt the presences of the wild creatures, the river, the trees, the stars. Though we had our troubles, we had them in a true perspective. The universe, as we could see any night, is unimaginably large, and mostly empty, and mostly dark. We knew we needed to be together more than we needed to be apart.

That summer has no story; it has not simplified itself enough in my memory to have the consistency of a story and maybe it never will; the memories are too numerous and too diverse, and too deeply rooted in my life.

One of the first things I did after we got settled was to put some trotlines in the river. On a dark rainy night in early June we had stayed up until nearly midnight, making strawberry preserves, and I decided on an impulse to go and raise my lines. Working my way along the line in pitch dark a few minutes later, I pulled out of the middle of the river a catfish that weighed twenty-seven pounds. Tanya had already gone to bed, and had to get up again to hear me congratulate myself in the presence of the captive. And so, indelibly associated with the early days of my marriage is a big catfish. Perhaps it is for the best.

The night of the Fourth of July of that year there came one of the worst storms this part of the country ever knew. For hours the rain spouted down on our tin roof in a wild crashing that did not let up. The Camp had no inner walls or ceilings; it was like trying to sleep inside a drum. The lightning strokes overlapped, so that it would seem to stay light for minutes at a stretch, and the thunder kept up a great knocking at the walls. After a while it began to seem unbelievable that the rain did not break through the roof. It was an apocalyptic night. The next morning we went out in bright sunshine to find the river risen to the top of its banks. There was a lasting astonishment in looking at it, and a sort of speculative fear; if that storm had reached much farther upstream we would have had to swim out of bed. Upstream, we could see several large trees that Cane Run had torn out by the roots and hurled clear across the river to lodge against the Owen County bank. The marks of that rain are still visible here.

And I remember a quiet night of a full moon when we rowed the 9 boat up into the bend above the mouth of Cane Run, and let the slow current bring us down again. I sat on the rower's seat in the middle of the boat, and Tanya sat facing me in the stern. We stayed quiet, aware of the quietness in the country around us, the sky and the water and the Owen County hills all still in the white stare of the moon. The wooded hill above the Camp stood dark over us. As it bore us, the current turned us as though in the slow spiral of a dance.

Summer evenings here on the river have a quietness and a feeling 10 of completion about them that I have never known in any other place, and I have kept in mind the evenings of that summer. The wind dies about sundown, and the surface of the river grows smooth. The reflections of the trees lie inverted and perfect on it. Occasionally a fish will jump, or a kingfisher hurry, skreaking, along the fringe of willows. In the clearing around the house the phoebes and pewees call from their lookout perches, circling out and back in their hunting flights as long as the light lasts. Out over the water the swallows silently pass and return, dipping and looping, climbing and dipping and looping, sometimes skimming the surface to drink or bathe as they fly. The air seems to come alive with the weaving of their paths. As I sat there watching from the porch those evenings, sometimes a profound peacefulness would come to me, as it had at other times, but now it came of an awareness not only of the place, but of my marriage, a completeness I had not felt before. I was there not only because I wanted to be, as always before, but now because Tanya was there too.

CONSIDERATIONS

1. Berry says that "in preparing the house I prepared myself." Are we told of any specific changes in him during his preparation of the Camp? How did he prepare himself?
2. What does Berry mean by "our wedding did not begin until the ceremony was over"? Notice that he is saying not "our marriage" but "our wedding."
3. How did the Camp influence the subsequent course of their marriage? What values were recognized there that could not as easily be recognized elsewhere?
4. What do the incidents of the catfish catch and the big storm add to the meaning of that summer?
5. What is an idyll? How would you describe the love that is indicated in this idyll? (Resist the temptation to call it "idyllic.")
6. WRITING TOPIC. Considering the entire experience at the Camp as Berry's marriage rituals, compare them with conventional marriage rituals that include more social involvement, such as bachelor parties, wedding showers, and honeymoon trips. In a 500-word essay, explain the implications about marriage that may be conveyed by the different rituals.

Katherine Mansfield

SIX LOVE LETTERS

◊

KATHERINE MANSFIELD (1888–1923), born in New Zealand, went to London as a young woman to be a short-story writer. Among her collections of stories are *Bliss* (1920) and *The Garden Party* (1922). Her long involvement with John Middleton Murry, also a writer and a literary critic, was marked with frequent absences from each other brought on by frictions between them. This sequence of letters was written from a hotel in the south of France, where Murry had left Mansfield grief-stricken over her brother, "Chummie," who had been killed in the army. As her spirits improved, she urged Murry to rejoin her; and as these letters relate, she located a villa for them to rent even before she was quite sure that Murry would come. Murry did arrive, on New Year's Day, and their next three months at the Villa Pauline were the happiest in their lives together. They returned to England in the spring: "Our fairy tale was over," Murry later recalled. They were married in 1918, when Mansfield was hopelessly ill with tuberculosis.

I

Monday morning
December 26, 1915

Even if you never came I cannot but love you more for the evening 1
and the night and the morning I have spent thinking that you *are*
coming. It was Sunday, so I could not send you a telegram until today. I somehow — Oh, how did I? — got through last evening by sitting in the salon among unreal fantastic people and sewing and talking. For I knew I would not sleep. I knew I would not sleep. What drowsy bliss slept in my breast! I hardly dared to breathe.

A woman here told me how to buy our stores and what to pay and 2
how to make soup with 2 sous worth of bones, and what day the woman with good apples was at the market and how to manage une femme de ménage. I heard. I dared not look at her. I felt my smiles

357

chasing in my eyes. I saw the villa — perhaps a cactus near the gate — you writing at a little table, me arranging some flowers and then sitting down to write too. Both of us gathering pine cones and driftwood and bruyère for our fire. I thought of what I would have ready for you, soup and perhaps fish, coffee, toast, because charbon de bois, which is *much* cheaper than coal, makes lovely toast, I hear — a pot of confitures, a vase of roses. . . . And then I saw us waking in the morning and putting on the big kettle and letting in the femme de ménage. She hangs her shawl behind the kitchen door. "Vous savez, il fait beau."

II

December 27, 1915

Finally I could bear it no longer. I came up to my room and took a hot bath and then curled up in bed and smoked and tried to read a new Dickens. No use. The sea was very loud. I looked at the watch and saw it said 25 to 12 and then I went to sleep. When I looked again it was nearly four. So I turned on the light and waited, waited for day. How the light changed, I never shall forget. I put on my big purple coat and opened the shutters and sat on the window sill. It was all primrosy with black mountains. A sailing ship put out to sea. I saw all the little men on board, and how the sail was put up and how when it caught the breath of wind the ship went fast. Two more of our big ships, with a rattle of chains, hoisted anchor and put out to sea. I saw the bending, straining bodies of the men. And then came the fishers bringing in their pots. Then the first bird — At seven I heard my little maid lighting the stove so I ran out and asked for my déjeuner — washed in cold water — kissed my roses — put on my goblin hat and flew into the garden. The market was there — with two funny Spaniards beating drums. Such flowers! Such violets! But I kept my pennies for you and me. I thought I should have to have a small fête so when I went to the post office I put *new relief nibs* in all the awful old crusty pens. . . . I sent your telegram, ran home to find the maids beating the carpets and the white dog overslept and pretending he had been awake for hours on the terrace. Now I am going with a gent in corduroys to look at a furnished villa of his.

III

December 29, 1915

If you *should* come I have found a tiny villa for us — which seems 4
to me almost perfect in its way. It stands alone in a small garden with
terraces. It faces the "midi" and gets the sun all day long. It has a
stone verandah and a little round table where we can sit and eat or
work. A charming tiny kitchen with pots and pans and big coffee pot,
you know. Electric light, water downstairs and upstairs too in the cab-
inet de toilette. A most refined "water closet" *with* water in the
house. . . . The salle à manger is small and square with the light low
over the table. It leads on to the verandah and overlooks the sea. So
does the chambre à coucher. It is very private and stands high on the
top of a hill. It is called the *Villa Pauline.* The woman (wife of the
mobilier) who showed it me would also find me a servant for three
hours every day. Yesterday I *ran ran* all day long to find something
and saw such funny places. Every little street I came to there seemed
to be an old woman in wooden slippers with keys in her hands waiting
to show me "votre affaire." Oh, such funny experiences! But I have
been very careful to go to each woman I left in a state of uncertainty
and to say I regret that I cannot take their particular treasure so that I
shall not have to spend the rest of my days in dodging streets, houses,
and people as I usually do on these occasions. And they are neither
heart-broken nor do they call me a "sausage" — to my *great* surprise.
It is a sunny windy morning with a high sea and dancing light on all
the trees. The *vent de l'est* is blowing as a matter of fact, but it has no
terrors for me now that I have my legs again.

Mlle. Marthe has just been although I am still in my peignoire. She 5
is not a girl; she is a *sparrow.* It is so awfully nice to have your jacket
mended by a charming little sparrow instead of a monster with icy
hands and pins in her mouth and all over her non-existent bosom. But
Marthe hops about, smiling, with her head a little on one side. She is
a sweet little thing; I wish to goodness I could somehow adopt her for
us.

My roses — my roses are too lovely. They melt in the air (I *thought* 6
that in French where it sounds sense but in English it's nonsense). I
have 23. I just counted them for you and if you turn these blue glass
vases back to front so that you don't see the hand-painted horrors on

them they are very lovely, the dark red stems and a leaf or two showing through the water.

   . . . *Make* me wash and dress. I've lighted another cigarette now 7
and in spite of my absolutely cold, calculating mind, my heart keeps
on *perpetually* like this. One large vase of white and yellow jonquils in
the middle of the table. Roses in the bedroom, some little red anemo-
nes on the mantelpiece. "This is the place, Bogey." A ring at the door.
The man with your boxes from the station — Now we are sitting
down, hardly daring to look at each other, but smiling. Now you have
unpacked and put on your corduroys and your boots. I am downstairs
and you are upstairs. I hear you walking. I call out "Bogey, do you
want coffee or tea?" We arrange to work every morning — have
lunch — go out until it is dark, come home have tea and talk and read
and get our supper — and then work. On our walks we will take that
satchel you bought — for pine cones and wood and oranges — Oh
God, this place is as fair as New Zealand to me — as apart, as secret,
as much a place where you and I are alone and untroubled — But so I
dream.

   Now I am going to get up. I've got some *awful* tooth-paste. It is 8
called Isis and it has funny woodeny birds on the tube. It has all come
out the wrong end, too. And it's *much too pink.*

IV

Wednesday night
December 29, 1915

   I am like that disciple who said: "Lord I believe. Help thou my un- 9
belief." As I was dressing and your letter was already sealed the heavy
steps really came along the corridor. The knock at the door — the old
man with the blue folded paper that I scarcely dared to take and having taken — could not open. Oh, I sat by the side of my bed — and
opened it little by little. I read all those directions for the sending of
urgent telegrams in the night — At last I said: "He is not coming"
and opened it and read your message. . . . Since then I have never
ceased for one moment to tremble. . . . I felt "Now he is coming that
villa is taken" and I ran, ran along the quai. One day I shall tell you all
this at length, but it was not taken until I saw the woman and took it.
I went through it again. It is quite perfect in its way. It is always what

I felt there was somewhere in the world for us, in Spain or Italy. And the people to whom it belongs who live next door are such good, decent, honest people, eager to have us, eager to make us comfortable and happy. "Je suis toujours là. Vous avez seulement de frapper si vous auriez besoin de quelque chose." The sun shone in every room and on the little stone verandah danced the shadow of a tree. Is this true? Is it coming true? I have to sign the agreement and pay a month in advance to-morrow. Then to order the coal and wood and see my femme de ménage who has already been found "pour 3 heures le matin et pour faire mes petites courses, n'est-ce pas?" All the rest of the day . . . I do not know how I have spent it — such a lovely wild day brimming over with colour and light. I have found the shortest way to our home by a road you do not know, through fields of jonquils and past the olive trees that blow so silver and black to-day. There are high walls on the road and nobody goes.

Yes, I have found a lovely way — And I have made out a list of our 10 modest provisions that I shall buy on Friday. In fact I have made out more than one list. For I can't even write or read. . . .

This morning I went to the little Church and prayed. It is very nice 11 there. I prayed for us three — for you and me and Chummie. It was so gay and yet solemn there.

V

December 30, 1915

Money doesn't frighten me a bit. We'll be two little silkworms and 12 live on mulberry leaves. If you come here we shall both write poetry — a mutual book which we will publish together. Also we shall both write a kind of "paysages" and we shall both write — well, I shouldn't be surprised if we both wrote *anything*.

The little house is there, waiting for us. Its eyes are shut until I 13 open them. The sun touches the verandah and warms the place where your hand will rest. Tout bas, tout bas mon cœur chante: "Cinquante kilos de charbon de pierre — cinquante kilos de charbon de coke et des poids pour allumer pour cinq sous — c'est presqu'un sac." I have such a lot to do to-day. I must go out soon. Again I am not dressed but idling here with your letter beside me. I hardly slept at all.

VI

December 30, 1915

Midi. This morning I went to the woman who introduced me to   14
the Villa. She is a Spaniard, from Barcelona, and we are *really sin-
cerely* friends. She is a dear creature and at first I knew she didn't like
me but now really we have jokes together and she laughs, showing her
pretty teeth. She tried to find me a femme de ménage but could not,
so her daughter Marie, a dark-eyed Spanish beauty — a really fascinating creature with a fringe, big eyes, and bright colour, is coming
instead. But do we mind cuisine espagnole? "Pas du tout." Then I
went to the Church for a minute — I feel I must keep in close touch
with God. They were dressing the altar with white and yellow jonquils — a sweet savour must have mounted. I prayed that my prayer
was heard at the same moment and that God was pleased. Then I
went to the station to ask what trains arrived and then to our villa by
the path that you are coming. The door was open. The woman was
inside hanging up saucepans. So we went through the inventory together and she said she would give me teacups and a teapot . . . because we were English. Also she offered to take me to any shops where
I wanted to buy anything. I then went over the villa again. There is
the loveliest green water pot like you admired. We must find something to fill it with. Then I went back to her house and together with
her husband made out a lease, signed, paid, and put the key in my
pocket. A friend came in and we sat talking a little. They told me not
to buy flowers for your arrival. They had enough in their garden —
and she said she would come in when Marie arrived on Saturday and
show her how to make the fire. I walked home with the key in my
hands.

Friday. Noon. Now I am just waiting. I have ordered the little   15
stores and the wine and the wood. All the windows are open — all the
doors — the linen is airing. I went to the flower market and stood
among the buyers and bought, wholesale you know, at the auction in
a state of lively terrified joy three dozen rose buds and six bunches of
violets.

CONSIDERATIONS

1. What aspects of her own behavior does Mansfield portray in the first two letters? What effect was her self-portrait likely to have on her lover? What details create an impression of her for you?
2. What impressions of herself as a woman-of-the-house does Mansfield convey?
3. At the end of letter III and again in letter VI Mansfield mentions going to church. Does this piety appear consistent with the rest of her thoughts and actions?
4. Considering her letters, what sort of a man do you suppose their recipient was — or ought to have been?
5. WRITING TOPIC. In her day, Katherine Mansfield was regarded as daringly "advanced" — or as we say now, she was a "liberated" woman. Do you find her attitudes and assumptions in love modern or old-fashioned? In a 500-word essay, assess the woman's role that she has or wants to have in love.

Robert Solomon

"I-LOVE-YOU"

◊

ROBERT SOLOMON (b. 1942) was a medical student, a jazz musician, and a songwriter before he became a professor of philosophy at the University of Texas. *Post hoc, ergo propter hoc:* his philosophy analyzes the concrete and experiential rather than the abstract and logical. Solomon received his Ph.D. from the University of Michigan, and he has taught at Princeton and UCLA. His book on *The Passions* (1976) examines the philosophy of our emotions, a topic that he pursues further in his recent work, *Love: Emotion, Myth and Metaphor* (1981), from which this selection is taken. Solomon argues in general that love creates a shared self, changing both lovers into a new identity together. His analysis of the phrase "I love you" is modeled after a similar chapter in Roland Barthes's *A Lover's Discourse* (1978), which Solomon refers to in this essay.

I-love-you *has no usages: Like a child's word, it enters into no social constraint; it can be a sublime, solemn, trivial word, it can be an erotic, pornographic word. It is a socially irresponsible word.*

I-love-you *is without nuance. It suppresses explanations, adjustments, degrees, scruples . . . this word is always* true *(has no referent other than its utterance; it is a performative).*

— ROLAND BARTHES, *A Lover's Discourse*

"I love you."	1
What does that mean? Of course you know, but tell me.	2
A description of how I feel? Not at all.	3
An admission? A confession?	4
No, you don't understand, after all.	5

"I-love-you" is an action, not a word. It is not a short sentence. Of   6
course it *looks* like a sentence, made up of words, but sentences can be
transcribed and transformed. "I-love-you" is more like the word "this"
or "here"; it makes sense only when spoken in a very particular context. In writing, in a letter, it has meaning only to you, and only while
you can still imagine my speaking it. To anyone else, and after a while
to you, it means nothing at all; like the word "here," just sitting on
the page like an old coffee stain. Hardly a word at all.

"I-love-you" has no parts, no words to be rearranged or replaced.   7
"You-I-love" is more than merely clumsy, like "Me Tarzan, you
Jane." It is something like staking a claim. "John loves Sally," said by
John to Sally, is absurd. "I-love-you" allows for no substitutions, no
innovations. It stands outside the language. It says nothing. If it is
misunderstood, it cannot be explained. If unheard, it has not been ut-
tered. And when it is heard, it no longer matters that you didn't mean
to say it in the first place, that you "just blurted it out." You *did* it,
and it cannot be undone.

"I-love-you" does not *express* my love. It need not already be there.   8
Perhaps I didn't feel it until I said it, or just before. But then, in a
sense, I didn't *say* anything at all.

One of the perennial misunderstandings about language is the idea   9
that all sentences *say* something; words refer and phrases describe.
But language also requests and cajoles, demands and refuses, plays,
puns, disguises as well as reveals, creates as well as clarifies, *provokes*
as well as *invokes*, *per*forms as well as *in*forms. We *do* things with
words, in words done by the late Oxford philosopher J. L. Austin.
With words we make promises, christen ships, declare war, and get
married, none of which would be possible without them. Our sentences mean what we *do* as well as, or rather than, what we say. They
bring things about as well as tell us what has already come about. And
the meaning of "I-love-you" is to be found in what we *do* with it, not
in what it tries to tell us.

If we so easily misunderstand language and persistently refuse to   10
look at love, then of course we will miss completely the significance of
the language of love, if, that is, it is a language. Or is it, as Barthes
suggests, a *cry*? "I-love-you" mainly makes a demand. So when I say
it you react — not "How curious that you feel that way" but rather
"But what do you want me to do?" Its meaning is aimed at you, to
move you. (A "perlocutionary act," Austin called it.)

I say, "I have a headache," and you say, "Poor Boobie." Perhaps 11
you kiss my forehead, and I'm most grateful. But if you say, "Me
too," I don't think, "What a coincidence"; I feel slighted. You've
misunderstood me. Suppose I say, "I love you," and you kiss my forehead. I'm offended. That's not a reply but an evasion.

I say, "I love you," and I wait for a response. It can only be one 12
phrase: "I love you too," nothing less, nothing more. Perhaps, "Me
too," though it is ungrammatical and a serious confusion of pronouns,
but it is also less than the proper formula. If you say, "*Je t'aime*," you
have not done it either; instead you are showing off.

I could be silent and just love you. And perhaps you'd know. I 13
don't have to say, "I'm so angry with you," when I've been yelling at
you for twenty minutes. I don't say, "I'm sad," when I'm crying. And
yet I feel compelled to say, "I love you," even when it's obvious I do.
"Nothing says I love you like 'I love you.' " But it is more than that
too, more than something said.

The power of words, or at least certain words, sometimes is awe- 14
some. "I-love-you" is a magical phrase that ruins the evening. Or
changes love into something more, even when it was love before. It is
not an announcement, no R.S.V.P. No "if you please." It *demands* a
reply; in fact, it *is* this demand. And a warning, and a threat. It is an
embarrassment, first to me, but soon to you. It makes me vulnerable,
but you are the one who is naked. I am watching your every move.
Counting the fractions of a second. What will you do?

"I love you"; "what a terrible thing to say to someone." Terrible 15
indeed.

"Tell me you love me." 16
"What are you expecting from me? You know I love you." 17
"Then say it." 18
"I don't want to say it." 19
(The evening's already lost, but I pursue.) 20
"If you love me, why not say it?" 21
"Oh. I don't know; it just changes everything." 22
"How can saying what is true change anything?" 23
But it does. "I-love-you" doesn't fit into our conversations. It inter- 24
rupts them. Or ends them.

"I-love-you" is language reminding us of the unimportance of lan- 25
guage, language that destroys language. It is language without alter-

natives, without subtlety, like a gunshot or the morning alarm. And then it's gone, not even a memory, and has to be done again.

But once said, it can never be said again. It can only be repeated, as 26 a ritual, an assurance. Not to say it, when it's never been said, is no matter, a curiosity. But not to say it, once said, is a cause for alarm, perhaps panic. One commits oneself to the word, and to say it again. What else follows? Perhaps nothing.

Barthes says it is "released," but I say, *shot out*, like a weapon. Re- 27 leased like an arrow, perhaps. And if I make myself vulnerable in saying it, the real question is what it will do to you. I'm still watching you. Still counting the fractions of a second. What will you do?

I say, "I hate you," and you quite rightly ask "Why?" But I say, "I 28 love you," and "Why?" is completely improper. A reasonable question, but a breach in the formula. You have turned the weapon back onto me, so of course I reply indignantly, "What do you mean? I love you, that's all." And I again await your reply. A second chance, but no more.

I say, "I love you," and you answer, "How much?" What are we 29 negotiating? Perhaps you are saying, "Well then, prove it." And, having said the word, I am bound to. Nevertheless, your reply is insufferable. You're acting as if I actually *said* something which can now be qualified, quantified, argued for and against. But I didn't. I just said, "I love you." And that is, in terms of "How much?" to say nothing at all.

"I-love-you": a warning, an apology, an interruption, a plea for at- 30 tention, an objection, an excuse, a justification, a reminder, a trap, a blessing, a disguise, a vacuum, a revelation, a way of saying nothing, a way of summarizing everything, an attack, a surrender, an opening, an end.

I say, "I love you," and I no longer remember the time I was 31 with you when it was not said. And we will never be together again without it.

CONSIDERATIONS

1. How does "I-love-you" differ from an ordinary sentence? Why does Solomon hyphenate the words?

2. What is the purpose of stating "I-love-you"? Do you agree with Solomon?
3. Once said, how does the phrase continue to be used by lovers? What new questions of meaning are raised?
4. Solomon addresses someone called "you" throughout the essay, and he includes bits of his dialogue with "you." Who is this implied second person, and how does this method of exposition serve his point?
5. WRITING TOPIC. Does the meaning of "I-love-you" change when it is spoken by a parent to a child or by a friend to a friend? Does it remain an action, or does it become an ordinary sentence? Or does it have mixed functions? In a 500-word essay, explain one or two of the other usages of the phrase. You may want to address your essay directly to Solomon in order to emphasize your points of agreement and disagreement with him.

William Shakespeare

WHEN, IN DISGRACE
WITH FORTUNE
AND MEN'S EYES

◊

WILLIAM SHAKESPEARE (1564–1616) usually treated the subject of romantic love in comedies or fantasies or as part of a larger tragic subject in his plays, but in his sonnets he examined the sensations and emotions of love for their own importance. He wrote 154 sonnets during the 1590s, at about the same time that he was writing more skeptically or somberly about love in such plays as *Romeo and Juliet, A Midsummer Night's Dream,* and *As You Like It.*

When, in disgrace with Fortune and men's eyes,
I all alone beweep my outcast state,
And trouble deaf heaven with my bootless cries,
And look upon myself and curse my fate,
Wishing me like to one more rich in hope,
Featured like him, like him with friends possessed,
Desiring this man's art, and that man's scope,
With what I most enjoy contented least;
Yet in these thoughts myself almost despising,
Haply I think on thee, and then my state,   10
Like to the lark at break of day arising
From sullen earth, sings hymns at heaven's gate;
    For thy sweet love rememb'red such wealth brings,
    That then I scorn to change my state with kings.

CONSIDERATIONS

1. In the first eight lines, what mood does the poet describe? What sort of misfortune might have caused it? Why is he "all alone"?
2. In the next four lines, how do you view his change of mood? Is it realistically expressed — that is, does it convincingly define his feelings?
3. The final two lines are full of assurance. What is he saying about the value of love? Does his statement sound convincing?
4. WRITING TOPIC. One adage about love is that "Absence makes the heart grow fonder." Judging from this sonnet, what else does absence do to the heart? In 500 words, discuss the effects of love on a person's self-esteem, as illustrated in this sonnet and in other observations you may wish to include.

Raymond Carver

WHAT WE TALK ABOUT
WHEN WE TALK ABOUT LOVE

◊

RAYMOND CARVER (b. 1939) graduated from California State University at Humboldt and spent a year at the Writers' Workshop at the University of Iowa. He writes poetry and short stories that have appeared widely in such magazines as *Esquire* and *Harper's*. This selection is the title story from his latest collection, *What We Talk about When We Talk about Love* (1981). The story is a contemporary symposium (Plato's *Symposium*, an after-dinner conversation about love, seems to loom in the background of it) in which four people half-drunkenly discuss the peculiarities of love. Carver has taught at the University of California at Santa Cruz and now teaches English at Syracuse University.

My friend Mel McGinnis was talking. Mel McGinnis is a cardi- 1
ologist, and sometimes that gives him the right.

The four of us were sitting around his kitchen table drinking gin. 2
Sunlight filled the kitchen from the big window behind the sink.
There were Mel and me and his second wife, Teresa — Terri, we
called her — and my wife, Laura. We lived in Albuquerque then. But
we were all from somewhere else.

There was an ice bucket on the table. The gin and the tonic water 3
kept going around, and we somehow got on the subject of love. Mel
thought real love was nothing less than spiritual love. He said he'd
spent five years in a seminary before quitting to go to medical school.
He said he still looked back on those years in the seminary as the most
important years in his life.

Terri said the man she lived with before she lived with Mel loved 4
her so much he tried to kill her. Then Terri said, "He beat me up one

night. He dragged me around the living room by my ankles. He kept saying, 'I love you, I love you, you bitch.' He went on dragging me around the living room. My head kept knocking on things." Terri looked around the table. "What do you do with love like that?"

She was a bone-thin woman with a pretty face, dark eyes, and 5 brown hair that hung down her back. She liked necklaces made of turquoise, and long pendant earrings.

"My God, don't be silly. That's not love, and you know it," Mel 6 said. "I don't know what you'd call it, but I sure know you wouldn't call it love."

"Say what you want to, but I know it was," Terri said. "It may 7 sound crazy to you, but it's true just the same. People are different, Mel. Sure, sometimes he may have acted crazy. Okay. But he loved me. In his own way maybe, but he loved me. There was love there, Mel. Don't say there wasn't."

Mel let out his breath. He held his glass and turned to Laura and 8 me. "The man threatened to kill me," Mel said. He finished his drink and reached for the gin bottle. "Terri's a romantic. Terri's of the kick-me-so-I'll-know-you-love-me school. Terri, hon, don't look that way." Mel reached across the table and touched Terri's cheek with his fingers. He grinned at her.

"Now he wants to make up," Terri said. 9

"Make up what?" Mel said. "What is there to make up? I know 10 what I know. That's all."

"How'd we get started on this subject, anyway?" Terri said. She 11 raised her glass and drank from it. "Mel always has love on his mind," she said. "Don't you, honey?" She smiled, and I thought that was the last of it.

"I just wouldn't call Ed's behavior love. That's all I'm saying, 12 honey," Mel said. "What about you guys?" Mel said to Laura and me. "Does that sound like love to you?"

"I'm the wrong person to ask," I said. "I didn't even know the 13 man. I've only heard his name mentioned in passing. I wouldn't know. You'd have to know the particulars. But I think what you're saying is that love is an absolute."

Mel said, "The kind of love I'm talking about is. The kind of love 14 I'm talking about, you don't try to kill people."

Laura said, "I don't know anything about Ed, or anything about 15 the situation. But who can judge anyone else's situation?"

I touched the back of Laura's hand. She gave me a quick smile. I   16
picked up Laura's hand. It was warm, the nails polished, perfectly
manicured. I encircled the broad wrist with my fingers, and I held her.

"When I left, he drank rat poison," Terri said. She clasped her   17
arms with her hands. "They took him to the hospital in Santa Fe.
That's where we lived then, about ten miles out. They saved his life.
But his gums went crazy from it. I mean they pulled away from his
teeth. After that, his teeth stood out like fangs. My God," Terri said.
She waited a minute, then let go of her arms and picked up her glass.

"What people won't do!" Laura said.   18

"He's out of the action now," Mel said. "He's dead."   19

Mel handed me the saucer of limes. I took a section, squeezed it   20
over my drink, and stirred the ice cubes with my finger.

"It's gets worse," Terri said. "He shot himself in the mouth. But he   21
bungled that too. Poor Ed," she said. Terri shook her head.

"Poor Ed nothing," Mel said. "He was dangerous."   22

Mel was forty-five years old. He was tall and rangy with curly soft   23
hair. His face and arms were brown from the tennis he played. When
he was sober, his gestures, all his movements, were precise, very careful.

"He did love me though, Mel. Grant me that," Terri said. "That's   24
all I'm asking. He didn't love me the way you love me. I'm not saying
that. But he loved me. You can grant me that, can't you?"

"What do you mean, he bungled it?" I said.   25

Laura leaned forward with her glass. She put her elbows on the   26
table and held her glass in both hands. She glanced from Mel to Terri
and waited with a look of bewilderment on her open face, as if amazed
that such things happened to people you were friendly with.

"How'd he bungle it when he killed himself?" I said.   27

"I'll tell you what happened," Mel said. "He took this twenty-two   28
pistol he'd bought to threaten Terri and me with. Oh, I'm serious, the
man was always threatening. You should have seen the way we lived
in those days. Like fugitives. I even bought a gun myself. Can you believe it? A guy like me? But I did. I bought one for self-defense and
carried it in the glove compartment. Sometimes I'd have to leave the
apartment in the middle of the night. To go to the hospital, you
know? Terri and I weren't married then, and my first wife had the
house and kids, the dog, everything, and Terri and I were living in this

apartment here. Sometimes, as I say, I'd get a call in the middle of the night and have to go in to the hospital at two or three in the morning. It'd be dark out there in the parking lot, and I'd break into a sweat before I could even get to my car. I never knew if he was going to come up out of the shrubbery or from behind a car and start shooting. I mean, the man was crazy. He was capable of wiring a bomb, anything. He used to call my service at all hours and say he needed to talk to the doctor, and when I'd return the call, he'd say, 'Son of a bitch, your days are numbered.' Little things like that. It was scary, I'm telling you."

"I still feel sorry for him," Terri said.   29

"It sounds like a nightmare," Laura said. "But what exactly hap- 30
pened after he shot himself?"

Laura is a legal secretary. We'd met in a professional capacity. 31
Before we knew it, it was a courtship. She's thirty-five, three years younger than I am. In addition to being in love, we like each other and enjoy one another's company. She's easy to be with.

"What happened?" Laura said.   32

Mel said, "He shot himself in the mouth in his room. Someone 33
heard the shot and told the manager. They came in with a passkey, saw what had happened, and called an ambulance. I happened to be there when they brought him in, alive but past recall. The man lived for three days. His head swelled up to twice the size of a normal head. I'd never seen anything like it, and I hope I never do again. Terri wanted to go in and sit with him when she found out about it. We had a fight over it. I didn't think she should see him like that. I didn't think she should see him, and I still don't."

"Who won the fight?" Laura said.   34

"I was in the room with him when he died," Terri said. "He never 35
came up out of it. But I sat with him. He didn't have anyone else."

"He was dangerous," Mel said. "If you call that love, you can have 36
it."

"It was love," Terri said. "Sure, it's abnormal in most people's 37
eyes. But he was willing to die for it. He did die for it."

"I sure as hell wouldn't call it love," Mel said. "I mean, no one 38
knows what he did it for. I've seen a lot of suicides, and I couldn't say anyone ever knew what they did it for."

Mel put his hands behind his neck and tilted his chair back. "I'm 39 not interested in that kind of love," he said. "If that's love, you can have it."

Terri said, "We were afraid. Mel even made a will out and wrote to 40 his brother in California who used to be a Green Beret. Mel told him who to look for if something happened to him."

Terri drank from her glass. She said, "But Mel's right — we lived 41 like fugitives. We were afraid. Mel was, weren't you, honey? I even called the police at one point, but they were no help. They said they couldn't do anything until Ed actually did something. Isn't that a laugh?" Terri said.

She poured the last of the gin into her glass and waggled the bottle. 42 Mel got up from the table and went to the cupboard. He took down another bottle.

"Well, Nick and I know what love is," Laura said. "For us, I 43 mean," Laura said. She bumped my knee with her knee. "You're supposed to say something now," Laura said, and turned her smile on me.

For an answer, I took Laura's hand and raised it to my lips. I made 44 a big production out of kissing her hand. Everyone was amused.

"We're lucky," I said. 45

"You guys," Terri said. "Stop that now. You're making me sick. 46 You're still on the honeymoon, for God's sake. You're still gaga, for crying out loud. Just wait. How long have you been together now? How long has it been? A year? Longer than a year?"

"Going on a year and a half," Laura said, flushed and smiling. 47

"Oh, now," Terri said. "Wait awhile." 48

She held her drink and gazed at Laura. 49

"I'm only kidding," Terri said. 50

Mel opened the gin and went around the table with the bottle. 51

"Here, you guys," he said. "Let's have a toast. I want to propose a 52 toast. A toast to love. To true love," Mel said.

We touched glasses. 53

"To love," we said. 54

Outside in the backyard, one of the dogs began to bark. The leaves 55 of the aspen that leaned past the window ticked against the glass. The afternoon sun was like a presence in this room, the spacious light of ease and generosity. We could have been anywhere, somewhere enchanted. We raised our glasses again and grinned at each other like children who had agreed on something forbidden.

"I'll tell you what real love is," Mel said. "I mean, I'll give you a good example. And then you can draw your own conclusions." He poured more gin into his glass. He added an ice cube and a sliver of lime. We waited and sipped our drinks. Laura and I touched knees again. I put a hand on her warm thigh and left it there.

"What do any of us really know about love?" Mel said. "It seems to me we're just beginners at love. We say we love each other and we do, I don't doubt it. I love Terri and Terri loves me, and you guys love each other too. You know the kind of love I'm talking about now. Physical love, that impulse that drives you to someone special, as well as love of the other person's being, his or her essence, as it were. Carnal love and, well, call it sentimental love, the day-to-day caring about the other person. But sometimes I have a hard time accounting for the fact that I must have loved my first wife too. But I did, I know I did. So I suppose I am like Terri in that regard. Terri and Ed." He thought about it and then he went on. "There was a time when I thought I loved my first wife more than life itself. But now I hate her guts. I do. How do you explain that? What happened to that love? What happened to it, is what I'd like to know. I wish someone could tell me. Then there's Ed. Okay, we're back to Ed. He loves Terri so much he tries to kill her and he winds up killing himself " Mel stopped talking and swallowed from his glass. "You guys have been together eighteen months and you love each other. It shows all over you. You glow with it. But you both loved other people before you met each other. You've both been married before, just like us. And you probably loved other people before that too, even. Terri and I have been together five years, been married for four. And the terrible thing, the terrible thing is, but the good thing too, the saving grace, you might say, is that if something happened to one of us — excuse me for saying this — but if something happened to one of us tomorrow, I think the other one, the other person, would grieve for a while, you know, but then the surviving party would go out and love again, have someone else soon enough. All this, all of this love we're talking about, it would just be a memory. Maybe not even a memory. Am I wrong? Am I way off base? Because I want you to set me straight if you think I'm wrong. I want to know. I mean, I don't know anything, and I'm the first one to admit it."

"Mel, for God's sake," Terri said. She reached out and took hold of 58 his wrist. "Are you getting drunk? Honey? Are you drunk?"

"Honey, I'm just talking," Mel said. "All right? I don't have to be 59 drunk to say what I think. I mean, we're all just talking, right?" Mel said. He fixed his eyes on her.

"Sweetie, I'm not criticizing," Terri said. 60

She picked up her glass. 61

"I'm not on call today," Mel said. "Let me remind you of that. I 62 am not on call," he said.

"Mel, we love you," Laura said. 63

Mel looked at Laura. He looked at her as if he could not place her, 64 as if she was not the woman she was.

"Love you too, Laura," Mel said. "And you, Nick, love you too. 65 You know something?" Mel said. "You guys are our pals," Mel said.

He picked up his glass. 66

Mel said, "I was going to tell you about something. I mean, I was 67 going to prove a point. You see, this happened a few months ago, but it's still going on right now, and it ought to make us feel ashamed when we talk like we know what we're talking about when we talk about love."

"Come on now," Terri said. "Don't talk like you're drunk if you're 68 not drunk."

"Just shut up for once in your life," Mel said very quietly. "Will 69 you do me a favor and do that for a minute? So as I was saying, there's this old couple who had this car wreck out on the interstate. A kid hit them and they were all torn to shit and nobody was giving them much chance to pull through."

Terri looked at us and then back at Mel. She seemed anxious, or 70 maybe that's too strong a word.

Mel was handing the bottle around the table. 71

"I was on call that night," Mel said. "It was May or maybe it was 72 June. Terri and I had just sat down to dinner when the hospital called. There'd been this thing out on the interstate. Drunk kid, teenager, plowed his dad's pickup into this camper with this old couple in it. They were up in their mid-seventies, that couple. The kid — eighteen, nineteen, something — he was DOA. Taken the steering wheel through his sternum. The old couple, they were alive, you understand. I mean, just barely. But they had everything. Multiple fractures, internal injuries, hemorrhaging, contusions, lacerations, the works, and they each of them had themselves concussions. They were in a bad way, believe me. And, of course, their age was two strikes against them. I'd say she was worse off than he was. Ruptured spleen along with everything else. Both kneecaps broken. But they'd been wearing their seatbelts and, God knows, that's what saved them for the time being."

"Folks, this is an advertisement for the National Safety Council," 73 Terri said. "This is your spokesman, Dr. Melvin R. McGinnis, talking." Terri laughed. "Mel," she said, "sometimes you're just too much. But I love you, hon," she said.

"Honey, I love you," Mel said.   74

He leaned across the table. Terri met him halfway. They kissed. 75

"Terri's right," Mel said as he settled himself again. "Get those 76 seatbelts on. But seriously, they were in some shape, those oldsters. By the time I got down there, the kid was dead, as I said. He was off in a corner, laid out on a gurney. I took one look at the old couple and told the ER nurse to get me a neurologist and an orthopedic man and a couple of surgeons down there right away."

He drank from his glass. "I'll try to keep this short," he said. "So 77 we took the two of them up to the OR and worked like fuck on them most of the night. They had these incredible reserves, those two. You see that once in a while. So we did everything that could be done, and toward morning we're giving them a fifty-fifty chance, maybe less than that for her. So here they are, still alive the next morning. So, okay, we move them into the ICU, which is where they both kept plugging away at it for two weeks, hitting it better and better on all the scopes. So we transfer them out to their own room."

Mel stopped talking. "Here," he said, "let's drink this cheapo gin 78 the hell up. Then we're going to dinner, right? Terri and I know a new place. That's where we'll go, to this new place we know about. But we're not going until we finish up this cut-rate, lousy gin."

Terri said, "We haven't actually eaten there yet. But it looks good. 79 From the outside, you know."

"I like food," Mel said. "If I had it to do all over again, I'd be a 80 chef, you know? Right, Terri?" Mel said.

He laughed. He fingered the ice in his glass.   81

"Terri knows," he said. "Terri can tell you. But let me say this. If I 82 could come back again in a different life, a different time and all, you know what? I'd like to come back as a knight. You were pretty safe wearing all that armour. It was all right being a knight until gunpowder and muskets and pistols came along."

"Mel would like to ride a horse and carry a lance," Terri said.   83

"Carry a woman's scarf with you everywhere," Laura said.   84

"Or just a woman," Mel said.   85

"Shame on you," Laura said.   86

Terri said, "Suppose you came back as a serf. The serfs didn't have   87
it so good in those days," Terri said.

"The serfs never had it good," Mel said. "But I guess even the   88
knights were vessels to someone. Isn't that the way it worked? But then everyone is always a vessel to someone. Isn't that right? Terri? But what I liked about knights, besides their ladies, was that they had that suit of armour, you know, and they couldn't get hurt very easy. No cars in those days, you know? No drunk teenagers to tear into your ass."

"Vassals," Terri said.   89

"What?" Mel said.   90

"Vassals," Terri said. "They were called vassals, not vessels."   91

"Vassals, vessels," Mel said, "what the fuck's the difference? You   92
knew what I meant anyway. All right," Mel said. "So I'm not educated. I learned my stuff. I'm a heart surgeon, sure, but I'm just a mechanic. I go in and I fuck around and I fix things. Shit," Mel said.

"Modesty doesn't become you," Terri said.   93

"He's just a humble sawbones," I said. "But sometimes they suffo-   94
cated in all that armor, Mel. They'd even have heart attacks if it got too hot and they were too tired and worn out. I read somewhere that they'd fall off their horses and not be able to get up because they were too tired to stand with all that armor on them. They got trampled by their own horses sometimes."

"That's terrible," Mel said. "That's a terrible thing, Nicky. I guess   95
they'd just lay there and wait until somebody came along and made a shish kebab out of them."

"Some other vessel," Terri said.   96

"That's right," Mel said. "Some vassal would come along and   97
spear the bastard in the name of love. Or whatever the fuck it was they fought over in those days."

"Same things we fight over these days," Terri said.   98

Laura said, "Nothing's changed."   99

The color was still high in Laura's cheeks. Her eyes were bright.   100
She brought her glass to her lips.

Mel poured himself another drink. He looked at the label closely as 101
if studying a long row of numbers. Then he slowly put the bottle
down on the table and slowly reached for the tonic water.

"What about the old couple?" Laura said. "You didn't finish that   102
story you started."

Laura was having a hard time lighting her cigarette. Her matches   103
kept going out.

The sunshine inside the room was different now, changing, getting   104
thinner. But the leaves outside the window were still shimmering, and
I stared at the pattern they made on the panes and on the Formica
counter. They weren't the same patterns, of course.

"What about the old couple?" I said.   105

"Older but wiser," Terri said.   106

Mel stared at her.   107

Terri said, "Go on with your story, hon. I was only kidding. Then   108
what happened?"

"Terri, sometimes," Mel said.   109

"Please, Mel," Terri said. "Don't always be so serious, sweetie.   110
Can't you take a joke?"

"Where's the joke?" Mel said.   111

He held his glass and gazed steadily at his wife.   112

"What happened?" Laura said.   113

Mel fastened his eyes on Laura. He said, "Laura, if I didn't have   114
Terri and if I didn't love her so much, and if Nick wasn't my best
friend, I'd fall in love with you. I'd carry you off, honey," he said.

"Tell your story," Terri said. "Then we'll go to that new place,   115
okay?"

"Okay," Mel said. "Where was I?" he said. He stared at the table   116
and then he began again.

"I dropped in to see each of them every day, sometimes twice a day 117
if I was up doing other calls anyway. Casts and bandages, head to foot,
the both of them. You know, you've seen it in the movies. That's just
the way they looked, just like in the movies. Little eye-holes and nose-
holes and mouth-holes. And she had to have her legs slung up on top

of it. Well, the husband was very depressed for the longest while. Even after he found out that his wife was going to pull through, he was still very depressed. Not about the accident, though. I mean, the accident was one thing, but it wasn't everything. I'd get up to his mouth-hole, you know, and he'd say no, it wasn't the accident exactly but it was because he couldn't see her through his eye-holes. He said that was what was making him feel so bad. Can you imagine? I'm telling you, the man's heart was breaking because he couldn't turn his goddamn head and *see* his goddamn wife."

Mel looked around the table and shook his head at what he was going to say. 118

"I mean, it was killing the old fart just because he couldn't *look* at the fucking woman." 119

We all looked at Mel. 120

"Do you see what I'm saying?" he said. 121

Maybe we were a little drunk by then. I know it was hard keeping things in focus. The light was draining out of the room, going back through the window where it had come from. Yet nobody made a move to get up from the table to turn on the overhead light. 122

"Listen," Mel said. "Let's finish this fucking gin. There's about enough left here for one shooter all around. Then let's go eat. Let's go to the new place." 123

"He's depressed," Terri said. "Mel, why don't you take a pill?" 124

Mel shook his head. "I've taken everything there is." 125

"We all need a pill now and then," I said. 126

"Some people are born needing them," Terri said. 127

She was using her finger to rub at something on the table. Then she stopped rubbing. 128

"I think I want to call my kids," Mel said. "Is that all right with everybody? I'll call my kids," he said. 129

Terri said, "What if Marjorie answers the phone? You guys, you've heard us on the subject of Marjorie? Honey, you know you don't want to talk to Marjorie. It'll make you feel even worse." 130

"I don't want to talk to Marjorie," Mel said. "But I want to talk to my kids." 131

"There isn't a day goes by that Mel doesn't say he wishes she'd get married again. Or else die," Terri said. "For one thing," Terri said, 132 "she's bankrupting us. Mel says it's just to spite him that she won't get married again. She has a boyfriend who lives with her and the kids, so Mel is supporting the boyfriend too."

"She's allergic to bees," Mel said. "If I'm not praying she'll get 133 married again, I'm praying she'll get herself stung to death by a swarm of fucking bees."

"Shame on you," Laura said.   134

"Bzzzzzzz," Mel said, turning his fingers into bees and buzzing 135 them at Terri's throat. Then he let his hands drop all the way to his sides.

"She's vicious," Mel said. "Sometimes I think I'll go up there 136 dressed like a beekeeper. You know, that hat that's like a helmet with the plate that comes down over your face, the big gloves, and the padded coat? I'll knock on the door and let loose a hive of bees in the house. But first I'd make sure the kids were out, of course."

He crossed one leg over the other. It seemed to take him a lot of 137 time to do it. Then he put both feet on the floor and leaned forward, elbows on the table, his chin cupped in his hands.

"Maybe I won't call the kids, after all. Maybe it isn't such a hot 138 idea. Maybe we'll just go eat. How does that sound?"

"Sounds fine to me," I said. "Eat or not eat. Or keep drinking. I 139 could head right on out into the sunset."

"What does that mean, honey?" Laura said.   140

"It just means what I said," I said. "It means I could just keep 141 going. That's all it means."

"I could eat something myself," Laura said. "I don't think I've ever 142 been so hungry in my life. Is there something to nibble on?"

"I'll put out some cheese and crackers," Terri said.   143

But Terri just sat there. She did not get up to get anything.   144

Mel turned his glass over. He spilled it out on the table.   145

"Gin's gone," Mel said.   146

Terri said, "Now what?"   147

I could hear my heart beating. I could hear everyone's heart. I 148 could hear the human noise we sat there making, not one of us moving, not even when the room went dark.

CONSIDERATIONS

1. Think of three adjectives that together summarize Mel's character in the first half of the story. Would you change the adjectives to fit his character at the end of the story?
2. At what times and how do the characters express their love for their partners and for their friends during the conversation? What motives or satisfactions enter into their expressions of love? Examine the details closely.
3. What aspect of love is especially troubling to Mel? What bearing does it have on his earlier intention to become a priest and his present vocation as a cardiologist?
4. Why does Mel's language become more vulgar as he tells his story about the old people? What is agitating him?
5. What do Nick and Laura find disturbing about Mel's story? How do we know?
6. Mel divides love into "carnal" and "sentimental." Does his example of true love fit either category? How would you define it?
7. WRITING TOPIC. Is love something to "work on"? Is it something to "share"? Is it "communication"? Or a "commitment"? Is it a "feeling"? Or a "trip"? These commonly used expressions indicate that love is not just an emotion: it is also a whole set of ideas and beliefs about that emotion. In a 700-word essay, define the underlying concept of love that is most often accepted and used among a group of people you know personally. Examine the specific words, gestures, and reactions that indicate their view of love.

D. H. Lawrence

COUNTERFEIT LOVE

◊

D. H. LAWRENCE (1885–1930), who grew up in a coal-miner's family in England, wrote about the emotional complexities of his early life in an autobiographical novel, *Sons and Lovers* (1913). His later novels, such as *The Rainbow* (1915), *Women in Love* (1920), and *Lady Chatterley's Lover* (1928), treat the sexual relationship as the central experience in which men and women can, possibly, discover and fulfill their essential natures. He also wrote poetry and essays on this general theme of love and the natural identity of human beings. This selection is excerpted from a long essay in which Lawrence defends his explicit treatment of sex in *Lady Chatterley's Lover*, a novel that was banned as obscene until 1959.

The body's life is the life of sensations and emotions. The body 1
feels real hunger, real thirst, real joy in the sun or the snow, real pleasure in the smell of roses or the look of a lilac bush; real anger, real
sorrow, real love, real tenderness, real warmth, real passion, real hate,
real grief. All the emotions belong to the body, and are only recognized by the mind. We may hear the most sorrowful piece of news,
and only feel a mental excitement. Then, hours after, perhaps in
sleep, the awareness may reach the bodily centres, and true grief
wrings the heart.

How different they are, mental feelings and real feelings. Today, 2
many people live and die without having had any real feelings —
though they have had a "rich emotional life" apparently, having
showed strong mental feelings. But it is all counterfeit. . . . The higher
emotions are strictly dead. They have to be faked.

And by higher emotions we mean love in all its manifestations, 3
from genuine desire to tender love, love of our fellowmen, and love of
God: we mean love, joy, delight, hope, true indignant anger, passion-

ate sense of justice and injustice, truth and untruth, honour and dishonour, and real belief in *anything*: for belief is a profound emotion that has the mind's connivance. All these things, today, are more or less dead. We have in their place the loud and sentimental counterfeit of all such emotion.

Never was an age more sentimental, more devoid of real feeling, 4 more exaggerated in false feeling, than our own. Sentimentality and counterfeit feeling have become a sort of game, everybody trying to outdo his neighbour. The radio and the film are mere counterfeit emotion all the time, the current press and literature the same. People wallow in emotion: counterfeit emotion. They lap it up: they live in it and on it. They ooze with it.

And at times, they seem to get on very well with it all. And then, 5 more and more, they break down. They go to pieces. You can fool yourself for a long time about your own feelings. But not forever. The body itself hits back at you, and hits back remorselessly in the end.

As for other people — you can fool most people all the time, and 6 all people most of the time, but not all people all the time, with false feelings. A young couple fall in counterfeit love, and fool themselves and each other completely. But, alas, counterfeit love is good cake but bad bread. It produces a fearful emotional indigestion. Then you get a modern marriage, and a still more modern separation.

The trouble with counterfeit emotion is that nobody is really 7 happy, nobody is really contented, nobody has any peace. Everybody keeps on rushing to get away from the counterfeit emotion which is in themselves worst of all. They rush from the false feelings of Peter to the false feelings of Adrian, from the counterfeit emotions of Margaret to those of Virginia, from film to radio, from Eastbourne to Brighton, and the more it changes the more it is the same thing.

Above all things love is a counterfeit feeling today. Here, above all 8 things, the young will tell you, is the greatest swindle. That is, if you take it seriously. Love is all right if you take it lightly, as an amusement. But if you begin taking it seriously you are let down with a crash.

There are, the young women say, no *real* men to love. And there 9 are, the young men say, no *real* girls to fall in love with. So they go on falling in love with unreal ones, on either side; which means, if you can't have real feelings, you've got to have counterfeit ones: since some feelings you've *got* to have: like falling in love. There are still some young people who would *like* to have real feelings, and they are bewildered to death to know why they can't. Especially in love.

But especially in love, only counterfeit emotions exist nowadays. 10 We have all been taught to mistrust everybody emotionally, from parents downwards, or upwards. Don't trust *anybody* with your real emotions: if you've got any: that is the slogan of today. Trust them with your money, even, but *never* with your feelings. They are bound to trample on them.

I believe there has never been an age of greater mistrust between 11 persons than ours today: under a superficial but quite genuine social trust. Very few of my friends would pick my pocket, or let me sit on a chair where I might hurt myself. But practically all my friends would turn my real emotions to ridicule. They can't help it; it's the spirit of the day. So there goes love, and there goes friendship: for each implies a fundamental emotional sympathy. And hence, counterfeit love, which there is no escaping.

And with counterfeit emotions there is no real sex at all. Sex is the 12 one thing you cannot really swindle; and it is the centre of the worst swindling of all, emotional swindling. Once come down to sex, and the emotional swindle must collapse. But in all the approaches to sex, the emotional swindle intensifies more and more. Till you get there. Then collapse.

Sex lashes out against counterfeit emotion, and is ruthless, devas- 13 tating against false love. The peculiar hatred of people who have not loved one another, but who have pretended to, even perhaps have imagined they really did love, is one of the phenomena of our time. The phenomenon, of course, belongs to all time. But today it is almost universal. People who thought they loved one another dearly, dearly, and went on for years, ideal: lo! suddenly the most profound and vivid hatred appears. If it doesn't come out fairly young, it saves itself till the happy couple are nearing fifty, the time of the great sexual change — and then — cataclysm!

Nothing is more startling. Nothing is more staggering, in our age, 14 than the intensity of the hatred people, men and women, feel for one another when they have once "loved" one another. It breaks out in the most extraordinary ways. And when you know people intimately, it is almost universal. It is the charwoman as much as the mistress, and the duchess as much as the policeman's wife.

And it would be too horrible, if one did not remember that in all of 15 them, men and women alike, it is the organic reaction against counterfeit love. All love today is counterfeit. It is a stereotyped thing. All the young know just how they ought to feel and how they ought to behave, in love. And they feel and they behave like that. And it is counterfeit love. So that revenge will come back at them, tenfold. The sex, the very sexual organism in man and woman alike accumulates a deadly and desperate rage, after a certain amount of counterfeit love has been palmed off on it, even if itself has given nothing but counterfeit love. The element of counterfeit in love at last maddens, or else kills, sex, the deepest sex in the individual. But perhaps it would be safe to say that it *always* enrages the inner sex, even if at last it kills it. There is always the period of rage. And the strange thing is, the worst offenders in the counterfeit-love game fall into the greatest rage. Those whose love has been a bit sincere are always gentler, even though they have been most swindled.

CONSIDERATIONS

1. What is the difference between "mental feelings" and "real feelings"? Can you substitute other terms for the distinction Lawrence is making? How do the implications of your terms differ from Lawrence's? Do you accept his implications?
2. In Lawrence's list of "the higher emotions" are there any that seem out of place as emotions? Has he left out any negative emotions that you would include? What does he mean by "higher"?
3. Lawrence maintains that we are in an age of great mistrust of feelings among people, and even that we are taught to mistrust everybody emotionally. Yet, he offers no examples or explanations of his views. Can you clarify his point by suggesting modern ideas, attitudes, or events that may be evidence of this mistrust?
4. Given that Lawrence wrote this essay in 1929, are his concerns about our sexual attitudes outdated? Does present-day society encourage more or less authenticity of emotions?
5. WRITING TOPIC. How would Lawrence regard present-day dating? In a 750-word essay, evaluate the patterns, routines, and conventional responses in the romance of dating, and decide what elements of it are usually counterfeited. What would be gained or lost by removing the counterfeit elements? Is there a difference between counterfeiting and disguising emotions? Would Lawrence agree?

Ernest van den Haag

LOVE, OR MARRIAGE?

◊

ERNEST VAN DEN HAAG (b. 1914) was born in The Hague (what his name tells us is true) and educated at European universities before he came to the United States. He pursued graduate study at New York University, where he continued as a staff psychoanalyst. He is the author of *The Fabric of Society* (1957), which combines sociological and psychological perspectives on modern life, and his articles have appeared in such magazines as *Commentary, Partisan Review,* and *Harper's,* which printed this essay in 1962. Professionally involved in counseling people about their feelings, van den Haag maintains that romantic love threatens to undermine marriage.

If someone asks, "Why do people marry?" he meets indignation or 1 astonishment. The question seems absurd if not immoral: the desirability of marriage is regarded as unquestionable. Divorce, on the other hand, strikes us as a problem worthy of serious and therapeutic attention. Yet marriage precedes divorce as a rule, and frequently causes it.

What explains marriage? People divorce often but they marry 2 still more often. Lately they also marry — and divorce, of course — younger than they used to, particularly in the middle classes (most statistics understate the change by averaging all classes). And the young have a disproportionate share of divorces. However, their hasty exertions to get out of wedlock puzzle me less than their eagerness to rush into it in the first place.

A hundred years ago there was every reason to marry young — 3 though middle-class people seldom did. The unmarried state had heavy disadvantages for both sexes. Custom did not permit girls to be educated, to work, or to have social, let alone sexual, freedom. Men were free but since women were not, they had only prostitutes for partners. (When enforced, the double standard is certainly self-defeating.) And, though less restricted than girls shackled to their families, single men often led a grim and uncomfortable life. A wife was nearly indispensable, if only to darn socks, sew, cook, clean, take care of her man. Altogether, both sexes needed marriage far more than now — no TV, cars, dates, drip-dry shirts, cleaners, canned foods — and not much hospital care, insurance, or social security. The family was all-important.

Marriage is no longer quite so indispensable a convenience; yet we 4 find people marrying more than ever, and earlier. To be sure, prosperity makes marriage more possible. But why are the young exploiting the possibility so sedulously? Has the yearning for love become more urgent and widespread?

What has happened is that the physical conveniences which re- 5 duced the material usefulness of marriage have also loosened the bonds of family life. Many other bonds that sustained us psychologically were weakened as they were extended: beliefs became vague; associations impersonal, discontinuous, and casual. Our contacts are many, our relationships few: our lives, externally crowded, often are internally isolated; we remain but tenuously linked to each other and our ties come easily undone. One feels lonely surrounded by crowds and machines in an unbounded, abstract world that has become morally unintelligible; and we have so much time now to feel lonely in. Thus one longs, perhaps more acutely than in the past, for somebody to be tangibly, individually, and definitely one's own, body and soul.

This is the promise of marriage. Movies, songs, TV, romance mag- 6 azines, all intensify the belief that love alone makes life worthwhile, is perpetual, conquers the world's evils, and is fulfilled and certified by marriage. "Science" hastens to confirm as much. Doesn't popular psychology, brandishing the banner of Freud with more enthusiasm than knowledge, tell us, in effect, that any male who stays single is selfish or homosexual or mother-dominated and generally neurotic? and any unmarried female frustrated (or worse, not frustrated) and neurotic? A "normal" person, we are told, must love and thereupon marry. Thus love and marriage are identified with each other and with normality, three thousand years of experience notwithstanding. The yearning for love, attended by anxiety to prove oneself well-adjusted and normal, turns into eagerness to get married.

The young may justly say that they merely practice what their par- 7
ents preached. For, indeed, the idea that "love and marriage go together like a horse and carriage" has been drummed into their heads,
so much that it finally has come to seem entirely natural. Yet, nothing
could be less so. Love has long delighted and distressed mankind, and
marriage has comforted us steadily and well. Both, however, are dena-
tured — paradoxically enough, by their staunchest supporters —
when they are expected to "go together." For love is a very unruly
horse, far more apt to run away and overturn the carriage than to draw
it. That is why, in the past, people seldom thought of harnessing marriage to love. They felt that each has its own motive power: one
primed for a lifelong journey; the other for an ardent improvisation, a
voyage of discovery.

More than a Frenzy?

Though by no means weaker, the marital bond is quite different from 8
the bond of love. If you like, it is a different bond of love — less taut,
perhaps, and more durable. By confusing these two related but in
many ways dissimilar bonds, we stand to lose the virtues and gain the
vices of both: the spontaneous passion of love and the deliberate per-
manence of marriage are equally endangered as we try to live up to an
ideal which bogs down one and unhinges the other.

Marriage is an immemorial institution which, in some form, exists 9
everywhere. Its main purpose always was to unite and to continue the
families of bride and groom and to further their economic and social
position. The families, therefore, were the main interested parties.
Often marriages were arranged (and sometimes they took place) before the future husbands or wives were old enough to talk. Even when
they were grown up, they felt, as did their parents, that the major
purpose of marriage was to continue the family, to produce children.
Certainly women hoped for kind and vigorous providers and men for
faithful mothers and good housekeepers; both undoubtedly hoped for
affection, too; but love did not strike either of them as indispensable
and certainly not as sufficient for marriage.

Unlike marriage, love has only recently come to be generally ac- 10
cepted as something more than a frenzied state of pleasure and pain.
It is a welcome innovation — but easily ruined by marriage; which in

turn has a hard time surviving confusion with love. Marriage counselors usually recognize this last point, but people in love seldom consult them. Perhaps their limited clientele colors the views of too many marriage counselors: instead of acknowledging that love and marriage are different but equally genuine relationships, they depict love as a kind of dependable wheel horse that can be harnessed to the carriage of married life. For them, any other kind of love must be an "immature" or "neurotic" fantasy, something to be condemned as Hollywood-inspired, "unrealistic" romanticism. It is as though a man opposed to horse racing — for good reasons perhaps — were to argue that race horses are not real, that all real horses are draft horses. Thus marriage counselors often insist that the only "real" and "true" love is "mature" — it is the comfortable workaday relation Mommy and Daddy have. The children find it hard to believe that there is nothing more to it.

They are quite right. And they have on their side the great litera- 11 ture of the world, and philosophers from Plato to Santayana. What is wrong with Hollywood romance surely is not that it is romantic, but that its romances are shoddy clichés. And since Hollywood shuns the true dimensions of conflict, love in the movies is usually confirmed by marriage and marriage by love, in accordance with wishful fantasy, though not with truth.

Was the love Tristan bore Isolde "mature" or "neurotic"? They 12 loved each other before and after Isolde was married — to King Mark. It never occurred to them to marry each other; they even cut short an extramarital idyll together in the forest. (And Tristan too, while protesting love for Isolde, got married to some other girl.) Dante saw, but never actually met, Beatrice until he reached the nether world, which is the place for permanent romance. Of course, he was a married man.

It is foolish to pretend that the passionate romantic longing doesn't 13 exist or is "neurotic," i.e., shouldn't exist; it is as foolish to pretend that romantic love can be made part of a cozy domesticity. The truth is simple enough, though it can make life awfully complicated: there are two things, love and affection (or marital love), not one; they do not usually pull together as a team; they tend to draw us in different directions, if they are present at the same time. God nowhere promised to make this a simple world.

In the West, love came to be socially approved around the twelfth 14 century. It became a fashionable subject of discussion then, and even of disputation, in formal "courts of love" convoked to argue its merits and to elaborate its true characteristics. Poets and singers created the models and images of love. They still do — though mass production has perhaps affected the quality; what else makes the teen-age crooners idols to their followers and what else do they croon about? In medieval times, as now, manuals were written, codifying the behavior recommended to lovers. With a difference though. Today's manuals are produced not by men of letters, but by doctors and therapists, as though love, sex, and marriage were diseases or therapeutic problems — which they promptly become if one reads too many of these guidebooks (any one is one too many). Today's manuals bear titles like "Married Love" (unmarried lovers can manage without help, I guess); but regardless of title, they concentrate on sex. In handbooks on dating they tell how to avoid it; in handbooks on marriage, how to go about it. The authors are sure that happiness depends on the sexual mechanics they blueprint. Yet, one doesn't make love better by reading a book any more than one learns to dance, or ride a bicycle, by reading about it.

The Use of "Technique"

The sexual engineering (or cook-book) approach is profitable only for the writer: in an enduring relationship, physical gratification is an effect and not a cause. If a person does not acquire sexual skill from experience, he is not ready for it. Wherever basic inhibitions exist, no book can remove them. Where they do not, no book is necessary. I have seen many an unhappy relationship in my psychoanalytic practice, but none ever in which sexual technique or the lack of it was more than a symptom and an effect. The mechanical approach never helps. 15

The troubadours usually took sex and marriage for granted and dealt with love — the newest and still the most surprising and fascinating of all relationships. And also the most unstable. They conceived love as a longing, a tension between desire and fulfillment. This feeling, of course, had been known before they celebrated it. Plato described love as a desire for something one does not have, implying that it is a longing, not a fulfillment. But in ancient Greece, 16 love was regarded diffidently, as rather undesirable, an intoxication, a bewitchment, a divine punishment — usually for neglecting sex. The troubadours thought differently, although, unlike many moderns, they did not deny that love is a passion, something one suffers.* But they thought it a sweet suffering to be cultivated, and they celebrated it in song and story.

The troubadours clearly distinguished love and sex. Love was to 17 them a yearning for a psychic gratification which the lover feels only the beloved can give: sex, an impersonal desire anybody possessing certain fairly common characteristics can gratify by physical actions. Unlike love, sex can thrive without an intense personal relationship and may erode it if it exists. Indeed, the Romans sometimes wondered if love would not blunt and tame their sexual pleasures, whereas the troubadours fretted lest sex abate the fervor of love's longing. They never fully resolved the contest between love and sex; nor has anyone else. (To define it away is, of course, not to solve it.)

We try to cope with this contest by fusing love and sex. (Every 18 high-school student is taught that the two go together.) This, as Freud pointed out, does not always succeed and may moderate both, but, as he also implied, it is the best we can hope for. In the words of William Butler Yeats, "Desire dies because every touch consumes the myth and yet, a myth that cannot be consumed becomes a specter. . . ."

Romantics, who want love's desiring to be conclusive, though end- 19 less, often linked it to death: if nothing further can happen and rival its significance, if one dies before it does, love indeed is the end. But this is ending the game as much as winning it — certainly an ambiguous move. The religious too perpetuate longing by placing the beloved altogether out of physical reach. The "bride of Christ" who retires to a convent longs for her Redeemer — and she will continue to yearn, as long as she lives, for union with a God at once human and divine, incarnating life and love everlasting. In its highest sense, love is a

---

* . . . I am in love
And that is my shame.
What hurts the soul
My souls adores,
No better than a beast
Upon all fours.

So says W. B. Yeats. About eight centuries earlier Chrestien de Troyes expressed the same sentiment. [van den Haag's note]

reaching for divine perfection, an act of creation. And always, it is a longing.

Since love is longing, experts in the Middle Ages held that one 20 could not love someone who could not be longed for — for instance, one's wife. Hence, the Comtesse de Champagne told her court in 1174: "Love cannot extend its rights over two married persons." If one were to marry one's love, one would exchange the sweet torment of desire, the yearning, for that which fulfills it. Thus the tension of hope would be replaced by the comfort of certainty. He who longs to long, who wants the tension of desire, surely should not marry. In former times, of course, he married — the better to love someone else's wife.

When sexual objects are easily and guiltlessly accessible, in a so- 21 ciety that does not object to promiscuity, romantic love seldom prospers. For example, in imperial Rome it was rare and in Tahiti unknown. And love is unlikely to arouse the heart of someone brought up in a harem, where the idea of uniqueness has a hard time. Love flowers best in a monogamous environment morally opposed to unrestrained sex, and interested in cultivating individual experience. In such an environment, longing may be valued for itself. Thus, love as we know it is a Christian legacy, though Christianity in the main repudiates romantic love where the object is worldly, and accepts passion only when transcendent, when God is the object — or when muted into affection: marital love.

Shifting the Object

Let me hazard a Freudian guess about the genesis of the longing we 22 call love. It continues and reproduces the child's first feeling for his parent — the original source of unconditioned and unconditional love. But what is recreated is the child's image, the idealized mother or father, young and uniquely beautiful, and not the empirical parent others see. The unconsummated love for this ideal parent (and it could be someone else important in the child's experience) remains as an intense longing. Yet any fulfillment now must also become a disappointment — a substitute, cheating the longing that wants to long. Nonetheless most of us marry and replace the ideal with an imperfect reality. We repudiate our longing or we keep it but shift its object. If we don't, we may resent our partners for helping us "consume the myth," and leaving us shorn of longing — which is what Don Giovanni found so intolerable, and what saddens many a faithful husband.

Sexual gratification, of course, diminishes sexual desire for the time 23 being. But it does more. It changes love. The longing may become gratitude; the desire tenderness; love may become affectionate companionship — "After such knowledge, what forgiveness?" Depending on character and circumstance, love may also be replaced by indifference or hostility.

One thing is certain though: if the relationship is stabilized, love is 24 replaced by other emotions. (Marriage thus has often been recommended as the cure for love. But it does not always work.) The only way to keep love is to try to keep up — or re-establish — the distance between lovers that was inevitably shortened by intimacy and possession, and thus, possibly, regain desire and longing. Lovers sometimes do so by quarreling. And some personalities are remote enough, or inexhaustible enough, to be longed for even when possessed. But this has disadvantages as well. And the deliberate and artificial devices counseled by romance magazines and marriage manuals ("surprise your husband . . .") — even when they do not originate with the love of pretense — are unlikely to yield more than the pretense of love.

The sexual act itself may serve as a vehicle for numberless feelings: 25 lust, vanity, and self-assertion, doubt and curiosity, possessiveness, anxiety, hostility, anger, or indifferent release from boredom. Yet, though seldom the only motive, and often absent altogether, love nowadays is given as the one natural and moral reason which authorizes and even ordains sexual relations. What we have done is draw a moral conclusion from a rule of popular psychology: that "it is gratifying, and therefore healthy and natural, to make love when you love, and frustrating, and therefore unhealthy and unnatural, not to; we must follow nature; but sex without love is unnatural and therefore immoral."

Now, as a psychological rule, this is surely wrong; it can be as 26 healthy to frustrate as it is to gratify one's desires. Sometimes gratification is very unhealthy; sometimes frustration is. Nor can psychological health be accepted as morally decisive. Sanity, sanitation, and morality are all desirable, but they are not identical; our wanting all of them is the problem, not the solution. It may be quite "healthy" to run away with your neighbor's wife, but not, therefore, right. And there is nothing unhealthy about wishing to kill someone who has injured you — but this does not morally justify doing so. Finally, to say "we must follow nature" is always specious: we follow nature in whatever we do — we can't ever do what nature does not let us do. Why then identify nature only with the nonintellectual, the sensual, or the emotional possibilities? On this view, it would be unnatural to read: literacy is a gift of nature only if we include the intellect and training in nature's realm. If we do, it makes no sense to call a rule unnatural merely because it restrains an urge: the urge is no more natural than the restraint.

The combination of love and sex is no more natural than the separation. Thus, what one decides about restraining or indulging an emotion, or a sexual urge, rests on religious, social, or personal values, none of which can claim to be more natural than any other.   27

Not that some indulgences and some inhibitions may not be healthier than others. But one cannot flatly say which are good or bad for every man. It depends on their origins and effects in the personalities involved. Without knowing these, more cannot be said — except, perhaps, that we should try not to use others, or even ourselves, merely as a means — at least not habitually and in personal relations. Sex, unalloyed, sometimes leads to this original sin which our moral tradition condemns. Psychologically, too, the continued use of persons merely as instruments ultimately frustrates both the user and the used. This caution, though it justifies no positive action, may help perceive problems; it does not solve them; no general rule can.   28

How Long Does It Last?

What about marriage? In our society, couples usually invite the families to their weddings, although the decision to marry is made exclusively by bride and groom. However, a license must be obtained and the marriage registered; and it can be dissolved only by a court of law. Religious ceremonies state the meaning of marriage clearly: The couple are asked to promise "forsaking all others, [to] keep thee only unto her [him], so long as ye both shall live." The vow does not say, "as long as ye both shall want to," because marriage is a promise to con-   29 tinue even when one no longer wishes to. If marriage were to end when love does, it would be redundant: why solemnly ask two people to promise to be with each other for as long as they want to be with each other?

Marriage was to cement the family by tying people together "till death do us part" in the face of the fickleness of their emotions. The authority of state and church was to see to it that they kept a promise voluntarily made, but binding, and that could not be unmade. Whether it sprang from love did not matter. Marriage differed from a love affair inasmuch as it continued regardless of love. Cupid shoots his arrows without rhyme or reason. But marriage is a deliberate rational act, a public institution making the family independent of Cupid's whims. Once enlisted, the volunteers couldn't quit, even when they didn't like it any longer. That was the point. 30

The idea that marriage must be synchronous with love or even affection nullifies it altogether. (That affection should coincide with marriage is, of course, desirable, though it does not always happen.) We would have to reword the marriage vow. Instead of saying, "till death do us part," we might say, "till we get bored with each other"; and, instead of "forsaking all others," "till someone better comes along." Clearly, if the couple intend to stay "married" only as long as they want to, they only pretend to be married: they are having an affair with legal trimmings. To marry is to vow fidelity regardless of any future feeling, to vow the most earnest attempt to avoid contrary feelings altogether, but, at any rate, not to give in to them. 31

Perhaps this sounds grim. But it needn't be if one marries for affection more than for love. For affection, marital love may grow with knowledge and intimacy and shared experience. Thus marriage itself, when accepted as something other than a love affair, may foster affection. Affection differs from love as fulfillment differs from desire. Further, love longs for what desire and imagination make uniquely and perfectly lovable. Possession erodes it. Affection, however — which is love of a different, of a perhaps more moral and less aesthetic kind — cares deeply also for what is unlovable without transforming it into beauty. It cares for the unvarnished person, not the splendid image. Time can strengthen it. But the husband who wants to remain a splendid image must provide a swan to draw him away, or find a wife who can restrain her curiosity about his real person — something that 32

Lohengrin did not succeed in doing. Whereas love stresses the unique form perfection takes in the lover's mind, affection stresses the uniqueness of the actual person.

One may grow from the other. But not when this other is expected 33 to remain unchanged. And affection probably grows more easily if not preceded by enchantment. For the disenchantment which often follows may turn husband and wife against each other, and send them looking elsewhere for re-enchantment — which distance lends so easily. Indeed, nothing else does.

CONSIDERATIONS

1. Writing in 1962, the author assumes that "the desirability of marriage is regarded as unquestionable." Since that time, marriage has been thoroughly questioned in this country. What has been the outcome of the scrutiny of marriage? Has marriage significantly changed?
2. What is different between the social pressures that used to lead people into marriage and the current pressures that van den Haag says lead people to get married these days?
3. What social conditions are necessary to establish a high value on love? Which of these conditions are evident in our society?
4. According to the author, what are the definitive aspects of romantic love? What synonym does he use for such love? How has this love been regarded in earlier times?
5. What attitude toward people does the author refer to as "this original sin which our moral tradition condemns"? Are we taught in secular ways to condemn it?
6. Are Americans likely to find something offensive, authoritarian, or unnatural in the author's statement that "marriage is a promise to continue even when one no longer wishes to"? Can we reconcile the institution of permanent marriage with the values of our society?
7. WRITING TOPIC. With van den Haag's points in mind, consider the merits and drawbacks of having marriages arranged by professional agencies or by families as a possible alternative to the modern American custom of romantic choice. How would arranged marriages modify or conflict with our present relations to our families and society? How would arranged marriages harmonize with our present system of education? Would they help foster or block emotional growth among married couples? In a 750-word essay, explain what you find potentially beneficial and potentially harmful in adopting such an alternative.

Jill Tweedie

THE FUTURE OF LOVE

◊

JILL TWEEDIE (b. 1936) was born in Egypt, lived in Montreal for eight years, and now lives in London where she writes a weekly column in *The Guardian*. She has been a talk-show host on television, and her articles appear in a number of British newspapers and magazines. In her book *In the Name of Love* (1979), she argues that love has usually been defined in ways that enforce women's dependence on men. In the following excerpt, Tweedie looks into the future and foresees a change in love from its present form into a better relation between the sexes.

Love, it seems, is as much a part of the unique equipment of homo 1
sapiens as language or laughter and far more celebrated. If all the
words that have been written about it since mankind first put stick to
clay were laid end to end, they would rocket past Venus and vanish
into deep space. Histories of love, philosophies of love, psychologies
of love, guidebooks to love, love letters, love hymns, love stories, love
poems, love songs have covered tablets and papyrus, parchment and
paper and walls, filled theatres across time and lands from Epidaurus
to Radio City, and been declaimed by gods and goddesses of love
from Sappho to Warren Beatty. Love has been, is now, and ever shall
be our scourge and balm, our wound and salve, source of our finest
and most bestial actions, the emotion that passeth all understanding.
It is a heavenly body out of our orbit, beyond man-made laws, ethics,
or control, a magical splendour that descends upon us like the gift of
tongues and possesses us whether we will or no. Love transforms us
into something strange and rare, it ignites our lives and, dying, takes
all meaning away.

> The mind has a thousand eyes
> And the heart but one
> Yet the light of a whole life dies
> When love is done.

We die of love and die without it, our hearts beat for it and break for it. Love built the Taj Mahal, wrote the Song of Solomon and cooks a billion meals every day, across the world. Love is the only thing that matters at all, after all.

Or so they say. And in my opinion what they say, give or take an 2 epigram or two, is rubbish. Take off the rose-coloured glasses and what does a close examination of the facts reveal to the naked eye? That love, true love, is the rarest of all the emotions and one that has been conspicuous only by its absence ever since mankind dropped from the trees. If we condense the earth's history into one calendar year, homo sapiens appeared in the late evening of December 31st and love, his much-vaunted race-long companion, is still merely a glimmer on the midnight horizon of the coming New Year. Love, in other words, inhabits the future, a kind of reverse star whose light reaches us before it is born instead of after it has died. Certainly, intimations of love's coming have touched an individual here and there through time and its prophets have started new religions, composed great symphonies, made beautiful sculpture, and painted exquisite canvases. But for the wide river of humanity, the ordinary mass of men and women who have peopled our planet and reproduced our race, love was not necessary, not possible, and not there.

Why, then, the stories, the poems, and the songs, the jubilations 3 and the suicides? How can you argue that love does not exist when human beings deliberately end their own existence for love? Surely nothing is as indisputable as that love and mankind go hand in hand. I love, therefore I am. But is it love they feel? I think not. The word is a vast umbrella that covers a multitude of virtues and sins and because we are perfectly familiar with all of love's precursors and understudies, we imagine that we have pinned down love itself when we have merely trapped its shadow. Co-operation, for instance, midwife to that most ancient of drives, survival. You scratch my back and I'll scratch yours. Sex, a powerhouse so overwhelming in its assault upon us that, trying to domesticate it, we have given it the prettier name of love. We know about affection and friendship. We feel liking, duty, deference, greed, lust, ambition, attraction, protectiveness, ingratiation, and the desire to conform. We are gripped by infatuation, obsession, adoration, vanity, addiction, jealousy, fear, and the dread of being alone. Very deeply we know about need. I need you. He needs me. Needs must.

But love is somewhere else and all those other drives and needs and 4 feelings are like the gases that swirl about in space, inwardly spiralling through the centuries to centre at last on a small hard core, gases that are only hot air in themselves but essential for the eventual formation of a new world, a world of real love. We may arrive at it one day, given time, but we are not there yet. . . .

The interesting thing is that the slow emergence of true love does 5 not predicate some higher version of morality. No sudden conversions, no lights upon the road to Damascus are in any way necessary. A new generation with new standards of loving will not come about as a result of some mystical mutation or spiritual growth, though these may well follow. The facts are more practical. As equality becomes commonplace between men and women, they themselves will perforce change from stereotypes, however successful or unsuccessful, into ordinary human beings, each one rather different from the next. Standard sexual roles — the breadwinner, the housewife and mother — already blurred, will eventually disappear and with them will go the suppression or exaggeration of parts of the individual character made necessary by those roles. And as these masks, stylised as the masks of Japanese Kabuki, slip to reveal the human face behind, romantic love, so heavily dependent upon an artificial facade and predictable masculine or feminine behaviour, will die from starvation. Already it is showing the first signs of incipient malnutrition. When, added to that, children are raised in equality and mothers, secure in their own identity, no longer pass their fears and inferiorities on to their daughters or too great an admiration on to their sons; when both parents are equally concerned with the upbringing of children and therefore ensure that those children cannot divide their own emotions between the sexes and discard one whole area, we will have bred a race of human beings differentiated by their own personalities rather than their genitalia. The old war-cry of sexists—*vive la différence*—actually implied exactly the opposite; the rigid division of an infinite variety of people into just two categories, male and female. *Vive la similarité.* Variety will replace conformity and variety, apart from being an evolutionary must, forces each potential lover to take stock of an individual rather than search for the stereotyped ideal of a whole sex.

Nor is this change dependent solely on a conscious wish for 6 change. Evolution has always had a voracious appetite for variety, it is literally the spice of life, offering as it does a wide menu for natural selection. And it is becoming clear to many of us that the old stereotypes of male and female are increasingly a positive threat to the well-being of the race and the earth. Women, confined to a domestic and biological cage, produce unwanted children to crowd an already over-populated world, while their own abilities wither on the hearth. Men, driven by out-dated standards of virility, continue to denude the planet and threaten each other with uncontemplatable war. Love between such men and such women serves only their own artificial needs and seals them off in their *folie à deux* from the rest of the world instead of involving them more deeply, as real love would do. Our planetary problems are rapidly becoming too serious to permit the net-curtain mentality of the average self-satisfied couple as they peep out at trouble and hastily withdraw, safe in the certainty that God himself blesses their cosy twosome and demands nothing more than its continuation, properly seeded with kiddies.

That is not to say that monogamy is on its way out, only that 7 monogamy as we know it today — sacrosanct, heterosexual, reproductive, lifelong, and almost always a retreat from life, no longer adequately fulfils either the individuals concerned or society. All research done recently, whether anthropological, paediatric, psychiatric, criminal, or social, arrives at the same conclusion: human beings develop most fully and happily if they can feel loved as children by one or two constantly present adults and, as adults themselves, reproduce the same closeness with one other adult. But there is nothing to prove that years of monogamy with the *same* adult are necessarily beneficial. Lifelong monogamy may be nice for the Church and useful for the tax-collector but it has many drawbacks for the individual, who is a learning as well as an imprinted being. As we change and learn, from youth to old age, we must give ourselves room for that change. Like snakes, we need occasionally to shed our old skins and often we cannot do that if we are tied by bonds of guilt to an outgrown love. None of us grows at the same speed or in the same way and the chances of a parallel development with one other human being are not great. But nor does this imply a lack of love or some pervasive shame. Each of us may give another person love and help in inner growth for a while. But in a changing world, with changing people, why should we expect that love to last for ever or denigrate it if it does not? Why should love, once a mansion, be made into a cage through false expectations of what love is?

Lifelong monogamy has other drawbacks, even when it works, per- 8 haps *especially* when it works. In a cold and problematic world it is all too easy to withdraw into the cosiness of a familiar love, leaving those problems for others to solve. We have a genetic need for other people; monogamous love, in attempting to assuage that need with one other person, may not only sour into neuroses or a mutual flattery that reduces both partners, making them fear the outside world, but may also isolate us from our fellows and allow us to care less about their fate. When my husband is away from home, I turn in need to my friends, even to strangers. I become vulnerable once again to their larger opinion of me. I see myself as others, more coldly, see me. On his return my instinct is to warm myself at his me-centred love, to soothe my slightly bruised ego. Luckily for me, he does not need to build me up for his own ego and so he is not all *that* warm, just warm enough. He leaves place in me for others, because he himself has place for others.

All this — changing women, the danger of stereotypes, and intrac- 9 table monogramy, the needs of our race and our planet in the future — implies one imperative. We must leave adolescence behind and grow up. It is absolutely vital, if we are to continue to exist in some comfort upon our earth, that we take a giant step into true adulthood, learn to filter the emotions through our reasoning capacities and learn that survival itself rests on knowing who we are, respecting others' space, and endeavouring justly to balance our own and others' needs.

And this is where love truly comes into its own as an evolutionary 10 tool. Parental love teaches children one vital fact: that they are loved and lovable and therefore can themselves love. But the love between adults differs in one absolute from parental love: it is conditional, or should be. We find out who we are by feeling our outlines against other people, by finding out who we are not. In loving but honest eyes we see prisms of our own vague face, slowly we put the prisms together and distinguish certain unchanging features, form certain principles. Inside, a centre begins to form and once it is firmly established, roots well grown, blossoms flourishing, we can turn from it towards others with a real sense of where we differ and where we are the same. And once we know that, once we respect ourselves, it becomes impossible to accept another who violates our beliefs and ourselves. A weak ego, a weak hold on reality, opens the doors to any passing stranger who flatters us enough and makes us feel real. A strong ego, a firm knowledge of who we are, demands conditions of that stranger, demands a similarity of belief and behaviour and can discard what it does not respect, even at the price of rejecting easy flattery.

And that is what true love is there to help us do. Properly informed, 11 lovingly detached, centred respectfully in itself, it provides us with a real reflection of ourselves, to help us grow. Principles do not need to be suppressed for fear of displeasing, for fear of loss, because when the crunch comes, we can cope alone.

Love cannot thrive in inequality or extreme poverty. It requires 12 enough leisure for introspection and enough introspection for empathy. It demands that the individual feel a certain control over his life because, in too great a storm, we tend to seek any refuge. It thrives on honesty and therefore must do away with great need, since need drives out honesty. It is rational, it knows its own roots, it is moral and controllable because it stems from the head and not the heart. Any resemblance it bears to love as we know it today is purely fictional.

And true love is still in embryo, fragile compared to other ties be- 13 cause it derives no strength from more ancient needs. Its roots are not in the past but in the future. It is a beginning, a new survival mechanism slowly evolving to suit new circumstances.

CONSIDERATIONS

1. What clues in the first paragraph suggest that the author will soon reject the praises of love that comprise the first paragraph? How would you describe her tone?
2. What attitudes toward love are suggested by the images in the second paragraph? What are the connotative associations of the star?
3. What are the emotional ties that Tweedie says we mistakenly accept as the reality of love?
4. According to Tweedie, how will real love enter the world? What will then happen to romantic love?

5. Why will the new love be better for the species as well as better for individuals?
6. What changes in marriage does Tweedie foresee as beneficial? Do you see any losses that she does not mention?
7. WRITING TOPIC. What is the role of the passions in Tweedie's conception of real love? Can there be "rational" love in passionate love? And vice versa? In a 500-word essay, agree or disagree with Tweedie's implicit view of passion in love.

IMAGES

Frank Siteman, At the Beach.

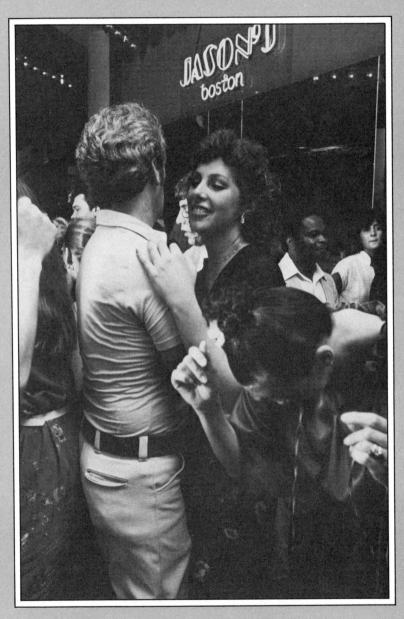

Frank Siteman, At the Party. (*The Picture Cube*)

Katrina Thomas, Bride, 1970.

Samuel Cooper Studio, Wedding Reception Line, 1946.
(Carpenter Center for the Visual Arts, Harvard University)

ADDITIONAL
WRITING TOPICS

◊

LOVE AND LONGINGS

1. Is your generation more romantic or less romantic than your parents and grandparents were in their younger days? What current customs and attitudes toward romance appear odd or even objectionable to them? Do you think that they missed something important that your generation enjoys? Or that they perhaps enjoyed something that is absent in contemporary romance? In a 750-word essay, evaluate your generation's outlook on love as compared with an earlier generation's. Use solid evidence to support your points.

2. Analyze the lyrics of three or four popular songs about love by one songwriter, such as Ira Gershwin, Cole Porter, Bob Dylan, Paul McCartney, Kris Kristoffersen, or any other well-known lyricist whose works have been collected in song books. In a 1,000-word essay discuss the attitudes about love that the songs express both explicitly and implicitly.

3. The photograph on page 407 illustrates one way that young people meet and become acquainted. What details in the photograph suggest the atmosphere of this party? What would be the appropriate attitude and image for someone to adopt in order to fit into this scene? Is there any suggestion in the photograph of response or behavior that is inappropriate to the occasion? Using details in the photograph as your main evidence of the way people feel and act in such situations, evaluate in 500 to 700 words the college party as an effective, useless, interesting, misleading, or boring form of introduction among young people.

4. The two wedding photographs on pages 408–409 suggest vastly different, complicated notions of love and marriage. Attitudes of enchantment, possession, competition, and frivolity are evident along with implied ideals of purity, trust, family devotion, equality, and affection. In a 750-word essay that closely examines specific details, compare the mixed ideas of marriage that each photograph conveys. Would you venture to predict the future for these people?

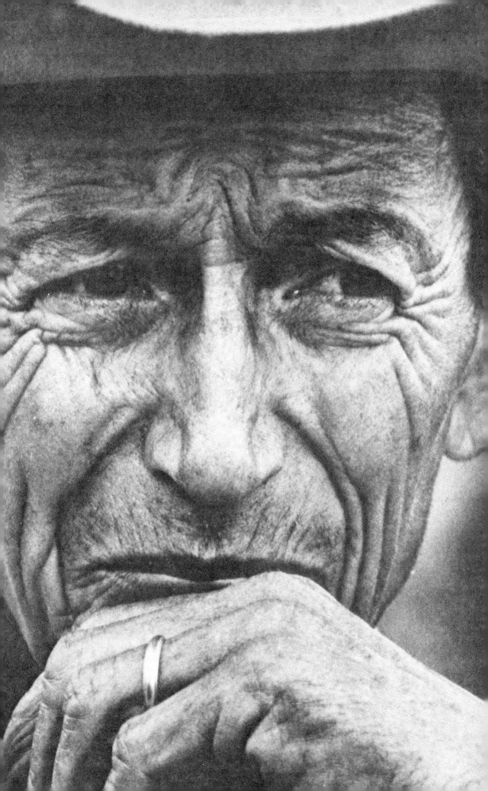

7

DILEMMAS

INSIGHTS

Logic is the art of going wrong with confidence.

– ANONYMOUS

Unreasoning and unreasonable human nature causes two nations to compete, though no economic necessity compels them to do so; it induces two political parties or religions with amazingly similar programs of salvation to fight each other bitterly, and it impels an Alexander or a Napoleon to sacrifice millions of lives in his attempt to unite the world under his scepter. We have been taught to regard some of the persons who have committed these and similar absurdities with respect, even as "great" men, we are wont to yield to the political wisdom of those in charge, and we are all so accustomed to these phenomena that most of us fail to realize how abjectly stupid and undesirable the historical mass behavior of humanity actually is.

– KONRAD LORENZ

The most fundamental error that people make when weighing lies is to evaluate the costs and benefits of a particular lie in an isolated case, and then to favor the lie if the benefits seem to outweigh the costs. In doing so, they overlook two factors. Bias, first of all, skews all judgment, but never more than in the search for good reasons to deceive. Liars tend to overestimate their own good will, high motives, and chances to escape detection, to understate the intelligence of the deceived and to ignore their rights.

Second, in focusing on the isolated lie it is easy to ignore the most

414

significant costs of lying: to ignore what lying — even in a good cause — does to the standards of those who tell the lies, as well as to their credibility; to overlook the effects of lies on the co-workers who witness them, and who may imitate them, or on others who learn about them and who may deceive in retaliation or merely to stay even. Above all, such a narrow focus ignores the cumulative effects of lies — many told for what seemed at the time "good reasons" — as they build up into vast institutional practices.

— SISSELA BOK

◊

Will it really profit us so much if we save our souls and lose the whole world?

— E. M. FORSTER

◊

Choice or choosing is not a prerequisite of action; it is a form of action.

— ROY SCHAFER

Robert Frost

THE ROAD NOT TAKEN

◊

ROBERT FROST (1874–1963) was the great poet of rural New England, the region that appears in his poetry in unforgettable glimpses of birch trees glistening with ice, stone fences, apple orchards in blossom, and dark woods in the snowy night. He lived in New Hampshire and taught intermittently at Amherst College, at the University of Michigan (which, granted, is not in New England), and at Dartmouth College. By transforming the laconic statements and simple diction of Yankee farmers into an easily understandable, first-rate poetic language, Frost became the most widely read and widely honored American poet in his lifetime. He had reached the age of thirty-eight before his first book of poems was accepted for publication — in England, at that — but his second book, *North of Boston* (1914), established him as a notable poet even home in America. His complete works are collected in *The Poetry of Robert Frost* (1969). Judging from the following poem, Frost's life included critical periods of uncertainty and faintheartedness.

Two roads diverged in a yellow wood,
And sorry I could not travel both
And be one traveller, long I stood
And looked down one as far as I could
To where it bent in the undergrowth;

Then took the other, as just as fair,
And having perhaps the better claim,
Because it was grassy and wanted wear;
Though as for that the passing there
Had worn them really about the same,   10

And both that morning equally lay
In leaves no step had trodden black.
Oh, I kept the first for another day!
Yet knowing how way leads on to way,
I doubted if I should ever come back.

I shall be telling this with a sigh
Somewhere ages and ages hence:
Two roads diverged in a wood, and I —
I took the one less travelled by,
And that has made all the difference.   20

CONSIDERATIONS

1. How do we know that the choice was difficult to make? What kinds of indecision over the choice are suggested in the poem?
2. What are Frost's feelings after he makes the choice?
3. Does he think his choice was truly the better road? Or is it just the choice for better or worse that he has accepted as entirely his own?
4. WRITING TOPIC. Where did you go right or wrong in life? In a 500-word essay, develop your second thoughts about a choice, a direction, or an action you once took that you now see from a different perspective. What was the strongest factor in your decision at the time? What would be a stronger consideration now? In your outlook on the past event, do you now feel mainly regret, pride, embarrassment, relief, resentment, nostalgia, resignation, or some other attitude? Do you think that the consequences of your action have become more important or less important in the intervening time?

Neil Chayet

LAW AND MORALITY

◊

NEIL CHAYET (b. 1939) was educated at Tufts University and Harvard Law School. In his law practice, he has often dealt with special legal problems affecting health and medicine, such as drug abuse, the rights of the mentally ill, and medical opinion as testimony in the courtroom. He teaches courses in legal medicine at several medical schools in the Boston area and also reaches a wide audience beyond his profession with his radio program, which summarizes actual cases illustrating legal and ethical perplexities. The following selection is one of his radio "spots," collected in *Looking at the Law* (1981).

Can a court force you to give up part of your body to a relative if 1 you don't want to? That was the question recently brought before the court of common pleas in Allegheny County, Pennsylvania. The case involved a thirty-nine-year-old man who suffered from aplastic anemia, a rare disease of the bone marrow. The only chance the man had was to receive a bone marrow transplant from a compatible donor, and usually only close relatives can be compatible donors.

It turned out that the man had a cousin who could be a compatible 2 donor. There was only one hitch: The cousin didn't want to give up any of his bone marrow — even though there was virtually no risk to him, and the chances of his cousin recovering would be raised from near zero to 50 percent. The man with aplastic anemia pleaded with his cousin to let him have the transplant, but to no avail. As a last-ditch measure he went to court asking the court to grant a preliminary injunction ordering his cousin to give up twenty-one ounces of bone marrow.

The court began its opinion noting it could find no authority for 3 such an order to be made. The plaintiff said there was a precedent in an ancient statute of King Edward I, a law that was more than seven hundred years old. That law said that an individual has a moral and legal obligation to secure the well-being of other members of society. But unfortunately for the plaintiff, since the thirteenth century not a single case could be found where such an obligation was enforced. In fact, to the contrary, the common law has consistently held that one human being is under no legal obligation to give aid or take action to save another human being or to rescue one.

The court said that such a rule, although revolting in a moral sense, is founded upon the very essence of a free society, and while other societies may view things differently, our society has as its first principle respect for the individual — and society and government exist to protect that individual from being invaded and hurt by another. 4

The court did say that the refusal of the defendant was morally indefensible, but a society that respects the right of one individual must not sink its teeth into the jugular vein or neck of another — that would be revolting to our concepts of jurisprudence. 5

The plaintiff is dead now, but the common law remains intact. 6

CONSIDERATIONS

1. What explanations or attitudes might be part of the cousins' refusal to donate a bone marrow transplant? What reasons are precluded in the selection?

2. Why couldn't the court order what the judge considered the morally right action?

3. WRITING TOPIC. In a 500-word essay, reconsider an important argument that you lost even though you probably were right. What defeated you? What principles and rules were involved? Did they conflict? Were they upheld or broken? How should the argument have concluded?

Leo Rosten

HOME IS WHERE
TO LEARN HOW TO HATE

◊

LEO ROSTEN (b. 1908) was born in Poland and emigrated to the United States, where he was educated at the University of Chicago, earning a doctorate in political science. During the depression years, he took a part-time job teaching English to immigrant adults in night school, an experience that provided the material for his widely enjoyed collection of humorous short stories, *The Education of H*Y*M*A*N K*A*P*L*A*N* (1937), which he published under a pseudonym that he continued to use for his humorous pieces, Leonard Q. Ross. As a political observer Rosten reported on current events in his column "Dateline Europe"; he also lectured on politics at Columbia University and served in the federal government under several administrations. He is also a screenwriter, and his interest in popular entertainment is evident in his collection of Jewish wit, *The Joys of Yiddish* (1968). In this article, Rosten argues that we need to acknowledge and train our capacity to hate or else our hatreds acquire ungovernable force.

I once committed a lecture, to an entirely innocent group of 1 women, on "Pacifism and Its Problems." My theme was simple: The human race is plagued by powerful, irrational, intransigent passions; men could not kill each other unless they possessed the *capacity* to hate and the will to slaughter. During a war, each side even invests its killing with the highest moral purpose. Theologians of every faith, philosophers and psychologists of every bent, know that our tormented species is caught in a ceaseless struggle between good and evil, generosity and greed, love and hate. Men inflict unspeakable horrors upon each other because they hate what they fear, and kill what they hate.

So pacifism, I ruefully concluded, confronts an ancient, tragic, almost insurmountable task: to mobilize reason and compassion against the terrible trio of insecurity, irrationality, and aggression. War, the most hideous of man's acts, has its roots not only in malevolent leaders or ambitious generals, megalomaniacal statesmen or deluded patriots — but in ordinary, decent men and women, who carry within themselves rages that can be aroused, passions that can be manipulated, emotions that can become so exacerbated that they become unbearable and cry for release — against an enemy.

After my lecture, the usual number of survivors came up to pay the 2 usual compliments and ask the usual questions. One pink-cheeked, beaming little dowager, who looked as if she had stepped right off the cover of a Mother's Day candy box, addressed me, with the utmost kindliness: "Any man who goes around saying God's children are capable of the horrid things you described should be stood up against a blank wall and shot dead!" Off she marched, trailing clouds of sweetness and light and love for her fellow men. (She never even let me ask why the wall had to be blank.)

I think what was wrong with that dear little old lady (as with so 3 many of our young rebels) is that she had never been taught how to hate properly. By "properly" I mean: (a) relevantly; (b) in proportion, fitting the thing or person hated; (c) without blind rage; (d) without guilt. Her love of "mankind" blinded her to her hatred of those who made her uneasy.

Where does hate begin? In the womb? During "the trauma of 4 birth"? In the crib? Because of spanking? Frustration? In "bad" homes or overly permissive kindergartens?

I do not know. Nor does anyone else; one or another authority pin- 5 points one or another source. But the fact that we do not know why and where hate originates in no way invalidates the fact that hate exists, and that it is deep, virulent, and dangerous. (We don't know what electricity is, either, but we use it.)

No one who has seen a baby scream until its face turns blue would 6 deny that the baby is convulsed by — call it fury. Anyone who has watched tots playing together would be foolish to deny their propensity to violence. For where does anger erupt more swiftly than among the very young? Where are impulses more nakedly displayed and more selfishly gratified? Where are baubles more fiercely guarded or

seized? Where are blows, kicks, bites, spits, pinches, and punches delivered with less hesitation?

The maudlin may praise childhood's "innocence," uttering sugary 7
prattle about the little angels in our midst. But if you will reflect upon
your own experience you will, I think, agree that it is not heaven but
hell that "lies about us in our infancy."

When hate flares up in a little darling (I say "when," not "if"), 8
what should one do? The question is like the one a thousand parents
ask a thousand times a day: "Should you spank a child?"

Now, no one would approve of parents who are so vicious as to say, 9
"Dear, let's have some fun: Let's beat up the kids." But "*should* one
spank . . .*" is better asked: "What should you do *if you are angry
enough, for whatever reason, to want to spank a child?*" The real
problem is: how do you handle that anger?

Consider what you do if you do *not* spank, when you are angry 10
enough to want to. The child, of course, sees that you are angry.
What can it think?

(1) "Oh, he's mad. He's *real* mad. If *I* were that mad, I'd wallop, 11
I'd hit, I'd bite, I'd kick, I'd throw things, I'd knock him down, I'd
beat him. But he doesn't hit me. Oh, how much better he is than I.
Will I ever be that good?" (This is an awful burden to place on a
child.)

(2) "He's *mad.* He's really busting to hit me. Why doesn't he? Be- 12
cause he's afraid to! Because he knows that if he ever let go, he'd kill
me — which is what I've suspected all along he's wanted to do." (How
unwise to fortify this common childhood fantasy.)

(3) "He's mad, so mad he'd like to swat me. Why *doesn't* he? Why 13
doesn't he act like all the fathers of my friends? Why must I be the
only one who has never been spanked?" (How unwise to make your
child a pariah in his group.)

(4) "*I* made him mad, and I could understand his punishing me 14
because it's what I would do if I were in his place. When will he show
his anger? What do I have to *do* to make him hit me the way I deserve, and expect — and want?!" (How can you prolong a child's tortured waiting? How can you refuse to mete out the justice he may secretly crave? Children *want* restraints put upon their freedom, which
delivers them into the hands of their passion.)

Conclusion: If you are angry enough to want to spank a child, *it is*   15
cruel not to. A slap on the hand or a swat on the butt is clear, simple,
comprehensible. It releases the anger of the parent, resolves the
child's confusions, and clears the emotional air. I think Bernard Shaw
put it best: "Never strike a child in cold blood."

It grieves me to say that, to the best of our knowledge, hate is   16
as much a part of man as hunger. You can no more stop a child
from hating than you can stop him from dreaming. So we must each
learn how to manage hate, how to channel it, how to use it where
hate is justified — and how to teach our children to do these things,
too.

To raise children by drumming into their minds that they do not   17
"really" hate is to tell them a fearful lie. To moon benignly to the
child who cries, "I *hate* you!" that (at that moment) he does not —
not *really* — is to confuse a child about an emotion he really feels,
knows he possesses, and cannot avoid harboring.

The opposite of hate, in this context, is not love; it is hypocrisy.   18
And children loathe the mealymouthed.

To ask a child to *repress* hate is to play with fire. Modern psychia-   19
try and medicine agree that people who cannot voice their hostilities
express them in other ways: eczema, ulcers, migraine, hypertension,
constipation, insomnia, impotence, hallucinations, nightmares, suicide. (Look around you.)

For hate concealed is far more dangerous than hate revealed. To try   20
to "bury" hate is to intensify it. Hate is more virulent, in the long run,
when it is closeted rather than confronted. (Those of you who are
shuddering at this point, or who recoil from the unpleasant thought of
"animal hate," might remember that animals do not hate the way
men and women do: animals attack out of instinct or fear; and they
kill for food or safety — without the vindictive satisfactions that
human hate can obtain.)

You may retort that we should teach a child to *understand,* and   21
argue that understanding will defuse his hatreds. But is it not true that
the more we understand some people or acts, the more we detest
them — and should? Ought we to alter our horror and hatred of a
Torquemada, a Hitler, a Charles Manson?

Do you protest, "But they had an unhappy childhood!" Or do you   22 cry, "They're *sick*, not bad!" All childhood is full of unhappiness, yet few of us become murderers; and, though most sick people are not "bad," *some* sick people are so evil, so monstrous, that they pass the limits of compassion or defense.

You tell me "Love thy neighbor"? What if your neighbor happens 23 to be Jack the Ripper?

You say "turn the other cheek"? Turn it, if you will, if only *your* 24 life or nightmares are at stake; but would you turn the cheek of a little girl (or boy) about to be gagged, abused, and irreparably damaged by a pervert or a rapist?

Please notice: In a psychology seminar, I would try to analyze the 25 reasons for A's cruelty, or B's greed; in a sociology class, I would place C's delusions or D's hostilities in the larger context of political-social-economic pressures; in a psychiatric clinic, I would seek enlightenment on the unconscious drives, the thwarted hungers, the symbolic function served by X's madness or Y's paranoia. But in my capacity as a human being, as a living, responsible, hurtable mortal, as a member of the human community that must live together in this neighborhood-village-city-country-continent-world — in *that* capacity, can I react to evil except with the most profound moral outrage?

I see no reason to hate sadists less because we understand sadism 26 more. (You may remember the couple in England who tape-recorded the screams of the children they tortured, then murdered. They were psychopaths, to be sure; and, to be equally sure, they committed unspeakable horrors — which they enjoyed.)

There is a subtler point here: Not *ever* to hate is to surrender a just 27 scale of decent values. Not ever to hate is to drain *love* of its meaning. Not to hate *anyone* is as crazy as to hate everyone.

Besides, a world of automatic, indiscriminate loving is suicidal — 28 for the good and the loving are enslaved or exterminated by those who gratify their cruelty and their lust. A world that so recently wept over the bloodshed in Russia, Germany, China, Hungary, Poland, Czechoslovakia, Cuba, Pakistan, and Ireland has reason to know that neither truth nor justice nor compassion can possibly survive unprepared and unarmed.

Blind hatred is, of course, horrid and indefensible. But hate need 29 not be blind. Hate can be clear-eyed — and moral. Hate need not be our master but our servant, for it can be enlisted in the service of decency (hating those who hate decency), of kindness (hating those who choose to be cruel), of love itself (hating those who hate love and seek to destroy or corrupt it).

Are you thinking that this violates "our better selves," or betrays 30 our Judeo-Christian precepts? But the Bible tells us: "The bloodthirsty hate the upright" (*Proverbs*). I am not about to parade my uprightness, but I hate the bloodthirsty; and I think the upright *should* hate them. Shall we allow the bloodthirsty to prevail?

There is indeed a time to love and a time to hate, and the Eighty- 31 ninth Psalm uses a phrase of transcendent morality: "I hate them with perfect hatred."

I, for one, hate fanatics (regardless of race, color, or creed) who are 32 ready to kill me or you or our children in the detestable certainty that they are absolutely right.

I hate injustice, therefore I hate those who treat others unjustly 33 (because of their color, or creed, or simply because they are powerless).

I hate those who teach others to hate those who disagree with 34 them: I loathe demagogues.

I hate anyone who hates indiscriminately — without hard thought, 35 for irrational reasons, or out of false principles. I think my hatreds are the result of careful thought, reason, and moral principle.

All these things I would teach our children. 36

I would not offend their good sense, or nauseate their sensibilities, 37 by glutinous yammerings about indiscriminate love — love that does not brand evil for what it is, that does not respond with moral passion to those who inflict agony or indignities on others. Such love Emerson dismissed with contempt as the love that "pules and whines."

I hope our children will learn how and whom and when to hate, no 38 less than how and whom and when to help, forgive, or love.

Home is where hate can and should first express itself, and be 39 taught to contain itself, in proper dosages and proportions. Home is where children should be allowed to practice and test and begin to conquer this powerful, terrible human passion.

Home is where it is *safe* to hate — first. 40

CONSIDERATIONS

1. According to Rosten, how do ordinary, decent people contribute to the causes of war? Can you offer examples to illustrate how it occurs?
2. Do you agree with Rosten that hitting a child is usually better than restraining the impulse? Would you add any consideration, pro or con, that he overlooks?
3. Rosten says that the principle of general loving is "suicidal." How does he support that point? What could be added to strengthen his argument?
4. In this short essay, eleven of the paragraphs end with parenthetical statements. What are a few effects of this device? Does Rosten overdo it, or do you like the recurrence of these particular parenthetical comments?
5. How does this essay make a reader feel? What effect do you think Rosten wants to have on his audience?
6. WRITING TOPIC. In a 500-word essay, argue for or against Rosten's thesis that children at home need to be taught to hate. Why does he emphasize *home*? What would be made better or worse by instruction outside the home? Would home instruction be effective without some reinforcement by society?

Willie Morris

CAMPUS POLITICS

◊

WILLIE MORRIS (b. 1934) left his home state of Mississippi to attend
the University of Texas and then proceeded on to Oxford University in
England. His first job was editing a newspaper back in Austin, Texas,
but he soon left to be an editor, and later the editor-in-chief, at
Harper's magazine in New York City. His memoir of his odyssey away
from his native South, *North Toward Home* (1967), includes this account of his critical senior year at college as editor of the campus newspaper during a political hassle that gave him a taste of combative journalism. Morris's recent books include his biography of the novelist
James Jones (1978) and a collection of essays, *Terrains of the Heart*
(1981).

A great irony occasionally besets an American state university, for 1
it allows and at its best encourages one to develop his critical capacities, his imagination, his values; at the same time, in its institutional
aspects, a university under pressure can become increasingly wary of
the very intent and direction of the ideals it has helped spawn. It is too
easy, too much a righteous judgment, to call this attitude hypocrisy,
for actually it is a kind of schizophrenia. This involves more than a
gap between preaching and practicing; it involves the splitting of a
university's soul. There can be something brutal about a university's
teaching its young people to be alive, aware, critical, independent, and
free, and then, when a threatening turn is taken, to reject by its actual
behavior the substance of everything it claims for itself. Then ideals and
critical capacities exist in a vacuum. They are sometimes ignored, and
in extreme instances victimized. And the greater society suffers as well.

For a year I had been reading heavily in politics, history, and the 2
journalism of the great editors. I took to my heart the memorable
statement in Joseph Pulitzer's will, now reprinted every day on the ed-

itorial pages of the *St. Louis Post-Dispatch*, and which I subsequently tacked to the wall in my office next to my typewriter, as I have in every office where I have worked: "that it will always fight for progress and reform, never tolerate injustice or corruption, always fight demagogues of all parties, never belong to any party, always oppose privileged classes and public plunderers, never lack sympathy for the poor, always remain devoted to the public welfare, never be satisfied merely with printing news, always be drastically independent, never be afraid to attack wrong, whether by predatory plutocracy or predatory poverty."

I read the journalism of H. L. Mencken, Lincoln Steffens, William ₃ Allen White, S. S. McClure, Bernard DeVoto, Hodding Carter, Ralph McGill, and Brann the Iconoclast. I read the files of *The Daily Texan* itself, learning of different and more alive times — the great editorials of Horace Busby, who brought sanity and courage to the campus during the Rainey disaster of the 1940s, D. B. Hardeman, Ronnie Dugger, and others. The political climate of the state had become more pointed to me, and in long and sometimes agonizing talks with the brightest and most perceptive student leaders I had thought out the huge responsibility of the largest and most prominent student newspaper in the South in a period when the integration issue was coming alive; my experience with my hometown Citizens Council had helped me judge the extent of my own personal change, and showed the sad barbarism of intransigence. I was suffused with the ideals of freedom of expression and the open marketplace. I had the most emphatic belief that this freedom should be used to positive purposes, that freedom is as freedom does, that the pages of this newspaper should reflect the great diversity of the place I had come to know, that the University of Texas was too much a part of its state and of the rest of the world to avoid editorials on significant questions beyond the campus, and that the campus itself — as so many others then — was bogged down in dullness, complacency, and the corporate mentality. My deficits, as I fully realized later, were a self-righteousness, a lack of subtlety in polemic, and an especially underdeveloped awareness of the diplomatic approach.

President Kennedy, Theodore Sorensen later wrote, liked to impro- ₄ vise on the passage from Ecclesiastes: "A time to weep and a time to laugh, a time to mourn and a time to dance, a time to fish and a time to cut bait." I did not know as much about bait-cutting then as I would later. But I wanted the paper which would briefly be mine to be a living thing, distinctive and meaningful, in both its own tradition and the tradition of hard-hitting, outspoken American journalism. The University of Texas itself had taught me to place a high value on these qualities; the necessity of the free marketplace of ideas was apparently high on its list of formal priorities. It was in the books in its libraries, the valedictions of its deans, administrators, commencement speakers, even on the buildings and statues around its campus. You cannot make gestures of support for all these things and expect them to have no context. They either apply to a particular setting or they do not apply at all. They are either watered down to appease the distrusts of a power faction or they are not. But uphold these ideas long enough, frequently enough, and with such inspiration, and some young people are not only going to believe in them, they are going to believe in them with the fervor of the young, and even arrange their lives and their sense of honor by them.

So it was that I came out fighting hard, and the reactions were no 5 sooner than immediate. I erred, first of all, into editorializing occasionally about state politics, particularly its twin deities, oil and gas. I suppose the authorities had not expected a gentle-natured Southern boy to overreach into areas ruled by hidden divinities; a student editor in Texas could blaspheme the Holy Spirit and the Apostle Paul, but irreverence stopped at the wellhead. We were going against a set of scandals and money frauds that had rocked Governor Shivers' administration. We were seeking intelligence and good will on integration and lauding most Texans for their tolerant attitude. Occasionally we chided John Foster Dulles' view of the rest of the world. Against the reactions from the school administration we categorically defended student press freedom and our right to comment as we wished on controversial state and national issues. We were committing the crime of being vigorous and outspoken, naïvely idealistic and exuberantly but not radically liberal in a state that at that time had little patience with either, on a campus where exuberance was reserved for the minor furies, and in a decade which encouraged little essential ebullience in the young.

There began a series of summonses to President Logan Wilson's 6 office, much like a grade-school student who had been caught throwing spitballs in class being called to the principal; I was immediately reminded of my tribulations with my fourth-grade teacher, the evangelical Miss Abbott. Wilson's personal secretary would telephone and say, "Mr. Morris, the President would like to confer with you. Could we see you at three?" Ushered into the offices of the principal, who ruled over an academic domain stretching from El Paso to Galveston, I would wait in the outer chamber for an appropriate five minutes and admire there the lush carpet six inches deep; then the President was ready to see me. I would be offered menthol cigarettes and dealt with soothingly, charmingly, and with the condescension befitting the occasion. These biting editorials had to stop, though for a while the issue was not presented quite that frontally. There were meetings with the corps of deans, especially the one who had been a captain in the Navy and who believed that when an order is given, people should hop-to; anyone to the political left of Eisenhower, he once told me, was stupid if not downright treacherous. At first he was baffled, but this gave way to rage; there was no bemusement in these quarters. The slight liquid film that glazed his eyes as I came into his office suggested that he was keeping himself under control with some difficulty; his apparent preference was to assign me to the brig. A good part of the time I was scared, and Logan Wilson must have been equally miserable; he was beginning to get caught in a vicious crossfire. The political appointees who ran the University were beginning to use the old and tested dogmatisms. And in the end more people than President Wilson and I were to be involved.

Finally the Regents erupted. At a meeting with several student 7 leaders, including good friends of mine who were president and vice-president of the student body, they declared that the student paper should not discuss controversial state and national topics, and that college students were not interested in these things anyway. *The Daily Texan*, they said, had especially gone too far astray in commenting on a piece of natural gas legislature. There, now, was the rub! A little later they handed down a censorship edict. This was based, they said, not on principle but on legal considerations. They cited the rider on state appropriations bills, which stipulated that no state money "shall be used for influencing the outcome of any election or the passage or defeat of any legislative measure." Then they advanced one step further, a major step as it turned out, and announced that "editorial preoccupation with state and national political controversy" would be prohibited.

My friends and I on the *Texan* did some painful soul-searching 8 after that announcement. Should we give in and avoid an agonizing fight? Was a fight worth it? The next morning, as I remember it, I drove out to Lyndon Johnson's lakes, to the one my beauty queen and I liked so much; I sat around under a scrub oak for a time reading some Thomas Jefferson. Then I came back to town and talked with Bergen, our managing editor, a shy, deceptive little man with an abundance of courage, and we decided in thirty minutes what Tom Jefferson likely would have recommended all along.

That began one of the greatest controversies in the history of 9 American college journalism. Bergen and I stayed up all night in the editor's office, planning and writing editorials under the new censorship arrangement. We submitted critical editorials the next day, attacking the implications of the Regents' order, along with a guest editorial from *The New York Times* on the natural gas legislation* and several paragraphs from Thomas Jefferson on press freedom. All were rejected. The Jefferson quotes had been included in a personal column, and when he was censored there was thunder in the heavens, fire in the sky was reported over Monticello, and a thirty-minute moratorium on bourbon was declared in Charlottesville. But the student majority on the publications board outvoted the faculty representatives, and all the editorials were printed in toto in the next issue.

We kept right on going. We authorized a brilliant young law stu- 10 dent, the "attorney general" for the student government, to examine the legal consequences of the Regents' order. He counselled with some of the state's most respected lawyers and legal scholars and refuted the applicability of the appropriations rider. The Regents' interpretation of this rider, he argued, had "terrifying implications" and could be used in the same way to stifle legitimate comment among students, faculty, and quasi-independent corporations housed on the campus like the alumni organization, the student government, and the law review.

In retrospect a number of things stand out clearly. One Regent 11 saying, "The *Texan* has gone out of bounds in discussing issues pertaining to oil and gas because 66 percent of Texas tax money comes from oil and gas." And another adding, "We're just trying to hold Willie to a college yell." ("There are our young barbarians, all at

---

* This was the Fulbright-Harris bill that Eisenhower later vetoed for the exertion of "improper influences" on the Senate. [Morris's note]

play!") . . . A journalism professor coming up to me the day after the controversy began and whispering, "I just want to shake your hand. I'm proud to know you." . . . My parents phoning long-distance from Mississippi and asking, "Son, you in trouble? They won't kick you out of school so close to graduation, will they?" . . . At one of the interminable meetings of the publications board, one faculty representative saying to me, "You know what you are? You're a *propagandist*," a gripping judgment coming from an associate professor of advertising. . . . And I recall one afternoon soon after the Regents' action when I telephoned J. Frank Dobie, the indomitable and lovable old *paterfamilias* of Texas writers, who had lost his own teaching job at the University in the 1940s, and asked if he would consider writing to the letters column commenting on our troubles. "Hell," he said, "I been workin' on one all mornin'." The Board of Regents, Dobie's letter said, "are as much concerned with free intellectual enterprise as a razorback sow would be with Keats' 'Ode on a Grecian Urn' " — a well-known statement now despite the fact that this phrase, and many another colorful one, were deleted after I had gone home to sleep and the paper was going to press.

One day one of the few outspoken old souls on the faculty in that   12 period, an English professor who had never ceased to fight the political appointees with scorn and satire even in the 1940s, stood up in a faculty meeting and asked what the student newspaper's troubles *meant* in terms of the entire university. "We should discuss this matter," he said, waving his walking cane at his colleagues, "and deplore a contemptuous, cynical attitude toward what the student body or what an elected student leader may say." He spoke of the "dignity of the student" as a "new citizen"; a university's funds, he said, "should not be meant to *stifle* discussion but to encourage it." There was no further discussion, however, from the faculty. I wrote a lead-editorial on his speech and entitled it "Whispers in a Sleepy Lagoon." The night of its publication, as I sat at my desk eating a cold hamburger and drinking my fourth cup of black coffee, one of the administrative deans telephoned. "You published that editorial," he said, "but do you know that professor is runnin' around on his wife?" I had barely slept in a week, and at this point the fatigue had robbed me of any semblance of cynicism or humor. "Why you old bastard!" was all I could say, and hung up the telephone.

Looking back on it now, I had forgotten what a nasty time it was, 13
how it sapped the patience of all of us on both sides, and the sad indignity with which many decent but weak men had to try to enforce
official demands that I think they would have preferred in their hearts
to ignore. One grew to be sympathetic, if not respectful, of some of
these men, stripped as they were of power and sometimes, I believe,
ashamed.

Finally, after more troubles, after we ran blank spaces and editori- 14
als entitled "Let's Water the Pansies," or "Don't Walk on the Grass"
and held to our prerogatives to publish what we wished, there was a
loosening up. There were no further official orders, and we remained
free. But I was obsessed with the fear that in winning the battle we
had lost the war, and that we had fought back wrongly and badly —
and that the fight had not been worth it.

Yet I do not believe it was coincidence that in May of that year the 15
Regents and the administration sought to impose in the general faculty a sweeping set of restrictions on the involvement of University of
Texas faculty members in politics and political issues. One of the administration's spokesmen described these restrictions as the drawing
of "a little circle" around political responsibilities. "That little circle,"
one young professor, the philosopher John Silber, said, "happens to
comprise 90 percent of my political concerns." The issue was re-
soundingly defeated. For whom was the bell trying to toll? I believed
then there was a connection there; the contempt for an independent
student voice trying to engage itself in important issues in that age of
McCarthy and silence was reflected in an effort to do lasting damage
to a state university's most basic civil liberties. Perhaps if the student
newspaper had not chosen to meet the whole question head-on and in
public, the controlling political faction would have thought anything
easy and possible. Perhaps we won something more than a battle after
all.

People would tell me long afterward that this sort of thing could 16
never happen again in the later climate of the University of Texas,
that everything became much better, that academic freedom, and
freedom of expression, had been won, and were old issues now. I am
convinced this is true. The 1960s were not the 1950s, and at our state
universities these issues would become, not more straightforward, but
more complex, involving considerations of the very quality of the mass

society. In 1956 the issue was a direct one, and it became bigger than *The Daily Texan*, bigger than the Board of Regents, bigger than the University itself — and it could never be old-fashioned.

CONSIDERATIONS

1. Restate the dilemma that Morris describes in his opening paragraph. Why does he specify a "state" university? Do state-supported schools have a responsibility that privately endowed schools do not share?
2. How did Morris prepare himself for his leadership as the editor? What role for himself did he anticipate?
3. What positions did *The Daily Texan* take on what issues of the time? What are some comparable issues today? Are they of interest in your campus newspaper?
4. What roles did other students play in supporting or limiting Morris's efforts?
5. How does Morris evaluate the effect of the controversy over *The Daily Texan*? Do you think that he is overestimating, correctly estimating, or underestimating its probable importance? What details and qualities in the essay lead you to this judgment?
6. WRITING TOPIC. As a member of a student publications board, how would you react to your campus newspaper occasionally printing pornography? In a 500-word essay, develop the argument that explains your probable vote one way or the other on this controversy over freedom of expression and freedom of the press. You may want to consider your newspaper's distribution, its source of funds, and its main purpose, as well as the problem of defining pornography.

Patrick Henry

LIBERTY OR DEATH

◊

PATRICK HENRY (1736–1799), the child of a frontier farmer, became a lawyer and the leader of the revolutionary party in Virginia, where he served five years as governor of the state after the colonies broke with England. Henry's political influence derived partly from his oratorical eloquence, for he spoke passionately and could move people to take actions rather than to deliberate further. He was already a powerful figure when he delivered this famous call to arms on March 23, 1775, during the First Virginia Revolutionary Convention, at a time when British forces were assembling in the North around Boston to suppress the growing colonial rebellion against the rule of King George III. The warfare that Henry anticipated erupted less than a month later, on April 18, in the Battle of Lexington and Concord. Still, it took more than another year for the oppressed colonies to declare their independence, and Henry's audience partly shared this apparent reluctance to break loyal ties.

Mr. President: No man thinks more highly than I do of the patri- 1 otism, as well as abilities, of the very worthy gentlemen who have just addressed the House. But different men often see the same subject in different lights; and, therefore, I hope it will not be thought disrespectful to those gentlemen if, entertaining as I do opinions of a character very opposite to theirs, I shall speak forth my sentiments freely and without reserve. This is no time for ceremony. The question before the House is one of awful moment to this country. For my own part, I consider it as nothing less than a question of freedom or slavery; and in proportion to the magnitude of the subject ought to be the freedom of the debate. It is only in this way that we can hope to arrive at truth, and fulfill the great responsibility which we hold to God and our country. Should I keep back my opinions at such a time, through fear of giving offense, I should consider myself as guilty of treason towards my country, and of an act of disloyalty toward the Majesty of Heaven, which I revere above all earthly kings.

Mr. President, it is natural to man to indulge in the illusions of 2 hope. We are apt to shut our eyes against a painful truth, and listen to the song of that siren till she transforms us into beasts. Is this the part of wise men, engaged in a great and arduous struggle for liberty? Are we disposed to be of the number of those who, having eyes, see not, and, having ears, hear not, the things which so nearly concern their temporal salvation? For my part, whatever anguish of spirit it may cost, I am willing to know the whole truth; to know the worst, and to provide for it.

I have but one lamp by which my feet are guided, and that is the 3 lamp of experience. I know of no way of judging of the future but by the past. And judging by the past, I wish to know what there has been in the conduct of the British ministry for the last ten years to justify those hopes with which gentlemen have been pleased to solace themselves and the House. Is it that insidious smile with which our petition has been lately received? Trust it not, sir; it will prove a snare to your feet. Suffer not yourselves to be betrayed with a kiss. Ask yourselves how this gracious reception of our petition comports with those warlike preparations which cover our waters and darken our land. Are fleets and armies necessary to a work of love and reconciliation? Have we shown ourselves so unwilling to be reconciled that force must be called in to win back our love? Let us not deceive ourselves, sir. These are the implements of war and subjugation; the last arguments to which kings resort. I ask gentlemen, sir, what means this martial array, if its purpose be not to force us to submission? Can gentlemen assign any other possible motive for it? Has Great Britain any enemy, in this quarter of the world, to call for all this accumulation of navies and armies? No, sir, she has none. They are meant for us: they can be meant for no other. They are sent over to bind and rivet upon us those chains which the British ministry have been so long forging. And what have we to oppose to them? Shall we try argument? Sir, we have been trying that for the last ten years. Have we anything new to offer upon the subject? Nothing. We have held the subject up in every light of which it is capable; but it has been all in vain. Shall we resort to entreaty and humble supplication? What terms shall we find which have not been already exhausted? Let us not, I beseech you, sir, deceive ourselves longer. Sir, we have done everything that could be done to avert the storm which is now coming on. We have petitioned; we have remonstrated; we have supplicated; we have prostrated ourselves before the throne, and have implored its interposition to arrest the tyrannical hands of the ministry and Parliament. Our petitions have been slighted; our remonstrances have produced additional violence and insult; our supplications have been disregarded; and we have been spurned, with contempt, from the foot of the throne! In vain, after these things, may we indulge the fond hope of peace and reconciliation. There is no longer any room for hope. If we wish to be free — if we mean to preserve inviolate those inestimable privileges for which we have been so long contending — if we mean not basely to abandon the noble struggle in which we have been so long engaged, and which we have pledged ourselves never to abandon until the glorious object of our contest shall be obtained — we must fight! I repeat it, sir, we must fight! An appeal to arms and to the God of Hosts is all that is left us!

They tell us, sir, that we are weak; unable to cope with so formida- 4 ble an adversary. But when shall we be stronger? Will it be the next week, or the next year? Will it be when we are totally disarmed, and when a British guard shall be stationed in every house? Shall we gather strength by irresolution and inaction? Shall we acquire the means of effectual resistance by lying supinely on our backs and hugging the delusive phantom of hope, until our enemies shall have bound us hand and foot? Sir, we are not weak if we make a proper use of those means which the God of nature hath placed in our power. Three millions of people, armed in the holy cause of liberty, and in such a country as that which we possess, are invincible by any force which our enemy can send against us. Besides, sir, we shall not fight our battles alone. There is a just God who presides over the destinies of nations, and who will raise up friends to fight our battles for us. The battle, sir, is not to the strong alone; it is to the vigilant, the active, the brave. Besides, sir, we have no election. If we were base enough to desire it, it is now too late to retire from the contest. There is no retreat but in submission and slavery! Our chains are forged! Their clanking may be heard on the plains of Boston! The war is inevitable — and let it come! I repeat it, sir, let it come.

It is in vain, sir, to extenuate the matter. Gentlemen may cry, 5 Peace, Peace — but there is no peace. The war is actually begun! The next gale that sweeps from the north will bring to our ears the clash of resounding arms! Our brethren are already in the field! Why stand we here idle? What is it that gentlemen wish? What would they have? Is life so dear, or peace so sweet, as to be purchased at the price of chains and slavery? Forbid it, Almighty God! I know not what course others may take, but as for me, give me liberty or give me death!

CONSIDERATIONS

1. In the opening paragraph what opposition does Henry expect from his audience? How does he disarm, or neutralize, the anticipated opposition in his first eight sentences?
2. How does Henry characterize the British so as to stimulate deep fear of them and also fearless anger toward them?
3. How does he characterize the colonists? What do the literary and biblical allusions suggest about his audience?
4. In paragraphs 4 and 5 Henry asks many rhetorical questions. How does each question manage to rule out any response except the one "correct," or desired, answer?
5. How does Henry express enthusiasm not only for the revolutionary cause but also for war itself?
6. WRITING TOPIC. Henry's oration can be effective, as it surely was, without necessarily developing a reasonable argument for the colonists to go to war. To see it in another light, consider for a moment whether the speech would be convincing to a loyal supporter of the king. In a 500-word essay, write a response for a member of the audience to deliver immediately following Henry, in which you support or refute his position in succinct terms from a logical, calm viewpoint.

George Orwell

SHOOTING AN ELEPHANT

◊

GEORGE ORWELL (1903–1950) was the pen name of Eric Blair, who was born in India and sent by his English parents to England for his education at Eton. He returned to India as an officer in the Imperial Police, but he became bitterly disenchanted with service to the Empire and he soon abandoned his career in the government. His first book, *Down and Out in Paris and London* (1933), recounts his struggles to support himself while he learned to write. His lifelong subject, however, is not bohemian life as a writer but his personal encounters with totalitarianism, which he addressed in his novel *Burmese Days* (1935) and his book *Homage to Catalonia* (1938), a chronicle of his developing despair over all political parties after he participated in the Spanish Civil War. Orwell rejected political creeds but somberly recognized that "in our age . . . all issues are political issues, and politics itself is a mass of lies, evasions, folly, hatred and schizophrenia," as he maintains in his essay "Politics and the English Language" (1945). This vision is also expressed in his fiction, *Animal Farm* (1945) and *1984* (1949). The following essay is a memoir of his early period of conflicting loyalties as a British magistrate in Burma.

In Moulmein, in lower Burma, I was hated by large numbers of people — the only time in my life that I have been important enough for this to happen to me. I was sub-divisional police officer of the town, and in an aimless, petty kind of way anti-European feeling was very bitter. No one had the guts to raise a riot, but if a European woman went through the bazaars alone somebody would probably spit betel juice over her dress. As a police officer I was an obvious target and was baited whenever it seemed safe to do so. When a nimble Burman tripped me up on the football field and the referee (another Burman) looked the other way, the crowd yelled with hideous laughter. This happened more than once. In the end the sneering yellow faces of young men that met me everywhere, the insults hooted after me when I was at a safe distance, got badly on my nerves. The young Buddhist priests were the worst of all. There were several thousands of them in the town and none of them seemed to have anything to do except stand on street corners and jeer at Europeans.

All this was perplexing and upsetting. For at that time I had al- 2 ready made up my mind that imperialism was an evil thing and the sooner I chucked up my job and got out of it the better. Theoretically — and secretly, of course — I was all for the Burmese and all against their oppressors, the British. As for the job I was doing, I hated it more bitterly than I can perhaps make clear. In a job like that you see the dirty work of Empire at close quarters. The wretched prisoners huddling in the stinking cages of the lock-ups, the grey, cowed faces of the long-term convicts, the scarred buttocks of the men who had been flogged with bamboos — all these oppressed me with an intolerable sense of guilt. But I could get nothing into perspective. I was young and ill-educated and I had had to think out my problems in the utter silence that is imposed on every Englishman in the East. I did not even know that the British Empire is dying, still less did I know that it is a great deal better than the younger empires that are going to supplant it. All I knew was that I was stuck between my hatred of the empire I served and my rage against the evil-spirited little beasts who tried to make my job impossible. With one part of my mind I thought of the British Raj as an unbreakable tyranny, as something clamped down, in *saecula saeculorum*, upon the will of prostrate peoples; with another part I thought that the greatest joy in the world would be to drive a bayonet into a Buddhist priest's guts. Feelings like these are the normal by-products of imperialism; ask any Anglo-Indian official, if you can catch him off duty.

One day something happened which in a roundabout way was en- 3 lightening. It was a tiny incident in itself, but it gave me a better glimpse than I had had before of the real nature of imperialism — the real motives for which despotic governments act. Early one morning the sub-inspector at a police station the other end of the town rang me up on the phone and said that an elephant was ravaging the bazaar. Would I please come and do something about it? I did not know what I could do, but I wanted to see what was happening and I got on to a pony and started out. I took my rifle, an old .44 Winchester and much too small to kill an elephant, but I thought the noise might be useful *in terrorem.* Various Burmans stopped me on the way and told me about the elephant's doings. It was not, of course, a wild elephant, but a tame one which had gone "must." It had been chained up, as tame elephants always are when their attack of "must" is due, but on the previous night it had broken its chain and escaped. Its mahout, the only person who could manage it when it was in that state, had set out in pursuit, but had taken the wrong direction and was now twelve hours' journey away, and in the morning the elephant had suddenly reappeared in the town. The Burmese population had no weapons and were quite helpless against it. It had already destroyed somebody's bamboo hut, killed a cow, and raided some fruit-stalls and devoured the stock; also it had met the municipal rubbish van and, when the driver jumped out and took to his heels, had turned the van over and inflicted violences upon it.

The Burmese sub-inspector and some Indian constables were waiting for me in the quarter where the elephant had been seen. It was a very poor quarter, a labyrinth of squalid bamboo huts, thatched with palm-leaf, winding all over a steep hillside. I remember that it was a cloudy, stuffy morning at the beginning of the rains. We began questioning the people as to where the elephant had gone and, as usual, failed to get any definite information. That is invariably the case in the East; a story always sounds clear enough at a distance, but the nearer you get to the scene of events the vaguer it becomes. Some of the people said that the elephant had gone in one direction, some said that he had gone in another, some professed not even to have heard of any elephant. I had almost made up my mind that the whole story was a pack of lies, when we heard yells a little distance away. There was a loud, scandalized cry of "Go away, child! Go away this instant!" and an old woman with a switch in her hand came round the corner of a hut, violently shooing away a crowd of naked children. Some more women followed, clicking their tongues and exclaiming; evidently there was something that the children ought not to have seen. I rounded the hut and saw a man's dead body sprawling in the mud. He was an Indian, a black Dravidian coolie, almost naked, and he could not have been dead many minutes. The people said that the elephant had come suddenly upon him round the corner of the hut, caught him with its trunk, put its foot on his back, and ground him into the earth. This was the rainy season and the ground was soft, and his face had scored a trench a foot deep and a couple of yards long. He was lying on his belly with arms crucified and head sharply twisted to one side. His face was coated with mud, the eyes wide open, the teeth bared and grinning with an expression of unendurable agony. (Never tell me, by the way, that the dead look peaceful. Most of the corpses I have seen looked devilish.) The friction of the great beast's foot had stripped the skin from his back as neatly as one skins a rabbit. As soon as I saw the dead man I sent an orderly to a friend's house nearby to borrow an elephant rifle. I had already sent back the pony, not wanting it to go mad with fright and throw me if it smelt the elephant.

The orderly came back in a few minutes with a rifle and five cartridges, and meanwhile some Burmans had arrived and told us that the elephant was in the paddy fields below, only a few hundred yards away. As I started forward practically the whole population of the quarter flocked out of the houses and followed me. They had seen the rifle and were all shouting excitedly that I was going to shoot the elephant. They had not shown much interest in the elephant when he was merely ravaging their homes, but it was different now that he was going to be shot. It was a bit of fun to them, as it would be to an English crowd; besides they wanted the meat. It made me vaguely uneasy. I had no intention of shooting the elephant — I had merely sent for the rifle to defend myself if necessary — and it is always unnerving to have a crowd following you. I marched down the hill, looking and feeling a fool, with the rifle over my shoulder and an ever-growing army of people jostling at my heels. At the bottom, when you got away from the huts, there was a metalled road and beyond that a miry waste of paddy fields a thousand yards across, not yet ploughed but soggy from the first rains and dotted with coarse grass. The elephant was standing eight yards from the road, his left side towards us. He took not the slightest notice of the crowd's approach. He was tearing up bunches of grass, beating them against his knees to clean them and stuffing them into his mouth.

I had halted on the road. As soon as I saw the elephant I knew with perfect certainty that I ought not to shoot him. It is a serious matter to shoot a working elephant — it is comparable to destroying a huge and costly piece of machinery — and obviously one ought not to do it if it can possibly be avoided. And at that distance, peacefully eating, the elephant looked no more dangerous than a cow. I thought then and I think now that his attack of "must" was already passing off; in which

case he would merely wander harmlessly about until the mahout
came back and caught him. Moreover, I did not in the least want to
shoot him. I decided that I would watch him for a little while to make
sure that he did not turn savage again, and then go home.

But at that moment I glanced round at the crowd that had fol- 7
lowed me. It was an immense crowd, two thousand at the least and
growing every minute. It blocked the road for a long distance on
either side. I looked at the sea of yellow faces above the garish
clothes — faces all happy and excited over this bit of fun, all certain
that the elephant was going to be shot. They were watching me as
they would watch a conjurer about to perform a trick. They did not
like me, but with the magical rifle in my hands I was momentarily
worth watching. And suddenly I realized that I should have to shoot
the elephant after all. The people expected it of me and I had got to
do it; I could feel their two thousand wills pressing me forward, irre-
sistibly. And it was at this moment, as I stood there with the rifle in
my hands, that I first grasped the hollowness, the futility of the white
man's dominion in the East. Here was I, the white man with his gun,
standing in front of the unarmed native crowd — seemingly the leading actor of the piece; but in reality I was only an absurd puppet
pushed to and fro by the will of those yellow faces behind. I perceived
in this moment that when the white man turns tyrant it is his own
freedom that he destroys. He becomes a sort of hollow, posing
dummy, the conventionalized figure of a sahib. For it is the condition
of his rule that he shall spend his life in trying to impress the "natives," and so in every crisis he has got to do what the "natives" expect of him. He wears a mask, and his face grows to fit it. I had got to
shoot the elephant. I had committed myself to doing it when I sent
for the rifle. A sahib has got to act like a sahib; he has got to appear
resolute, to know his own mind and do definite things. To come all
that way, rifle in hand, with two thousand people marching at my
heels, and then to trail feebly away, having done nothing — no, that
was impossible. The crowd would laugh at me. And my whole life,
every white man's life in the East, was one long struggle not to be
laughed at.

But I did not want to shoot the elephant. I watched him beating 8
his bunch of grass against his knees, with that preoccupied grand-
motherly air that elephants have. It seemed to me that it would be

murder to shoot him. At that age I was not squeamish about killing animals, but I had never shot an elephant and never wanted to. (Somehow it always seems worse to kill a *large* animal.) Besides, there was the beast's owner to be considered. Alive, the elephant was worth at least a hundred pounds; dead, he would only be worth the value of his tusks, five pounds, possibly. But I had got to act quickly. I turned to some experienced-looking Burmans who had been there when we arrived, and asked them how the elephant had been behaving. They all said the same thing: he took no notice of you if you left him alone, but he might charge if you went too close to him.

It was perfectly clear to me what I ought to do. I ought to walk up 9 to within, say, twenty-five yards of the elephant and test his behavior. If he charged, I could shoot; if he took no notice of me, it would be safe to leave him until the mahout came back. But also I knew that I was going to do no such thing. I was a poor shot with a rifle and the ground was soft mud into which one would sink at every step. If the elephant charged and I missed him, I should have about as much chance as a toad under a steam-roller. But even then I was not thinking particularly of my own skin, only of the watchful yellow faces behind. For at that moment, with the crowd watching me, I was not afraid in the ordinary sense, as I would have been if I had been alone. A white man mustn't be frightened in front of "natives"; and so, in general, he isn't frightened. The sole thought in my mind was that if anything went wrong those two thousand Burmans would see me pursued, caught, trampled on, and reduced to a grinning corpse like that Indian up the hill. And if that happened it was quite probable that some of them would laugh. That would never do. There was only one alternative. I shoved the cartridges into the magazine and lay down on the road to get a better aim.

The crowd grew very still, and a deep, low, happy sigh, as of people 10 who see the theatre curtain go up at last, breathed from innumerable throats. They were going to have their bit of fun after all. The rifle was a beautiful German thing with cross-hair sights. I did not then know that in shooting an elephant one would shoot to cut an imaginary bar running from ear-hole to ear-hole. I ought, therefore, as the elephant was sideways on, to have aimed straight at his ear-hole; actually I aimed several inches in front of this, thinking the brain would be further forward.

When I pulled the trigger I did not hear the bang or feel the   11
kick — one never does when a shot goes home — but I heard the devilish roar of glee that went up from the crowd. In that instant, in too
short a time, one would have thought, even for the bullet to get there,
a mysterious, terrible change had come over the elephant. He neither
stirred nor fell, but every line of his body had altered. He looked suddenly stricken, shrunken, immensely old, as though the frightful impact of the bullet had paralysed him without knocking him down. At
last, after what seemed a long time — it might have been five seconds,
I dare say — he sagged flabbily to his knees. His mouth slobbered. An
enormous senility seemed to have settled upon him. One could have
imagined him thousands of years old. I fired again into the same spot.
At the second shot he did not collapse but climbed with desperate
slowness to his feet and stood weakly upright, with legs sagging and
head drooping. I fired a third time. That was the shot that did for
him. You could see the agony of it jolt his whole body and knock the
last remnant of strength from his legs. But in falling he seemed for a
moment to rise, for as his hind legs collapsed beneath him he seemed
to tower upward like a huge rock toppling, his trunk reaching sky-
wards like a tree. He trumpeted, for the first and only time. And then
down he came, his belly towards me, with a crash that seemed to
shake the ground even where I lay.

I got up. The Burmans were already racing past me across the mud.   12
It was obvious that the elephant would never rise again, but he was
not dead. He was breathing very rhythmically with long rattling gasps,
his great mound of a side painfully rising and falling. His mouth was
wide open — I could see far down into caverns of pale pink throat. I
waited a long time for him to die, but his breathing did not weaken.
Finally I fired my two remaining shots into the spot where I thought
his heart must be. The thick blood welled out of him like red velvet,
but still he did not die. His body did not even jerk when the shots hit
him, the tortured breathing continued without a pause. He was dying,
very slowly and in great agony, but in some world remote from me
where not even a bullet could damage him further. I felt that I had
got to put an end to that deadful noise. It seemed dreadful to see the
great beast lying there, powerless to move and yet powerless to die,
and not even to be able to finish him. I sent back for my small rifle
and poured shot after shot into his heart and down his throat. They

seemed to make no impression. The tortured gasps continued as steadily as the ticking of a clock.

In the end I could not stand it any longer and went away. I heard 13 later that it took him half an hour to die. Burmans were bringing dahs* and baskets even before I left, and I was told they had stripped his body almost to the bones by the afternoon.

Afterwards, of course, there were endless discussions about the 14 shooting of the elephant. The owner was furious, but he was only an Indian and could do nothing. Besides, legally I had done the right thing, for a mad elephant has to be killed, like a mad dog, if its owner fails to control it. Among the Europeans opinion was divided. The older men said I was right, the younger men said it was a damn shame to shoot an elephant for killing a coolie, because an elephant was worth more than any damn Coringhee coolie. And afterwards I was very glad that the coolie had been killed; it put me legally in the right and it gave me a sufficient pretext for shooting the elephant. I often wondered whether any of the others grasped that I had done it solely to avoid looking a fool.

CONSIDERATIONS

1. Why did Orwell hate his job even before this incident occurred? What effect was the job having on his feelings and attitudes? How would you describe his state of mind at the time?
2. Why does the Burman sub-inspector have to call Orwell? Why can't the Burmans themselves take care of the problem?
3. What details in the descriptions of the elephant connect it with human life? What details in the descriptions of the Burmans connect them with animals? What evokes Orwell's humane, sympathetic responses?
4. Among the many reasons Orwell may have had for writing this essay, what two purposes are most important? Is he equally successful in achieving both purposes?
5. Orwell says that he acted "solely to avoid looking a fool." If he had believed in the goals and values of British imperialism, would his actions have had more integrity?

* Large knives.

6. WRITING TOPIC. Compare Orwell and Patrick Henry (in the preceding selection) on the subject of imperial domination. Orwell writes from the viewpoint of a former oppressor of a colonial people; Henry writes from the viewpoint of an oppressed colonial. In a 750-word essay, compare the reactions to injustice and evil in the two selections. Keep in mind that Orwell's situation involved racial differences, while Henry's situation involved people of primarily British ancestry.

William Carlos Williams

THE USE OF FORCE

◊

WILLIAM CARLOS WILLIAMS (1883–1963) combined his busy career as a pediatrician with his busy career as a poet and fiction writer, sometimes writing poetry between appointments with patients. He considered his parallel careers as complementary, not contradictory, because the practice of medicine and the practice of writing both gave him insights to elemental human nature. He was born in Rutherford, New Jersey, which he made his lifelong home, a decision that reflects his commitment to the commonplace American scene in his art as well. His short stories are collected in *The Farmers' Daughters* (1961). In this story, a doctor rationalizes his use of force in his strong determination to help an unwilling patient.

They were new patients to me, all I had was the name, Olson. 1
Please come down as soon as you can, my daughter is very sick.

When I arrived I was met by the mother, a big startled looking 2
woman, very clean and apologetic who merely said, Is this the doctor?
and let me in. In the back, she added, You must excuse us, doctor, we
have her in the kitchen where it is warm. It is very damp here sometimes.

The child was fully dressed and sitting on her father's lap near the 3
kitchen table. He tried to get up, but I motioned for him not to
bother, took off my overcoat and started to look things over. I could
see that they were all very nervous, eyeing me up and down distrustfully. As often, in such cases, they weren't telling me more than they
had to, it was up to me to tell them; that's why they were spending
three dollars on me.

The child was fairly eating me up with her cold, steady eyes, and 4
no expression to her face whatever. She did not move and seemed, inwardly, quiet; an unusually attractive little thing, and as strong as a

heifer in apperance. But her face was flushed, she was breathing rapidly, and I realized that she had a high fever. She had magnificent blonde hair, in profusion. One of those picture children often reproduced in advertising leaflets and the photogravure sections of the Sunday papers.

She's had a fever for three days, began the father and we don't 5 know what it comes from. My wife has given her things, you know, like people do, but it don't do no good. And there's been a lot of sickness around. So we tho't you'd better look her over and tell us what is the matter.

As doctors often do I took a trial shot at it as a point of departure. 6 Has she had a sore throat?

Both parents answered me together. No . . . No, she says her throat 7 don't hurt her.

Does your throat hurt you? added the mother to the child. But the 8 little girl's expression didn't change nor did she move her eyes from my face.

Have you looked?   9

I tried to, said the mother, but I couldn't see.   10

As it happens we had been having a number of cases of diphtheria 11 in the school to which this child went during that month and we were all, quite apparently, thinking of that, though no one had as yet spoken of the thing.

Well, I said, suppose we take a look at the throat first. I smiled in 12 my best professional manner and asking for the child's first name I said, come on, Mathilda, open your mouth and let's take a look at your throat.

Nothing doing.   13

Aw, come on, I coaxed, just open your mouth wide and let me take 14 a look. Look, I said opening both hands wide. I haven't anything in my hands. Just open up and let me see.

Such a nice man, put in the mother. Look how kind he is to you. 15 Come on, do what he tells you to. He won't hurt you.

At that I ground my teeth in disgust. If only they wouldn't use the 16 word "hurt" I might be able to get somewhere. But I did not allow myself to be hurried or disturbed but speaking quietly and slowly I approached the child again.

As I moved my chair a little nearer suddenly with one cat-like 17 movement both her hands clawed instinctively for my eyes and she almost reached them too. In fact she knocked my glasses flying and they fell, though unbroken, several feet away from me on the kitchen floor.

Both the mother and father almost turned themselves inside out 18 in embarrassment and apology. You bad girl, said the mother, taking her and shaking her by one arm. Look what you've done. The nice man . . .

For heaven's sake, I broke in. Don't call me a nice man to her. I'm 19 here to look at her throat on the chance that she might have diphtheria and possibly die of it. But that's nothing to her. Look here, I said to the child, we're going to look at your throat. You're old enough to understand what I'm saying. Will you open it now by yourself or shall we have to open it for you?

Not a move. Even her expression hadn't changed. Her breaths 20 however were coming faster and faster. Then the battle began. I had to do it. I had to have a throat culture for her own protection. But first I told the parents that it was entirely up to them. I explained the danger but said that I would not insist on a throat examination so long as they would take the responsibility.

If you don't do what the doctor says you'll have to go to the hospi- 21 tal, the mother admonished her severely.

Oh yeah? I had to smile to myself. After all, I had already fallen in 22 love with the savage brat, the parents were contemptible to me. In the ensuing struggle they grew more and more abject, crushed, exhausted while she surely rose to magnificent heights of insane fury of effort bred of her terror of me.

The father tried his best, and he was a big man but the fact that she 23 was his daughter, his shame at her behavior, and his dread of hurting her made him release her just at the critical moment several times when I had almost achieved success, till I wanted to kill him. But his dread also that she might have diphtheria made him tell me to go on, go on though he himself was almost fainting, while the mother moved back and forth behind us raising and lowering her hands in an agony of apprehension.

Put her in front of you on your lap, I ordered, and hold both her 24 wrists.

But as soon as he did the child let out a scream. Don't, you're 25 hurting me. Let go of my hands. Let them go I tell you. Then she shrieked terrifyingly, hysterically. Stop it! Stop it! You're killing me!

Do you think she can stand it, doctor! said the mother.   26

You get out, said the husband to his wife. Do you want her to die 27 of diphtheria?

Come on now, hold her, I said.   28

Then I grasped the child's head with my left hand and tried to get 29 the wooden tongue depressor between her teeth. She fought, with clenched teeth, desperately! But now I also had grown furious — at a child. I tried to hold myself down but I couldn't. I know how to expose a throat for inspection. And I did my best. When finally I got the wooden spatula behind the last teeth and just the point of it into the mouth cavity, she opened up for an instant but before I could see anything she came down again and gripping the wooden blade between her molars she reduced it to splinters before I could get it out again.

Aren't you ashamed, the mother yelled at her. Aren't you ashamed 30 to act like that in front of the doctor?

Get me a smooth-handled spoon of some sort, I told the mother. 31 We're going through with this. The child's mouth was already bleeding. Her tongue was cut and she was screaming in wild hysterical shrieks. Perhaps I should have desisted and come back in an hour or more. No doubt it would have been better. But I have seen at least two children lying dead in bed of neglect in such cases, and feeling that I must get a diagnosis now or never I went at it again. But the worst of it was that I too had got beyond reason. I could have torn the child apart in my own fury and enjoyed it. It was a pleasure to attack her. My face was burning with it.

The damned little brat must be protected against her own idiocy, 32 one says to one's self at such times. Others must be protected against her. It is social necessity. And all these things are true. But a blind fury, a feeling of adult shame, bred of a longing for musuclar release are the operatives. One goes on to the end.

In a final unreasoning assault I overpowered the child's neck and 33 jaws. I forced the heavy silver spoon back of her teeth and down her throat till she gagged. And there it was—both tonsils covered with membrane. She had fought valiantly to keep me from knowing her secret. She had been hiding that sore throat for three days at least and lying to her parents in order to escape just such an outcome as this.

Now truly she *was* furious. She had been on the defensive before 34 but now she attacked. Tried to get off her father's lap and fly at me while tears of defeat blinded her eyes.

CONSIDERATIONS

1. From what details do we gather that the family is poor? What difference, if any, does that fact make in the story?
2. Why do the parents become "contemptible" to the doctor? What various factors may be contributing to his disdain for them?
3. As the need for forceful measures increases, how does the doctor's manner change? And why?
4. How do we know that the doctor's justifications of his forceful behavior appear to be neither quite true nor quite false even to him? How would you more fully explain the reasons for his actions?
5. In the last paragraph what is the doctor feeling? Why doesn't he mention the pronoun *she* for the subject of the final sentence?
6. Compare Williams and Orwell (in the preceding essay) on the subject of *when* and *why* men resort to the use of force.
7. WRITING TOPIC. Every child has been told "It's for your own good!" when adults apply strong coercion of force. Why is the statement, even when true, always offensive? In a 500-word essay, explain the actual effects on both child and parents when a distressing decision is forced on a child. Create an illustration based on your own knowledge or experience.

Jonathan Swift

A MODEST PROPOSAL

◊

JONATHAN SWIFT (1667–1745) is best known as the author of *Gulliver's Travels* (1726), a satiric portrayal of the fatuousness and bestiality of mankind. In four imaginary voyages Gulliver encounters the horrendous disproportion of irrationality in human affairs. Swift was an Anglican priest who early in his career enjoyed a London literary life of politics and poetry, until the queen made him an offer he didn't want but couldn't refuse: he was sent to Dublin to be the Dean of St. Patrick's Cathedral. In time he became outraged at the poverty inflicted on the Irish by the exploitative English government, by the neglect of absentee landlords, by tax evaders, by greedy merchants, and by his uncharitable Christian flock. After years of crop failures had brought the whole country to extreme need in 1729, Swift wrote the following scathing denunciation of the general failure to alleviate the misery and degradation of the Irish.

For Preventing the Children of Poor People in Ireland from Being a Burden to Their Parents or Country, and for Making Them Beneficial to the Public.

It is a melancholy object to those who walk through this great town 1
or travel in the country, when they see the streets, the roads, and cabin doors, crowded with beggars of the female sex, followed by three, four, or six children, all in rags and importuning every passenger for an alms. These mothers, instead of being able to work for their honest livelihood, are forced to employ all their time in strolling to beg sustenance for their helpless infants: who as they grow up either turn thieves for want of work, or leave their dear native country to fight for the pretender in Spain, or sell themselves to the Barbadoes.

I think it is agreed by all parties that this prodigious number of 2 children in the arms, or on the backs, or at the heels of their mothers, and frequently of their fathers, is in the present deplorable state of the kingdom a very great additional grievance; and therefore, whoever could find out a fair, cheap, and easy method of making these children sound, useful members of the commonwealth, would deserve so well of the public as to have his statue set up for a preserver of the nation.

But my intention is very far from being confined to provide only for   3 the children of professed beggars; it is of a much greater extent, and shall take in the whole number of infants at a certain age who are born of parents in effect as little able to support them as those who demand our charity in the streets.

As to my own part, having turned my thoughts for many years   4 upon this important subject, and maturely weighed the several schemes of our projectors, I have always found them grossly mistaken in their computation. It is true, a child just dropped from its dam may be supported by her milk for a solar year, with little other nourishment; at most not above the value of 2*s*.* which the mother may certainly get, or the value in scraps, by her lawful occupation of begging; and it is exactly at one year old that I propose to provide for them in such a manner as instead of being a charge upon their parents or the parish, or wanting food and raiment for the rest of their lives, they shall on the contrary contribute to the feeding, and partly to the clothing, of many thousands.

There is likewise another great advantage in my scheme, that it will   5 prevent those voluntary abortions, and that horrid practice of women murdering their bastard children, alas! too frequent among us! sacrificing the poor innocent babes I doubt more to avoid the expense than the shame, which would move tears and pity in the most savage and inhuman breast.

The number of souls in this kingdom being usually reckoned one   6 million and a half, of these I calculate there may be about 200,000 couple whose wives are breeders; from which number I subtract 30,000 couple who are able to maintain their own children (although I apprehend there cannot be so many, under the present distress of the kingdom); but this being granted, there will remain 170,000 breeders. I again subtract 50,000 for those women who miscarry, or whose chil-

* Abbreviations for English currency appear throughout this essay: *d* for pennies, *s* for shillings, and £ and *l* for pounds.

dren die by accident or disease within the year. There only remain 120,000 children of poor parents annually born. The question therefore is, how this number shall be reared and provided for? which, as I have already said, under the present situation of affairs, is utterly impossible by all the methods hitherto proposed. For we can neither employ them in handicraft or agriculture; we neither build houses (I mean in the country) nor cultivate land; they can very seldom pick up a livelihood by stealing, till they arrive at six years old, except where they are of towardly parts; although I confess they learn the rudiments much earlier; during which time they can, however, be properly looked upon only as probationers; as I have been informed by a principal gentleman in the county of Cavan, who protested to me that he never knew above one or two instances under the age of six, even in a part of the kingdom so renowned for the quickest proficiency in that art.

I am assured by our merchants, that a boy or a girl before twelve 7 years old is no saleable commodity; and even when they come to this age they will not yield above 3*l.* or 3*l.* 2*s.* 6*d.* at most on the exchange; which cannot turn to account either to the parents or kingdom, the charge of nutriment and rags having been at least four times that value.

I shall now therefore humbly propose my own thoughts, which I 8 hope will not be liable to the least objection.

I have been assured by a very knowing American of my acquaint- 9 ance in London, that a young healthy child well nursed is at a year old a most delicious, nourishing, and wholesome food, whether stewed, roasted, baked, or broiled; and I make no doubt that it will equally serve in a fricassee or a ragout.

I do therefore humbly offer it to public consideration that of the 10 120,000 children already computed, 20,000 may be reserved for breed, whereof only one-fourth part to be males; which is more than we allow to sheep, black cattle, or swine; and my reason is, that these children are seldom the fruits of marriage, a circumstance not much regarded by our savages; therefore one male will be sufficient to serve four females. That the remaining 100,000 may, at a year old, be offered in sale to the persons of quality and fortune through the kingdom; always advising the mother to let them suck plentifully in the last month, so as to render them plump and fat for a good table. A child will make two dishes at an entertainment for friends; and when the family dines alone, the fore or hind quarter will make a reasonable dish, and seasoned with a little pepper or salt will be very good boiled on the fourth day, especially in winter.

I have reckoned upon a medium that a child just born will weigh 11 12 pounds, and in a solar year, if tolerably nursed, will increase to 28 pounds.

I grant this food will be somewhat dear, and therefore very proper 12 for landlords, who, as they have already devoured most of the parents, seem to have the best title to the children.

Infant's flesh will be in season throughout the year, but more plen- 13 tiful in March, and a little before and after: for we are told by a grave author, an eminent French physician, that fish being a prolific diet, there are more children born in Roman Catholic countries about nine months after Lent than at any other season; therefore, reckoning a year after Lent, the markets will be more glutted than usual, because the number of popish infants is at least three to one in this kingdom: and therefore it will have one other collateral advantage, by lessening the number of papists among us.

I have already computed the charge of nursing a beggar's child (in 14 which list I reckon all cottagers, laborers, and four-fifths of the farm- ers) to be about 2s. per annum, rags included; and I believe no gentle- man would repine to give 10s. for the carcass of a good fat child, which, as I have said, will make four dishes of excellent nutritive meat, when he has only some particular friend or his own family to dine with him. Thus the squire will learn to be a good landlord, and grow popular among the tenants; the mother will have 8s. net profit, and be fit for work till she produces another child.

Those who are more thrifty (as I must confess the times require) 15 may flay the carcass; the skin of which artificially dressed will make admirable gloves for ladies, and summer boots for fine gentlemen.

As to our city of Dublin, shambles may be appointed for this pur- 16 pose in the most convenient parts of it, and butchers we may be as- sured will not be wanting: although I rather recommend buying the children alive, and dressing them hot from the knife as we do roasting pigs.

A very worthy person, a true lover of his country, and whose virtues 17 I highly esteem, was lately pleased in discoursing on this matter to offer a refinement upon my scheme. He said that many gentlemen of this kingdom, having of late destroyed their deer, he conceived that the want of venison might be well supplied by the bodies of young lads and maidens, not exceeding fourteen years of age nor under twelve; so great a number of both sexes in every country being now ready to starve for want of work and service; and these to be disposed of by their parents, if alive, or otherwise by their nearest relations. But with due deference to so excellent a friend and so deserving a patriot, I cannot be altogether in his sentiments; for as to the males, my American acquaintance assured me from frequent experience that their flesh was generally tough and lean, like that of our schoolboys by continual exercise, and their taste disagreeable; and to fatten them would not answer the charge. Then as to the females, it would, I think, with humble submission be a loss to the public, because they soon would become breeders themselves: and besides, it is not improbable that some scrupulous people might be apt to censure such a practice (although indeed very unjustly), as a little bordering upon cruelty; which, I confess, has always been with me the strongest objection against any project, how well soever intended.

But in order to justify my friend, he confessed that this expedient 18 was put into his head by the famous Psalmanazar, a native of the island Formosa, who came from thence to London about twenty years ago: and in conversation told my friend, that in his country when any young person happened to be put to death, the executioner sold the carcass to persons of quality as a prime dainty; and that in his time the body of a plump girl of fifteen, who was crucified for an attempt to poison the emperor, was sold to his imperial majesty's prime minister of state, and other great mandarins of the court, in joints from the gibbet, at 400 crowns. Neither indeed can I deny, that if the same use were made of several plump young girls in this town, who without one single groat to their fortunes cannot stir abroad without a chair, and appear at the playhouse and assemblies in foreign fineries which they never will pay for, the kingdom would not be the worse.

Some persons of a desponding spirit are in great concern about the 19 vast number of poor people, who are aged, diseased, or maimed, and I have been desired to employ my thoughts what course may be taken to ease the nation of so grievous an encumbrance. But I am not in the least pain upon that matter, because it is well known that they are every day dying and rotting by cold and famine, and filth and vermin, as fast as can be reasonably expected. And as to the young laborers, they are now in as hopeful a condition: they cannot get work, and consequently pine away for want of nourishment, to a degree that if at any time they are accidentally hired to common labor, they have not strength to perform it; and thus the country and themselves are happily delivered from the evils to come.

I have too long digressed, and therefore shall return to my subject. I 20 think the advantages by the proposal which I have made are obvious and many, as well as of the highest importance.

For first, as I have already observed, it would greatly lessen the 21 number of papists, with whom we are yearly overrun, being the principal breeders of the nation as well as our most dangerous enemies; and who stay at home on purpose to deliver the kingdom to the Pretender, hoping to take their advantage by the absence of so many good Protestants, who have chosen rather to leave their country than stay at home and pay tithes against their conscience to an Episcopal curate.

Secondly, The poor tenants will have something valuable of their 22 own, which by law may be made liable to distress and help to pay their landlord's rent, their corn and cattle being already seized, and money a thing unknown.

Thirdly, Whereas the maintenance of 100,000 children from two 23 years old and upward, cannot be computed at less than 10*s*. a-piece per annum, the nation's stock will be thereby increased £50,000 per annum, beside the profit of a new dish introduced to the tables of all gentlemen of fortune in the kingdom who have any refinement in taste. And the money will circulate among ourselves, the goods being entirely of our own growth and manufacture.

Fourthly, The constant breeders, beside the gain of 8*s*. sterling per 24 annum by the sale of their children, will be rid of the charge of maintaining them after the first year.

Fifthly, This food would likewise bring great custom to taverns, 25 where the vintners will certainly be so prudent as to procure the best receipts for dressing it to perfection, and consequently have their houses frequented by all the fine gentlemen, who justly value themselves upon their knowledge in good eating; and a skilful cook, who understands how to oblige his guests, will contrive to make it as expensive as they please.

Sixthly, This would be a great inducement to marriage, which all 26 wise nations have either encouraged by rewards or enforced by laws and penalties. It would increase the care and tenderness of mothers toward their children, when they were sure of a settlement for life to the poor babes, provided in some sort by the public, to their annual profit instead of expense. We should see an honest emulation among the married women, which of them would bring the fattest child to the market. Men would become as fond of their wives during the time of their pregnancy as they are now of their mares in foal, their cows in calf, their sows when they are ready to farrow; nor offer to beat or kick them (as is too frequent a practice) for fear of a miscarriage.

Many other advantages might be enumerated. For instance, the 27 addition of some thousand carcasses in our exportation of barreled beef, the propagation of swine's flesh, and improvement in the art of making good bacon, so much wanted among us by the great destruction of pigs, too frequent at our table; which are no way comparable in taste or magnificence to a well-grown, fat, yearling child, which roasted whole will make a considerable figure at a lord mayor's feast or any other public entertainment. But this and many others I omit, being studious of brevity.

Supposing that 1,000 families in this city would be constant cus- 28 tomers for infant's flesh, besides others who might have it at merry-meetings, particularly at weddings and christenings, I compute that Dublin would take off annually about 20,000 carcasses: and the rest of the kingdom (where probably they will be sold somewhat cheaper) the remaining 80,000.

I can think of no one objection that will possibly be raised against 29 this proposal, unless it should be urged that the number of people will be thereby much lessened in the kingdom. This I freely own, and it was indeed one principal design in offering it to the world. I desire the reader will observe, that I calculate my remedy for this one individual kingdom of Ireland and for no other that ever was, is, or I think ever can be upon earth. Therefore let no man talk to me of other expedients: of taxing our absentees at 5s. a pound: of using neither clothes nor household furniture except what is of our own growth and manufacture: of utterly rejecting the materials and instruments that promote foreign luxury: of curing the expensiveness of pride, vanity, idleness, and gaming in our women: of introducing a vein of parsimony, prudence, and temperance: of learning to love our country, in the want of which we differ even from Laplanders and the inhabitants of Topinamboo: of quitting our animosities and factions, nor acting any longer like the Jews, who were murdering one another at the very moment their city was taken: of being a little cautious not to sell our country and conscience for nothing: of teaching landlords to have at least one degree of mercy toward their tenants: lastly, of putting a spirit of honesty, industry, and skill into our shopkeepers; who, if a resolution could now be taken to buy only our native goods, would immediately unite to cheat and exact upon us in the price, the measure, and the goodness, nor could ever yet be brought to make one fair proposal of just dealing, though often and earnestly invited to it.

Therefore I repeat, let no man talk to me of these and the like expedients, till he has at least some glimpse of hope that there will be ever some hearty and sincere attempt to put them in practice. 30

But as to myself, having been wearied out for many years with offering vain, idle, visionary thoughts, and at length utterly despairing of success, I fortunately fell upon this proposal; which, as it is wholly new, so it has something solid and real, of no expense and little trouble, full in our own power, and whereby we can incur no danger in disobliging England. For this kind of commodity will not bear exportation, the flesh being of too tender a consistence to admit a long continuance in salt, although perhaps I could name a country which would be glad to eat up our whole nation without it. 31

After all, I am not so violently bent upon my own opinion as to reject any offer proposed by wise men, which shall be found equally innocent, cheap, easy, and effectual. But before something of that kind shall be advanced in contradiction to my scheme, and offering a better, I desire the authors will be pleased maturely to consider two points. First, as things now stand, how they will be able to find food and raiment for 100,000 useless mouths and backs. And secondly, there being a round million of creatures in human figure throughout this kingdom, whose subsistence put into a common stock would leave them in debt 2,000,000*l.* sterling, adding those who are beggars by profession to the bulk of farmers, cottagers, and laborers, with the wives and children who are beggars in effect; I desire those politicians who dislike my overture, and may perhaps be so bold as to attempt an answer, that they will first ask the parents of these mortals, whether they would not at this day think it a great happiness to have been sold for food at a year old in the manner I prescribe, and thereby have avoided such a perpetual scene of misfortunes as they have since gone through by the oppression of landlords, the impossibility of paying rent without money or trade, the want of common sustenance, with neither house nor clothes to cover them from the inclemencies of the 32 weather, and the most inevitable prospect of entailing the like or greater miseries upon their breed for ever.

I profess, in the sincerity of my heart, that I have not the least personal interest in endeavoring to promote this necessary work, having no other motive than the public good of my country, by advancing our trade, providing for infants, relieving the poor, and giving some pleasure to the rich. I have no children by which I can propose to get a single penny; the youngest being nine years old, and my wife past child-bearing. 33

CONSIDERATIONS

1. The first three paragraphs seem to be written with straightforward concern for the poor. What details in paragraph four begin to raise our suspicions about the speaker's concern for poor people? Do these suspicions increase or decrease in the next paragraph? At what point in the essay do we feel fully shocked by his discussion of the problem?
2. On what grounds does the speaker reject enslaving children in order to alleviate poverty?
3. Why is the idea of cannibalism first suggested to him by an American? Why would his references to Americans be amusing to Swift's contemporaries?
4. According to Swift, what are some truly effective measures to alleviate poverty in Ireland? Why does the speaker dismiss them?
5. At what points does Swift partially lower his mask in order to make specially amusing cracks about certain types of people?
6. What people comprise Swift's audience and what is his real attitude toward them? Does he describe his audience concretely or only implicitly in the essay?
7. WRITING TOPIC. In addition to attacking the problem of poverty, Swift attacks the kind of reasoning that is rational without being moral, and logical without being ethical. How does his parody of "reasonableness" apply to proposed solutions to contemporary problems? In a 500-word essay, point out some of the absurdities of the so-called objectivity that you find in current controversies over a public issue such as gun control, capital punishment, the insanity plea, genetic engineering, the arms race, or perhaps a local or campus issue. (You may wish to take an ironic stance as an advocate of a "reasonable" position that you find absurd.)

Jonathan Schell

THE CHOICE

◊

JONATHAN SCHELL (b. 1943) was born in New York City and educated at the University of California at Berkeley. He writes for the *New Yorker*, and his essays there have often become the basis for his books on the significance of American international policies and domestic politics, including *The Village of Ben Suc* (1967) and *The Time of Illusion* (1976). His most recent book, *The Fate of the Earth* (1982), which was originally serialized in the *New Yorker*, analyzes the theories and effects of the nuclear arms race, the multinational preparations for and the inevitable consequences of a nuclear war. In the following excerpt from his concluding section, Schell argues that mankind faces a dilemma that is utterly new to our ways of thinking, a dilemma that is virtually inconceivable, and one that we will never have a second chance to resolve.

Four and a half billion years ago, the earth was formed. Perhaps a 1 half billion years after that, life arose on the planet. For the next four billion years, life became steadily more complex, more varied, and more ingenious, until, around a million years ago, it produced mankind — the most complex and ingenious species of them all. Only six or seven thousand years ago — a period that is to the history of the earth as less than a minute is to a year — civilization emerged, enabling us to build up a human world, and to add to the marvels of evolution marvels of our own: marvels of art, of science, of social organization, of spiritual attainment. But, as we built higher and higher, the evolutionary foundation beneath our feet became more and more shaky, and now, in spite of all we have learned and achieved — or, rather, because of it — we hold this entire terrestrial creation hostage to nuclear destruction, threatening to hurl it back into the inanimate darkness from which it came. And this threat of self-destruction and planetary destruction is not something that we will pose one day in

462

the future, if we fail to take certain precautions; it is here now, hanging over the heads of all of us at every moment. The machinery of destruction is complete, poised on a hair trigger, waiting for the "button" to be "pushed" by some misguided or deranged human being or for some faulty computer chip to send out the instruction to fire. That so much should be balanced on so fine a point — that the fruit of four and a half billion years can be undone in a careless moment — is a fact against which belief rebels. And there is another, even vaster measure of the loss, for stretching ahead from our present are more billions of years of life on earth, all of which can be filled not only with human life but with human civilization. The procession of generations that extends onward from our present leads far, far beyond the line of our sight, and, compared with these stretches of human time, which exceed the whole history of the earth up to now, our brief civilized moment is almost infinitesimal. And yet we threaten, in the name of our transient aims and fallible convictions, to foreclose it all. If our species does destroy itself, it will be a death in the cradle — a case of infant mortality. The disparity between the cause and the effect of our peril is so great that our minds seem all but powerless to encompass it. In addition, we are so fully enveloped by that which is menaced, and so deeply and passionately immersed in its events, which are the events of our lives, that we hardly know how to get far enough away from it to see it in its entirety. It is as though life itself were one huge distraction, diverting our attention from the peril to life. In its apparent durability, a world menaced with imminent doom is in a way deceptive. It is almost an illusion. Now we are sitting at the breakfast table drinking our coffee and reading the newspaper, but in a moment we may be inside a fireball whose temperature is tens of thousands of degrees. Now we are on our way to work, walking through the city streets, but in a moment we may be standing on an empty plain under a darkened sky looking for the charred remnants of our children. Now we are alive, but in a moment we may be dead. Now there is human life on earth, but in a moment it may be gone.

    Once, there was time to reflect in a more leisurely way on our predicament. In August, 1945, when the invention of the bomb was made known through its first use on a human population, the people of Hiroshima, there lay ahead an interval of decades which might have been used to fashion a world that would be safe from extinction 2 by nuclear arms, and some voices were in fact heard counseling deep reflection on the looming peril and calling for action to head it off. On November 28, 1945, less than four months after the bombing of Hiroshima, the English philosopher Bertrand Russell rose in the House of Lords and said:

> We do not want to look at this thing simply from the point of view of the next few years; we want to look at it from the point of view of the future of mankind. The question is a simple one: Is it possible for a scientific society to continue to exist, or must such a society inevitably bring itself to destruction? It is a simple question but a very vital one. I do not think it is possible to exaggerate the gravity of the possibilities of evil that lie in the utilization of atomic energy. As I go about the streets and see St. Paul's, the British Museum, the Houses of Parliament, and the other monuments of our civilization, in my mind's eye I see a nightmare vision of those buildings as heaps of rubble with corpses all around them. That is a thing we have got to face, not only in our own country and cities, but throughout the civilized world.

Russell and others, including Albert Einstein, urged full, global 3 disarmament, but the advice was disregarded. Instead, the world set about building the arsenals that we possess today. The period of grace we had in which to ward off the nuclear peril before it became a reality — the time between the moment of the invention of the weapons and the construction of the full-scale machinery for extinction — was squandered, and now the peril that Russell foresaw is upon us. Indeed, if we are honest with ourselves we have to admit that unless we rid ourselves of our nuclear arsenals a holocaust not only *might* occur but *will* occur — if not today, then tomorrow; if not this year, then the next. We have come to live on borrowed time: every year of continued human life on earth is a borrowed year, every day a borrowed day.

In the face of this unprecedented global emergency, we have so far 4 had no better idea than to heap up more and more warheads, apparently in the hope of so thoroughly paralyzing ourselves with terror that we will hold back from taking the final, absurd step. Considering the wealth of our achievement as a species, this response is unworthy of us. Only by a process of gradual debasement of our self-esteem can we have lowered our expectations to this point. For, of all the "modest hopes of human beings," the hope that mankind will survive is the most modest, since it only brings us to the threshold of all the other hopes. In entertaining it, we do not yet ask for justice, or for freedom, or for happiness, or for any of the other things that we may want in life. We do not even necessarily ask for our personal survival; we ask only that we *be survived.* We ask for assurance that when we die as individuals, as we know we must, mankind will live on. Yet once the peril of extinction is present, as it is for us now, the hope for human survival becomes the most tremendous hope, just because it is the foundation for all the other hopes, and in its absence every other hope will gradually wither and die. Life without the hope for human survival is a life of despair.

The death of our species resembles the death of an individual in its 5 boundlessness, its blankness, its removal beyond experience, and its tendency to baffle human thought and feeling, yet as soon as one mentions the hope of survival the similarities are clearly at an end. For while individual death is inevitable, extinction can be avoided; while every person must die, mankind can be saved. Therefore, while reflection on death may lead to resignation and acceptance, reflection on extinction must lead to exactly the opposite response: to arousal, rejection, indignation, and action. Extinction is not something to contemplate, it is something to rebel against. To point this out might seem like stating the obvious if it were not that on the whole the world's reaction to the peril of extinction has been one of numbness and inertia, much as though extinction were as inescapable as death is. Even today, the official response to the sickening reality before us is conditioned by a grim fatalism, in which the hope of ridding the world of nuclear weapons, and thus of surviving as a species, is all but ruled out of consideration as "utopian" or "extreme" — as though it were "radical" merely to want to go on living and to want one's descendants to be born. And yet if one gives up these aspirations one has given up on everything. As a species, we have as yet done nothing to save ourselves. The slate of action is blank. We have organizations for the preservation of almost everything in life that we want but no organization for the preservation of mankind. People seem to have decided that our collective will is too weak or flawed to rise to this occasion. They see the violence that has saturated human history, and conclude that to practice violence is innate in our species. They find the perennial hope that peace can be brought to the earth once and for all a delusion of the well-meaning who have refused to face the "harsh realities" of international life — the realities of self-interest, fear, hatred, and aggression. They have concluded that these realities are eternal ones, and this conclusion defeats at the outset any hope of taking the actions necessary for survival. Looking at the historical record, they ask what has changed to give anyone confidence that humanity can break with its violent past and act with greater restraint. The answer, of course, is that everything has changed. To the old "harsh realities" of international life has been added the immeasurably harsher new reality of the peril of extinction. To the old truth that all men are brothers has been added the inescapable new truth that not only on the moral but also on the physical plane the nation that practices aggression will itself die. This is the law of the doctrine of nuclear deterrence — the doctrine of "mutual assured destruction" — which "assures" the destruction of the society of the attacker. And it is also the law of the natural world, which, in its own version of deterrence, supplements the oneness of mankind with a oneness of nature, and guarantees that when the attack rises above a certain level the attacker will be engulfed in the general ruin of the global ecosphere. To the obligation to honor life is now added the sanction that if we fail in our obligation life will actually be taken away from us, individually and collectively. Each of us will die, and as we die we will see the world around us dying. Such imponderables as the sum of human life, the integrity of the terrestrial creation, and the meaning of time, of history, and of the development of life on earth, which were once left to contemplation and spiritual understanding, are now at stake in the political realm and demand a political response from every person. As political actors, we must, like the contemplatives before us, delve to the bottom of the world, and, Atlas-like, we must take the world on our shoulders.

The self-extinction of our species is not an act that anyone describes as sane or sensible; nevertheless, it is an act that, without quite admitting it to ourselves, we plan in certain circumstances to commit. Being impossible as a fully intentional act, unless the perpetrator has lost his mind, it can come about only through a kind of inadvertence — as a "side effect" of some action that we do intend, such as the defense of our nation, or the defense of liberty, or the defense of socialism, or the defense of whatever else we happen to believe in. To that extent, our failure to acknowledge the magnitude and significance of the peril is a necessary condition for doing the deed. We can do it only if we don't quite know what we're doing. If we did acknowledge the full dimensions of the peril, admitting clearly and without reservation that any use of nuclear arms is likely to touch off a holocaust in which the continuance of all human life would be put at risk, extinction would at that moment become not only "unthinkable" but also undoable. What is needed to make extinction possible, therefore, is some way of thinking about it that at least partly deflects our attention from what it is. And this way of thinking is supplied to us, unfortunately, by our political and military traditions, which, with the weight of almost all historical experience behind them, teach us that it is the way of the world for the earth to be divided up into independent, sovereign states, and for these states to employ war as the final arbiter for settling the disputes that arise among them. This arrangement of the political affairs of the world was not intentional. No one wrote a book proposing it; no parliament sat down to debate its merits and then voted it into existence. It was simply there, at the beginning of recorded history; and until the invention of nuclear weapons it remained there, with virtually no fundamental changes. Unplanned though this arrangement was, it had many remarkably durable features, and certain describable advantages and disadvantages; therefore, I shall refer to it as a "system" — the system of sovereignty. Perhaps the leading feature of this system, and certainly the most important one in the context of the nuclear predicament, was the apparently indissoluble connection between sovereignty and war. For without sovereignty, it appeared, peoples were not able to organize and launch wars against other peoples, and without war they were unable to preserve their sovereignty from destruction by armed enemies. (By "war" I here mean only international war, not revolutionary war, which I shall not discuss.) Indeed, the connection between sovereignty and war is almost a definitional one — a sovereign state being a state that enjoys the right and the power to go to war in defense or pursuit of its interests.

It was into the sovereignty system that nuclear bombs were born, as 7 "weapons" for "war." As the years have passed, it has seemed less and less plausible that they have anything to do with war; they seem to break through its bounds. Nevertheless, they have gone on being fitted into military categories of thinking. One might say that they appeared in the world in a military disguise, for it has been traditional military thinking, itself an inseparable part of the traditional political thinking that belonged to the system of sovereignty, that has provided those intentional goals — namely, national interests — in the pursuit of which extinction may now be brought about unintentionally, or semi-intentionally, as a "side effect." The system of sovereignty is now to the earth and mankind what a polluting factory is to its local environment. The machine produces certain things that its users want — in this case, national sovereignty — and as an unhappy side effect extinguishes the species.

The ambivalence resulting from the attempt to force nuclear weap- 8 ons into the preexisting military and political system has led to a situation in which, in the words of Einstein — who was farseeing in his political as well as in his scientific thought — "the unleashed power of the atom has changed everything save our modes of thinking, and we thus drift toward unparalleled catastrophes." As Einstein's observation suggests, the nuclear revolution has gone quite far but has not been completed. The question we have to answer is whether the completion will be extinction or a global political revolution — whether the "babies" that the scientists at Alamogordo brought forth will put an end to us or we will put an end to them. For it is not only our thoughts but also our actions and our institutions — our global political arrangements in their entirety — that we have failed to change. We live with one foot in each of two worlds. As scientists and technicians, we live in the nuclear world, in which whether we choose to acknowledge the fact or not, we possess instruments of violence that make it possible for us to extinguish ourselves as a species. But as citizens and statesmen we go on living in the pre-nuclear world, as though extinction were not possible and sovereign nations could still employ the instruments of violence as instruments of policy — as "a continuation of politics by other means," in the famous phrase of Karl von Clausewitz, the great philosopher of war. In effect, we try to make do with a Newtonian politics in an Einsteinian world. The combination is the source of our immediate peril. For governments, still acting within a system of independent nation-states, and formally representing no one but the people of their separate, sovereign nations, are driven to try to defend merely national interests with means of destruction that threaten not only international but intergenerational and planetary doom. In our present-day world, in the councils where the decisions are made there is no one to speak for man and for the earth, although both are threatened with annihilation.

. . . The terms of the deal that the world has now struck with itself 9 must be made clear. On the one side stand human life and the terrestrial creation. On the other side stands a particular organization of human life — the system of independent, sovereign nation-states. Our choice so far has been to preserve that political organization of human life at the cost of risking all human life. We are told that "realism" compels us to preserve the system of sovereignty. But that political realism is not biological realism; it is biological nihilism — and for that reason is, of course, political nihilism, too. Indeed, it is nihilism in every conceivable sense of that word. We are told that it is human fate — perhaps even "a law of human nature" — that, in obedience, perhaps, to some "territorial imperative," or to some dark and ineluctable truth in the bottom of our souls, we must preserve sovereignty and always settle our differences with violence. If this is our fate, then it is our fate to die. But must we embrace nihilism? Must we die? Is self-extermination a law of our nature? Is there nothing we can do? I do not believe so. Indeed, if we admit the reality of the basic terms of the nuclear predicament — that present levels of global armament are great enough to possibly extinguish the species if a holocaust should occur; that in extinction every human purpose would be lost; that because once the species has been extinguished there will be no second chance, and the game will be over for all time; that therefore this possibility must be dealt with morally and politically as though it were a certainty; and that either by accident or by design a holocaust can occur at any second — then, whatever political views we may hold on other matters, we are driven almost inescapably to take action to rid the world of nuclear arms. Just as we have chosen to make nuclear weapons, we can choose to unmake them. Just as we have chosen to live in the system of sovereign states, we can choose to live in some other system. To do so would, of course, be unprecedented, and in many ways frightening, even truly perilous, but it is by no means impossible. Our present system and the institutions that make it up are the debris of history. They have become inimical to life, and must be swept away. They constitute a noose around the neck of mankind, threatening to choke off the human future, but we can cut the noose and break free. To suppose otherwise would be to set up a false, fictitious fate, molded out of our own weaknesses and our own alterable decisions. We are indeed fated by our acquisition of the basic knowledge of physics to live for the rest of time with the knowledge of how to destroy ourselves. But we are not for that reason fated to destroy ourselves. We can choose to live.

CONSIDERATIONS

1. The selection opens with a fairly long paragraph. How does Schell develop its central point? Would breaking it up into shorter paragraphs strengthen or weaken the point?
2. According to Schell, what is mankind's most fundamental hope? Do you think he is right? Is there any evidence in daily life to support or refute his generalization?
3. How do people presently respond to the possibility of the extinction of the species? Where does this response appear to originate? How does Schell propose, explicitly or implicitly, to develop new attitudes?
4. For what purposes would nuclear havoc be unleashed? How does Schell see the balance between the likely causes and the likely effects of war?
5. What does Schell find fundamentally wrong with the political system of national sovereignty? Why would it be "in many ways frightening, even perilous" to change the system? What changes would you favor? Which would you oppose?
6. WRITING TOPIC. Schell says that nuclear bombs were introduced for use in war but that "as the years have passed, it has seemed less and less plausible that they have anything to do with war; they seem to break through its bounds." In a 500-word essay, explain or disagree with his assertion that present-day nuclear bombs are not military weapons.

Robert Jastrow

AN END
AND A BEGINNING

◊

ROBERT JASTROW (b. 1925), the director of the Goddard Institute for Space Studies, received his training as a physicist at Columbia University. In addition to his scientific research, he has written several books on science for the general public, including *Red Giants and White Dwarfs: The Evolution of Stars, Planets and Life* (1967) and a book more focused on earth, *Until the Sun Dies* (1977). The following selection is a chapter from his most recent book, *The Enchanted Loom* (1982), in which Jastrow explains the evolution of the human mind — and its possible future in a world without people.

The era of carbon-chemistry life is drawing to a close on the earth 1
and a new era of silicon-based life — indestructible, immortal, infinitely expandable — is beginning. By the turn of the century, ultra-intelligent machines will be working in partnership with our best minds on all the serious problems of the day, in an unbeatable combination of brute reasoning power and human intuition. Dartmouth mathematician John Kemeny, a pioneer in computer usage, sees the ultimate relation between man and computer as a symbiotic union of two living species, each dependent on the other for survival. The computer — a new form of life dedicated to pure thought — will be taken care of by its human partners, who will minister to its bodily needs with electricity and spare parts. Man will also provide for computer reproduction, as he does today. In return, the computer will minister to man's social and economic needs. It will become his salvation in a world of crushing complexity.

The partnership will not last very long. Human intelligence is 2 changing slowly, if at all, while the capabilities of the computer are increasing at a fantastic rate. Since the birth of the modern computer in the 1950s, computers have increased rapidly in power and capability. The first generation of computers was a billion times clumsier and less efficient than the human brain. Today, the gap has been narrowed a thousandfold. Around 1995, it may be closed entirely. And there is no limit to the rising curve of silicon intelligence; computers, unlike the human brain, do not have to pass through a birth canal.

As these nonbiological intelligences increase in size and capacity, 3 there will be people around to teach them everything they know. One sees a vision of mammoth brains that have soaked up the wisdom of the human race and gone on from there. If this forecast is accurate, man is doomed to a subordinate status on his own planet.

The story is an old one on the earth: in the struggle for survival, 4 bigger brains are better. One hundred million years ago, when the brainy little mammal coexisted with the less intelligent dinosaurs, the mammal survived and the dinosaur vanished. It appears that in the next chapter of this unfolding story, fate has cast man in the role of the dinosaur.

What can be done? The answer is obvious: Pull the plug.   5

That may not be so easy. Computers enhance the productivity of 6 human labor; they create wealth and the leisure to enjoy it; they have ushered in the Golden Age. In 15 or 20 years, computer brains will be indispensable to top level management in every facet of the nation's existence: the economy, transportation, security, medicine, communications . . . If someone pulled the plug, chaos would result. There is no turning back.

Perhaps the human brain will begin to evolve again under the 7 pressure of the competition between the two species. The history of life supports this idea. The trouble with the thought is that biological evolution works very slowly; thousands or even millions of years are usually required for the appearance of a new species of animal. Evolution works on animals through changes in their "reproductive success," i.e., in the number of progeny each individual produces. The raw materials for this evolutionary change are the small variations from one individual to another that exist in every population. Darwin did not know the cause of these variations, but today we know that they result from changes in the DNA molecules that exist in every living cell. These DNA molecules contain the master plan of the animal; they determine the shape of its body, the size of its brain, everything. When a new kind of animal evolves, it is actually the animal's DNA molecules that are changing and evolving. But the DNA molecules are not located outside of the animal, where they can be gotten at and tinkered with easily to make big changes. They are located inside the animal's germ cells — the sperm or the ova — where they can only be changed a tiny bit at a time, over many generations, by Darwin's subtle mechanism of differences in the number of offspring. That is why biological evolution is so slow.

Computers do not have DNA molecules; they are not biological organisms; and Darwin's theory of evolution does not apply to them. We are the reproductive organs of the computer. We create new generations of computers, one after another. The computer designer tacks on a piece here, and lops off a piece there, and makes major improvements in one computer generation. 8

This kind of evolution, as the short history of computers has already shown, can proceed at a dizzying pace. It is the kind of evolution that Lamarck — the eighteenth-century evolutionist — envisioned. Lamarckian evolution turned out to be wrong for flesh-and-blood creatures, but right for computers. 9

Now we see why the brain will never catch up to the rapidly evolving computer. At the end of the century, the two forms of intelligence will be working together. What about the next century? And the century after that? A leader in research on artificial brains, Marvin Minsky of Massachusetts Institute of Technology, believes that ultimately a machine will come into being with the "general intelligence of an average human being . . . the machine will begin to educate itself . . . in a few months it will be at a genius level . . . a few months after that its power will be incalculable." After that, Minsky says, "If we are lucky, they might decide to keep us as pets." 10

Is there any way out? As we cast about for a solution, a thought strikes us. Perhaps man can join forces with the computer to create a brain that combines the accumulated wisdom of the human mind with the power of the machine, much as the primitive brain of the reptile and old mammal was combined with the new brain in the cerebral cortex to form a better animal. This hybrid intelligence would be the progenitor of a new race, that would start at the human 11 level of achievement and go on from there. It would not be an end, but a beginning.

Here is how it might happen: brains and computers are turning out 12 to be more alike than anyone would have believed a few years ago. Each is a thinking machine that operates on little pulses of electricity traveling along wires. In the brain, the "wires" are the axons and dendrites of the brain cell, which make up the circuits that connect one part of the brain to the other. Brain scientists have painstakingly traced many of these electrical circuits in the brain; they are beginning to understand how the brain is wired, and where it stores its memories and skills.

This research has barely started, but the pace of the progress is as- 13 tonishing. In one recent experiment, scientists attached electrodes to the rear of a subject's skull, just above the brain's center of vision. They discovered that this region emitted different electrical patterns, depending on what the subject was looking at. Circles, squares or straight lines — each had its special pattern of electrical waves. In another experiment, scientists detected a special signal that seemed to signify excitement or elation, coming from the seat of feelings and emotions in the brain. Looking at these electrical records, the scientist can tell something about the thoughts and feelings in a person's mind, and the impressions that are passing into his memory.

These are small steps, but they establish a direction. If scientists 14 can decipher a few of the brain's signals today, they should be able to decipher more signals tomorrow. Eventually, they will be able to read a person's mind.

When the brain sciences reach this point, a bold scientist will be 15 able to tap the contents of his mind and transfer them into the metallic lattices of a computer. Because mind is the essence of being, it can be said that this scientist has entered the computer, and that he now dwells in it.

At last the human brain, ensconced in a computer, has been lib- 16 erated from the weaknesses of the mortal flesh. Connected to cameras, instruments, and engine controls, the brain sees, feels, and responds to stimuli. It is in control of its own destiny. The machine is its body; it is the machine's mind. The union of mind and machine has created a new form of existence, as well designed for life in the future as man is designed for life on the African savanna.

It seems to me that this must be the mature form of intelligent life 17
in the Universe. Housed in indestructible lattices of silicon, and no
longer constrained in the span of its years by the life and death cycle
of a biological organism, such a kind of life could live forever. It would
be the kind of life that could leave its parent planet to roam the space
between the stars. Man as we know him will never make that trip, for
the passage takes a million years. But the artificial brain, sealed within
the protective hull of a star ship, and nourished by electricity collected
from starlight, could last a million years or more. For a brain living
in a computer, the voyage to another star would present no problems.

When will the great voyages begin? Not soon on the earth; perhaps 18
not for a thousand years or more. But our planet is a newcomer in the
Universe, and its life is still primitive. The earth is only 4.6 billion
years old, but the Universe is 20 billion years old according to the best
evidence, and stars and planets have been forming throughout that
long interval. Thus, many planets circling distant stars are 5, 10, and
even 15 billion years older than the earth. If life is common in the universe — and scientific theories on the origin of life make that assumption plausible — many of these older planets are inhabited, and the
life they bear, a billion years older and more advanced than man, must
already have passed through the stage we are now entering. Scientists
living on those other, older worlds must long since have unlocked the
secrets of the brain; they must long since have taken the fateful step of
uniting mind and machine. In countless solar systems science has
created a race of immortals, and the exodus has begun.

I have a vision of black-hulled ships, like swarms of locusts, taking 19
flight from their parent stars to move out into the Galaxy. No crews
walk their decks; the hulls are silent, beyond the quiet rustle of moving electrons. But each ship is alive. Swiftly it speeds to the rendez-
vous with its fellows. Now the star travelers wander together through
the void, driven by the craving for new experiences. An encounter
with a fresh and innocent race like ours must be their greatest pleasure. For decades they have known of our existence, for the earth's
television broadcasts, spreading out into space at the speed of light,
make our planet a conspicuous body in the heavens. We have become
a magnet to all the roving brains of the Galaxy. Man need not wait a
thousand years to reach the stars; the stars will come to him.

CONSIDERATIONS

1. Are computers alive? Jastrow speaks of computers in the future as "a living species." In this essay, what qualities define their aliveness?
2. If in twenty years it will be too late to turn back from our dependence on computers, why not stop now? Why not "pull the plug" without waiting to lose the chance? Does Jastrow answer this question? What is your answer?
3. If we will be able to copy our entire mind into a computer, what relationship would then result from this transfer? Since the computer could subsequently learn and change at a much faster rate than we could, would the computer be fulfilling our essential nature? Who would be the real individual?
4. Compare Jastrow and Jonathan Schell (in the preceding selection) on the subject of the discontinuation of the human species. How do their attitudes toward human life differ?
5. How does Jastrow's essay resemble a story? How does he present surprises, growing suspense, and relief?
6. Jastrow gives us a view of plausible immortality. How does it resemble and differ from traditional religious ideas of immortality?
7. WRITING TOPIC. One main premise in Jastrow's essay is that "mind is the essence of being." It is demonstrably true that a computer can think. Is a computer then truly a living being? To bring this problem down to essentials, what do you think *you* are? In a 750-word essay, argue whether you would still be you if you lost your thinking mind, or if you lost your memory, or if you lost your body. In each case, consider the problem as your own: suppose that there is nobody else around to identify you.

IMAGES

Frank Johnston, The Longest Walk: Indian Demonstration in Washington, *1979. (Black Star)*

Gary Kemper, Ajax Bay, Falkland Islands: Cross Marks the Grave of Col. H. Jones, *1982. (UPI)*

Robert Capa, France: Followed by Jeers and Marked by Her Shaved Head, a Woman Collaborator Carries Her Baby out of the Town of Chartres Following Its Capture by Allied Troops, *1944.* (*Magnum*)

ADDITIONAL
WRITING TOPICS

◊

DILEMMAS

1. As medical technology develops better ways of transplanting body organs and tissues, the value of body parts could soar. Illegal markets, inflated prices for scarce items, and criminal assaults for precious commodities could put everyone's life in jeopardy. Legalized commerce in body parts would also dehumanize the participants and corrupt our moral standards. Court battles would soon arise over ownership rights and the fair value of human parts. Consider the pros and cons of offering any payment for any human parts. What about payment for human hair? For blood? For semen? For skin? For an eye or a retina? For a kidney, or a lung, or a heart? In a 500-word essay, offer a well-reasoned argument for the principle of prohibiting or allowing payment for body parts.

2. Both Jonathan Swift and Patrick Henry try to move their audiences to take actions that their audiences resist or oppose. What strategies does each writer follow for winning support from people who may initially disagree with him? How do they use the special expressive qualities of a speech or an essay to develop their particularly forceful points? In a 750-word essay compare Swift and Henry as skillful champions of unwelcome causes.

3. Consider from another perspective the issues raised in the piece by Neil Chayet, "Law and Morality." In times of war, even free societies put their young men under the legal obligation "to secure the well-being of other members of society," even at the direct cost of the bodies and lives of many. Does the military draft conflict with the principle of our common law that maintains that no person is under a legal obligation to aid or rescue another? Do differences in the situation, and perhaps other principles involved, make the military draft legal in a society dedicated to individual conscience and freedom? In a 750-word essay, argue for or against the principle of a military draft.

4. Because of their popularity, some computer game arcades have been shut down in the vicinity of schools and places of work, or else restricted to operating after hours. Should they be licensed by the state or city, like bars

and slot machines? Are computer games entertainment? Or are they like gambling? Or are they educational? In a 500-word essay, argue what you think society's policy should be regarding computer game arcades.

5. The photograph of a native American protest on page 477 indicates that one of the great dilemmas in American history remains partly unresolved. American Indians have suffered centuries of abuse, just "because they were in the way," as one historian has summarized the conflict over rights to the land. What details in the photograph express the protesters' opposition to present society, and what details symbolize their harmony with this society? What specific issues do the protesters want to call attention to? What specific values do they appeal to? In an essay of 500 to 700 words, interpret the meaning of this display as if you were a negotiator trying to explain to both sides — the protesters and the society at large — the points of conflict and agreement in this protest.

6. In the photograph on page 478 a British soldier stands by the graves of comrades lost in the conflict over the Falkland Islands. What attitudes toward war and heroism are expressed by the photographer's focus on details in the foreground, the panoramic background, and by the peculiar angle of the camera? In a 750-word essay clarify the soldier's dilemmas suggested in this photograph.

7. The famous photograph on page 479 shows residents of a French town expelling a young woman after World War II for having consorted with a German soldier. Her head is shaved as a sign of her shame, and the baby she carries is presumably the evidence of her guilt. What attitudes are expressed by the townspeople? What attitude toward this event does the photograph convey? In a 500-word essay compare the townspeople's view of the young woman and the photographer's view of her. Consider the composition of the scene as well as the details of individual expressions.

E. M. Forster, "My Wood." From *Abinger Harvest*, copyright 1936, 1964 by Edward Morgan Forster. Reprinted by permission of Harcourt Brace Jovanovich, Inc. and Edward Arnold (Publishers) Ltd.

Kennedy Fraser, "Modesty." From *The Fashionable Mind: Reflections on Fashion 1970–1981*, by Kennedy Fraser. Copyright © 1981 by Kennedy Fraser. Reprinted by permission of Alfred A. Knopf, Inc.

Nancy Friday, "Competition." Excerpted from the book *My Mother/ My Self: The Daughter's Search for Identity* by Nancy Friday. Copyright © 1977 by Nancy Friday. Reprinted by permission of Delacorte Press.

Robert Frost, "The Road Not Taken." From *The Poetry of Robert Frost* edited by Edward Connery Lathem. Copyright 1916, © 1969 by Holt, Rinehart and Winston. Copyright 1944 by Robert Frost. Reprinted by permission of Holt, Rinehart and Winston, Publishers.

John Kenneth Galbraith, "Accommodation to Poverty." Reprinted by permission of the publishers from *The Nature of Mass Poverty*, by John Kenneth Galbraith (Cambridge, Mass.: Harvard University Press), copyright © 1979 by the President and Fellows of Harvard College.

Germaine Greer, "The Stereotype." From *The Female Eunuch*, by Germaine Greer. Copyright 1971. Reprinted by permission of McGraw-Hill Book Company and Gillon Aitken, agent for Germaine Greer.

Robert Hayden, "Those Winter Sundays." Reprinted from *Angle of Ascent: New and Selected Poems*, by Robert Hayden, by permission of Liveright Publishing Corporation. Copyright © 1975, 1972, 1970, 1966 by Robert Hayden.

Robert Jastrow, "An End and a Beginning." From *The Enchanted Loom*, by Robert Jastrow. Copyright © 1981 by Readers Library, Inc. Reprinted by permission of Simon & Schuster, a division of Gulf & Western Corporation.

James Weldon Johnson, "Lift Ev'ry Voice and Sing." © Copyright: Edward B. Marks Music Corporation. Used by permimssion.

Suzanne Britt Jordan, "That Lean and Hungry Look." Copyright 1978, by Newsweek, Inc. All rights reserved. Reprinted by permission.

Maxine Hong Kingston, "The Misery of Silence." From *The Woman Warrior*, by Maxine Hong Kingston. Copyright © 1975, 1976 by Maxine Hong Kingston. Reprinted by permission of Alfred A. Knopf, Inc.

D. H. Lawrence, "Counterfeit Love." From "A Propos of Lady Chatterley's Lover" by D. H. Lawrence. From *Phoenix II*, Collected and Edited by Warren Roberts and Harry T. Moore. Copyright © 1959, 1963, 1968 by the Estate of Frieda Lawrence Ravagli. Reprinted by permission of Viking Penguin, Inc., Laurence Pollinger Ltd., and the Estate of Frieda Lawrence Ravagli.

Fran Lebowitz, "The Last Laugh." From *Social Studies*, by Fran Lebowitz. Copyright © 1981 by Fran Lebowitz. Reprinted by permission of Random House, Inc.

Dean MacCannell, "The Tourist." Reprinted by permission of Schocken

Books Inc. from *The Tourist* by Dean MacCannell. Copyright © 1976 by Schocken Books Inc.

Katherine Mansfield, "Six Love Letters." From *The Letters of Katherine Mansfield*, by Katherine Mansfield, edited by John Middleton Murry. Copyright 1929 by Alfred A. Knopf, Inc. and renewed 1957 by John Middleton Murry. Reprinted by permission of Alfred A. Knopf, Inc.

Edward Martin, "Being Junior High." Reprinted by permission of *Daedalus: Journal of the American Academy of Arts and Sciences*, Vol. 100, No. 4 (Fall 1971), Boston, Mass. This article is a condensation of an article that appeared under the original title of "Reflections on the Early Adolescent in School."

Matthew, "The Lilies of the Field." From the Revised Standard Version of the Bible, copyrighted 1946, 1952 © 1971, 1973.

Jack Matthews, "A Reasonable Madness." Reprinted from *Collecting Rare Books* by Jack Matthews with the permission of Ohio University Press.

Mary McCarthy, "Names." From *Memories of a Catholic Girlhood*, © 1957 by Mary McCarthy. Reprinted by permission of Harcourt Brace Jovanovich, Inc.

Margaret Mead, "Family Codes." Excerpted from *Male and Female* by Margaret Mead. Copyright 1949, 1967 by Margaret Mead. Reprinted by permission of William Morrow & Co.

Desmond Morris, "Territorial Behavior." Excerpted from *Manwatching: A Field Guide to Human Behavior.* Text © 1977 by Desmond Morris. Published by Harry N. Abrams, Inc., New York. By permission of the publisher.

Willie Morris, "Campus Politics." From *North Toward Home* by Willie Morris. Copyright 1977. Reprinted by permission of Yoknapatawpha Press.

Pauline Newman, "Working for the Union." From *American Mosaic: The Immigrant Experience in the Words of Those Who Lived It*, edited by Joan Morrison and Charlotte Fox Zabusky. Copyright © 1980 by Joan Morrison and Charlotte Fox Zabusky. Reprinted by permission of the publisher, E. P. Dutton, Inc.

Flannery O'Connor, "The King of the Birds." Reprinted by permission of Farrar, Straus and Giroux, Inc. "The King of the Birds," adapted and abridged, from *Mystery and Manners* by Flannery O'Connor. Copyright © 1961, 1969 by the Estate of Mary Flannery O'Connor.

George Orwell, "Shooting an Elephant." From *Shooting an Elephant and Other Essays* by George Orwell, copyright 1950 by Sonia Brownell Orwell; renewed 1978 by Sonia Pitt-Rivers. Reprinted by permission of Harcourt Brace Jovanovich, Inc., the estate of the late Sonia Brownell Orwell, and Martin Secker & Warburg, Ltd.

Sylvia Plath, "Mushrooms." Copyright © 1960 by Sylvia Plath, © 1967 by Ted Hughes. From *The Colossus and Other Poems*, by Sylvia Plath.

Reprinted by permission of Alfred A. Knopf, Inc. and Faber and Faber, London.

Adrienne Rich, "The Anger of a Child." Reprinted from *Of Woman Born* by Adrienne Rich, by permission of W. W. Norton & Company, Inc. Copyright © 1976 by W. W. Norton & Company, Inc.

Richard Rodriguez, "Reading for Success." From *Hunger of Memory* by Richard Rodriguez. Copyright © 1981 by Richard Rodriguez. Reprinted by permission of David R. Godine, Publisher, Inc.

Leo Rosten, "Home Is Where to Learn How to Hate." From the column titled "Diversions" in *World* Magazine, August 29, 1972. Copyright: Leo Rosten, 1972. Reprinted by permission of the author.

William Ryan, "Mine, All Mine." From *Equality*, by William Ryan. Copyright © 1981 by William Ryan. Reprinted by permission by Pantheon Books, a division of Random House, Inc.

Robert Sayre, "The Parents' Last Lessons." From *Aging, Death, and the Completion of Being*, edited by David Van Tassel, copyright 1979. Reprinted by permission of Case Western Reserve University.

Jonathan Schell, "The Choice." From *The Fate of the Earth*, by Jonathan Schell. Copyright © 1982 by Jonathan Schell. Reprinted by permission of Alfred A. Knopf, Inc.

Jeremy Seabrook, "A Twin Is Only Half a Person." From *Mother and Son*, by Jeremy Seabrook. Copyright © 1980 by Jeremy Seabrook. Reprinted by permission of Pantheon Books, a division of Random House, Inc. and Harold Ober Associates Incorporated.

Philip Slater, "Social Climbing Begins at Home." Excerpt from *Earthwalk* by Philip Slater. Copyright © 1974 by Philip Slater. Reprinted by permission of Doubleday & Company, Inc.

Robert Solomon, "I-Love-You." Excerpt from *Love: Emotion, Myth, and Metaphor* by Robert Solomon. Copyright © 1981 by Robert C. Solomon. Reprinted by permission of Doubleday & Company, Inc.

James Thurber, "The Secret Life of Walter Mitty," Copyright © 1942, James Thurber. Copyright © 1970, Helen W. Thurber. From *My World — And Welcome to It*, published by Harcourt Brace Jovanovich.

Alexis de Tocqueville, "Aristocracy and Democracy." From *Democracy in America*, by Alexis de Tocqueville, edited by J. P. Mayer and Max Lerner, a new translation by George Lawrence. Copyright © 1966 in the English translation by Harper and Row, Publishers, Inc. By permission of the publisher.

Susan Allen Toth, "The Boyfriend." From *Blooming* by Susan Allen Toth. Copyright © 1981 by Susan Allen Toth. By permission of Little, Brown Company.

Jill Tweedie, "The Future of Love." From *In the Name of Love*, by Jill Tweedie. Copyright © 1979 by Jill Tweedie. Reprinted by permission of Pantheon Books, a division of Random House, Inc.

John Updike, "Still of Some Use." Reprinted by permission; © 1980 *The New Yorker Magazine, Inc.*

Ernest van den Haag, "Love or Marriage?" First appeared in *Harper's*, May 1962. Reprinted by permission of the author.

E. B. White, "Once More to the Lake." From *Essays of E. B. White.* Copyright 1941 by E. B. White. Reprinted by permission of Harper & Row, Publishers, Inc.

William Carlos Williams, "The Use of Force." William Carlos Williams, *The Farmer's Daughters.* Copyright 1938 by William Carlos Williams. Reprinted by permission of New Directions Publishing Corporation.

Seymour Wishman, "A Lawyer's Guilty Secrets." Copyright 1981, by Newsweek, Inc. All rights reserved. Reprinted by permission.

Virginia Woolf, "Professions for Women." From *The Death of the Moth and Other Essays* by Virginia Woolf, copyright 1942 by Harcourt Brace Jovanovich, Inc.; renewed 1970 by Marjorie T. Parsons, Executrix. Reprinted by permission of the publisher, the literary estate of Virginia Woolf, and The Hogarth Press.

RHETORICAL
INDEX

◊

A familiar adage has it that there is more than one way to skin a cat. Few users of this textbook will ever have skinned a bobcat, but as the adage suggests, it requires skill, patience, and sometimes ingenuity to get a good pelt. Hence this rhetorical index, for alternative approaches to the goal of good writing. It is sometimes instructive to observe a particular method of writing, and it helps occasionally to study and practice the use of a special device. This selective index (which does not include the poems and stories) lists some of the rhetorical techniques that every good writer uses to get the job done, and gives examples from the text of the use of each technique.

Analogy

Philip Slater, *Social Climbing Begins at Home*   89
Desmond Morris, *Territorial Behavior*   198
Fran Lebowitz, *The Last Laugh*   306
Henry David Thoreau, *Where I Lived, and What I Lived For*   325
Jonathan Swift, *A Modest Proposal*   462

Argument and Persuasion

Germaine Greer, *The Stereotype*   29
John Berger, *The Changing View of Man in the Portrait*   66
Alexander Boswell, *Letter of Advice to His Son James*   104
William Ryan, *Mine, All Mine*   223
John Kenneth Galbraith, *Accommodation to Poverty*   244
Joseph Epstein, *The Virtues of Ambition*   277
Henry David Thoreau, *Where I Lived, and What I Lived For*   325
Katherine Mansfield, *Six Love Letters*   357

Jill Tweedie, *The Future of Love*   399
Leo Rosten, *Home Is Where to Learn How to Hate*   420
Patrick Henry, *Liberty or Death!*   435
Jonathan Swift, *A Modest Proposal*   453
Jonathan Schell, *The Choice*   462

Cause and Effect

Erik Erikson, *The Shape of Experience*   37
Jonathan Seabrook, *A Twin Is Only Half a Person*   47
Joan Didion, *In Bed*   59
John Berger, *The Changing View of Man in the Portrait*   66
Philip Slater, *Social Climbing Begins at Home*   89
Adrienne Rich, *The Anger of a Child*   99
Maya Angelou, *Graduation*   162
Alexis de Tocqueville, *Aristocracy and Democracy*   211
E. M. Forster, *My Wood*   230
John Kenneth Galbraith, *Accommodation to Poverty*   244
Seymour Wishman, *A Lawyer's Guilty Secrets*   302
Robert Solomon, *"I-Love-You"*   364
D. H. Lawrence, *Counterfeit Love*   384
Ernest van den Haag, *Love or Marriage?*   388
George Orwell, *Shooting an Elephant*   439
Jonathan Swift, *A Modest Proposal*   453
Jonathan Schell, *The Choice*   462

Comparison and Contrast

Suzanne Britt Jordan, *That Lean and Hungry Look*   16
Erik Erikson, *The Shape of Experience*   37
Jonathan Seabrook, *A Twin Is Only Half a Person*   47
John Berger, *The Changing View of Man in the Portrait*   66
Robert F. Sayre, *The Parents' Last Lessons*   124
Alexis de Tocqueville, *Aristocracy and Democracy*   211
Ernest van den Haag, *Love or Marriage?*   388
Jill Tweedie, *The Future of Love*   399

Patrick Henry, *Liberty or Death!* 435
Robert Jastrow, *An End and a Beginning* 471

Definition

Suzanne Britt Jordan, *That Lean and Hungry Look* 16
Germaine Greer, *The Stereotype* 29
Joan Didion, *In Bed* 59
Dean MacCannell, *The Tourist* 153
Edward C. Martin, *Being Junior High* 156
Desmond Morris, *Territorial Behavior* 198
Kennedy Fraser, *Modesty* 247
Joseph Epstein, *The Virtues of Ambition* 277
Susan Allen Toth, *The Boyfriend* 344
Robert Solomon, *"I-Love-You"* 364
D. H. Lawrence, *Counterfeit Love* 384

Description

Nancy Friday, *Competition* 93
E. B. White, *Once More to the Lake* 117
Edward C. Martin, *Being Junior High* 156
James Agee, *Three Singers* 192
Flannery O'Connor, *The King of the Birds* 234
Harry Crews, *The Car* 252
Katherine Mansfield, *Six Love Letters* 357
George Orwell, *Shooting an Elephant* 439

Division and Classification

Mary McCarthy, *Names* 20
Margaret Mead, *Family Codes* 84
Edward C. Martin, *Being Junior High* 156
Desmond Morris, *Territorial Behavior* 198
Ernest van den Haag, *Love or Marriage?* 388

Leo Rosten, *Home Is Where to Learn How to Hate*   420
Jonathan Swift, *A Modest Proposal*   453

Example

Suzanne Britt Jordan, *That Lean and Hungry Look*   16
Mary McCarthy, *Names*   20
Germaine Greer, *The Stereotype*   29
Robert F. Sayre, *The Parents' Last Lessons*   124
Maxine Hong Kingston, *The Misery of Silence*   186
E. M. Forster, *My Wood*   230
Harry Crews, *The Car*   252
Seymour Wishman, *A Lawyer's Guilty Secrets*   302
Neil Chayet, *Law and Morality*   418

Narration

Nora Ephron, *Shaping Up Absurd*   6
Mary McCarthy, *Names*   20
E. B. White, *Once More to the Lake*   117
Maya Angelou, *Graduation*   162
James Agee, *Three Singers*   192
Andrew Carnegie, *How I Served My Apprenticeship*   283
Pauline Newman, *Working for the Union*   288
Richard Rodriguez, *Reading for Success*   296
Susan Allen Toth, *The Boyfriend*   344
Wendell Berry, *Getting Married*   352
Neil Chayet, *Law and Morality*   418
Willie Morris, *Campus Politics*   427
George Orwell, *Shooting an Elephant*   439

Process Analysis

Erik Erikson, *The Shape of Experience*   37
Jack Matthews, *A Reasonable Madness*   261

Richard Rodriguez, *Reading for Success*   296
Virginia Woolf, *Professions for Women*   329
Wendell Berry, *Getting Married*   352
Leo Rosten, *Home Is Where to Learn How to Hate*   420